Samuel Sebastian Wesley

A Life

PETER HORTON

OXFORD
UNIVERSITY PRESS

OXFORD
UNIVERSITY PRESS

Great Clarendon Street, Oxford OX2 6DP

Oxford University Press is a department of the University of Oxford.
It furthers the University's objective of excellence in research, scholarship,
and education by publishing worldwide in

Oxford New York

Auckland Bangkok Buenos Aires Cape Town Chennai
Dar es Salaam Delhi Hong Kong Istanbul Karachi Kolkata
Kuala Lumpur Madrid Melbourne Mexico City Mumbai Nairobi
São Paulo Shanghai Taipei Tokyo Toronto

Oxford is a registered trade mark of Oxford University Press
in the UK and in certain other countries

Published in the United States
by Oxford University Press Inc., New York

British Library Cataloguing in Publication Data
Data available

Library of Congress Cataloging in Publication Data
Data available

ISBN 0–19–816146–8

1 3 5 7 9 10 8 6 4 2

Typeset by Hope Services (Abingdon) Ltd
Printed in Great Britain
on acid-free paper by
Biddles Ltd.,
King's Lynn, Norfolk

To the memory of my parents,
who encouraged my research but did not live to see its completion

The completion of the book was made possible by a generous grant
from the Ouseley Trust in memory of Watkins Shaw

EDITOR'S FOREWORD

The church music of Britain, like its church buildings and liturgical texts, is a national heritage that transcends religious controversy and the decline of faith. Unlike them—because of the ephemeral nature of music—it needs revival, interpretation, and advocacy if it is to be preserved and appreciated. Such processes must rest on a sound basis of fact and understanding. This series serves to encourage and present some of the best efforts of modern scholarship in the field.

The great Anglican cathedral tradition, with its roots in the Middle Ages, naturally takes the central place in this heritage. For centuries it has raised the music of worship to a high art, with its own style and history and its own series of composers, performers, and critics. It constitutes a school of musical art that is effortlessly distinctive, recognizably English, without being in the least nationalistic.

Samuel Sebastian Wesley, without any question, is one of the key figures in this unique tradition. In his time he stood for the highest artistic ideals, pursuing excellence in both performance and composition almost without regard to practical difficulties and discouragements. He won widespread admiration in spite of his near-fatal propensity to give offence. In our time, his genius is still recognized by the few of us who really know him, but his cathedral music is in danger of gradually disappearing from the public scene as its original function becomes ever more marginal to modern life.

Similarly, a century ago William Byrd was little more than a name to any but a few devotees. Through the research and advocacy of William Barclay Squire, Richard Terry, Edmund Fellowes, Frank Howes, and Edward Dent, Byrd's music attracted the notice of conductors and performers, and soon came into its own again as a vital part of the repertory, in the home and the concert hall as well as in church. The same could very well happen to Wesley. If it does, Peter Horton will be the prime mover. He has already published critical editions of all Wesley's anthems in three splendid volumes of Musica Britannica. Now he is offering the first thoroughly researched book on the composer.

Dr Horton's investigations have taken him to a range of sources that were untapped by earlier writers on Wesley. One of the most important results is a new and reliable chronology of the principal works. This in turn has opened the way to an analysis of Wesley's stylistic development, the first of its kind. It turns out that although he was strongly influenced by several Continental composers, his own development was fascinatingly individual. Horton shows how it is linked to both the circumstances of Wesley's career and his inner motivations. Another important feature of this study is that it gives full consideration to Wesley's achievements outside the church, including his early theatre music, his secular songs, and his piano music.

Here we have a full portrait of a complex man and musician, considered from all sides. At long last, Wesley has got his due.

NICHOLAS TEMPERLEY

Urbana, Illinois,
November 2003

PREFACE

MY first encounter with the music of Samuel Sebastian Wesley was when, as a child, I sang his hymn tune 'Aurelia'. At the time it made little impression, and when I was later introduced to 'Thou wilt keep him in perfect peace' this also—to my ears—lacked the immediate appeal of such other Victorian works as John Goss's 'O Saviour of the World' or the hymn tunes of J. B. Dykes. But I gradually came to realize that Wesley's music yields up its secrets slowly and that its inner toughness and richness of invention repay repeated hearing and study. Over thirty years later it continues to fascinate me, and the fruits of that fascination are to be found in the following pages.

Since his death in 1876 much has been written about Wesley's life, but considerably less about his music, and it was with the aim of making good this deficiency that I embarked on a survey of the latter for a doctoral thesis. Although the present book has its roots in that study, I have attempted to weave a discussion of his music into the fabric of his life, relating it to the circumstances of his eventful career and placing it in a wider musical context. Thus the steady development of his individual style is seen against the background of his restless moves from the vibrant and cosmopolitan musical life of the capital to the provincial obscurity of Hereford—albeit enlivened by the triennial Three Choirs Festival—and thence to Exeter, Leeds, Winchester, and Gloucester. While the resultant picture broadly conforms to the familiar image of a gifted but difficult composer and organist, it differs in many details. We see, for example, something of the privations of his childhood, his immersion in the musical life of London during the late 1820s and early 1830s, his leading role in music-making in Exeter and Leeds, his lectures on sacred music in Liverpool, his growing disenchantment with music at Winchester, and, most significantly, his activity as a composer in a wide variety of forms. Even the accepted opinion that his work as conductor of the Gloucester Three Choirs Festival was of little importance is contradicted by contemporary accounts, with many of the poor performances due as much to insufficient rehearsal time as to his idiosyncratic conducting. But most significant is the evidence of the work-list, which belies the widely held view that he wrote little but church and organ music—and it is through his early secular works, many of which have lain undisturbed since the 1830s, that his links with the mainstream of European music are most apparent.

No author can be insensitive to the work of his predecessors, and I must record a particular debt to Paul Chappell's biography, which provided the first detailed account of Wesley's life. No less valuable have been the personal accounts and reminiscences of his former pupils William Spark, J. Kendrick Pyne, and George Garrett, or the pioneering researches of F. G. Edwards who, writing in the early 1900s, was able to draw on the memories of many who had known Wesley. More recently several writers have brought critical scrutiny to bear on particular aspects of Wesley's life and music, in particular Nicholas Temperley with his discussion of Wesley's sacred music in *The Romantic Age* and William Gatens in the chapter devoted to Wesley in *Victorian Cathedral Music in Theory and Practice*. Gatens was also the first to develop a more general theory of Victorian cathedral music, which inevitably touches on Wesley's work at a number of points. So, too, do two more specialized studies to which I am also indebted, Temperley's magisterial *The Music of the English Parish Church* and Nicholas Thistlethwaite's *The Making of the Victorian Organ*.

There is, in addition, a wealth of primary source material, some of it untapped by previous authors. Close on 400 of Wesley's letters survive, and using these, contemporary archival material, and newspaper accounts, it has been possible to piece together more of the day-to-day events of his career. Newspapers, in particular, have provided valuable information not only on his involvement in more general musical activity in the various towns and cities in which he lived, but also on the repertoires at Leeds Parish Church and Winchester and Gloucester cathedrals. Despite this, there are still many gaps in the picture, and information about his family life remains sparse in the extreme—a situation which appears unlikely to change.

In conclusion I should like to thank the large number of people who have provided assistance. The initial suggestion that I should study Wesley's music came from Bernard Rose and Watkins Shaw, and the latter provided welcome encouragement when progress was slow. I owe a similar debt to Harry Johnstone who, as my supervisor, saw my thesis through to completion. As general editor of the series Oxford Studies in British Church Music, Nicholas Temperley has made innumerable helpful suggestions, and I have benefited greatly both from his great knowledge of English nineteenth-century music and from his concern for detail. In addition I must acknowledge the help I have received from the many institutions containing source materials, particularly those who so kindly answered last-minute enquiries: the British Library; the Bodleian Library, Oxford (particularly Peter Ward Jones and Robert Bruce); Cambridge University Library (Richard Andrewes); Exeter Cathedral Library (Audrey Erskine and Angela Doughty); Gloucester Cathedral Library (Lowinger Maddison); Guildhall Library, London; Hereford Cathedral Library (the late Penelope Morgan and Joan Williams); Hymns Ancient and Modern Archive (Gordon Knights); Lancashire County Record Office; Leeds Parish

Church (Simon Lindley); the National Library of Scotland (Almut Boehme); Novello and Co. (Leslie Ellis); the Rowe Library, King's College, Cambridge; the Royal Academy of Music Library (particularly Bridget Palmer); the Royal Archives, Windsor; the Royal College of Organists Library (Duncan Johnstone, Robin Langley, and Andrew McCrea); the Three Choirs Festival Archive (Anthony Boden); Winchester Cathedral Library (particularly Frederick Bussby and John Hardacre); Wonford House Hospital, Exeter (Gill Meredith). Among my colleagues at the Royal College of Music, Celia Clarke and Oliver Davies have been especially helpful, while Paul Collen took the photographs of all RCM material. Philip Olleson and Michael Kassler answered questions on Samuel Wesley, while Jan Fisher generously provided me with details of Wesley's descendants in Australia.

The following institutions and individuals have kindly allowed me to quote from material in their possession: the Bodleian Library; the British Library; Devon and Exeter Record Office; Edinburgh University Library; Robert Woodruff Library Emory University Library; Exeter Cathedral Library; the Fitzwilliam Museum, Cambridge; Gloucester Cathedral Library; the Guildhall Library; Hereford Cathedral Library; the Dean of Blackburn Cathedral; Leeds Parish Church; the Methodist Archives, Manchester; Novello and Co.; the Royal Academy of Music; the Royal College of Music; the Royal College of Organists; the Royal School of Church Music; the Three Choirs Festival Archive; Winchester Cathedral Library; Wonford House Hospital; Douglas Carrington; the late Sir John Dykes Bower; David Greer; the Revd Brian Findlay; the late Betty Matthews; Angela Parkes; Robert Pascall; Laura Ponsonby and Kate Russell (who made me most welcome at Shulbrede Priory).

It is with much gratitude that I acknowledge the financial and other help I received from various sources: a grant from the *Music and Letters* Trust which allowed me to take some unpaid leave, a very generous grant from the Ouseley Trust which enabled me to take study leave, and a further grant of study leave from the Royal College of Music. I must also thank those at Oxford University Press for waiting so patiently while the book gradually took shape: Bruce Phillips, Sophie Goldsworthy, Jacqueline Smith, Sarah Holmes, and Fiona Little, whose eagle eye spotted so many inconsistencies. My final debts, however, are to my family for whom Wesley became part of the household: my wife Elaine, and Edward, John, and Alice (who have never known life without him).

Writing in 1976 at the centenary of Wesley's death, Watkins Shaw sought in his article 'Samuel Sebastian Wesley (d. 19 April 1876): Prolegomenon to an Imagined Book' 'to consider in outline what might be some aspects of any book about him if, *per impossible*, one might ever be published'.[1] As someone who benefited from his advice and support, I should like to think that this might indeed be the book he had in mind.

P.H.

November 2002

---

[1] Watkins Shaw, 'Samuel Sebastian Wesley', *ECM*, 20 (1976), 22.

CONTENTS

PLATES

TABLES

MUSIC EXAMPLES

Unless otherwise stated all examples are by S. S. Wesley (and retain his sometimes idiosyncratic spelling of accidentals).

ABBREVIATIONS

General

A	alto (chorus)
a	alto solo (verse)
B	bass (chorus)
b	bass solo (verse)
bar	baritone
Can.	Cantoris
Dec.	Decani
S	soprano (chorus)
s	soprano solo (verse)
T	tenor (chorus)
t	tenor solo (verse)

Pitch references are styled CC (16'); C (8'); c (4'); c^1 (2'); c^3 (1').

Periodical and Newspaper Titles

ABG	*Aris's Birmingham Gazette*
At	*The Atlas*
Ath	*The Athenaeum*
BIOSJ	*The BIOS Journal*
BMSJ	*British Music Society Journal*
ChR	*The Christian Remembrancer*
CMJ	*The Choir and Musical Journal*
CMS	*Church Music Society Annual Report*
ECM	*English Church Music*
GJ	*The Gloucester Journal*
GM	*The Gentleman's Magazine*
HA	*The Hampshire Advertiser*
Har	*The Harmonicon*
HC	*The Hampshire Chronicle*
HJ	*The Hereford Journal*
HSB	*The Hymn Society Bulletin*
HT	*The Hereford Times*
ILN	*The Illustrated London News*
LiM	*The Liverpool Mercury*

LI	The Leeds Intelligencer
LM	The Leeds Mercury
M	The Minim
ME	The Musical Examiner
MG	The Musical Gazette
ML	Music and Letters
MM	The Musical Magazine
MMR	The Monthly Musical Record
MN	Musical News
MO	Musical Opinion
MP	The Morning Post
MQ	The Musical Quarterly
MR	The Methodist Recorder
MS	The Musical Standard
MT	The Musical Times
MW	The Musical World
Org	The Organ
PC	The Parish Choir
PDSH	The Plymouth, Devonport, and Stonehouse Herald
PDWJ	The Plymouth and Devonport Weekly Journal
PMA	Proceedings of the Musical Association
QMMR	The Quarterly Musical Magazine and Review
Sp	The Spectator
T	The Times
TEFP	Trewman's Exeter Flying Post
WEPG	Woolmer's Exeter and Plymouth Gazette
WL	The Western Luminary

Libraries and Archives

Wherever possible the appropriate sigla from Répertoire International des Sources Musicales have been used, but without the national prefixes.

Atu	Robert Woodruff Library, Emory University, Atlanta
CA	Harvard University Libraries
Cfm	Fitzwilliam Museum, Cambridge
En	National Library of Scotland, Edinburgh
Eu	Edinburgh University Library
EXc	Exeter Cathedral Library
EXce	Exeter Central Library

GL	Gloucester Cathedral Library
H	Hereford Cathedral Library
HA&M	Hymns Ancient and Modern, Norwich
Lam	Royal Academy of Music Library, London
Lbl	British Library, Reference Division, London
Lcm	Royal College of Music Library, London
Lco	Royal College of Organists Library, London
Lgc	Guildhall Library, London
LRO	Liverpool Record Office
LPC	Leeds Parish Church
Mp	Henry Watson Music Library, Manchester
Mr	John Rylands University Library, Deansgate Branch, Manchester
NWr	Norfolk and Norwich Record Office
Ob	Bodleian Library, Oxford
OM	Magdalen College Library, Oxford
RSCM	Royal School of Church Music Library, Cleveland Lodge, Dorking
ShP	Shulbrede Priory, Lynchmere, Sussex
ThCh	Three Choirs Festival Archive, Gloucester
WC	Chapter Library, Winchester Cathedral
WCc	Winchester College Library
WRch	St George's Chapter Library, Windsor

I

London

. . . he will remain with his unprincipled Mother to be trained up with the Vicious, and incorporated with the Vulgar . . . We would have rescued this poor Boy, and given him a chance of becoming a good Member of Society.[1]

WHEN Sarah Wesley penned those damning words in 1817, the possibility that her seven-year-old nephew Samuel Sebastian would become the foremost church musician of his generation would surely have filled her with amazement and disbelief. But such is the power of human determination when allied with true talent that, even with such an inauspicious start as an illegitimate birth and a home in which he would often have experienced real poverty, 'this poor Boy' quickly rose to the top of his profession and, at the end of his career, received official recognition with the offer of a knighthood or Civil List pension.

Samuel Sebastian Wesley had been born on 14 August 1810 at 11 Adam's Row, Hampstead Road, London, on the northern outskirts of the city.[2] A grandson of Charles Wesley, the celebrated hymn-writer, and a great-nephew of John Wesley, the founder of Methodism, he was the first of seven children of an irregular union between the renowned organist and composer Samuel Wesley and his housemaid Sarah Suter. It was not, however, merely that he had been born out of wedlock which so damned him in the eyes of his aunt, but that he had been born to a woman who had lured his father away from his wife and lawful family. Samuel Sebastian consequently passed his earliest years under the shadow of extreme family disapproval both of his father's lifestyle and of his mother and all that she stood for; that he initially took her surname cannot have helped matters.[3] Whilst there were occasional visits to his paternal grandmother, he and his siblings were pointedly ignored in the wills of his

[1] Letter dated 26 Aug. 1817 from Sarah Wesley to William Kingston (*Atu* John Wesley Collection, BV 2, no. 85).

[2] There appears to be no documentary evidence to support the oft-repeated statement that his birth took place at 1 Great Woodstock Street, the home of his paternal grandmother.

[3] In a letter dated 4 March 1818 to Samuel's eldest son Charles, his sister wrote that 'the Boy should never have borne her [Sarah Suter's] name if I could have prevented it' (*Atu* John Wesley Collection, BV 2, no. 86).

uncle Charles and aunt Sarah, both of whom left bequests to Samuel's three
legitimate children. What effect this had on him can only be conjectured,
although such near-rejection by the Wesley family must surely have contributed to those feelings of self-doubt and suspicion of others which so
plagued him later in life. Similarly, his constant worries about money must
surely have had their roots in childhood memories of his father's ever-present
financial problems and arrest for debt. But what had led Samuel to defy the
accepted standards of behaviour and thereby bring down opprobrium and
hardship on himself and his family?

Born in Bristol in 1766, Samuel was the youngest of the three surviving
children of the Revd Charles Wesley and his wife, Sarah (1726–1822). Like his
elder brother Charles (1757–1834) he showed great musical promise and
achieved considerable fame as an infant prodigy. By his early teens he was
already an accomplished organist and composer and seemed set to embark on
a successful musical career. But (as he later wrote to his mother) the necessity
of having to make his living from music had robbed it of all enjoyment:

I have every Day more and more Cause to curse the Day that ever my good Father
suffered <u>Musick</u> to be my Profession—In this country Experience continually shews
that only impudent and ignorant Wretches make any considerable Emolument by it,
excepting a few Singers . . . But the whole is a trivial & a degrading Business to any
Man of Spirit or of any Abilities to employ himself more usefully.[4]

But it was not only a natural disinclination to rub shoulders with 'impudent
and ignorant Wretches' which was to hamper the development of his career.
Irritable under interference, too outspoken where those in authority were
concerned, and determined to have freedom of action, he was a natural rebel.
Conversion to Roman Catholicism in 1784 and a flirtation with the controversial views on marriage propounded by his godfather the Revd Martin
Madan in *Thelyphthora, or A Treatise on Female Ruin* (1780) merely served to
strain relations with his family, quite apart from hindering his professional
advancement. But such was Samuel's nature. Whilst his allegiance to the
Catholic faith was to be short-lived, his receptiveness to the arguments in
Thelyphthora—most notably that marriage should be instituted by betrothal
and physical union, irrespective of any ceremony, and that the Bible sanc-
tioned a man 'putting aside' his wife for good cause and taking another—was
to colour the remainder of his life. It could indeed be held responsible for his
subsequent separation from his wife and liaison with Sarah Suter—and thus for
the birth of Samuel Sebastian. In the 1780s, however, the immediate consequence was the beginning of a liaison in 1784 with Charlotte Louisa Martin

<hr>

[4] Letter dated 1 April 1806 (*Cfm* Letters of Samuel Wesley, no. 11).

(1761–1845), the daughter of a demonstrator in anatomy at St Thomas's Hospital. The couple had met two years earlier in October 1782,[5] and by 1792 (if not before) were living together in Samuel's 'wooden Cottage'[6] at Ridge, a small village between Barnet and St Alban's. Samuel, following Madan's line that marriage required no formal ceremony, could see no reason (as he later wrote) to submit to 'a few empty, ridiculous Words . . . in the presence of a drunken Parson'[7] and, despite persistent appeals from his sister to make Charlotte an 'honourable woman', was adamant: 'I have but two objections to marrying. The first is I am not rich enough: the second that to tie my person wd be to lose my heart: and she who valued it would hardly consent to that. It is impossible for me to explain . . . and I can only declare this truth, that my aversion to constraint is invincible.'[8]

Only the imminent birth of a child to Charlotte compelled him to compromise his principles, and they were married on 5 April 1793 at St Paul's Church, Hammersmith; their son Charles was born on 25 September. No members of the Wesley family were present at the ceremony and, to judge from Sarah Wesley's comment in January 1794 that her brother had 'at last made known his Marriage, which I understand took place a year ago',[9] they were allowed to remain in ignorance for some months. Samuel had earlier prophesied to his sister that were Charlotte 'to reproach me with the Injury done to her Reputation, I wd marry her & hate her to-morrow',[10] and no truer words were spoken in jest. Within a short time relations had begun to turn sour on account of what he claimed to be 'the ill-founded jealousy of . . . [his] Wife respecting a Woman',[11] but Charlotte's fears were only too justified, and matters came to a head in 1795 when both desired a separation. Sarah Wesley succeeded in achieving a reconciliation but further quarrels erupted in 1796 and 1798, and in 1804 they finally separated, Charlotte taking lodgings in Pimlico and Samuel returning to live with his mother, brother, and sister. 1805 found them living together again but, with strife never far from the surface and neither able to speak a good word of the other, it was only a matter of time before a further eruption resulted in a further and irrevocable parting. This appears to have taken place in early 1810, and the catalyst was the liaison which had developed between Samuel and the new housemaid. That

---

[5] See the letter dated 7 Nov. 1792 from Samuel to his mother (*Mr* Methodist Archives DDWF/15/5).
[6] Ibid.
[7] Letter (undated but 22 Aug. 1793?) to Sarah Wesley (*Mr* Methodist Archives, DDWF/15/6).
[8] Letter dated 5 June [1791] to Sarah Wesley (*Cfm* Letters of Samuel Wesley, no. 3).
[9] Letter dated 28 Jan. 1794 to Mrs P. Maitland (*Ob* MS Eng. Misc. c.502, fo. 98ᵛ).
[10] Letter dated 5 June [1791] (*Cfm* Letters of Samuel Wesley, no. 3).
[11] Letter dated 2 Sept. 1807 from Sarah Wesley to Samuel, 'to be deliver'd after my Death' (*Atu* John Wesley Collection, box 6).

fifteen-year-old Sarah Suter subsequently became pregnant would merely have added insult to injury, although (in Sarah Wesley's eyes) Charlotte had only herself to blame: 'she herself flung the temptation in the way by admitting a Girl (whom she knew was not good) to wait upon him many years ago—and with her he has continued to live to our Heart Ache!'[12]

Events had turned full circle and Samuel, who had earlier written to his mother stoutly defending Charlotte from the accusation that she was of a 'careless, prodigal Disposition . . . [and] a Coquette, nay more; a Wanton',[13] was now forced to protect his latest paramour from the charge that she was 'a worthless abandoned Strumpet'.[14] He continued:

Time will prove the Truth, & it will not be very long before Experience will shew whether I have deserted my Family, because I will no longer remain with an abominable Creature in female Shape, whose Extravagance was hurrying me to Ruin, & whose Insolence & Vulgarity were not longer to be borne . . .

I mean not to leave my Enemy distressed, or even straitened, as far as my Circumstances can afford, & shall certainly do the best in my Power for my Children, whom I love: but I will not again enter my House to meet the disgusting & violent Behaviour I experienced the last Time I went thither on Business . . .[15]

A deed of separation was drawn up in 1812 under which Samuel was obliged to make monthly payments of £10 16s. 8d. for his wife's maintenance, although the divorce for which he had hoped never materialized. Such a detail was not, however, allowed to get in the way, and from henceforth he and Sarah lived together as man and wife. Whatever the rights and wrongs of his conduct Samuel had finally found contentment at home. Although Sarah (or 'Pexy' as he playfully called her) was young enough to be his daughter and had a limited experience of life, she was able to give him the companionship and support he needed. He in turn adopted a somewhat paternal attitude (as when writing whilst on a visit to Tunstall in Suffolk), although nothing could disguise his very real affection:

I ride on Horseback, & went down Yesterday to the Seaside: You cannot think what a fine Sight it is: You may a little imagine something about it when I tell you that it is a great Body of Water to which you can see no End, & this you will not very much wonder at when I tell you also, that in the Part of the Coast where I viewed it, it is full a Hundred & twenty Miles across before you come to any Land; & when the Wind blows hard, the Waves are lifted up much higher than the highest House you

---

[12] Letter dated 23 May 1825 to John Gaulter (*Atu* John Wesley Collection, box 7, no. 23).

[13] Letter dated 7 Nov. 1792 (*Mr* Methodist Archives DDWF/15/5).

[14] Letter (undated but probably Feb.–March 1810) to his mother (*Mr* Methodist Archives DDWes/6/53).

[15] Ibid.

ever saw, so that the Sea in a Storm is the very grandest Object in the World, & quite as astonishing as Sebastian Bach.[16]

She, for her part, provided the material comforts he so welcomed:

I am just as well contented to sit down to a Beef Steak broiled by Pexy, & a Glass of Brandy & Water as all the Delicacies which we have here every Day.—It is not Luxury but <u>Comfort</u> that Mr. Pug wants, & he has that in Adam's Row, quite as much as at Tunstall where the Folks are making much of him from Morning till Night.[17]

But to return to 1810. Following the final separation from Charlotte, Samuel had left their home in Arlington Street, Camden Town, and he and Sarah had moved a few hundred yards south and taken lodgings at 11 Adam's Row, part of a new development lying east of Hampstead Road in Somers Town, close to where Euston station now stands; it was here, on 14 August, that Sarah's first child, Samuel Sebastian, was born and named after his father's musical idol, '<u>Saint</u> Sebastian' Bach.[18] Misleading rumours had reached Samuel's mother and, anxious that relations should not be strained further, he provided as favourable an account as possible:

You have been grossly misinformed concerning the State of my Household. The sole People who have been Inmates in my Lodgings are the Nurse (the elderly Person whose Appearance you so much liked) & Sarah's Sister, who has saved the Expence of Washerwomen, & during a Confinement of the Sort, you well know that <u>some</u> extra Assistance is utterly unavoidable. I believe that a lying-in Month was never gone through with <u>less</u> Expence: I know that it was a very different Business in the Reign of Mrs Wesley, for then the House was full of Gossips & Hangers on from Morning till Night.[19]

The need to economize was of particular importance as Samuel never had sufficient money. Financial responsibility was not his forte and now, with two households to support on an income derived from teaching, concert appearances, and the receipts from occasional publications, he was in debt more often than not. Appeals to his family became ever more frequent, and on several occasions he was thrown into gaol for failing to pay his wife's allowance on time. Yet for a few years after Samuel Sebastian's birth not even the never-ending shortages of cash could dampen his spirits. The Wesley household might be poor but it was not, by all accounts, unhappy.

---

[16] Letter dated 15 Jan. 1811 to Sarah Suter (*Lbl* Add. MS 35012, fo. 36).

[17] Ibid., fo. 37ʳ.

[18] Letter dated 17 Sept. 1808 to Benjamin Jacob (*Lcm* MS 2130, fo.1). It has proved impossible to discover any documentation of Samuel Sebastian's birth or baptism.

[19] Letter dated 12 Sept. 1810 (*Mr* Methodist Archives, DDWes/6/51).

Information on the young Samuel Sebastian is scanty and almost entirely restricted to occasional references in his father's letters. *En route* to Tunstall in January 1811 he was very concerned to learn that 'little Boy blue' was 'poorly' and sent instructions to Sarah to 'try and cure him before I come back',[20] while some twenty months later he wrote from Ramsgate to say that 'Mrs. S. has got a fine Lot of pretty Shells, & Sea Weed & I know not what, all for him'.[21] The family had by now moved to 13 Tottenham Court, New Road (now Euston Road), and here, in mid November 1812, a daughter was born to Sarah; she only lived for five months, dying on 29 March 1813.[22] July 1813 found Samuel in East Anglia again, this time in Ipswich, where he and Charles Hague (Professor of Music at the University of Cambridge) gave a less-than-successful benefit concert:

I am extremely concerned to hear such a bad Account of my dear Sammy.—I agree with Mr. Wakefield that Change of Air may be serviceable to him, & yet I am very loth to trust him any where without either You or me about him . . .

You must keep what I write to yourself about Boy Blue—I cannot bear the Thought of his being snubbed or teazed by <u>any Body</u> who does not belong to him: I wish to God you could manage to have him at some <u>near</u> Place, where you or I could see him almost every Day.[23]

Three days later he wrote on a more positive note to report that 'Mrs. J. . . . has sent Sammy a nice Handkerchief with S.W. marked by herself'.[24]

Not until October 1814 do we learn anything more about 'little Boy Blue', who was missing his father and under the weather again. This was not, however, Samuel's only worry:

I'm afraid by your Way of Writing about Sammy Sixpence that he is but poorly: do hearten him up as much as possible, & you may safely tell him now that he is likely to see me very soon again.

I am in a great Passion with you for not packing up a Pair of Drawers in my Trunk. I have worn the only Pair almost off my Arse, not to mince the matter.[25]

By now the family had again been augmented with the birth of another daughter, Rosalind, in the autumn of 1814, and it was doubtless this which had necessitated a further move, to 4 Gower Place, Euston Square, New Road.[26]

---

[20] Letter undated [9 Jan. 1811] (*Lbl* Add. MS 35012, fo. 32ᵛ).

[21] Letter dated 29 Sept. [1812] (ibid., fo. 43ʳ).

[22] See Michael Kassler and Philip Olleson, *Samuel Wesley (1766–1837): A Source Book* (Aldershot: Ashgate, 2001), 6.

[23] Letter dated 6 July 1813 (*Lbl* Add. MS 35012, fo. 45ʳ–44ᵛ).

[24] Letter dated 9 July 1813 (ibid., fo. 46).

[25] Letter dated 15 October [1814] (ibid., fo. 49).

[26] See Kassler and Olleson, *Samuel Wesley*, 6. The precise date of Rosalind's birth is unknown, but was before 16 Oct.

Here they were to remain for some six fateful years which embraced one of the darkest periods of Samuel's life, as in the late summer of 1816 the black clouds of depression again appeared on the horizon. These periodic but severe attacks which caused him such misery were long thought to have been precipitated by his refusal to undergo the operation of trepanning following a severe head injury in 1787. Yet there is no contemporary evidence to support this theory (and some doubt about whether the accident took place), and it is more likely that they were merely one symptom of the violent alternations between 'mad fun, & excessive depression' which Mary Sabilla, wife of his good friend Vincent Novello, was later to describe: 'I knew him unfortunately too well, pious Catholic raving atheist, mad, reasonable, drunk, & sober. The dread of all wives & regular families, a warm friend, a bitter foe, a satirical talker, a flatterer at times of those he cynically traduced at others—a blasphemer at times, a puking Methodist at others.'[27]

The death in August 1816 of an infant son, whose loss (as his sister recorded) 'drove him frantic on the road to Norwich', triggered off a particularly severe bout.[28] Some months later he wrote to Novello requesting his 'candid & unreserved Opinion . . . of my <u>whole</u> present State, both mental, public, & domestic',[29] and matters came to a head in early May 1817 when (as his sister related) he was persuaded to leave Sarah and go to his mother's house:

We had just taken him out of his Snares, and he left his Mistress Saturday Sevennight [3 May], coming to my Mother's House: his Mind in such a state of derangement that we were obliged to have a Keeper, and were removing him into a Lodging in our Neighbourhood, when last Tuesday, while my dear Mother was sitting by his side, he flung up the Window, and Himself out it—25 Feet deep—on <u>Stones</u>.[30]

Elsewhere she recorded that he 'precipitated himself out of the window in a fit of frenzy, pressed, as he thought, by creditors, as writs were issued against him by his wife, and threats by his Landlord; miraculously his life was preserved'.[31] Samuel now endured perhaps the lowest point in his life, as a pitiful appeal to Novello bears witness:

---

[27] Undated letter to Henry Phillips (*Lbl* Add. MS 31764, fos. 33–4).

[28] Letter dated 26 Aug. 1817 from Sarah Wesley to William Kingston (*ATu* John Wesley Collection, BV 2, no. 85). Samuel set out for Norwich on 10 Aug.: see his letter to Vincent Novello dated 1 Aug. [1816] (*Lbl* Add. MS 11729, fo. 144).

[29] Letter (undated but *c*.April 1817) (*Lbl* Add. MS 11729, fo. 152).

[30] Letter (dated 1817 in a later hand) to William Wilberforce (*ATu* John Wesley Collection, box 7, no. 3).

[31] Memorandum dated 6 May 1817 (see Kassler and Olleson, *Samuel Wesley*, 359), quoted in J. T. Lightwood, *Samuel Wesley, Musician: the Story of his Life* (London: Epworth Press, 1937), 183. Its present whereabouts is not known.

My dear Friend

Here I am in the greatest Agonies of Mind & Body too tho' the latter are the less.—
All forsake me: Why is this?—If you think you ought not to come & comfort me I
must submit, but I trust this is not So.—O come my dear Novello, & leave me not
utterly in my deep Distress.—My Prayer is unavailing, else how do I long for a Release
from my offended Maker!—It is hardest that even my little ones are with-holden from
seeing me. Alas alas, Despair is for ever in Prospect.

Will you come this Evening, Do for Pity's Sake.[32]

In July he was entrusted to the care of Dr Alexander Sutherland and placed
in Blacklands House, a private asylum in Chelsea. It was here that his friend
William Kingston acquainted him with the offer by a Mr Bridge of Heywood
Hall, near Manchester, to act as guardian and educate seven-year-old Samuel
Sebastian. Kingston wrote to Sarah Wesley:

It was the wish of your mother that he should be told that his little boy was about to
be provided for in the way proposed. He greatly objected to the distance yet seemed
to think that it might be for his advantage—then the separation—the distance again
recurred to his thoughts—& every time with increased force of a sentiment of repug-
nance. He should never see him again! It was a plan to send him out of his reach![33]

It was, of course, also necessary to gain Sarah Suter's consent, to do which
the assistance of another friend was enlisted. His failure led Sarah Wesley to
unleash a bitter diatribe on the moral failings of her poor brother's family:

Mr Swan . . . said he should use all his interest with Mrs Suitor [*sic*] not to stand in her
own right; not having heard anything further, I conclude Mrs Suitor did not choose
to send the Child, and he will remain with his unprincipled Mother to be trained up
with the Vicious, and incorporated with the Vulgar . . .

Having thus discharged the Duties of Humanity, and our Efforts being defeated, the
matter ends: poor Sams children are likely to be involved in the Misfortunes of their
Father, and probably may live to be sad memorials of his mispent [*sic*] Youth. We
would have rescued this poor Boy, and given him a chance of becoming a good
Member of Society, & shall therefore have no Self-reproaches. If He be now sent to
a School, it must at the Expence of Others—for such liberal Offers are rare.[34]

In the event Robert Glenn, fellow guardian with Kingston of Samuel's
affairs and organist of Christ's Hospital (the Blue Coat School), was able to
gain Samuel Sebastian admission to the school which he attended for a short
time in 1817, on an unofficial basis 'without a nomination, and without wear-

---

[32] Letter dated 30 May 1817 to Vincent Novello (*Lbl* Add. MS 11729, fo. 154).
[33] Letter dated 24 Aug. 1817 (*ATu* John Wesley Collection, BV 2, no. 98).
[34] Letter dated 26 Aug. 1817 to William Kingston (*ATu* John Wesley Collection, BV 2, no. 85).

ing the costume'.[35] Within a few months, however, a more secure future beckoned following his acceptance as one of the Children of the Chapel Royal at St James's Palace (see Pl. 1). Samuel, although in no position to make the arrangements himself, wrote to thank William Hawes, the Master of the Children, and in so doing provided the earliest reference to the youngster's keen interest in music:

Pray accept my best Thanks for your extremely kind Offer relative to my little Boy. He is a very apprehensive Child & very fond of Music; how far he may have Talent & Voice sufficient to do Credit to your valuable Instructions, Experiment will best shew: his Temper & Disposition I believe to be good, wanting only due Direction, & I know him to be susceptible of Kindness, which with you I am confident he will meet.—My good Friend Glenn will doubtless confer with you fully upon Points of necessary arrangement . . .[36]

Throughout this time Sarah and Rosalind had been left to fend for themselves, for such was the antipathy of the Wesley family that no help could be expected from that quarter. Indeed, when in March 1818 the question of his possible 'release' was under discussion Sarah Wesley reported that 'Mr Glenn & Kingston thought the more time was allowed, the greater chance of his Mistress disposing of herself (which she doubtless would do) and then, half the danger would be removed', adding for good measure that 'It would be very horrible if he wishd to return to Her'.[37] But even the best laid plans can go awry, and despite her hope that 'his Friends will doubtless find some Apartments which are eligible'[38] Samuel had no desire to do anything but return to his old life with Sarah and their children. A new home was found at 16 Euston Street, Euston Square, and here they remained until March 1830. Not until 1823 or 1824, however, did he finally succeed in shaking off the debilitating feelings of depression which had caused him such mental anguish and, with a still-growing family, considerable physical hardship. Only Samuel Sebastian, following his acceptance by Hawes, was to enjoy an escape from much of the unhappiness of these years: for him there was the prospect of a new beginning as a chorister.

[35] George J. Stevenson, *Memorials of the Wesley Family* (London: S. W. Partridge & Co., [1876]), 544. Precise details of this episode remain unclear. Stevenson stated (presumably from information supplied by Wesley) that he had attended the school for a year, but as other aspects of his account are slightly inaccurate this may be so too. Certainly (as F. G. Edwards wrote) 'The statement that he was educated at Christ's Hospital . . . is not confirmed by the records of that charity . . . [while] an 'old Blue,' in the person of the late Mr. Frederick Cox, C.C. (born in 1809), had no recollection of a schoolfellow named Wesley, and his (Mr. Cox's) father was a personal friend of the Rev. Charles Wesley' ('Samuel Sebastian Wesley', *MT*, 41 (1900), 297).

[36] Letter dated 28 Nov. 1817 (*Lbl* Loan 79).

[37] Letter dated 4 March 1818 to Samuel's son Charles (*ATu* John Wesley Collection, BV 2, no. 86).

[38] Letter (undated but c.May 1818) from Sarah Wesley to Miss Ogle (ibid., no. 91).

At the time of Samuel Sebastian's entry, late in 1817, the distinguished days of the Chapel Royal were past. Nevertheless, as the personal ecclesiastical establishment of the sovereign it continued to enjoy prestige and could still boast a considerable array of musical talent to support the twice-daily services on Sundays and holy days: two organists (Charles Knyvett and John Stafford Smith), a composer (Thomas Attwood), a 'lutenist' (Hawes), ten priests-in-ordinary, sixteen Gentlemen, and ten Children. Hawes also held the post of Master of the Choristers of St Paul's Cathedral, and the boys of both choirs were boarded, lodged, and educated together at his large house, 7 Adelphi Terrace. Their life, by the standards of a later age, was far from one of ease, and their training rough and ready.

For their general education Hawes engaged 'a parochial schoolmaster' who provided rudimentary instruction (mainly arithmetic, worked on slates) for an hour and a half twice a week, and for piano playing they were passed to one of the men of the Chapel Royal choir, Henry Mullinex.[39] Hawes himself was responsible for their singing, though this included nothing that we should regard as voice-training. Mistakes in rendering the music were corrected by him, 'aided by a charming little riding-whip, which he applied to their backs with benevolent impartiality'.[40] On other occasions misdemeanours would be punished by the 'gating' of the whole choir.[41]

Hawes used his dual role to make some of his chapel boys do extra work to supplement those of St Paul's on Sundays. For example, a later child of the Chapel Royal, Edward Hopkins (born in 1818 and later organist of the Temple Church), would leave the 9.45 service at St Paul's early, dash back to Adelphi Terrace, and change into Chapel Royal court dress for the morning service there. Then, after 'a frugal and hasty dinner'[42] he would return to St Paul's in ordinary clothes for 3.15 p.m., and finally, after changing once more, to St James's Palace for Evening Prayer at 5.30.

In spite of the evident shortcomings of this regime, the routine of learning and singing the music for the regular services provided an education in itself. It need cause no surprise that the repertoire in the 1820s looked back mainly to the late seventeenth century and eighteenth century, with emphasis on works by Blow, Purcell, Croft, Greene, and Boyce, though with glances to a little music dating from before the Civil War and with an admixture of recent work by Thomas Attwood, John Stafford Smith, John 'Christmas' Beckwith, and Haydn ('The heavens are telling' from *The Creation*). The direction which

---

[39] From John Goss's experience. See William Spark, *Musical Memories*, 3rd edn. (London: W. Reeves, [1909]), 111.

[40] Recollection by W. H. Cummings (b. 1815). See *MT*, 48 (1907), 111.

[41] See *Lgc* MS 10189/4, fo. 179.   [42] 'Dr. Edward John Hopkins', *MT*, 38 (1897), 585.

the style of Samuel Sebastian's own compositions was afterwards to take is the more striking when seen against the conservative nature of this background. And the strength of that conservative continuity is emphasized when it is recalled that among the sets of manuscript part-books still used in his boyhood is one which had been in use since the days of Henry Purcell.[43] By the early 1820s Samuel Sebastian was beginning to make his mark as one of the leading boys—Hawes declaring him to have been 'the best boy he had ever had'[44]— and in 1823 was one of the two selected to sing in the recently consecrated chapel of the Royal Pavilion, Brighton, when the King (George IV) was in residence. Week by week he would travel down by post-chaise on Saturday, take part in the Saturday evening concert, sing at the Sunday services (at which the King's private wind band would play), and return on Monday morning. The court's residence was always reported in *The Morning Post*, with occasional references to 'Master Wesley'. The first was in March 1823: 'Master Wesley, from His Majesty's Choir at the Royal Chapel, St. James's, took the soprano and leading parts in the anthem, &c and with sweet and divine effect.'[45] The following December his singing was again appreciated: 'The soprano of Master Wesley was remarkably clear; his shake was open, his every intonation distinct and correct. The King's Band, with Mr. Attwood at the organ, were on duty.'[46]

Royal approval came in the form of a gold watch which 'His Majesty ordered to be presented to the lad'.[47] Occasionally, too, the choir's visits were prolonged to enable it to take part in further concerts, and it thus came about that on Monday 29 December 1823 the thirteen-year-old Samuel Sebastian was a fellow performer with Rossini at 'The King's Grand Music Party'. Not surprisingly, the visits to Brighton were an important part of his life, as a request to his mother for a new coat makes clear:

I write to let you know that I am going to Brighton next Saturday week so I hope you will let me have a new coat as this is to small . . . Dont forget to send my box and those Wooden things . . . I hope you will send me word about the Coat as I should not like to go in the same one as I did last year mind you send those bits of wood out of the Catherine wheels.[48]

---

[43] For the Chapel Royal repertoire of the time, see Thomas Pearce, *A Collection of Anthems . . . Used in His Majesty's Chapels Royal, and Most Cathedral Churches in England and Ireland*, new edn., with additions (London: C. and J. Rivington, 1826); information about the Chapel Royal part-books (*Lbl* RM 27.a.1–6 (formerly RM 23.m.1–6)) kindly supplied by Watkins Shaw.

[44] Stevenson, *Memorials of the Wesley Family*, 545.

[45] *MP* (11 March 1823), [3]. [46] *MP* (30 Dec. 1823), [3].

[47] Stevenson, *Memorials of the Wesley Family*, 544.

[48] Undated letter (?1824) (*Lbl* Add. MS 35019, fo. 8).

Even in London the choristers' musical fare was by no means restricted to the services and anthems sung at the chapel services, as Hawes would hire them out to sing at the many city dinners for whose musical arrangements he was responsible (and then pocket the fees himself),[49] while in 1825 they took part in a complete performance of Weber's *Der Freischütz* at his benefit concert.[50] The best boys would also be taken to assist in the various other musical activities with which he was connected, among them those of the Madrigal Society and the Concert of Ancient Music. Samuel Sebastian's name also appears twice on Sir George Smart's annotated copies of the programmes for the Vocal Concerts.[51] On Tuesday 11 May 1824 he took part with Messrs Evans, Hawes, and Leete in performances of the four-part glees 'The fairy beam upon you' (C. S. Evans) and 'You pretty birds' (William Horsley), while a year later, on Tuesday 10 May, he joined Messrs Terrail, Hawes, and Sale in his master's 'Oh! Where is the flower that bloomed in the vale'. On this occasion he shared a place in the programme with 'Master Bailey (William Bayley?)' of St Paul's; by 1826 his voice had broken and Bailey had the stage to himself.

Hawes was not alone, however, in appreciating young Sam's musical talent, as his father had also begun to take him—Chapel Royal duties permitting—on some of his concert tours. August 1824 thus found them in Margate where, as Samuel reported to Sarah, 'Sam is very useful & attentive, and as stingy as you can wish him'.[52] A few months later in December his help was required for a private performance of Samuel's newly published *A Morning & Evening Church Service* (Service in F) which an old acquaintance, Sir Robert Peat, parson of Brentford, had expressed a wish to hear. Never one to turn down an invitation combining both music and a social visit, Samuel was eager to make the arrangements and enlisted Vincent Novello to play the piano. Young Sam was to take the treble part: 'The only <u>Hitch</u> is the Probability of our worthy Friend Hawes's Interference, who will not suffer Sam to budge from his Prison on any Day that he can rob him of a Guinea.'[53] Some five weeks later at the end of January it was Graun's Te Deum that Samuel wished to try out: 'I shall try for Sam on Thursday Evening, but you know that Mr. Hawes is Mr. Hawes: to say any Thing more of him that is <u>true</u> would be libellous.'[54]

The days of such gatherings would, however, soon be drawing to a close as Samuel Sebastian was now in his fifteenth year. Shortly before his birthday he

---

[49] See Samuel Wesley's letter of 14 June 1826 to his sister Sarah in which he wrote that 'Hawes used always to get 3 Guineas at every Place where he sent my Sam, and always gave him afterwards, what?—not even Thanks' (*Mr* MA DOWes/6/38).

[50] See *QMMR*, 7 (1825), 197.   [51] See *Lbl* Case 61.h.4.

[52] Letter dated 3 Aug. [1824] (*Lbl* Add. MS 35012, fo. 51).

[53] Letter dated 6 Dec. 1824 (*Lbl* Add. MS 11729, fo. 214). Peat subscribed to the service.

[54] Letter dated 31 Jan. 1825 to Novello (ibid., fo. 235).

was the recipient of a long, typically chatty letter from his father which ended thus:

Give me a <u>full true & particular</u> Account of all Things you can cram into <u>three Pages</u>, for you must not leave an Inch of Paper unoccupied, and as with a <u>good</u> Knife you <u>may</u> make a good Pen, with a good Pen you <u>may</u> write a good Hand, which I assure you Master Sammy (I beg your Pardon, <u>Doctor</u> I meant) I wish you would set about to do.—At all Events you ought now to be a forward <u>English</u> Scholar, and I do not despair even of your becoming a Latin one, if you make good Use of the most valuable Article in Life, which is Time . . .
Spell <u>Wantes</u>, <u>so</u>—Wants
& <u>Knive</u>—Knife[55]

His father's optimism notwithstanding, mastery of the Latin language eluded Samuel Sebastian. But of more immediate concern to Samuel was his son's advancing years. Writing to Novello on 17 August (three days after Sam's birthday), he informed him that 'Sam will be with us on Sunday, but alas! his Voice betrays Symptoms of Anti-Vellutism, & moreover he begins to shew Signs that a Razor must before very long form one Article of his Toilette'.[56] In the event it was not until March 1826 that he left the Chapel Royal, taking with him a testimonial which stated that 'Mr. Samuel Sebastian Wesley was formerly a Chorister of His Majesty's Chapel, St. James's, and . . . has received his musical education among the gentlemen of that establishment, and . . . is fully competent to undertake the musical duties of any Cathedral'.[57] Even before leaving, however, he had been one of the applicants for the organist's post at the city church of St Stephen, Walbrook, although his name was not on the shortlist drawn up on 5 December 1825. Undaunted, he applied for the vacant post at St James's Chapel, Hampstead Road (see Pl. 2)—only a short distance from his birthplace—and on 25 March wrote to inform his father's friend J. G. Emett of his success, concluding in a most grown-up fashion: 'I hope Mrs. Emett and your daughters are well, pray come and see us soon.'[58] Within a matter of weeks he was again a candidate, this time for the post at St Mary at Hill (30 May). His failure here, however, seems to have made him more content with his lot, and not until 1 November 1827 does his name again appear on a shortlist (for St Stephen, Coleman Street).

But work as a church organist was by no means Samuel Sebastian's only occupation, and other openings—particularly at the English Opera House— soon came his way. Before looking more closely at these and the unfolding of

---

[55] Letter dated 1 Aug. 1825 (*Lbl* Add. MS 35012, fos. 109–10).
[56] Letter dated 17 Aug. 1825 (*Lbl* Add. MS 11729, fo. 277). The reference is to the castrato singer G. B. Velluti, who was the talk of London in 1825.
[57] *Lbl* Add. MS 35020, fo. 5ᵛ.   [58] *Lbl* Add. MS 35019, fo. 131.

his career, it is worthwhile to pause to consider the rich and varied musical life of the capital which had earned London a place alongside Vienna and Paris as one of the three great musical centres of the world and which could offer abundant opportunities to a young musician of talent intent on making his way professionally.

England in the 1820s was prosperous. Freed from the burden of sustaining a lengthy war with France, it was now able to devote all its energies to the development of industry and commerce, and thus to reinforce its position as the world's most powerful nation, at the centre of a fast-growing empire. Hand in hand with this prosperity went the emergence of a new, well-to-do, middle class, for whom music held an important place in the social calendar. As the *London Magazine* commented, 'Music is now, indeed, so universally cultivated, that scarcely a house can be found without a pianoforte or harp',[59] and it was the support of this body of musical amateurs that ensured that concert life in London flourished and also attracted a number of the leading continental musicians (who also appreciated the political freedom that England offered). The roll-call of those who arrived, whether at the end of the eighteenth century or during the early years of the nineteenth, is impressive. Some, like Ries, Viotti, Kalkbrenner, J. B. Cramer, and Moscheles, settled there for several years, while Clementi stayed for life and established a flourishing instrument-building and publishing business. Spohr made the first of several visits in 1820, while six years later Weber crossed the channel to conduct the first performances of *Oberon*, commissioned by Charles Kemble for the Theatre Royal, Covent Garden. But the best-known continental visitor was the young Mendelssohn, who first went to England in 1829 and was to return regularly until his death eighteen years later. What drew them all was the wide range of musical activity on offer: formal series of concerts, notably those of the aristocratic and increasingly old-fashioned Concert of Ancient Music and the more forward-looking Philharmonic Society (founded in 1813 and enjoying the support of professional musicians), 'benefits' given by individual performers, private soirées in the homes of the well-to-do, various societies cultivating glees and madrigals, and opera and other forms of musical drama. Italian opera, the delight of the aristocracy, remained the preserve of the King's Theatre, while English spoken drama (with or without music) was restricted to the two 'patent' theatres, Covent Garden and Drury Lane. Under the terms of the Licensing Act of 1737 the various minor theatres were precluded from producing straight tragedy or comedy, with the result that they staged a motley collection of genres, all more or less dependent on music. In addition the

---

[59] 'Report of Music. No. 1', *The London Magazine*, 1 (1820), 92.

city could boast flourishing music publishing and instrument-making busi-
nesses, as well as two serious periodicals, *The Quarterly Musical Magazine and
Review* (1818–28) and *The Harmonicon* (1823–33). Yet despite such intense
activity the status of professional musicians remained low. Two, it is true, had
had the honour of receiving a knighthood (but only from the Lord Lieutenant
of Ireland)—John Stevenson (1803) and George Smart (1811)—but the majority suffered from the long-held belief that music was not a respectable profession for an Englishman and were accordingly classed with tradesmen and
servants.[60] The opening in 1823 of the Royal Academy of Music had gone one
step towards raising the status of music, but it would be a long time before
musicians were finally able to shake the image of belonging 'below the salt'.

Church musicians, as Wesley would soon discover, fared no better than
their secular counterparts. Cathedral lay clerks or vicars choral were paid only
a pittance, and while those in London could augment their incomes by holding several positions simultaneously, the only options in the provinces were to
juggle the conflicting demands of trade and music or to build up a teaching
practice. Neither was the situation any more promising for composers, who
received little encouragement to venture beyond those fields for which there
was either a steady demand or little foreign competition: songs, piano and
instrumental works for domestic use, music for the pleasure gardens, 'English'
opera, glees, and church music. Even the Philharmonic Society, organized and
run by professional musicians, did little to help. During its first two seasons
only two instrumental works by native-born English men were given—a
string quartet by George Griffin (28 February 1814) and a symphony by
Crotch (16 May 1814)—and the same pattern continued for the remainder of
the decade: after ten years 83 British works had been heard (56 of them vocal)
out of a total of 964.[61] Yet this was only a generation after Haydn's symphonies
had taken London by storm and, with a few notable exceptions, had signally
failed to take root.[62] An anonymous correspondent to *The Harmonicon* encap-
sulated the situation:

He [a young composer] may probably write a symphony or overture, which, by dint
of manœvering, he may *possibly* have the satisfaction of hearing it played once; and it

---

[60] For a broad discussion of the musical profession in England see Deborah Rohr's *The Careers of British
Musicians, 1750–1850: A Profession of Artisans* (Cambridge: Cambridge University Press, 2001).

[61] See Myles Birket Foster, *History of the Philharmonic Society of London, 1813–1912: A Record of a Hundred
Years' Work in the Cause of Music* (London: John Lane, 1912), 59.

[62] Among their few English offspring were Samuel Wesley's fine Symphony in B flat (1802), his two
minuets and trios for string quartet (1800, 'An Imitation of the Stile of Haydn', and 1807, 'in the German
Style'—see the copies by Vincent Novello in *Lcm* MS 5251), and William Crotch's two symphonies (1808
and 1814), but these were isolated examples. The first English-born composer of the post-Haydn period to
make a significant contribution to the development of the symphony was Cipriani Potter (born 1791) who
completed nine during the 1820s and 1830s—but significantly only after studying in Vienna.

is very problematical whether it be ever performed or not, whatever its merit may be. In the mean time, his invention is dulled by disappointment, want of employment, and the indifference of those about him; and, to gain a livelihood, he must have recourse to writing ballads and teaching music. This is what many young men of talent arrive at, who, had they met with fair encouragement, might have become ornaments to their profession, and have rescued us from the imputation . . . of having no music of our own . . . When a system like this prevails, can we be surprised that we have no English school of composition?[63]

It was into such an environment that young Samuel Sebastian now stepped. Unlike several of his contemporaries who studied at the Royal Academy of Music, he never benefited from a rigorous course in harmony, counterpoint, orchestration, or the handling of musical form, but was at once thrown into the hurly-burly of professional life, playing at church on Sundays, continuing to assist his father and Hawes in various undertakings, teaching at a school (where his sister Eliza was among his pupils),[64] taking private pupils—among them Josiah Pittman—and within a few years (if not already) starting to compose. But what he lacked in formal training, he largely made up through practical experience and the 'apprenticeship' he served in the cosmopolitan musical environment of the London theatres and concert-halls, so that as early as June 1826 his father could write that 'he has (God be praised) a pretty good Prospect of being able to scramble for a decent Livelihood himself, tho' in a Profession that I hate & despise'.[65] Some months later Samuel vigorously rebutted the charge that his son's career would be harmed should details of his parentage become known:

after the <u>numerous Instances</u> in which his Name has stood in a Concert Bill, it were absurd, & <u>impossible</u> (were I so minded, which I am <u>not</u>) to prevent its being known <u>who he really is</u>, a Son of mine, gifted with extraordinary Musical Powers, of whom born it matters not . . .

. . . Mr <u>Scott</u>, my <u>Son John's former Master in the Coal Trade</u>, who is one of the Active Members in the Royal Institution, particularly invited Sam to the Conversazione on Friday Evenings there, and moreover sent him a Ticket of Admission for the whole Season.

You will not affirm that <u>Scott</u>, knowing the whole Story from Drummer concerning John & Samuel, and knowing also my total Separation from the Mother of the former, could possibly believe them both to be the Sons of the <u>Same</u> Mother.[66]

[63] 'On the Formation of an English School of Music' *Har*, 9 (1831), 110.

[64] See the letter dated 20 May 1895 from Robert Glenn Wesley to F. G. Edwards in which he referred to Eliza gaining her musical education from her father '. . . & more particularly from S. S. Wesley at a school where he used to [teach]' (*Lbl* Add MS 41574, fo. 79).

[65] Letter dated 14 June [1826] (*Mr* Methodist Archives, DDWes/6/38).

[66] Letter dated 20 April 1827 (*Mr* Methodist Archives, DDWes/6/37). Samuel's second son John (1799–1860) was later one of the lay secretaries of the Wesleyan Mission House.

Exactly how or when Samuel Sebastian gained that mastery of the organ which would stand him in such good stead it is impossible to say. Hawes was no great player, and neither he nor the two Chapel Royal organists, Charles Knyvett and John Stafford Smith (even if they had anything to do with the education of the choristers), possessed any skill in the department in which he was to excel, pedal playing. One can only assume, therefore, that he gained his prowess largely unaided. We do, however, have tangible evidence of the part played by Samuel in introducing his son to the keyboard in the form of a volume of printed music inscribed 'Samuel Wesley junr. The Gift of his Father. March 22. 1822'.[67] The composers represented include Thomas Adams, J. S. Bach (the first three of the six 'Little' Preludes BWV 933–8 in an edition by Samuel), Handel, Mozart, Pleyel, Samuel Webbe the younger, and Samuel himself, and several of the pieces have been fingered and show signs of regular use. It would also have been through his father that Samuel Sebastian came to know the still little-known organ music of Bach of which Samuel was an early exponent (although only in the form of duets or with the pedal part assigned to a double bass); as early as August 1825 his son was the proud possessor of a copy of 'Bach's Exercises' (part 1 of *Clavierübung*).[68] Whether his father also gave him any grounding in the theory of music remains unknown, although here too one suspects that much of his knowledge was casually acquired as he went along. Be that as it may, by September 1825 he was sufficiently well versed to be able to rally to Samuel's defence when the latter's Service in F was criticized by William Horsley in *The Quarterly Musical Magazine and Review*: 'My worthy Correspondent [Horsley] has forgotten a few of the Liberties he himself takes in his Harmony, & (I cannot but think) those as reprehensible as what he quarrels with in my Text: <u>Sam</u> furnished me with them from the Canon "Audivi Vocem" . . .'[69]

By the autumn of 1826, barely six months after he had left the Chapel Royal, Samuel Sebastian's talents were becoming more widely known, and in November his name was suggested by Thomas Greenwood for the important post at the newly rebuilt parish church in Blackburn, Lancashire. Greenwood had known the vicar, Dr John Whittaker, since their days as students at St John's College, Cambridge:

---

[67] Now *Lcm* LXXVIII.E.18. The majority of works are for the piano, and none of those for organ have pedal parts.

[68] See the letter dated 9 Aug. [1825] from Samuel Wesley to Vincent Novello in which he requests the return of the 'Exercises' which were 'Sam's Property' (*Lbl* Add. MS 11729, fo. 271). A copy, inscribed 'S. Sebn. Wesley. 1827', is now *Lcm* H417.

[69] Letter dated Sept. 1825 to Novello (*Lbl* Add. MS 11729, fo. 281). The service had been reviewed in the previous January (*QMMR*, 7 (1825), 95–101) and Horsley's canon in April (ibid. 224).

. . . having learnt that the celebrated Sam. Wesley had a son of extraordinary musical abilities who was desirous of obtaining a situation as an organist . . . [my brother] applied to the father through a friend to know whether an appointment like that a[t] Blackburn would be acceptable. The lad, though only 17 [*recte* 16] years inheriting a large share of his father's extraordinary talent, appeared to my brother even a more eligible person than one of more advanced age, who perhaps with less ability might require a larger salary.[70]

Two weeks later he wrote again, providing the earliest description of 'young Sam. Wesley's playing:

On Wednesday last I had the pleasure of hearing young Sam. Wesley perform on the Organ of St. Sepulchre's church in the City. I think that the performance was upon the whole highly creditable to him; and I have no doubt that when his hand acquires its full strength, and a little more experience is added to his present stock he will be one of the <u>best</u> organists in the kingdom. Let me give you a list of his performances: The <u>first</u> piece was a voluntary (extempore) in which he showed a considerable acquaintance with the principles of harmony . . . and without deficiency of musical ideas (Melody). His transitions were smooth and legitimate and continuous; never venturing out of his depth & therefore never awkward or at a loss. He manages the pedals well, which is a very difficult & very important part of a modern organist's duty. He next played with correctness two organ fugues by Sebastian Bach, a severe trial for any performer: Next common psalmody quite to my satisfaction. He ended with a second extempore performance which I liked even more than the first. I listened to him attentively, for more than an hour, and found little to object to except a want of experience in the management of the swell and stops. He was a little too noisy for me . . . A year or two will no doubt add these to his other accomplishments. As it is there are in all probability not a great many better organists in London.

In appearance he is very young and good looking, short in stature, and modest in his manner, devoted I understand to his profession, and diligent in the study of it.[71]

Given Samuel Sebastian's youth it had been necessary to involve his father in the discussions, and from Greenwood's reports we learn that Samuel spoke 'very highly' of his son's musical ability and considered, perhaps wistfully, that, as far as teaching was concerned, he was already 'on the high road to prosperity'.[72] He also had another worry:

The lad, he tells me, is so exclusively devo[ted] to Musick that he has hitherto not shown as much inclination for other and more important studies as he (the father) could wish. He seemed therefore anxious to ascertain whether any opportunity of classical & other more general instruction was likely to offer. S. Wesley himself is an

---

[70] Letter dated 14 Nov. 1826 in St Mary the Virgin, Blackburn, coucher book 1820–31 (Lancashire County Record Office, MS PR 3073/2/43, p. 74).

[71] Letter dated 12 Dec. 1826 (ibid. 76).   [72] Letter dated 28 Nov. 1826 (ibid. 75).

excellent scholar so that you can hardly be surprised that he should desire his son should partake in some degree of the same advantage.[73]

Ultimately it was only Samuel Sebastian's youth that stood against him, an opinion from which Greenwood did not demur: 'I agree with you that he is not of an age to exercise great control over grown up singers who have to be cured of many bad habits'.[74] We do not, unfortunately, know which fugues Greenwood heard, although, if his account can be trusted, the occasion constituted the first known solo performance—or more accurately 'play-through'—of any of Bach's organ fugues in this country. That this distinction should have fallen on a youth of sixteen merely serves to emphasize the great changes taking place in the field of organ playing and Samuel Sebastian's place at the forefront of a new generation of players for whom mastery of the pedals was a sine qua non. Close on a year later it also fell to him to give one of the first two recorded solo performances of the 'St Anne' Fugue, which both he and H. J. Gauntlett played on 17 October 1827 at the trial for the organist's post at St Stephen's, Coleman Street. Despite what was described as an 'extraordinary' performance which did the 'greatest credit' to the two men, neither was elected and the position went to the otherwise unknown Miss Sarah Alder Bradfield.[75] Finally, on 8 January 1829, Samuel Sebastian was successful in obtaining another post when he was elected organist of St Giles', Camberwell (see Pl. 3). Not content with this, he also applied for the position of organist at St John's, Waterloo Road (see Pl. 4), vacant after the death of his father's friend Benjamin Jacob, and was duly elected on 29 November; for some months he held both posts in addition to that at Hampstead Road. Although such plurality was not uncommon, it led in this instance to bitter resentment on the part of an older, disappointed rival. Joshua Doane (d. 1848), author of *Remarks on Thirty-One Elections for Church Organists Exposing Various Intrigues thereat and the Shameful Practice of Pluralities which are, Manifestly, to the Injury of Science, and the Utter Disgust of Many Congregations*, directed his wrath widely. He had a particular antipathy towards blind or female organists and 'young W——', however:

St. Giles's Camberwell. Here young W— was returned by the umpire as far superior to any of his fellow candidates, although his psalmody was played in a style that would preclude the possibility of any children singing to it. The trial of skill . . . was a mere mockery, as it was generally understood . . . that the place would be given to young

---

[73] Ibid.   [74] Letter dated 17 Dec. 1826 (ibid. 76).
[75] See F. G. E[dwards], 'Bach's Music in England', *MT*, 37 (1896), which quotes a contemporary report from *MP*.

W—. In consequence of that election, the singing children at that church have ever since been much neglected.[76]

But it was not only at Camberwell that Doane found himself thwarted. Having acted as Jacob's deputy at St John's, Waterloo Road, he had had every expectation of being appointed in his place, but it was not to be: 'here we have a lad enjoying the emoluments of two, if not three, organists' situations, to the prejudice of a man whose abilities as a church organist have been proved to be of a superior order.'[77]

At Camberwell Samuel Sebastian found himself a near neighbour of another of his father's band of Bach enthusiasts, Thomas Adams. Adams had been appointed to the new church of St George in 1824, and G. J. Stevenson (with information provided by Wesley) recorded that:

About that period, 1829–30, the celebrated Thomas Adams was organist at the new church, Camberwell, where the service continued longer than at the parish church, which gave Dr. Wesley many opportunities of calling at the new church, on which occasions Mr. Adams frequently left the organ to his young friend, for him to extemporise a fugue as a concluding voluntary, notwithstanding the possibility of Wesley's playing being mistaken for his own. The favour thus shown him Dr. Wesley greatly appreciated, for he held Thomas Adams in the highest esteem.[78]

Adams was also well known for his performances on the Apollonicon, the large mechanical-cum-manual instrument completed by Messrs Flight and Robson in 1817. Designed to imitate an orchestra, it must be held at least partially responsible for encouraging the new 'orchestral' style of organ playing (of which Adams was a leading exponent) that came to the fore in the 1820s. Not unnaturally some of the latter's influence rubbed off onto his young colleague, and Samuel Sebastian's two earliest organ works, the Andante in A and the Variations on 'God save the King', are both concert pieces employing 'orchestral' effects. Indeed, the main theme of the former bears such an uncanny likeness to the opening of the slow movement of Beethoven's Symphony No. 2 (which Wesley was to conduct on several occasions) that a reviewer suggested that it could have been intended as a deliberate paraphrase.[79] But what most impresses is the finished nature of the music. The Andante may contain little that would identify its composer, but one cannot help admiring such moments as the second subject, with its delightful

---

[76] *Remarks on Thirty-One Elections* (quoted by Stanley Lucas in 'Samuel Sebastian Wesley', *MO*, 47 (1933), 245).

[77] Ibid.   [78] Stevenson, *Memorials of the Wesley Family*, 545.

[79] See *MT*, 19 (1878), 36. The dating of the Andante (not published during Wesley's lifetime) is conjectural and based on its musical style.

Ex. 1.1. Andante in A, second subject

exchange between the Open Diapason and Cremona stops (Ex. 1.1), or the later staccato pedal arpeggios, so reminiscent of pizzicato cellos and double basses.

A similar concern for instrumental colour characterises the highly virtuoso Variations. The second variation, for example, contrasts the sound of the Great Diapasons (right hand) with a Swell reed (left hand), supported by 8' and 16' pedal stops, while the seventh has the character of a lightly scored scherzo with three carefully differentiated layers of sound. In the third variation Wesley included a running pedal part in semiquavers which demonstrates in the clearest possible way his considerable technique: 'Where the author will meet with a performer, himself excepted, to play the pedal part . . . we cannot guess'[80] declared *The Harmonicon* two years later, hazarding that it would not be in England. The work concludes with a fugue, cleverly constructed around the first two lines of the tune.

The Variations had received one of their earliest performances—if not the first—at St Mary Redcliffe, Bristol, in 1829 during one of the three recitals given by Samuel Wesley to mark the opening of the rebuilt organ. Samuel had first intended to take George Cooper, organist of St Sepulchre's, Holborn, to assist him, but his West Country host, Dr Daniel Wait, Vicar of Blagdon, thought otherwise. '. . . let Sam come down, <u>not Cooper</u>'[81] he wrote to Sarah, and despite Samuel's protestation that he 'must be the Person to decide whether his Assistance be absolutely necessary or not',[82] Sam it was who travelled down for 'Three Performances of Sacred Music . . . from the works of Handel, Haydn, Mozart, &c.'.[83] Although not large, his contribution was well received:

> The great praise of Mr. W. and his able and interesting Son, who occasionally accompanied him in a Duet, and gave also *'God save the King,'* with variations of his own composition, is, that to that powerful instrument, the Organ, they have so far beyond their compeers,
>
> > 'Enlarged the former narrow bounds
> > And added length to solemn sounds.'[84]

Relations between father and son were still uneasy and were not improved by the latter's appropriation of some of the Bristol profits and less-than-enthusiastic account of their success. It was a decidedly disgruntled Samuel who wrote to Sarah on 18 October:

---

[80] *Har*, 9 (1831), 197.
[81] Letter dated 23 Sept. [1829] from Daniel Wait and Samuel Wesley to Sarah Suter (*Lbl* Add. MS 35012, fo. 78).
[82] Ibid.   [83] *BG* (1 Oct. 1829), [3].
[84] *BG* (8 Oct. 1829), [3].

I am exceedingly angry that Master Sam did not give you (after paying his travelling Expenses) <u>all</u> the Cash which he took from me: his lousy Tailor's Bill might have been settled quite soon enough upon my Return.

I find that he has tried to alarm you as much as possible about my Success, which is very wicked & very foolish, for altho' I have certainly been ill used by the shabby scabby Churchwardens of Redcliff, yet there is a Certainty of my making Money in <u>two</u> if not <u>three</u> other Places . . .[85]

Three days later he returned to the subject of 'Master Sam': 'I hope that Master Sam does not worry you, if he cannot or will not <u>help</u> you: if ever he should have a Family of his own he will then know what his Duty to them is, & how much ought to be sacrificed to <u>their</u> Welfare, whatever Inconvenience it might occasion him.'[86] Early in the following year father and son parted company, Samuel commenting to Sarah that he was 'not sorry that Master Sam has taken his roosting Perch with Atkins: he will begin before long to know the Value of what he was dissatisfied with before'.[87]

But it was not merely as an organist that Wesley (as we shall hereafter refer to him) had started to make his mark. Not only do his earliest compositions date from around this time, but he was also associated with the theatrical and concert-giving activities of his former choirmaster, William Hawes. He had apparently been tempted by the stage—the one field into which his father had never ventured—as early as 1825 when, according to his sister Eliza, he had contemplated writing an opera to a libretto by Samuel's friend Dr Daniel Wait.[88] All that survives is a sequence of twenty five brief but well-wrought instrumental movements, some of them clearly dances, whose lack of originality is offset by a simple charm and whose scoring—for a small orchestra of two flutes, clarinet, bassoon, two horns, trumpet, bugle, two violins, and bass—is always idiomatic.

Hawes had taken over the musical direction of the English Opera House—the name given to the Lyceum Theatre for the three-month season (3 June–3 October) when it was licensed for the performance in English—in 1824, and under his charge the company were to give a number of notable performances. Foremost among these were the English premières of Weber's *Der Freischütz* in 1824 (arranged and adapted by Hawes) and Mozart's *Così fan tutte* (as *Tit for Tat*) in 1828, together with revivals of *Don Giovanni* (1830) and *Le nozze di*

---

[85] Letter dated 18 Oct. 1829 to Sarah Suter (*Lbl* Add. MS 35012, fo. 85).

[86] Letter dated 21 Oct. 1829 to Sarah Suter (ibid., fo. 88).

[87] Letter dated 26 Jan. 1830 to Sarah Suter (ibid., fo. 106ᵛ). 'Atkins' was probably I. O. Atkins, two of whose glees were published by Hawes, *c*.1830.

[88] See *Cfm* MS MU 698, on which Eliza has written 'This MS is by my brother Samuel Sebastian Wesley and I believe it to be movements for the Opera he purposed writing in <u>1825</u>, as in a letter from Dr. Wait in my possession he promised to send the Words of the Opera without delay'.

Figaro (1832). The company's main fare, however, consisted of a wide range of shorter works in the various 'illegitimate' genres to which the 'minor theatres' in the capital were restricted—operettas, musical farces, musical dramas, melodramas, pantomimes, and musical entertainments.[89] Given the public's love of spectacle all would probably have drawn upon the expertise of Mr O. Smith, 'Director of the Melo-Dramatick Department'.

Exactly when, or in what capacity, Wesley joined Hawes is not clear. All we do know is that at the beginning of the 1829 season he was announced as 'Pianist' and 'Conductor of the Chorus' (in the place of James Thomas Harris) and in all probability had previously been assisting in a less official way, perhaps since soon after leaving the Chapel Royal. To have seen his name on a playbill for *Tit for Tat* (29 June 1829) must have given him a great sense of pride and achievement. Other performances that season included the première of Ferdinand Ries's *Die Räuberbraut* (as *The Robber's Bride*) and revivals of *Der Freischütz* and John Goss's *The Serjeant's Wife*.

Wesley continued as pianist and chorus conductor for the next three seasons, and the experience he gained during these years had a considerable bearing on his subsequent development as a composer. Not only did he become fully conversant with the contemporary early romantic idiom, but he also experienced the use of music in a dramatic context. Both were to reappear in his anthems, notably 'The Wilderness' (1832) and 'Blessed be the God and Father' (1834). In addition he made several useful professional acquaintances, among them W. H. Kearns and John Barnett. Kearns (1794–1846), a Dubliner by birth, had settled in London in 1817 as a violinist at the Theatre Royal, Covent Garden, but soon became involved with the English Opera House as violinist and musical adviser, re-scoring Purcell's *King Arthur* (as *Arthur and Ermeline*) in 1827. It was from him that Wesley gained much of his knowledge of the orchestra, and it was doubtless around this time that he arranged his father's early March in B flat for full orchestra, making it one of the earliest English orchestral works to include trombones.[90] It was also to Kearns that he turned a few years later for an opinion of an overture and his Benedictus 'newly scored' (see Chapter 2).

By the time their paths crossed in the later 1820s, John Barnett (1802–1890), Wesley's senior by eight years, was already established as a composer. His own first stage work, the musical farce *Before Breakfast*, had been produced at the

[89] For a fuller discussion of contemporary theatre music in London, see Bruce Carr's 'Theatre Music: 1800–1834' in Nicholas Temperley (ed.), *The Romantic Age, 1800–1914*, The Athlone History of Music in Britain, 5 (London: Athlone Press, 1981), 288–306.

[90] See Nicholas Temperley's 'Samuel Wesley', *MT*, 107 (1966), 109, in which he writes that the Overture in E (1834) 'seems to be the first English orchestral work with trombone parts'. This distinction should probably apply to the March.

English Opera House in 1826, and during the next few years he had many opportunities of observing his younger colleague at work as 'Choragus (or Conductor of the Chorus) having had frequent opportunities of witnessing the able and masterly manner in which he conducted the Chorus at the English Opera House some years ago, when the production of some of my own works brought me into Contact with him'.[91] Wesley's opinion (as expressed to Kearns in 1832) was less complimentary: 'It appears to me that he [Barnett] has talked himself into notice. I don't think he has so much real feeling for music as even Bishop'.[92]

After the Lyceum was destroyed by fire on 16 February 1830 the company performed at the Adelphi and Olympic theatres, and it was at the latter (see Pl. 8) that Wesley's theatrical career reached its peak with the production on 30 July 1832 of a new melodrama, *The Dilosk Gatherer; or The Eagle's Nest* (see Pl. 6). The libretto was by Edward Fitzball, the music composed and arranged by Wesley and Hawes.[93] In the context of early nineteenth-century English opera a 'melodrama' was a spoken play in which music was extensively used 'to accompany entrances and exits . . . and to underscore and heighten any dialogue, action, or motion of particular importance to the plot';[94] with Hawes merely arranging the vocal numbers, it fell to Wesley to produce an overture and fourteen short numbers of 'melo-dramatick' music. This he did with no little success, and his contributions reveal an obvious familiarity with German Romantic opera and an ability to create music of some emotional power. The *Theatrical Observer* thought otherwise: 'Messrs. Hawes and S. S. Wesley claim the honour of composing the music; but, to our thinking, it is scarcely to the reputation of either of those gentlemen'.[95] Fitzball's libretto, which has little bearing on the music, is set in Ireland and relates a typical story of the triumph of true love over adversity, with the largely irrelevant activities of the comic schoolmaster, Mick Mugwussel, and his pupils adding light relief. Norah Cavanagh, the daughter of a local fisherman and the dilosk (seaweed) gatherer of the title, has secretly married Fergus, the nephew of the local squire, Sir Bryan O'Beg, and borne him a son. Not surprisingly Norah is very unhappy at the need to maintain secrecy, especially when Sir Bryan threatens to evict her aged father from his cottage. Her grief is compounded when the child escapes and, after climbing a rock to play with the seaweed, is plucked up by an eagle and taken to its lair in a ruined tower. Only after Fergus has climbed up the ruins to rescue the child is all revealed and the work ends on a note of happiness and rejoicing.

[91] From a testimonial dated 3 Feb. 1844 [*recte* 1848] (author's collection).
[92] Letter (undated but *c*.28 Dec. 1832) (*Lbl* Add. MS 69435, fo. 5).
[93] The opening glee was the work of George Hargreaves.
[94] Carr, 'Theatre Music: 1800–1834', 293.
[95] Quoted in F. G. E[dwards], 'Samuel Sebastian Wesley', *MT*, 41 (1900), 299. It has not proved possible to trace a copy.

Of the various movements the overture—a well-constructed movement in ABA form—is by far the most substantial. One of its most striking features is the sense of breadth conveyed by the long musical paragraphs of the outer sections, whether at the opening where sustained harmonies, ostinato figures in the first violin part, and a slowly descending horn solo conjure up a vision of the gently rocking sea, or in the equally expansive second subject group. Ominous string tremolandos presage a change of mood and introduce the central Allegro agitato (in the tonic minor), dominated by a vigorous passage of imitative counterpoint, before slowly falling woodwind chords over an inner pedal and a long timpani roll lead to a silent pause and the recapitulation of the opening. Wesley subsequently used the main theme of the Allegro to accompany a moment of great drama—Norah's ascent of the rock in pursuit of her child. The libretto and stage directions at this point give an idea of the work's flavour (Norah was played by Frances Kelly):

Music—She [Norah] rushes frantically up the rock—she springs forward! falls! Her hair streaming over the edge of the precipice.
[After which the chorus of dilosk girls sing:]

> Oh, sight of horror!
> Oh, wretched mother!
>   In vain thou rendst thy floating hair
> Thy child is lost
> Each hope is cros't
>   Nought is left thee but despair
> Thus kneeling
> Thus appealing
>   Hear kindly fate for her own pray'r.[96]

The remaining numbers consist of brief instrumental movements to accompany moments of particular drama and contain further rudimentary examples of themes associated with particular persons or actions. One, to accompany Fergus's precarious ascent of the ruined tower to rescue the child, is based on a descending whole tone scale in the bass, but its novel mixture of diminished sevenths, augmented sixths, and chromatic triads is more remarkable for boldness of conception than for harmonic logic. Overall, however, the minor place accorded to music and the absence of any opportunities for characterization placed severe limitations on what Wesley was able to achieve. After its initial run of twelve performances *The Dilosk Gatherer* was never revived, and sank without trace. By now Wesley's time at the English Opera House had in any case drawn to a close, following his unexpected appointment on 10 July as

---

[96] Ex. 1.2. See Plays from the Lord Chamberlain's Office, June–July 1832 (*Lbl* Add. MS 42,917, fo. 381).

Ex. 1.2. *The Dilosk Gatherer*, 'When Miss Kelly goes up rock'

organist of Hereford Cathedral. Before following him westwards, however, we must turn back a few years and glance at other aspects of his developing career.

For the past three seasons Wesley had also been organist (and perhaps 'Director of the Chorus' as well) at the Lent Oratorio Concerts, courtesy no doubt of Hawes, the conductor in 1830.[97] The performances were given twice weekly (on Wednesdays and Fridays) at Covent Garden and Drury Lane theatres respectively, and at the former on 31 March 1830 he had the opportunity to repeat his Variations on 'God save the King', between parts 1 and 2 of *Messiah*. Opportunities for solo performance were not, however, frequent, and for most of the time he was merely required to join the orchestra in accompanying the miscellaneous selections of choral and solo numbers (both sacred and secular) which made up the programmes. On 30 March 1832, however, he accompanied a distinguished group of singers—Anna Bishop, Tom Cooke, Francis [?] Robinson, and Henry Phillips—in the first performance of his '*New Quartetto . . . Benedictus*'. Fluently written, it inhabits the same world as *The Dilosk Gatherer* and shows him entirely at ease with the early romantic idiom. Delicate chromatic inflexions add piquancy to the harmony, while two bold examples of tonal parenthesis to the flat submediant—a technique he had learnt from Spohr—provide dramatic colour.[98] But throughout it is echoes of the opera house that one can hear most clearly, particularly where the four voices join together in unison in the coda (see Ex. 1.3).

In falling victim to the seductive charms of Spohr's highly chromatic idiom, Wesley was by no means alone, as Henry Bishop, John Barnett, George Macfarren, and Henry Smart likewise succumbed. But its influence, although powerful at first, was not destined to last and by the mid-1830s was beginning to wane. In addition to the Benedictus, a further two mass movements survive from this period, both scored for two flutes, solo cello, and strings: a setting of the Agnus Dei for high voice and the opening fragment of a Gloria in excelsis for four-part choir. Whether they were also written for the Lent Oratorio Concerts is not known, but the only obvious alternative would be for use at one of the Roman Catholic chapels (where his father had connections). Another early work is a setting for male voices and large orchestra of a drinking song, 'Young Bacchus in his lusty prime', on whose manuscript he later scribbled 'A very young production'.

[97] James Thomas Harris, Wesley's predecessor as director of the chorus at the English Opera House, performed a similar function at the Oratorio Concerts—see Betty Matthews (ed.), *The Royal Society of Musicians of Great Britain: List of Members, 1738–1984* (London: Royal Society of Musicians, 1985), 68.

[98] The term 'tonal parenthesis' was first used by Gerald Abraham in his discussion of Chopin's derivation of the technique from Spohr (see *Chopin's Musical Style* (London: Oxford University Press, 1939), 91–92).

Organ playing on Sundays continued much as before, although by the spring of 1832 his posts had been reduced to two—or, more accurately, one and a half. Following what he later described as 'a fuss about my holding three posts together'[99] he had resigned from both St John's, Waterloo Road (where he played for the last time on 27 March 1831), and Hampstead Road Chapel, and for close on nine months retained only the Camberwell appointment. At Camberwell, however, there was no Sunday evening service, and this fact doubtless prompted him to look for an extra post. The upshot was that on 21 November, having canvassed the parish of Hampton (Middlesex) 'with the express undertaking that I could only attend the Evening service',[100] he was appointed organist of the rebuilt church (reopened on 1 September) and subsequently settled in the village (see Pl. 5). The fishing prospects it offered—rather better, one imagines, than in the Surrey Commercial Docks where he had hitherto pursued his hobby (see Pl. 7)—are reputed to have been one of the major attractions.[101]

While the early 1830s saw Wesley gradually making a name for himself as a rising organist, pianist, and conductor, they also saw the appearance of his earliest printed works, the majority published by Hawes. The first to be issued had been a short Waltz for piano, contributed to *The Harmonicon* in 1830, but this was soon followed by a further two works for the piano—an *Introduction and Rondo on an Air from Spohr's Azor and Zemira* and *An Original Air, with Variations*, dedicated to Clementi (both now lost)—the Variations on 'God save the King' for organ, and the song 'You told me once', all published in 1831. Those that were reviewed received favourable notices, although both sets of variations were criticized for the excessive difficulty of their keyboard (and pedal) writing. Even at the age of twenty-one Wesley clearly had a technique to be reckoned with. Writing in *The Atlas* Edward Holmes considered that the 'fingering [of the piano variations] will be found immensely difficult': 'Music of this kind will perplex the most practised performer, and is in most cases left to the author to execute if he can. Young Mr. Wesley has, we think, advanced his reputation by this production, but it will never get into general circulation unless the passages are in some way distributed between four hands.'[102]

---

[99] Letter dated 25 Nov. 1874 to W. H. Blanch (repr. in the *South London Press*: see *Lbl* Add MS 35020, fo. 32).

[100] Letter dated 22 June 1832 to W. H. Kearns (*Lbl* Add. MS 69435, fo. 1).

[101] A season ticket, issued on 9 June 1830 by the Commercial Docks, Rotherhithe, permitting 'Mr. Samuel Wesley . . . to ANGLE . . . in the TIMBER DOCKS, No. 4, 5, & 6, until the THIRTY-FIRST Day of DECEMBER, 1830, SUNDAYS *excepted*' is preserved in the *Lbl* (Add. MS 35019, fo. 185).

[102] *At*, 7 (1832), 92.

Ex. 1.3. 'Benedictus qui venit': *a* tonal parenthesis; *b* coda

a)

William Ayrton also welcomed the work, noting that it showed 'very considerable ability in the author, who is still a youthful, but most promising, one'.[103] Only the issue by Hawes of 'O God, whose nature and property', a short but effective *stile antico* setting in a series entitled A Collection of Anthems and other Sacred Music as Used at His Majesty's Chapels Royal and the Various Cathedrals throughout the Kingdom (1831), provided a hint of the direction in which his career would move. Although largely eschewing a contemporary idiom (and containing his earliest use of the 'English' cadence), it makes telling use of a touch of enharmony at the words 'thy great mercy' with a progression he was to reuse in a number of other works. But the most distinctive feature is the bold handling of diatonic dissonance in the freely contrapuntal 'Amen' where, for the first time, we see the shape of things to come (see Ex. 1.4): 'a fine specimen of the use of the ninth in transition', H. J. Gauntlett wrote approvingly a few years later.[104] Although the work was welcomed by *The Harmonicon* as 'a composition no less pleasing than devotional',[105] Wesley's attention was drawn to the unsatisfactory underlay of the sixth and seventh bars, and in the autograph manuscript copied at Hereford in 1834 this has been altered in accordance with the reviewer's suggestion.

To a casual observer it would have appeared as though Wesley, the holder of two organists' posts on the fringe of the metropolis, developing and earning recognition as a composer, and becoming involved in London's varied secular musical activities, could have looked forward to a fruitful career in the capital, not by any means confined to church music. It is therefore unexpected to find that early in July 1832 he was one of three candidates for the post of organist at Hereford Cathedral. His competitors, Moss and Smith by name, were nonentities; yet he himself, the successful candidate, was not yet twenty-two and almost certainly the youngest of the three.[106] And thus began his career as a cathedral organist which, whether or not he then realised it, would take him away from London and its musical life for ever. It was a move he would ever regret, and when, seventeen years later, he looked back on this, his first major appointment, he did so with feelings bordering on despair:

Painful and dangerous is the position of a young musician who, after acquiring great knowledge of his art in the Metropolis, joins a country Cathedral. At first he can scarcely believe that the mass of error and inferiority in which he has to participate is habitual and irremediable. He thinks he will reform matters, gently, and without

---

[103] *Har*, 10 (1832), 15.

[104] H. J. Gauntlett, 'English Ecclesiastical Composers of the Present Age', *MW*, 2 (1836), 118.

[105] *Har*, 9 (1831), 222.

[106] There remains a possibility that Moss was Matthew Moss, another composer associated with the English Opera House.

Ex. 1.4. 'O God, whose Nature and Property', 'Amen'

giving offence; but he soon discovers that it is his approbation and not his advice that is needed. The choir is 'the best in England,' (such being the belief at most Cathedrals,) and, if he give trouble in his attempts at improvement, he would be, by some Chapters, at once voted a person with whom they 'cannot go on smoothly,' and 'a bore.' The old man knows how to tolerate error, and even profit by it; but in youth, the love of truth is innate and absorbing.[107]

---

[107] S. S. Wesley, *A Few Words on Cathedral Music and the Musical System of the Church, with a Plan of Reform* (London: F. & J. Rivington, 1849), 11–12.

2

Hereford

> I left London when very young for Hereford, intending to compose chiefly
> for the Church.[1]

WHEN the new Dean, John Merewether, DD, arrived at Hereford Cathedral
in June 1832 he found much to claim his immediate attention. Not only was
the building in a poor state, but the conduct of services also left much to be
desired, and at his first chapter meeting on 16 June the latter was discussed.
Whilst it was recognized that this proceeded from the disability of the organist, John Clarke Whitfeld, it was now considered that the chapter's 'long . . .
forbearance' could be extended no further. Accordingly, they felt it to be 'their
indispensable duty to communicate to him their decision that the Office of
organist . . . [would become] vacant at Midsummer next', unless he wished to
retire earlier. The blow was softened by the grant of an annual allowance of
£40 'in proof of their kindly feelings towards him'—a gesture whose generosity was more apparent than real because the sum was to be deducted from
the emoluments of his successor.[2]

These decisions were rapidly followed by the election on 10 July of 'Mr.
Wesley the Organist of Hampton Church near London . . . as Organist of this
Cathedral on a Salary of Fifty Two pounds', plus £8 paid by the College of
Vicars Choral and the expectation of a further £40 on the death of his predecessor.[3] That Dean Merewether had also moved to Hereford from Hampton
(where he had been curate at the parish church) was surely no coincidence,
and one can sense his influence in the surprising decision of his brilliant young
organist to exchange his burgeoning career in London for work at a remote
country cathedral. At the same meeting it was further resolved that 'Mr.
Bishop a person recommended by the Dean' should be invited to Hereford 'as

---

[1] Letter dated 10 Dec. 1875 to his sister Eliza (*Lbl* Add. MS 35019, fo. 124ᵛ).
[2] See the Hereford Cathedral Chapter act book, 1814–34 (*H MS* 7031/18, 356, 360).
[3] The meagreness of Wesley's salary becomes even more apparent when compared with the £42 Edward
Hopkins was offered as organist of Mitcham Parish Church in 1834 (see C. W. Pearce, *The Life and Works
of Edward John Hopkins* (London: Vincent Music Co., [1910], 21).

soon as convenient . . . to repair and tune the Cathedral Organ'.[4] It was not until 18 September that J. C. Bishop finally reached the city; his original brief had by then been expanded, no doubt after consultation with the new organist, to include a number of alterations, among them a change to the action of the Choir manual 'to form a Recess of a Foot deep for knee-room for Action upon the Pedals'.[5] Work began immediately, resulting in the temporary discontinuation of choral services.

When Wesley arrived in Hereford in September he thus had no cathedral duties and had little else to do, in surroundings, moreover, which were markedly different from those to which he had been accustomed. Though a cathedral city, it was then only a sleepy country market town with a population little more than a third of that of his familiar Camberwell.[6] Contemporary effects of industrial progress and upheaval, political and social ferment, all largely passed it by, leaving it as simply the centre of an agricultural neighbourhood which retained much of its eighteenth-century character. Finding himself 150 miles from family and friends and in a small town which completely lacked the hustle and bustle of the capital, Wesley initially felt isolated and lonely, although his enforced idleness gave time for correspondence and allowed him to unburden himself in long letters to his mother and father. Writing to the latter in early October, he provided a glimpse of his first few weeks away from London:

My Dear Father,

. . . I am very anxious to learn what has been done since your last letter—how you all are . . . The distance between us, and the impossibility of my affording any immediate assistance, makes me request that you will not give a worse account than need be . . . I have taken comfortable lodgings near the Cathedral for the present, I think it probable that soon I shall be allowed rooms in the College here. I should then have to get furniture.

I find that much teaching may be had within fifteen miles of Hereford. I should, of course, have been better pleased to have lived quietly, without this tiresome and somewhat degrading occupation, the salary at the cathderal is, however, insufficient, and by teaching I hope shortly to be able to send you money to town . . . I must hire, or keep a horse when I commence—as the pupils live many miles away, and apart.

I shall not do any duty at the Cathedral until the sixth of November. The organ is being enlarged considerably. My payment will however be the same, I am, therefore, glad of the liberty. If I can afford it, I think of going a short distance into Wales should

---

[4] Hereford Cathedral Chapter act book, 1814–34, 365 (*H MS* 7031/18, 365). Bishop had earlier provided the organ for Hampton Parish Church.

[5] Ibid. 372. Details of the work were entered into Bishop's ledger in two instalments—on 11 Sept. and on 12 Oct. (see the transcript of the original, now lost, provided in 1898 for F. G. Edwards and among his papers in the private library of Novello & Co.).

[6] At the 1831 census the population of Hereford was 10,180, that of Camberwell 28,231.

the weather permit. Lately we have had rain night and day. Hawes, Atkins, etc: have been down here giving a concert at which I played a piano forte and violin Duet with [J. D.] Loder of Bath. We got on tolerably well but I hate playing the mountebank on these occasions—Nothing is to me so pleasant as to join in the performance of good music. But when a certain quantity of twaddle is to be played that some imposter may beg money, I'd rather be far off than mix in the mess. The 'concert' was for the benefit of a resident singer of Hereford. I got nothing for my share . . .

Write and let me know what you are all about. I have not been able to go and buy poultry yet. Tell me when you want it most. Fine Geese cost about three and six-pence. Fowls, two and threepence a couple. Ducks, in proportion . . . Tell mother to make you write directly . . . take care what you say to me in your letter, being idle, I am in course nervous. Tell mother to think of my knives and forks, and the other things, but be careful how you mention them in your letter, as it (the letter) may miscarry, and be opened.[7]

We learn more from a less deferential letter to his mother, and one senses that the dispatch of various trivial errands—chasing the money he was owed by Atkins for a fender, getting some visiting cards printed, ordering a new pair of dress shoes, and so on—provided some relief from the feelings of melan-choly which had gripped him:

I have no teaching, the cathedral is not open, and until it is, I shall scarcely see any-one about the place, I must be patient, and so must everybody else . . .

How is Father? He might as well write better letters to me. If your lodgings are let you must get him out of town. A Change of scene would do him immense good. I want a copy of his Church service to perform at the Cathedral. Glenn has a copy, Cooper also. Pray send one in the parcel. Has Novello done anything. How can I get Father's Manuscripts. Must I come to London for them . . . ? Pray attend to these things as I am getting very melancholy here. I am obliged to change my lodging, this week. According to an agreement I made. I must pay 10 shillings a week which I can't afford. It cost me one pound three [shillings] for my boxes coming from Hampton [and] they arrived today. Tell Ros [his sister] to get a Dictionary and look out any word she don't know the way to spell. Her letter was imperfect—and Father did not cor-rect all mistakes.

I shall try and come to London shortly.[8]

Whether he managed a journey to London is doubtful, but by the end of October he was in better spirits and (as he wrote to Kearns who had taken his post at Hampton):

well, and tolerably happy—and very anxious to hear from you . . . How do you get on at Hampton. What have you been at in London. What is [Henry?] Smart's music

[7] Letter dated Oct. 1832 (*Lbl* Add. MS 35019, fos. 6–7ᵛ).
[8] Letter postmarked 26 Oct. 1832 (ibid., fos. 10–11ᵛ).

like at the theatre . . . Pray write to me and answer all these questions and give all the
news, if you have ever been away from your friends you [will] know how desirous
you were to receive a letter.[9]

But some letters were more welcome than others. Henry Smart, he complained to Kearns, had written 'a long letter of abuse <u>because</u> I talked to him
of theatrical Ladies in <u>your</u> fashion'.[10] What, one wonders, had he, Kearns
('my dear, drunken, brother Psalm Smiter'),[11] and these 'theatrical ladies' got
up to in London?

But all was not gloom. The cathedral, he told Kearns, was 'a fine old
place',[12] while the countryside also gave him great pleasure: 'The Country is
indeed beautiful. Such a river the Wye. I went about 14 miles up it the other
day—such scenery—it beats Pomkins and Jits hollow.'[13]

It was perhaps during this or another excursion that the idea for a new
anthem to commemorate the reopening of the cathedral organ came to him,
and it may not be too fanciful to read an extra significance into his choice of
texts. Were the verses from Isaiah 35 with their references to 'The wilderness
and the solitary place' and 'the wilderness . . . [where] waters break out, and
streams in the desert' perhaps suggested by the wild unspoilt countryside he
had just encountered for the first time? Was he even aware that his uncle
Charles had already set the opening words as a verse anthem for two trebles?[14]
Be this as it may, having finally found himself with the opportunity to write a
large-scale work for church use he quickly completed 'The Wilderness' and it
was ready for performance at Mattins on 8 November, the last of the three
annual Audit days (when the cathedral's accounts were audited). A glowing
account of the opening day's services—the first at which he played—appeared
in *The Hereford Journal*: 'The Audit was never more fully attended . . . and
never were the full powers of the beautiful instrument more successfully and
skilfully developed, very much to the admiration and gratification of all present'.[15]

One has only to compare the new anthem with the works by the other
composers performed at the Audit services—settings of the canticles and
anthems by Robert Cooke (1768–1814) and Wesley's immediate predecessors

---

[9] Letter postmarked 29 Oct. 1832 (*Lbl* Add. MS 69435, fo. 2).
[10] Undated letter (*c*.28 Dec. 1832) (ibid., fo. 5).   [11] Ibid.
[12] Letter postmarked 29 Oct. (*Lbl* Add. MS 69435, fo. 4).
[13] Ibid. The ref. to 'Pomkins and Jits' remains obscure.
[14] *Lam* MS 190 contains four anthems by and in the hand of Charles Wesley. The first is dated 13 Aug.
1802, the third is dated 19 Oct. and the last ('The Wilderness') is entitled 'Anthem (Compos'd for a Private
harmonic meeting.) Duett. For Two Trebles. CW. London. Dec: 11th.' Curiously, both Charles and
Samuel Sebastian Wesley omitted the word 'even' from v. 2.
[15] *HJ* (7 Nov. 1832).

at Hereford, Clarke-Whitfeld and Aaron Hayter (organist from 1818 to 1820)—to appreciate how fundamentally Wesley had departed from the accepted style of cathedral music. While both Cooke and Clarke-Whitfeld had made a conscious break with the past and, together with the Irishman John Stevenson and Thomas Attwood, had adopted a 'classical' style for their sacred works, even this modest attempt to step outside conventional stylistic propieties had caused considerable upset.[16] To some ears it represented the infiltration of native church music by an alien culture, and Attwood was roundly criticized for concluding 'I was glad' (written for the coronation of George IV in 1821) 'in imitation of HAYDN, or, if you please, of ROSSINI!':

in the present instance we have an Englishman of taste and talent, who has so far caught the infection under which our Continental neighbours labour, that he has thought it incumbent on him to introduce to us all sorts of remote combinations and modulations, before he concludes a passage [the Gloria Patri] which should only be remarkable for its touching simplicity![17]

In this context it is not without significance that both Attwood and Stevenson had first become known for their work in the theatre, and a surprisingly large number of musicians in both London and Dublin either had a foot in both camps or moved easily from one to the other. Hawes was a prime example, as were his Chapel Royal colleagues Sir George Smart (joint organist) and Thomas Welsh (gentleman), and all three were also active in London concert life. Their example had not been lost on the young Wesley, who, presented with the opportunity to write his first important work for church use, had no hesitation in transferring his enthusiasm for the works of Weber, Spohr, and their contemporaries from the concert-hall to the chancel. While a simple listing of the anthem's movements might suggest a verse anthem not unlike Attwood's 'Teach me, O Lord' (1796) or Goss's 'Have mercy upon me, O God' (1833), the reality is very different.[18] In place of the steady rhythms and old-fashioned notation (in minims) of Attwood and Goss one finds varied musical phrases supported by an imaginative orchestrally conceived accompaniment laid out on three staves. Indeed, the heady mixture of German romantic harmony, Bachian diatonic dissonance, and solid English diatonicism immediately proclaims a new and potent voice, able to marry

---

[16] For a detailed discussion of the subject, see the chapter 'Proprieties and constraints' in William Gatens, *Victorian Cathedral Music in Theory and Practice* (Cambridge: Cambridge University Press, 1986), 60–81.

[17] *QMMR*, 4 (1822), 92.

[18] In the discussion of anthems the following definitions, from John Stainer and William Barrett, *Dictionary of Musical Terms*, rev. edn. (London: Novello & Co., 1898), have been adopted: a verse anthem begins with a section intended to be sung by single voices to a part (verse); a full-with-verse anthem opens and closes with movements for full choir but includes movements for verse ensemble.

something of the excitement of the theatre with the age-old forms of church music, and the work provides an object lesson in Wesley's re-invention of the multi-movement anthem in a new romantic guise. Something of this can be seen from its varied key relationships and musical links (see Table 2.1).

TABLE 2.1. *Internal structure of 'The Wilderness'*

Movement	Scoring	Text	Key
Verse	satb	The wilderness	E–B–E
Aria	b	Say to them	a–F–a
Recitative★	t	Then shall the lame man	A–E
Verse/Full★	satb, SATB	For in the wilderness	E–G#–C–E
Recitative★	ATB, ssat	And a highway shall be there	c#–B
Full★	SSATB	And the ransomed of the Lord	E–G#–E
Verse, full	ssattb, SATB	And sorrow and sighing	E

★Ending with imperfect cadence or musical link to the next movement.

From its solemn opening the music exudes seriousness and a sense of purpose, as though to offer a practical demonstration of Wesley's observation that 'it is a duty . . . incumbent on all . . . that our best gift is brought to the Altar'.[19] The initial bass solo metamorphoses into an elegant trio (and subsequently quartet), with delicate touches of chromatic harmony (bar 16) and the organ weaving a delicate filigree around the voices (bars 7–11, 17–23). But perhaps the most significant feature is the sense of breadth. Although only forty-six bars long, the movement has a feeling of substance, of providing the foundation for a work of some stature. The same freshness and vitality characterize the succeeding bass solo with its relentless stalking obbligato pedal part and 'classical' descending chromatic fourth in the bass line (bars 49–50—compare the opening of the Prelude in A minor from book 2 of Bach's *Das wohltemperirte Clavier*).[20] Here, too, one can see Wesley experimenting with formal structures and producing a movement whose ternary thematic organization (ABA, but with several statements of the A and B material) is at cross purposes with its ternary tonal structure (A minor, F major, A minor). A similar dichotomy can be seen in the central movement, 'For in the wilderness'. While the concept of a movement scored for a combination of verse ensemble and full choir was not unusual, Wesley's material and handling of the medium were anything but conventional: the imaginative accompaniment with its descending parallel 6–3 chords in the organ part (perhaps illustrative

[19] *Lcm* MS 2041f, fo. 49v.

[20] As Peter Williams has demonstrated, use of the chromatic fourth runs like a thread through music of the 16th to 20th centuries. See his *The Chromatic Fourth during Four Centuries of Music* (Oxford: Clarendon Press, 1997), 77.

of the 'streams in the desert'),[21] the cumulative effect of a succession of upward modulations through keys a major third apart (E major, G sharp major, C major, E major), and the series of clashing parallel thirds in contrary motion—subsequently softened—when the full choir enters are all quite new (see Ex. 2.1*a*). Although a brief recapitulation imparts a sense of thematic resolution, both here and in the following recitative 'And a highway shall be there', Wesley relied principally on harmony and tonality to shape the music. Indeed, the latter movement is crowned by one of those master strokes at which he excelled, the dramatic juxtaposition of tonalities a semitone apart, B flat minor and B major. Yet, as Ex. 2.1*b–d* demonstrates, the passage as we know it today is the product of considered revision, as neither the ethereal sound of high voices (SSAT) at the words 'But the redeemed shall walk there' nor the silent pause preceding their entry were part of the original conception. Note, too, how the rhythm was subtly altered and longer note values introduced to provide a natural rallentando.

Even the well-wrought fugue ('And the ransomed of the Lord'), which proclaims a link with the past, is crowned by a bold modern gesture—a totally unexpected modulation to C major. The composed rallentando that forms the coda itself provides a fine climax (note the powerful effect of the re-entry of the pedals), but the sudden move away from the tonic is a master stroke. As Nicholas Temperley has written, 'the key transition itself was not unusual . . . but the sequence and spacing of the chords, and the position of the passage at the climax of a long and arduous fugal movement make it electrifying'.[22] It was a technique Wesley was to employ in several other works written during the 1830s and 1840s, among them 'O Lord, thou art my God', and the *Choral Song* and Andante in E flat from the first set of *Three Pieces for a Chamber Organ*, and surely reflects Walter Parratt's comment that he was 'especially good at "extraneous modulation"'[23] (defined as 'modulation to an extreme or unrelated key').[24] Rather than ending triumphantly (as Goss was to do in his setting), Wesley chose to conclude with a quiet, glee-like movement for verse ensemble in which the full choir only enters for the final cadence. Such an ending had no obvious precedent, and this, combined with the music's decorative chromaticism, led to mixed reactions among contemporary critics. But with the benefit of hindsight we can view the music more dispassionately

---

[21] Did Gustav Holst have these chords in mind when making his arrangement of 'Personent hodie'? See *The Oxford Book of Carols* (London: Oxford University Press, 1928), 166–8.

[22] *The Romantic Age*, 198.   [23] 'Oxford', *MT*, 58 (1917), 182.

[24] Stainer and Barrett, *Dictionary of Musical Terms*, 166. For a more extended discussion of the topic see my article 'Modulation Run Mad' in Jeremy Dibble and Bennett Zon (eds.), *Nineteenth Century British Music Studies*, 2 (Aldershot: Ashgate, 2002), 223–34.

Ex. 2.1. 'The wilderness': *a* 'For in the wilderness'; *b–d* 'And a highway shall be there', 1834, 1840, and 1868 versions

and see it for what it was surely intended to be—a peaceful conclusion to an outstanding work.

'The Wilderness' was also the first work to illustrate Wesley's characteristic method of compiling anthem texts. Unlike many composers who were content to take verses from a single source and set them to music with the minimum of alteration, he invariably rearranged his texts, omitting sections or changing their order until he had the perfect vehicle for his purpose. It is particularly interesting to compare his selection from Isaiah 35 with Goss's almost complete setting, chosen not by himself but by the Succentor of St Paul's, the Revd W. C. F. Webber,[25] which lacks the simple directness and immediacy of Wesley's. Take, for example, verses 8–9, where the picturesque references to the 'wayfaring men' and the lion or 'ravenous beast' serve more to obscure than to enlighten (see Table 2.2).

TABLE 2.2. *Comparison of the texts from Isaiah 35 set by Wesley and Goss in 'The Wilderness'*

Wesley	Goss
vv. 8, 9. And a highway shall be there: it shall be called The way of holiness; the unclean shall not pass over it, but the redeemed shall walk there.	v. 8. And an highway shall be there, and a way, and it shall he called The way of holiness; the unclean shall not pass over it, but it shall be for those: the wayfaring men, though fools, shall not err therein.
	v. 9. No lion shall be there, nor any ravenous beast shall go up thereon, it shall not be found there; but the redeemed shall walk there.

One can only speculate on how the Hereford choir coped with the anthem's considerable technical demands, but the resumption of choral services had revealed serious deficiencies in its ranks. Foremost was a shortage of boys able to sing, and at a chapter meeting on 8 November it was decided to advertise a voice trial for three new choristers, who were required to have 'a correct ear' as well as a 'good voice'.[26] Doubtless of no less concern to Wesley was the fact that the men of the choir, the vicars choral, had become extremely erratic in their attendance. They were also regularly absent on Sundays, a situation which arose because all were in holy orders and, to augment their stipends, held livings in or near the city which necessitated their attending to parochial duties. Despite its unsatisfactory nature the practice had been toler-

---

[25] According to Robert Sloman (who heard it from Wesley in 1866), Goss's anthem was commissioned by the Dean and Chapter of St Paul's after Wesley turned down their request for the loan of a set of copies of his setting. Wesley's action was apparently motivated by the earlier refusal of the Dean and Chapter to subscribe to the *Anthems* (see *Lbl* Add. MS 35020, fo. 57ᵛ—an unidentified newspaper clipping dated 16 Jan. 1895).

[26] Hereford Cathedral Chapter act book, 1814–34 (*H MS* 7031/18, 404).

ated as a necessary evil, and to cater for these occasions Clarke-Whitfeld had composed three settings of the Communion service for treble voices alone. So, too, did Wesley, and his early settings of the Creed and Responses to the Commandments (to reappear in his Service in E) were, as he put it, 'written for treble voices only, to meet an emergency which occasionally arose at one of the Cathedrals with which he [Wesley] was connected'.[27] After his first Easter Sunday, Dean Merewether had determined to remedy this situation and in June 1833 appointed two lay singing men from Hampton as 'Deacons to take part in the Musical Services of the Choir on Sundays, festivals, State Days and at the Audit on the Morning and Evening Services of those days'.[28] But Easter Sunday 1834 proved to be little better as only one 'Deacon' turned up, and Wesley's specially written anthem, 'Blessed be the God and Father' had perforce to be sung by 'Trebles and a single Bass voice' when it was performed at Evensong.[29]

But to return to November 1832. With the excitement of the audit now past, and in the knowledge that he had written something of more than passing worth, Wesley decided to enter 'The wilderness' for the Gresham Prize Medal. Little can he have realized what a hornet's nest he would stir up, or that the repercussions of the affair would continue to resound for the next twenty years. The prize, for a newly composed anthem or service setting, had been established the previous year by Miss Maria Hackett (1783–1874), better known for her lifelong work on behalf of the welfare and general education of cathedral choristers. To encourage young composers she offered an annual prize, with a gold medal worth 5 guineas. The contest took its name from Sir Thomas Gresham, and the prizewinning entry would be sung at a commemorative service in his honour at St Helen's, Bishopsgate. There were three umpires: Miss Hackett appointed William Crotch and R. J. S. Stevens, and they in turn selected William Horsley. All three subscribed to the view that church music had witnessed a 'golden age' in the sixteenth and seventeenth centuries, and that thereafter it had had been in a state of decline.

For Crotch and the other members of this small but influential group 'The introduction of novelty, variety, contrast, expression, originality, etc., is the very cause of the decay so long apparent in our Church music'.[30] Making an

---

[27] S. S. Wesley, *A Morning & Evening Cathedral Service* (London: Chappell, [1845]), vi.

[28] Hereford Cathedral Chapter act book, 1814–34 (*H* MS 7031/18, 404). For a full discussion of Dean Merewether's difficulties with the vicars choral, see Gerald Aymler and John Tiller (eds.), *Hereford Cathedral: A History* (London: The Hambledon Press, 2000), 416–19.

[29] S. S. Wesley, *Anthems* (1853), 229. The tradition that the solitary bass was the Dean's butler becomes more comprehensible in the knowledge of the appointment of the two lay singers.

[30] Letter to Maria Hackett, quoted by John S. Bumpus in *A History of English Cathedral Music*, 2 vols. (London: T. Werner Laurie, 1908), 2. 370.

analogy with painting and drawing on the views of Sir Joshua Reynolds, Uvedale Price and others, he had proposed that 'Music, like painting, may be divided into three styles—the sublime, the beautiful, and the ornamental'.[31] Church music, he believed, should be in the sublime style of the sixteenth and early seventeenth centuries:

The sublime is founded on principles of vastness and incomprehensibility. The word sublime originally signifies high, lofty, elevated; and this style, accordingly, never descends to any thing small, delicate, light, pretty, playful, or comic. The grandest style in music is therefore the sacred style—that of the church and oratorio . . . where the words convey the most awful and striking images. Infinity, and, what is next to it, immensity, are among the most efficient causes of this quality; and when we hear innumerable voices and instruments sounding the praises of God in solemn and becoming strains, the most sublime image that can fill the mind seldom fails to present itself—that of the heavenly host described in the Holy Scriptures . . .

    In music, the great compass of notes employed in a full orchestra conveys an idea of vastness undefined. A uniform succession of major chords, the most agreeable of all sounds, resembles a blaze of light; while the unintelligible combination of extraneous discords conveys a feeling like that caused by darkness.[32]

In contrast were the beautiful and the ornamental:

When . . . the melody is vocal and flowing, the measure symmetrical, the harmony simple and intelligible, and the style of the whole soft, delicate, and sweet, it may with as much propriety be called beautiful, as a small, perfect, Grecian temple, or a landscape of Claude Lorraine.

    The ornamental style is the result of roughness, playful intricacy, and abrupt variations. In painting, splendid draperies, intricate architecture, gold or silver cups and vases, and all such objects are ornamental; aged heads, old hovels, cottages, or mills, ruined temples or castles, rough animals, peasants at a fair, and the like, are picturesque. In music, eccentric and difficult melody; rapid, broken, and varied rhythm; wild and unexpected modulation, indicate this third style.[33]

    Crotch even supplied a simple rule of thumb for identifying the style of a work: 'It is sublime if it inspires veneration, beautiful if it pleases, ornamental if it amuses'.[34] But when he wrote that composers who had written in the style he designated 'the pure sublime'[35] had trodden 'in the highest walks of the art', in contrast to 'those of the ornamental [who] are far below',[36] it was immediately obvious that a work so self-consciously modern and full of 'wild and unexpected modulation' as 'The Wilderness' was unlikely to be successful.

---

[31] William Crotch, *Substance of Several Courses of Lectures on Music* (London: Longman, Rees, Orme, Brown, and Green, 1831), 28. Although not published until 1831, Crotch's lectures were a revised version of those he had given at Oxford in 1800–4.

[32] Ibid. 32–4.   [33] Ibid. 35–6.   [34] Ibid. 43.   [35] Ibid. 39.   [36] Ibid. 43.

Indeed, given that both Horsley and Stevens held similar views, its failure was almost a foregone conclusion. Wesley, who had already encountered Horsley's pedantry, was quite aware of this. 'I have sent an Anthem for the Gresham Prize', he wrote to Kearns, '—more fool me, say you. I like the music very well, it was done here in the Cathedral. If I am unsuccessful, I shall print it with a long preface of abuse of the umpires, Crotch, Horsley, Stevens; I should like your opinion of it . . .'[37]

But despite such ill omens he had decided to make his bid, and had already dispatched last-minute instructions to his mother to collect the parcel from the coach office:

Call on Monday Morning at the coach office for a parcel. It is an anthem I have written for a prize in London and must be delivered on Monday or it is too late . . . Pray don't fail to meet the coach and open the parcel when you get it and then do as I will tell you in the letter. You must keep Father at home as he will have to write something in a letter, it is only just to write a Motto in Latin, you had better mention it a once, tell him I wish it to be—Let justice be done, or—weigh and consider, or anything he chooses—only, in Latin it must be . . .[38]

Samuel Wesley duly endorsed his son's letter with the words 'Fiat Justitia', but the anthem had arrived too late and was held over until the following year's competition. Unaware of this, Samuel Sebastian wrote again to ask his mother to treat him to a copy of *The Harmonicon*:

I suppose an account of the Gresham prize will be in that. If anybody else gets it, you must go and fetch my Manuscript back. You can send the Harmonicon in the parcel—do send it if you can afford it, dont on any account distress yourself though, as I can perhaps borrow it here at any rate get Glenn to look at it.[39]

When, in November 1833, 'The Wilderness' finally came up for consideraton, it found little favour with the judges. According to anecdote Crotch 'expressed his dislike of the whole design . . . by drawing on the copy . . . the portrait of a chorister boy with his face distorted with agony in the effort to reach the high A in the concluding verse, "And sorrow and sighing" ',[40] while Stevens dismissed it (in a letter to Miss Hackett) with the memorable words 'a

---

[37] Letter (undated but *c*.31 Dec. 1832) (*Lbl* Add. MS 69435, fo. 5ᵛ).

[38] Letter dated 15 Dec. [1832] (*Lbl* Add. MS 35019, fo. 12ʳ).

[39] Letter postmarked 1 Jan. 1833 (ibid., fo. 14ᵛ).

[40] Bumpus, *A History of English Cathedral Music*, 2. 370. Kellow J. Pye, winner of the 1832 competition, later described how Crotch had informed him that he had preferred a different work but had been dissuaded by Horsley and Stevens. When he added that Crotch had subsequently told him that his preferred work was by 'young Wesley' his memory was clearly muddled, as the two anthems were judged in different years, although he persisted in believing that he and Wesley were fellow competitors in 1832. (See the letter from A. H. D. Prendergast to F. G. Edwards, dated 31 March 1885, in the private library of Novello & Co.)

clever thing, but not Cathedral Music'.[41] In the event the medal went to John Goss for his fluently written (and stylistically 'correct') setting of 'Have mercy upon me', which, like all the other prize compositions, has fallen into oblivion. There the matter might have ended, but news of the failure had got abroad and reached the ears of H. J. Gauntlett. Although they were later to fall out, the mid-1830s saw Gauntlett and Wesley on cordial terms, and in 1836 Gauntlett brought Wesley's name before the musical public at large in the course of two strongly worded and cogently argued articles entitled 'The Gresham Prize' and 'English Ecclesiastical Composers of the Present Age' in *The Musical World* (of which he was editor).[42]

It was in the latter that Gauntlett most effectively dissected Crotch's arguments and demonstrated the futility of trying to prohibit the use of certain chords on the grounds that they were 'secular' rather than 'sacred'. Taking the example of Purcell—another composer as much at home in the theatre as in the church—he noted that 'Purcell, and with him all great writers, introduced in their church-music *all harmonies that were then invented and in use*. These great spirits did not recognise the dogma, that *an isolated harmony was in its nature purely secular, and improper for the sanctuary*.'[43]

No less importantly, he also took the opportunity to eulogize 'The Wilderness', commenting that he 'would have given a dozen Gresham medals'[44] to have written the concluding bars of 'And the ransomed of the Lord'. For Gauntlett, as for most of his contemporaries, the art of music was steadily moving towards a state of greater perfection, and neither he nor Wesley had any time for the views of Crotch and his followers. '. . . if the system pursued by Messrs. Crotch and Horsley . . . should unhappily obtain general favour and adoption', observed Gauntlett, 'it will ultimately affect a total change in our cathedral style of composition, and lead to its destruction rather than to its improvement'.[45] Wesley, in contrast, he hailed as the inventor of a 'school (yet in its infancy) founded on a union of Purcell, Bach, and Beethoven', noting that his works contained 'the two great requisites for Church composition: *learning*, as distinguished from *pedantry*,—and *expression*'.[46] '*Expression*', he wrote, 'appears in ideas of majesty, solemnity, and pathos, contrasted with energy, vivacity, grace, beauty, and force of colouring'[47]—in short, those qualities most removed from the 'pure sublime'. The battle between the two schools rumbled on for several years, but with the ending of the Gresham competition in 1845 it quickly ran out of steam. This was not, however, before there had been accusations of foul play. The Revd W. H.

---

[41] Letter dated 30 Nov. 1833 (*Lgc* MS 10 189/2, fo. 346).
[42] See *MW*, 2 (1836), 81–6, 97–101, 113–20.   [43] Ibid. 114–15.   [44] Ibid. 117.
[45] 'The Gresham Prize', 98.   [46] Ibid. 84.   [47] Ibid.

Havergal, winner in 1836 and 1841, felt particularly aggrieved (as he complained to Miss Hackett):

I wished, also, to offer a suggestion or two about the wording of the advertisement which occasionally appears for the direction of candidates who send in compositions for the prize. Would it not be well <u>expressly to state</u> the <u>style</u> of composition which the Umpires (or those who appoint them!) wish to be adopted?—viz—the genuine <u>English</u> Cathedral style of such & such periods? . . . Such a notice wd., I think, save either the efforts or the disappointment, of many a candidate. At all events it wd. be likely to stop the <u>silly</u> clamour of certain scribblers (<u>writers</u> I cannot call them) in the Musical World, about the narrow-mindedness (!!!) and other <u>little</u> defects of the Gresham Umpires.[48]

Despite its short lifespan, the Gresham competition cast a long shadow over church music. Not only had its avowed intention of encouraging the composition of church music ended in failure, but it had also left a sour taste behind it. Wesley certainly felt bitter and could not resist a sarcastic comment in the preface to his Service in E:

In London, a Lady annually awards a Gold Medal, value Five Pounds, for encouragement of the *true Church School*. This donation . . . has existed some years; and, even now . . . competition has not fallen into such perfect disrepute, but that some few among the earliest beginners in Musical Composition are observed to make their first essay, with a view towards publication, in this direction.[49]

But in 1833, with 'The Wilderness' dispatched on its fateful journey, Wesley was free (as he told Kearns) to turn his attention to other matters:

I . . . am now going to address you on a subject very near my heart as you will know. I saw an account of Mendelssohn's intended proceedings at the Philharmonic [Society]. <u>I will send something</u>. A friend of mine will leave Hereford on Monday . . . [and] I shall <u>send</u> by him, an Overture and my Benedictus newly <u>scored</u>, will you do me the <u>very great kindness</u> to overlook them? I dont know anything for which I could be more grateful than this <u>assistance</u> . . . I know it is a tiresome job but any <u>return</u> I can make shall not be neglected, and I keep my word in <u>some matters</u> . . .[50]

Rivalry with Mendelssohn was a major factor, as Wesley's letter to the secretary of the Philharmonic Society makes clear:

Sir

I take the liberty of troubling you with two compositions of mine for the inspection of the Philharmonic Society's Committee.

---

[48] Letter dated 20 Feb. 1837 (*Lgc* MS 10 189/3, fo. 265).
[49] *A Morning & Evening Cathedral Service*, vii.
[50] Letter dated 31 Dec. 1832 (*Lbl* Add. MS 69435, fo. 5).

I am not unacquainted with the suspicious view with which the Musical writings of Englishmen are received by your Society, I cannot but admit that those suspicions are most justly founded, but from the liberal patronage you have lately bestowed on a foreigner, 'of distinguished merit, truly' I have ventured to hope that even the accompanying productions may not be thrown aside <u>unexamined</u>. Should they be <u>favorably</u> received, I shall esteem the good opinion of the Society as a mark of high honor.[51]

'This is a canting Epistle' he told Kearns, 'but it is a canting society, [and] I have no expectation that they will perform these things, but their refusal will give me a <u>spur</u>'.[52] For once his pessimism was misplaced, and on Wednesday 24 January he wrote in some excitement to say that provided the orchestral parts were available, the overture would be 'tried' on the 31st:

This of course pleased me much for should it be successful I shall receive a <u>spur</u> which may be highly useful to <u>me</u> in future proceedings . . .

Now to return to (as Atkins would say) Almighty, Eternal, and everlasting—<u>self</u>. Are you going to London on Friday? If you are, I want you to get the Score of the overture and take it to any copyist you prefer and desire him to get it ready by the 27th.—Sunday Evening or Monday the 28th. Can you do this much for me[?][53]

Wesley travelled to London to be present at the trial, but beyond a report in *The Harmonicon* that among the compositions played were 'symphonies by Mr. W. Griesbach, Mr. Cipriani Potter . . . and M. Rousselot; also an overture, by Mr. S. B. Wesley [*sic*]'[54] nothing more is known of the occasion. As the work was never repeated one can only assume that it failed to impress, and today even its identity remains unclear. What is certain, however, is that in January 1833 Wesley had two overtures to hand, the 'Philharmonic' one and another (as he wrote to Kearns): 'Would there be any chance of getting an Overture done at Covent Garden[?] I did one for their instruments, if there is, I would have it copied and get <u>you</u> to attend rehearsals. I like it better than the one I send, but it would require <u>more</u> practice.'[55]

While the latter can be identified fairly positively as the Overture in E major (which calls for four horns and trombones and was apparently not performed until the 1834 Hereford Three Choirs Festival), the only contender for the former—the so-called Symphony in C major/minor—would appear to be ruled out by the watermark date of its sole source—a roughly written manuscript, much of it on paper dated 1834. Was there a third work which has since disappeared?

---

[51] Letter dated 1 Jan. 1833 (*Lbl* Loan 48.13/35).
[52] Letter dated 1 Jan. 1833 (*Lbl* Add. MS 69435, fo. 7).   [53] Ibid., fo. 9.   [54] *Har*, 11 (1833), 64.
[55] Letter dated 31 Dec. 1832 (*Lbl* Add. MS 69435, fo. 5).

Although his partial success at the Philharmonic Society must have been gratifying, it did little to advance Wesley's career. Indeed, once he was back in Hereford the thrill of hearing his overture played in the Hanover Square Rooms must soon have seemed like a distant memory, and his hopes of making a name for himself as a composer an unattainable dream. Now, surely, the reality of the situation must have been only too apparent. How could he, a young and obscure musician from the provinces, hope to achieve recognition on the musical stage of London when with every passing day his links with the capital became more tenuous and any memories of him ever weaker? The Philharmonic Society had provided a lifeline, and a performance at one of their concerts would both have kept his name alive and brought his music before a wider public. But it was not to be. The events of January 1833 formed a watershed in his career, and thenceforth he remained an outsider, on the periphery of national musical life. In consequence the focus of his career now turned inexorably from the concert-hall to the church and cathedral, and during the next six to eight years secular works steadily yielded pride of place to sacred ones. While the change was neither immediate nor absolute (though it gained momentum after his move away from Hereford and the Three Choirs Festival in 1835), it poses an intriguing question: would his development have proceeded as it did had he not suffered such enforced artistic isolation, or would he ultimately have concentrated on church music regardless of circumstances? Although such speculation must remain unanswered, it is worth bearing in mind that it was the opportunity to compose his first large-scale anthem, 'The Wilderness', in 1832 that had suddenly brought him to artistic maturity, and that a large proportion of his most inspired works are settings of sacred words, be they church music or sacred songs. Words, too, imposed a degree of discipline, and many of his vocal works have a tighter structure than the instrumental pieces, which have a tendency to ramble. Yet the fact that he had served an 'apprenticeship' in the demanding environment of the opera-house meant that, irrespective of the ultimate direction of his career, he was ideally equipped to inject new life into the traditional forms of anthem and service. Indeed, it is because their roots were so firmly planted in the vital soil of a living musical tradition—and a style, incidentally, which came naturally to him—that 'The Wilderness' and the works which followed it were so successful.

Having demonstrated so convincingly that the verse anthem could be adapted to the changing conditions of the nineteenth century, and paying scant regard to the verdict of the Gresham Prize umpires, Wesley proceeded to build on his achievement, most notably in 'Blessed be the God and Father'. Written to meet the unusual situation existing on Easter Day 1834, it sets

verses about Christ's resurrection from the First Epistle of Peter and demonstrates an even greater reliance than 'The Wilderness' on a contemporary harmonic idiom (with its inevitable secular overtones), as well as an increasing
concern for the overall shape of a work. Although following the outward form
of a full-with-verse anthem, the mixture of declamatory and lyrical material
and the manner in which its five linked but contrasted sections—an opening
four-part chorus, an arioso for male voices in unison, a central treble arioso
and duet, a male voice recitative, and a concluding four-part fughetta—coalesce to form a convincing arch-like structure, unimpeded by strong internal
cadences, suggest a conscious debt to the operatic or oratorio writing of Spohr.
Consider, for example, the opening vocal numbers of the second part of *Die
letzten Dinge*. The first (no. 14) is an extended bass solo, 'So spricht der Herr',
containing a mixture of arioso and recitative, and leads directly into the
soprano and tenor duet 'Sei mir nicht schrecklich in der Noth', which in turn
is linked to the chorus 'So ihr mich von ganzem Herzen suchet':[56] the ear,
however, does not hear the internal divisions, but perceives a continuous
musical span.

    While the circumstances at Hereford were no doubt responsible for the
prominence of unison writing, this also reflects Wesley's readiness to expand
the stylistic boundaries of what was admissable. Even its appearance on the
printed page is quite different from that of other contemporary anthems, with
comparatively little four-part writing and a very pianistic accompaniment to
the treble solo 'Love one another'. The latter also provides a good illustration
of his concern for word-setting and of his refusal to allow melodic lines to be
dictated by musical rather than verbal considerations (see Ex. 2.2*a*). Contrast
this with a contemporary work by his most distinguished predecessor, Thomas
Attwood's 'Bow down thine ear' (*c*.1833; Ex. 2.2*b*). Although the musical
styles are not dissimilar, Wesley's melody is shaped by the rhythm and nuances
of the text, with important words or syllables falling on strong beats or high
notes. Attwood's, in contrast, gives every impression of having been conceived independently, resulting in an unfortunate stress on 'unto' (bar 23) and
the compression of 'daily unto' (bar 27). As if to point the difference, Wesley
subsequently broke up his original phrase structure to create a perfectly balanced alternation of four- and three-bar phrases.

---

[56] William Gatens has put forward the alternative suggestion that this and other anthems derive their
shape from the concert aria. While this could be argued for 'Blessed be the God and Father'—though
Wesley's considerable theatrical experience would still suggest the *scena* as a more likely source of influence—his attempt to broaden the analogy to include all Wesley's anthems moves on to much shakier
ground. For all their differences in musical style or in the proportions of their movements, such works as
'The Wilderness', 'O give thanks unto the Lord', 'Trust ye in the Lord', and 'O Lord, thou art my God'
follow clearly in the long tradition of Boyce, Clarke-Whitfeld, and Attwood. (See Gatens, *Victorian
Cathedral Music*, 140–3.)

Ex. 2.2. *a* Thomas Attwood: 'Bow down thine ear'; *b* 'Blessed be the God and Father', 'Love one another'

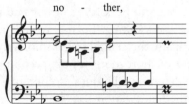

Throughout the work the organ plays a vital part in the musical argument, underpinning the vocal writing, linking the sections, providing colour (as in the mournful combination of Clarabella and Swell reeds at the words 'The grass withereth'), and, at the fortissimo dominant seventh which introduces the final fugato, making an exhilarating gesture which still retains the power to thrill. The choir's subsequent fanfare-like opening and forceful organ inter-jections show Wesley at his best, writing naturally in a free and unforced style and paying scant regard to the niceties of a 'church' idiom. With its direct appeal and youthful vigour, this is unquestionably one of his most effective works and has justifiably retained its popularity.

Yet despite the anthem's undoubted success Wesley never repeated its *scena*-like structure. He did, however, continue to experiment and in 'Trust ye in the Lord' (c.1835) produced an unusual work in da capo form in which the short opening chorus frames the two linked movements for solo treble. Other unorthodox features include a lengthy organ interlude linking the first two movements—the second an arioso in the Neapolitan key—and an elaborate obbligato organ part in the following treble solo. The last is a particularly sub-stantial movement which admirably demonstrates the subtlety of his vocal writing, with phrases of varying lengths dovetailing to produce a variegated patchwork, held together by a four-times repeated bass-line (see bars 79–82).

A similar desire to stretch boundaries can been seen in his setting of the Nicene Creed. Abandoning the customary sequence of short self-contained sections in favour of a single ABAC structure, he produced a remarkably uni-fied movement, bound together and driven forward by the almost continous crotchet movement in the accompaniment. Not until the final clause 'And I believe in the Holy Ghost' does the pace slacken, with the chant-like setting imparting an appropriate sense of dignity to these solemn words. But the most striking feature is the modernity of the harmonic language. To a generation for whom the once-exotic sound of the diminished seventh has been cheapened by over-exposure, its use at the words 'God of God, Light of Light' may seem to be in poor taste, but in the 1830s it was a far from hackneyed device and in rural Hereford would have sounded novel and exciting. So too would the delicious chromatic auxiliaries which accompany the central treble solo 'Who for us men', while the use and development of short motifs in the accompa-niment demonstrates an early alliance between the techniques of contempo-rary instrumental music and the English cathedral tradition (Ex. 2.3).

But as with so much of his music, Wesley looked backwards as well as for-wards and, at the words 'And the third day he rose again', incorporated, with due acknowledgement, a brief chromatic progression used by both Bach in the Credo of the Mass in B minor (at the words 'et expecto resurectionem') and

Ex. 2.3. Service in E, Creed, 'Who for us men'

Spohr in *Die letzten Dinge* (at the words 'Das Grab gibt seine Todten!'); as later
works demonstrate, he was to become adept at marrying Bach's essentially linear chromaticism with Spohr's extended harmonic palette. Although the
church music he wrote remains the best memorial to Wesley's years at
Hereford, it is doubtful whether, 'The Wilderness' excepted, he ultimately set
great store by it. 'Trust ye in the Lord' was allowed to remain unpublished,
and when writing to Vincent Novello several years later to enquire about the
possibility of his publishing 'two little anthems [probably 'Blessed be the God
and Father' and 'Trust ye in the Lord'] and a creed', he asked for his 'indulgence of the music':

Allow me to inquire whether it would be agreeable to you to publish of mine, two
little anthems and a creed which I am disposed to print together . . . They are chiefly
for treble voices and I set no store by them as they are fitter for the drawing room than
the church, although this may be in their favour in one respect . . .
   The creeds of the Protestant Church, I mean their music, is very short, scarcely a
word sung twice. I publish this one of mine really because so many persons inquire
for copies which it is impossible for me to give them, [and] I cannot recommend its
music to you, but I do not now presume to address you as an artist but as [a publisher.]
If you desire to see them before you oblige me with a reply they shall be forwarded,
but I bespeak your indulgence for the music, [as] they are written for country folk,
and the ignorance of such people is I think beyond your conception.[57]

Although Wesley's self-depreciation should be taken with a pinch of salt, it
is highly likely that by the 1840s he had begun to feel rather self-conscious
about the markedly secular tone of these early works. Certainly by 1865 when
he wrote to a certain Alderman Dyson of Windsor he played down the importance of 'Blessed be the God and Father':

I assure you I view it merely as a sort of shewy sketch, or a little thing just made to
stop a gap, and never meant for publication. It may be something new in its style, and
certainly is effective, but it does not satisfy me as to being true Church music.
However, people all seem to like it, and perhaps it may lead people to look at better
things of mine.[58]

But even in the 1830s church music formed only one part of his output, and
it should not be forgotten than he was still best known as a composer of songs
and piano pieces. Two new songs had appeared in the autumn of 1832—
'When we Two Parted' (to words by Byron) and 'The Smiling Spring' (to a
translation of De Beranger)—and he completed another, 'Wert thou like me'
(to words quoted by Sir Walter Scott in *A Legend of Montrose*), on 29 December

[57] Letter dated 29 Jan. 1840 (*Lbl* Add. MS 11730, fos. 227–8).
[58] Letter quoted in *MT*, 36 (1895), 407.

1832. Publication had to wait until summer 1835, by which time a further three songs, 'Blessed are the dead', 'There be none of beauty's daughters' (both settings of Byron), and 'Did I possess the magic art' (to words by Samuel Rogers), were ready for issue. Although not on a par with his finest sacred works, they are all charming, if sometimes slight pieces. 'Wert thou like me', for example, demonstrates a skilful handling of tonality (with the mediant major and minor as the main subsidiary keys), a well-integrated thematic structure (ABB'AC), and an effective use of a simultaneous false relation to depict pain—'To weep' or 'To wound'. But perhaps the strongest evidence of his growing skill is the economy with which he was able to achieve this. There is, one feels, not a note too many, and a sense of true pathos in the move to A minor ('But parted by severe decree far diff'rent must our fortunes be'), with its striking Neapolitan harmony (Ex. 2.4*a*). In contrast to such studied simplicity, 'Did I possess the magic art' is a more sophisticated work, full of those chromatic inflexions so characteristic of the early romantic style, and one of the few works in which he demonstrates a true lightness of touch.[59] But it is the role of the accompaniment that most sets it apart from his earlier songs. Now elevated to the status of equal partner, its function is twofold: to provide a clearly defined formal structure, with the opening theme used as a ritornello, and to allow the music to 'breathe' by means of brief interludes between the vocal phrases (Ex. 2.4*b*). In both it succeeds admirably and the song remains one of Wesley's most polished scores.

While the majority of the songs are strophic ballads, 'Blessed are the dead' adopts the cavatina–cabaletta pattern of the operatic aria, while 'There be none of beauty's daughters' is a through-composed work in the new English art-song tradition. In contrast to the delicacy of 'Did I possess', the former possesses an almost Beethovenian grandeur and exploits the extremes of the keyboard with some typical flights of harmonic fancy—a sudden plunge from the tonic (E flat), via the tonic minor and flattened mediant (G flat), to the triad on the flat seventh (D flat), juxtaposed with its own Neapolitan sixth, D major (I–i–♭III♮⁶₄–♭iii♮⁶₄–♭VII–♮VII⁶). Wide leaps in the vocal part add to the excitement, while the final pages of the cabaletta are equally dramatic, with expanding melodic intervals and rapid descending scales (spanning over five octaves) bringing the work to an exhilarating close.

In comparison with such virtuoso display, 'There be none of beauty's daughters' is an altogether more elegant settting whose through-composed

---

[59] Among the several small alterations Wesley made to Rogers's verses one stands out, the substitution of 'Mary' for 'Chloe' in the line 'Its lustre caught Mary's eye'. Given that the song was published in Aug. or Sept. 1835, only a few months after Wesley had married Mary Anne Merewether, it is not hard to divine his reasons.

Ex. 2.4. *a* 'Wert thou like me'; *b* 'Did I possess the magic art'

(ABA') form, atmospheric piano writing, and increasing harmonic independence represent the pinnacle of Wesley's songwriting to date. It also makes an interesting comparison with Mendelssohn's simpler, but arguably more polished, setting of the same words, completed in 1833 but unpublished until 1836. The comparison is particularly apposite because Wesley had based his main theme on the introduction to Mendelssohn's *Lied ohne Worte* Op. 19 No. 4 (published in London in 1830). Yet despite its inevitable Mendelssohnian overtones 'There be none of beauty's daughters' shows him following a more individual path, less dependent upon decorative chromaticism than 'Did I possess the magic art' and likewise more confident in his tonal explorations, venturing into such remote keys as A sharp and E sharp major. Some of the most poetic writing is found in the central section, where, at the words 'And the midnight moon is weaving her bright chain o'er the deep', the essentially mechanical figuration in the accompaniment is transformed into an array of shimmering chords, unique in his output (see Ex. 2.5).

Since leaving London Wesley had written very little for the piano, and the only substantial piece to date from his time at Hereford is the Rondo in G, probably completed in 1834 and published by Mori & Lavenu a year or two later. Fluently written and containing more than a hint of Spohr, it does, however, contain two pointers to the future—a characteristic disregard for the passing dissonance involved in the strict pursuit of sequential passages and a clear demonstration of the growing importance of counterpoint, seen in the manner in which the simple homophonic opening gives way to episodes based on strings of suspensions (see Ex. 2.6).

Another, but very different, contemporary keyboard work is *A Selection of Psalm Tunes Adapted Expressly to the English Organ with Pedals*, issued by J. Dean about February 1834. The custom of preceding the singing of metrical psalms (or hymns) with an elaborate 'giving-out' of the tune and of linking the verses with instrumental interludes was an old one. Common throughout the eighteenth century, it was becoming obsolescent by the 1830s but Wesley, with his strong links with the previous generation of organists, chose to continue it and provided a series of givings-out, interludes, and varied harmonizations for nineteen psalm tunes. Casting his net widely to embrace both the simplest chorale preludes of J. S. Bach and Spohr's pervasive chromatic harmony, he attempted to inaugurate a new style of hymn tune prelude, seen at its best in the givings-out for 'Angel's Hymn', Psalm 104 ('Hanover'), and 'Irish'. Yet despite running to a second, much revised, edition eight years later, *A Selection of Psalm Tunes* had few followers.[60] Indeed, like Wesley's extended anthems it

---

[60] For a comprehensive list of publications including interludes see David Burchell, 'The Role of Pedals in the Accompaniment of English Hymnody, 1810–1860', *BIOSJ*, 25 (2001), 56–77.

Ex. 2.5. 'There be none of beauty's daughters'

Ex. 2.6. Rondo in G

represented the final flowering of an old tradition rather than the beginning of a new one. Given that the accompaniment of congregational singing formed a very minor part of his duties at Hereford, it seems likely that the collection grew out of his pre-Hereford experience as a parish church organist in London, while such an early date would also account for the often bizarre chromatic harmony, which he later attempted to blame on the machinations of a 'friend'. Although typographical errors certainly abound, it is hard to believe that the character of the work was so altered by a third party as to necessitate 'immediate' (i.e. after eight years) re-engraving. What surely changed were his views on what was stylistically appropriate:

How such strange things got into the first Edition can only be accounted for by my supposing that a rather obtrusive friend of mine in London corrected! my proofs, and as this Friend interfered greatly in my affairs & afterwards published a Book of his own in the very style, as to harmony, of what I object to as regards these proofs, I feel sure that my suspicion is well founded. As soon as I saw the work I had it all re-engraved for however fond I may be of fine harmony I certainly do not think extravagance should have a place in any kind of Music whatever, in this respect. The correct Edition is headed '2nd Edition'.[61]

For all its uneven nature *A Selection of Psalm Tunes* remains a fascinating work, demonstrating again his flair—already seen in 'Blessed be the God and Father'—for colourful organ registration. It is also one of the earliest English publications to promote the technique of trio playing on the organ and had a clear didactic purpose, explained in Wesley's preface to the revised edition: 'to assist the young church organist in his accompaniment of congregational psalmody, and to furnish him, at the same time, with a work to which he may refer in his endeavours to make use of the Pedals, and acquire an independent command of the left hand',[62] words which mirror the brief introduction to Bach's *Orgel-Büchlein*:

Little Organ Book
In which a Beginner at the Organ is given Instruction in Developing a Chorale in many divers ways, and at the same time in Acquiring Facility in the Study of the Pedal since in the Chorales contained therein the Pedal is treated as Wholly Obbligato.[63]

---

[61] Letter dated 19 May 1854 to an unknown correspondent (collection of the late Betty Matthews). While the identity of the 'friend' remains a mystery, it could conceivably have been Smart, although his arrangements lack the harmonic exuberance of Wesley's.

[62] *A Selection of Psalm Tunes*, 2nd edn., 1.

[63] Trans. from Hans David and Arthur Mendel, *The Bach Reader*, rev. edn. (London: J. M. Dent & Sons, 1966), 75.

The giving-out to Psalm 104 provides a perfect illustration of the techniques required, demanding an independent command of the left hand and mastery of the pedals, besides illustrating a clear indebtedness to Bach (see Ex. 2.7).

Wesley's predilection for all things German is also evident in his most successful secular works of this period, the four glees written for the Manchester Gentlemen's Glee Club. Defined as a 'piece of unaccompanied vocal music in at least three parts, and for solo voices, usually those of men',[64] the glee was a specifically English genre which flourished during the second half of the eighteenth century and the first quarter of the nineteenth; by the end of this period few towns of any size did not boast their own glee clubs, meeting monthly at an inn (or similar venue) to combine musical and gastronomic pleasures. Membership was open to middle-class amateurs, though 'professional' members (i.e. professional musicians) were always welcome and usually undertook the bulk of the singing. Manchester, however, had been an exception, and until the foundation of the Gentlemen's Glee Club in 1830 glee singing had formed but one part of the programmes of the Gentlemen's Concerts. As though to demonstrate its seriousness of purpose, the third of the new club's rules was that 'one object . . . shall be to offer premiums for Glees to be written purposely for the Club',[65] and the resolve was immediately put into practice, with the first competition held in 1831. Two years later Wesley was one of seven contenders for the prize for a 'cheerful' glee with his five-part setting (ATTBB) of a translation by Byron of Anacreon's *To his Lyre* ('I wish to tune my quiv'ring lyre'). At its first hearing (on 5 September) it so impressed the committee that it received nine votes in favour and none against, and, after faring equally well on the second and third hearings, it was duly awarded the prize. One of the members recorded his impressions: 'A good Glee but not [str]ictly cheerful tho' [an]imated and with [var]iety of expression'.[66] A little over a year later, on 11 October 1834, he was again successful, though now in the 'serious' class. Details of the voting do not survive, but his four-part (ATTB) setting of verses by William Linley, 'At that Dread Hour', was judged to be the best of twelve entries. Linley had earlier published his own setting in his *Eight Glees* (1832), to which Wesley had been a subscriber; that both works are in F minor/major seems more than coincidental. 'Fill me Boy as Deep a Draught', Wesley's 'cheerful' entry, was less fortunate, and the prize went to George Hargreaves of Livrpool, winner of the 'serious' prize in 1833; a note

[64] George Grove (ed.), *A Dictionary of Music and Musicians (A.D. 1540–1889)* (London: Macmillan & Co., 1879–90), I, 598.

[65] Henry Watson, *A Chronicle of the Manchester Gentlemen's Glee Club* (Manchester: Charles H. Barber, 1906), 14.

[66] Manchester Gentlemen's Glee Club: words of candidate glees, 1833 (*Mp* R 780.68 Me 75). The mutilated state of the source accounts for the incomplete text.

Ex. 2.7. *A Selection of Psalm Tunes*, 1st edn., giving-out for Psalm 104

by Wesley on the score informing the singers that 'it can hardly be sung too fast . . . [and] must not take seven minutes in performance'[67] suggests that its first hearing had left something to be desired.

Although the techniques he employed to reflect the different sentiments of the text—changes of mood, texture, scoring, and key—had all been used before, they had rarely been handled more effectively. All can be seen in the five sections into which the first movement of 'I wish to tune my quiv'ring lyre' falls—a vigorous opening theme in the tonic, C major ('I wish to tune my quiv'ring lyre'), a turbulent, dissonant fugal exposition in the tonic minor ('When Atreus' sons advanc'd to war'), a resolute linking passage in the mediant ('Fired with the hope of future fame'), a repetition of the opening theme in the mediant minor ('The dying chords are strung anew, | To war, to war my harp is due'), and a tranquil conclusion, replete with yearning chromatic appoggiaturas, in the mediant major ('All, all in vain my wayward harp | Wakes silver notes of soft desire'). By maintaining the same pulse but varying the note values he was able to provide both variety and a sense of unity (see Ex. 2.8).

With these glees Wesley had once again successfully injected new life into an old-established form, so much so that when 'I wish to tune my quiv'ring lyre', 'At that Dread Hour' and a third, 'When Fierce Conflicting Passions Rend the Breast', written for the 1837 competition, were published in 1839, Edward Holmes seized upon them as 'most interesting and meritorious productions . . . [and] the best things in the style that we have seen for many years'. 'They show eminent talent and feeling' he continued, 'and are worthy to find a place in every classical library'. But his greatest praise was still to come: 'We regret that the modern Germans, who, in their *lieder-tafeln*, so highly cultivate part singing, are likely to know nothing of this collection; were they but to hear it, they would perceive that their present composers must bestir themselves to compete successfully with the rising talent in England.'[68]

Holmes noted with approval Wesley's use of 'modern *German* harmonies', and his musical idiom in these works is as rich as anywhere in his output. The second movement of 'When Fierce Conflicting Passions', for example, consists of a lilting barcarolle in F sharp major, whose octave writing was likened to that of a double quartet by Spohr, while attention was also drawn to the final page where the second bass is faced with a phrase which 'would, perhaps, be produced with greater certainty upon a violoncello'. Perhaps Wesley, who by 1837 had few outlets for his inspiration, was channelling his ideas into

---

[67] *Mp* MS 471.1 Me 51.   [68] *MW*, 11 (1839), 212.

Ex. 2.8. 'I wish to tune my quiv'ring lyre', openings of the five sections of the first movement

whatever medium was available to him, regardless of whether it was the most appropriate.

By now, however, greater success than a prize for glee composition had come his way, for in 1834 it had been the turn of Hereford to host the Three Choirs Festival. Wesley's first contact with the festivals had been in 1833 when he had acted as pianist at the Worcester meeting, accompanying the solo items at the secular evening concerts, but his thoughts had turned to the subject as early as December 1832, when, in a reference to Kearns's employment at a future festival, he informed him that 'The Dean intends to <u>rouse the world</u>! and bring it here'.[69] Another plan had been to invite his father to come and conduct his setting of Psalm 111, 'Confitebor tibi, Domine', but Samuel Wesley was now too old and this fell through. Kearns, however, was not forgotten, and from Wesley's letter confirming his appointment 'as a violin at your terms of the last Festival. 15 Guineas'[70] it would appear that his reward had come a year earlier than expected.

The annual 'Music Meetings' had been taking place since the early eighteenth century in rotation at Hereford, Gloucester, and Worcester, and formed the most important musical events in the local calendar.[71] By Wesley's time they had settled into a regular pattern, with an opening service in the cathedral on the first (Wednesday) morning and oratorio performances on the two subsequent ones, and a concert and ball in a secular venue each evening. Hitherto the cathedral performances had always been in the choir, but this year were transferred to the nave where, the stewards hoped, 'the more ample accommodation for the auditory, the impressive character of the architecture, and the improved sphere for the undulation of harmonious sounds, will combine to augment that unspeakable fascination which is the never-failing effect of the grand compositions selected for the occasion'.[72] While the three cathedral choirs formed the backbone of the choral forces, it had long been the practice to draw on orchestral players from the capital. François Cramer was as usual to lead the band for the morning performances, sharing his duties in the evening with J. D. Loder and Nicholas Mori, while the names of many of the leading players and singers of the day are to be found among the other performers. Wesley even repaid his debt to Hawes, who, though hardly one of the best-known singers, was numbered among the 'Principal Vocal

---

[69] Letter dated 31 Dec. 1832 (*Lbl* Add. MS 69435, fo. 5).

[70] Letter postmarked 12 June 1834 (ibid., fo. 11).

[71] For a detailed history of the festival see Anthony Boden, *Three Choirs: A History of the Festival* (Stroud: Alan Sutton, 1992).

[72] Daniel Lysons *et al.*, *Origin and Progress of the Meeting of the Three Choirs of Gloucester, Worcester & Hereford, and of the Charity Connected with it* (Gloucester: Chance and Bland, 1895), 123.

Performers' and was paid the handsome sum of £31 10s. 0d. for singing tenor in a couple of glees.

Details of the arrangements are well documented, both in the printed programme and wordbooks and in the pocketbook Wesley used to note down the names and terms of the participants.[73] This last makes fascinating reading. The young Italian singer Giulia Grisi (who had made her London début the previous April) had been his first choice for principal soprano—for a proposed fee of £300—but the position ultimately went to Maria Caradori-Allen, who received £160 for a mere three days' work! Instrumentalists were in a different league. Cramer received £63, the cellist Robert Lindley £42, and the famous double bass player Dragonetti £40: the last was also informed that 'the expence of bringing your Instrument must be paid by yourself'.[74] Wesley considered his own services to be worth £100, nearly double his annual salary, although as no official accounts survive it is not known whether he received as much.

While individual soloists chose their own solo items, ultimate responsibility for the programmes—subject to approval by the festival stewards—lay with Wesley. The music thus reflects his own preferences and affords an interesting comparison with previous festivals. The beginnings of a move away from overdependence on the choral music of Handel had been felt two years earlier when John Amott, newly appointed to Gloucester, had included a selection from Spohr's *Die letzten Dinge*, Neukomm's *Mount Sinai*, and Mozart's *Requiem*. Charles Clarke repeated the first two at Worcester the following year, together with a selection from Friedrich Schneider's *Die Sündfluth* and Crotch's *Palestine*, but it was left to Wesley (who had a particular fondness for the work) to give *Die letzten Dinge* complete. To allow time for both this and a complete performance of Mozart's *Requiem* only a selection from *Messiah* was included. 'This departure from all precedent', Amott later observed drily, 'has . . . never been repeated, and, it is hoped, never will be'.[75]

The people of Hereford were treated to more music by Spohr in the evening concerts, with performances of the overture to *Jessonda* and an extended selection from *Azor und Zemira* (with the 'Chorus of Hags' from *Faust* interpolated).[76] First heard in England in 1831 in an adaptation by Sir George Smart at Covent Garden, the opera came close to being omitted from the programme. Only a direct appeal from Wesley to Messrs Goulding & D'Almaine saved the day:

---

[73] Now *Lcm* MS 2141e.   [74] Letter dated 9 June 1834 (*Lbl* Add. MS 56411, fo. 20).

[75] Lysons *et al.*, *Origin and Progress of the Meeting of the Three Choirs*, 124.

[76] A piano arrangement of the last by Wesley survives in MS as the Witches' Rondo (*Cfm* MS MU 691).

Gentlemen

The Post is just leaving this place so I have little time to make my question. I have advertised to perform Spohr's opera Azor & Zemira at the Hereford Musical Festival. I can not get the parts [—] the copyist at the theatre does not like to part with them as he hopes to get a job to copy new ones—which is absurd as it is <u>my own whim</u> that this fine music should be played—no one elses. Can you through Sir G. Smart insist on this fellow's compliance. I must have an immediate reply—it would surely be to your advantage.[77]

Mozart was the other composer best represented, with the overture to *Don Giovanni* and the second half of the finale to Act I of *Così fan tutte* included, in addition to the Requiem and various operatic arias; his Serenade for wind instruments in C minor, K. 375, was a casualty of last-minute changes, as was Beethoven's cantata *Meeresstille und glückliche Fahrt* (Calm Sea and Prosperous Voyage). The programme however still included the latter's 'Pastoral' Symphony, together with Mendelssohn's overture to *A Midsummer Night's Dream* and an overture by Wesley himself—probably the one he had hoped to have had performed at Covent Garden in 1833—which now received its first performance.[78] Also included were three other works from his pen: the Benedictus, now framed by choral settings of the Sanctus and Osanna (both lost), the canzonet 'When we two parted', and a 'sacred song' with orchestral accompaniment, *Abraham's Offering*. The text of the last had been written by his friend W. H. Bellamy, and its first performance was entrusted to an old acquaintance from the English Opera House, Henry Phillips. 'Mr. Phillipps [sic] was evidently new to the subject, which circumstance was much against the effect of the performance', declared the critic of *The Hereford Times*, who clearly did not know what to make of the piece. Hedging his bets, he merely observed that 'of the music it is difficult, on one hearing only, to give an opinion; but its spirit is congenial with that of the poetry'.[79]

Bellamy's text tells the story of Abraham and Isaac and evoked a ready response from Wesley. Taking as his model the operatic *scena*, he produced a powerful two-movement setting (with introductory and linking recitatives), whose brooding opening in the dark key of E flat minor perfectly catches the mood of the words. Both the key and the scoring for wind alone immediately recall Spohr's overture to *Jessonda* (and remind one of Wesley's later comment to Hubert Parry that Spohr 'excelled . . . because he could bring such a

---

[77] Letter dated 7 Aug. 1834 (*Cfm* MU MS 691).

[78] The work in question can quite safely be identified as the Overture in E major, hitherto attributed to his father on the basis of the name 'S. Wesley' on the professionally copied orchestral parts. Its survival solely as a set of parts, on paper bearing the watermark date 1834 and copied by the festival copyist, I. Hedgley, points to Samuel Sebastian as the composer.

[79] *HT* (13 Sept, 1834), [3].

marvellous tone out of his orchestra'),[80] while the influence of his distinctive chromatic harmony is never far away. From this tentative beginning Wesley gradually increased the tension to build up to a searing climax over double tonic and dominant pedals. The soloist's subsequent hushed entry and the unexpected shift to E major (the Neapolitan key) introduces a sense of other-worldliness, as though to underline Abraham's acceptance that he has no choice but to obey God's command. But even the tone of resignation with which the final movement (in the tonic major) opens is soon dispelled as the reality of a lonely old age and death strikes home. The scoring for low wind and strings is striking, and the bleakness of Abraham's vision is emphasized by the harshly dissonant simultaneous false relations in bar 121 (see Ex. 2.9). That a work of such emotional power should thereafter have been condemned to lie unheard is one of the tragedies of Wesley's life.

Described by *The Hereford Journal* as 'a very fine Composition',[81] the Overture in E is an equally impressive if less original work—and in many ways the exact opposite of *Abraham's Offering*. Where the latter is dark-hued, inward-looking, and close to the music of such German romantics as Spohr and Weber, the overture is an extrovert work, whose clear-cut textures, deft orchestration, and general lightness of touch are more reminiscent of Mendelssohn (with several hints of the overture to *A Midsummer Night's Dream*). So too is the almost continuous quaver movement in the strings, which, together with the regular return of the energetic first subject, gives it such a compelling forward drive; only Wesley's awkward handling of the formal structure and tonal scheme, notably two false recapitulations and an inability to keep away from the tonic in the middle of the movement, reveal his inexperience in handling extended forms. One of its most strikingly romantic features is the series of sustained harmonies in the second subject (which returns in the development section), sometimes maintained for a dozen bars or more, against which the melodic instruments weave their own path with some yearning chromatic appoggiaturas (see Ex. 2.10). The coda is equally fine, with rapid figuration in the violin parts and slowly rising arpeggios for the trombones combining to reinforce the insistent subdominant harmony and create a truly splendid conclusion.

All in all the festival left Wesley with plenty to be satisfied about, and, writing to his mother some four weeks later, he was able to report that he had been 'spoken very highly of in the newspaper'.[82] Had he too been among those for whom 'Mr. Jones's excellent quadrille band kept the 'light fantastic toe' in activity until a late hour in the morning'?[83]

[80] Parry's diary entry for 6 Jan. 1866 (*ShP*).
[82] Letter postmarked 16 Oct. 1834 (*Lbl* Add. MS 35019, fo. 22).
[81] 17 Sept. 1834 [3].
[83] *HT* (13 Sept. 1834) [3].

Ex. 2.9. *Abraham's Offering*

Ex. 2.10. Overture in E, development section

To Mr. S. S. Wesley . . . no common praise is due—deprived of those benefits which a long residence amongst us would have imparted in appreciating the public taste, his selections have given general satisfaction; the musical departments were ably filled, and the noble band greatly surpassed that of any former meeting—the talents selected, vocal and instrumental, were first rate, and most creditable to his judgement.[84]

But words of praise do not keep body and soul together, and it is clear from his letters that he was still finding it difficult to make ends meet—and certainly could not justify the expense of travelling to London in May 1834 for the wedding of his sister Rosalind to Robert Glenn, 'for mere personal amusement'.[85] Even though there was no music master within fifty miles of Hereford 'that a respectable person would learn of',[86] pupils were few and far between, so that (as he wrote) 'I intend advertizing in all the papers my intention to teach, [as] it appears people are afraid to apply to me because I visit the <u>Dean</u>'.[87] But teaching brought further worry:

I am obliged to think twice or thrice before I spend a shilling. I dread Xmas. Some thing I must do to get <u>ready</u> money . . . at present my whole time is taken up in thinking how I shall get money. These great people are so fanciful and whimsical that I have more trouble in getting an opportunity to give a lesson than in giving it <~~and God only knows when I shall get paid~~>.[88]

His particular concern, however, was that lack of money would stand in the way of future happiness (as he wrote to his mother):

What will you think when I tell you I have a very excellent opportunity of settling in this <u>county</u>—I have the permission to <u>marry</u> the daughter of one of the most respectable Clergymen in the neighbourhood. At present—she will have but little money but at the death of her parents will have something <u>useful</u>. This would of course give me great reason to be thankful as I should not only have a <u>companion</u>, (and the misery of living <u>alone</u> I have borne till I am quite tired thereof[)]—but it would so establish me in my profession here that I think I might look to the future with a reasonable hope for prosperity.

I should have mentioned this sooner but I scarcely hoped it could ever happen. Now if Mr Glenn who is the only rich friend I have, would come forward and assist me I should indeed remember with thankfulness his kindness to the day of my death. Do you think if I were to write a copy of what I here state he would be the friend in need. And greater need there cant be when you think how I may to the end of my life regret the loss of this opportunity of being happy. But dont object to me on that

---

[84] *HJ* (17 Sept. 1834) [3].   [85] Letter to his mother dated 2 April 1834 (*Lbl* Add. MS 35019, fo. 16).
[86] Ibid., fo. 17ᵛ).   [87] Ibid.
[88] Letter to his mother postmarked 16 Oct. 1834 (*Lbl* Add. MS 35019, fo. 22). Angle brackets indicate sections of text deleted in the original.

account. If I could but secure <u>150</u> pounds <u>what might I be</u>—however there is no hope, but I cannot refrain from telling you all.[89]

The identity of the lady in question remains a mystery as nothing came of the match, but if the impediment was indeed financial it must have been particularly galling when, as he believed, the dean was made a 'Canon of Windsor, which adds about 14 hundred a year to his income!!'; 'I wish I was a Dean!' he wrote to his mother.[90] Dean Merewether had, in fact, been appointed only one of the deputy clerks of the closet, a position which is unlikely to have brought such generous remuneration, but within a little over a year the 'misery of living <u>alone</u>' was a thing of the past. On 4 May 1835 he married Mary Anne, the Dean's younger sister. That the wedding was by special licence (thus obviating the need for banns) and took place on a Monday at Ewyas Harold, a small village some eleven miles south-west of Hereford in the neighbouring diocese of St David's, with none of the bride's relations present, is proof enough that family approval on her side was not forthcoming.

Mary Anne (b. 1809) was the only daughter and youngest of the four children of John Merewether of Blackland, Wiltshire, and before her marriage had lived with her brother at both Hampton and Hereford. Whether she had met Wesley at the former is uncertain, but there can be little doubt that their friendship developed out of a shared love of music. Did Mary Anne perhaps take lessons from the cathedral organist, explaining Wesley's earlier comment about visiting the Dean? Since September 1830 she had been compiling a manuscript album of songs and operatic arias, and to this, probably in 1833, her husband-to-be started to make some additions.[91] Initially these took the form of short piano pieces by his father and himself—including two dated April 1834 and his sacred song 'The Bruised Reed' (6 March 1834)—but within a short time he had taken over much of the copying with the aim, one suspects, of introducing music he especially admired. Interestingly, Mary Anne shared her husband's enthusiasm for the works of Spohr; whether he was equally enamoured of the music of Donizetti and Bellini is another matter! Other works to survive from her library include J. B. Cramer's *Reminiscences of Paganini* and Hummel's *Recollections of Paginini* (both dated 24 November 1833) and the vocal score of Spohr's *Azor und Zemira*. The last bears two inscriptions in Wesley's hand, 'M. Merewether' and 'Mary Anne Wesley. May 13th. 1835'—the latter dated just nine days after their marriage.[92]

[89] Letter dated 2 April 1834 (ibid., fos. 16ᵛ–17ʳ).
[90] Letter postmarked 16 Oct. 1834 (ibid., fo. 22ᵛ).   [91] Now *Lcm* MS 4038.
[92] The works are now in *Lcm* as LXXVIII.E.7 (Cramer and Hummel) and XXXII.E.46 respectively.

Beyond these brief snippets of information we know very little about Mary Anne, but the mere fact that she was prepared not only to defy her family but also to forsake a comfortable life in the deanery for the organist's lodgings and a meagre salary bespeaks no little courage and determination. The ability to cope with a sometimes difficult husband was clearly another of her attributes, and there must have been numerous occasions when her calming influence was needed to defuse an explosive situation. All in all it was, on the surface, an unlikely match—she the daughter of a respectable county family, he the illegitimate son of a gifted but impoverished musician—but by all accounts the marriage was a happy one, and several of Wesley's pupils later spoke of the kindness they had invariably received from his wife. Details of their domestic affairs, or indeed of Wesley's activity away from the cathedral, are few and far between, but it is interesting to discover that on 17 September 1833 he had followed in his father's footsteps and been initiated into the Freemasons, but apparently without great enthusiasm: his only subsequent attendance was on the following day to play the organ in All Saints' Church after the inauguration of the Provincial Grand Lodge.[93]

Doubtless anticipating that life in Hereford would not now be so easy, Wesley had already made one attempt to escape when, in April 1835, he had been a candidate for the post of organist at St George's Chapel, Windsor. His fellow competitors had included two well-known musicians of an older generation, Sir George Smart and the opera composer Henry Bishop, as well as Edward Hodges, Philip Knight, and the nineteen-year-old George Elvey. The King (William IV) claimed the final vote and on being told that the Chapter considered that Elvey was the best but was too young replied that 'The best man is to have it'.[94] That he should have been defeated by a mere youth 'arrayed in a blue tail-coat with brass buttons and a yellow waistcoat'[95] rankled with Wesley who from henceforth had nothing good to say about either Elvey or Windsor.[96]

[93] See *HJ* (25 Sept. 1833). Information kindly supplied by Bruce Hogg.

[94] Mary Elvey, *Life and Reminiscences of George J. Elvey, Knt* (London: Sampson Low, Marston & Co., 1894), 25.

[95] Ibid. 22.

[96] Despite Lady Elvey's statement that only one of the candidates 'stood the smallest chance against young Elvey, and this was not from ability, but because one of the Canons was determined to have, if possible, a candidate of his own appointed' (p. 24), it is difficult to believe that the election was either unbiased or a true test of ability. Wesley had already made a name for himself as an organist, but Elvey never enjoyed great renown as a player. Could it be that the name Wesley was viewed with suspicion at Windsor, and that the odds were against him from the outset? According to Faustina H. Hodges, the other favoured candidate was her father, Edward Hodges, who was passed over in favour of Elvey because it was thought that the latter 'would be easier to manage than Dr. Hodges' (*Edward Hodges* (New York: G. P. Putnam's Sons, 1896), 71).

But all was not lost. The death on 14 June of James Paddon, organist of Exeter Cathedral, created another vacancy, and this time Wesley's application was successful and he was appointed on 15 August. Events had ultimately worked to his advantage, for not only was the salary at Exeter (about £175) more generous than the £130 offered at Windsor, but the choir he inherited was also considerably more efficient; Elvey found himself with an aged body of minor canons, only four of whom could sing.[97]

A fortnight was to elapse before Wesley wrote to offer his resignation from the end of the quarter, and this was duly accepted at the Chapter meeting on 2 September. On the same occasion it was also minuted that 'the other matters included in his [Wesley's] announcement relating to his past services & salary—must necessarily await the Deans return'.[98] Three weeks later he received the following reply from the Chapter Clerk:

Sir,

At the Chapter specially convened to consider your applications made thro' me on the 31st of August, the Dean & Chapter have fully examined & compared them with the correspondence & Capitular Acts which passed at the time of your Election & I am instructed to inform you that it does not appear that you are intitled to any payment beyond that proportion of the Salary of the Organist hitherto paid by them & acknowledged by you.[99]

Wesley, perhaps emboldened by his imminent departure and revealing that taste for controversy which was so characteristic of his later career, had claimed that the £40 per annum subtracted from his nominal salary as a pension for Clarke-Whitfeld should rightfully have been his from the start. That the action was against his brother-in-law seems not to have deterred him in the slightest, and in the following December he sought legal assistance to pursue his claim. On 11 January 1836 the Chapter Clerk 'read a Letter from Mr. Lanwarne an Attorney in Hereford of which the following is a Copy':

Dear Sir

I have received a Letter from a friend of Mr. Wesleys (an Attorney) desiring me to communicate with the Dean and Chapter thro' you respecting payment by them to Mr. Wesley of a proper recompense for his services for 3 years as Organist of Hereford Cathedral—it appears by the statement sent me that Mr. Wesley was to have been paid 100£ per annum and a place of abode found him—he however only received 52£ a year and paid £30 out of it for rooms. Will you therefore please ascertain the intention of the Dean & Chapter on this subject and let me know.[100]

---

[97] Mary Elvey, *Life and Reminiscences of George J. Elvey*, 38.
[98] Hereford Cathedral Chapter act book, 1834–44, 31 (*H*).
[99] Ibid. 32.   [100] Ibid. 47.

It was then 'Resolved that the following reply be sent to Mr. Lanwarne', and there the matter rested: 'The Dean and Chapter of Hereford having fully satisfied all their engagements with Mr. Wesley as their late organist decline all further communication on the subject.'[101]

Having submitted his resignation Wesley must have been impatient to leave, and this doubtless accounts for his less-than-wholehearted attention to his duties during his remaining weeks at Hereford. On Tuesday 22 September, for example, the Hebdomary (canon in residence) 'reported that the organ was not played on Saturday Evening, the whole of Sunday & on Monday Morning last',[102] and when the conditions of employment for his successor were drawn up particular attention was paid to the subject of absence without leave. After the trial for the post on 1 October it was offered to John Hunt, a lay clerk from Lichfield Cathedral and a gentle, conscientious personality, but without the outstanding musical gifts of his controversial predecessor.

Shortly before moving to Exeter Wesley had made what would be his last appearance at the Three Choirs Festival for thirty years when he acted as pianist at Gloucester. Two new works of his had been announced, a 'Concertante' for wind instruments and 'Millions of Spiritual Creatures', a setting of words from the fourth book of Milton's *Paradise Lost*. Only the latter was subsequently performed, suggesting that the concertante was never finished—or possibly even started. No score survives, and only the names of the prospective performers indicate that it was intended for pairs of flutes, oboes, clarinets, and bassoons and four horns. Scored for solo quartet and orchestra, 'Millions of Spiritual Creatures' consists of a single well-planned sonata-form movement containing many imaginative touches of harmony and scoring. Surprisingly, given the increasing prominence of counterpoint in Wesley's music, the textures are almost entirely homophonic, and this inevitably results in a certain short-windedness—something which even the careful integration of the voices into the overall texture and sudden plunges to the flat submediant and flat supertonic cannot entirely redeem. Like previous works by Wesley it seemed to bewilder the critics, *The Musical Magazine* declaring it to be 'a singular composition . . . [which] possesses much originality',[103] but it suffered the same fate as Wesley's other larger non-church works and was never heard again.

Of rather more significance, however, was a general comment on Wesley's contribution—or lack of it—to the occasion:

We cannot help expressing our regret, that Mr. S. S. Wesley . . . should have had so little to do at this Festival, and we certainly think the Directors ought to have further

---

[101] Ibid.   [102] Ibid. 32.   [103] *MM*, 1 (1835), 154.

availed themselves of his presence. His extempore performance on the organ is very wonderful, and those persons who have heard him cannot fail to trace in him a great share of the musical genius so conspicuous in his family.[104]

By the time when these words appeared Wesley had departed south-westwards, but before following him to Exeter we must glance at another piece almost certainly begun at Hereford in 1834 or 1835, the single movement entitled 'Symphony'. Like *Abraham's Offering*, it is a troubled work whose predominantly contrapuntal and frequently dissonant textures set it apart from most contemporary orchestral music. Although extravagant in its thematic material—the exposition contains no fewer than five distinct ideas—it shows Wesley beginning to grasp the possibilities of thematic development and deriving several later ideas from the opening subject. The dotted rhythm recurs in the second subject group (bars 54, 110) and is later extended into a vigorous and powerful passage of contrapuntal writing in the development. No less significant is the part played by inner pedals. Take the very beginning, where the insistent tonic pedal immediately introduces a note of tension, or the way in which the recapitulation of the jaunty second subject theme for horns develops into a sinister series of rising 6–3 chords against an insistent tonic pedal (bar 292).

But it is in the development, with its novel twists of chromatic harmony, that the work's greatest individuality lies. Here we find a chorale-like passage (see Ex. 2.11*a*) based on a slowly rising sequential pattern of 5–3 and 6–3 triads whose striking false relations are reminiscent of the more experimental Italian composers of the late Renaissance, a sequential series of 6–3 and 4–2 chords with an idiosyncratic combination of sharps and flats (Ex. 2.11*b*), a characteristic juxtaposition of dominant sevenths with roots a tritone apart and decorative foreground chromaticism (Ex. 2.11*c*), and an exciting passage in which the free use of enharmonic change allows the music to lurch thrillingly through pairs of keys a semitone apart—E to F major, D flat major to D minor, B flat major to B minor (Ex. 2.11*d*). Such passionate writing is far removed from the generally urbane tone of Spohr, and one senses that Wesley is on the brink of freeing himself from such inherited influence and striding forth as his own man.

But for all its originality the Symphony, like the Overture, is compromised by weaknesses of design—the exposition is too diffuse, and there is too much tonic harmony. It is as though without a text to help support and shape a work Wesley reverted to the habits of a practised extempore player and allowed formal considerations to become subsidiary to the maintenance of a ready flow of

[104] *MM*, 1 (1835), 154.

Ex. 2.11. Symphony, examples of idiosyncratic chromatic harmony

Ex. 2.11. cont.

musical ideas. Whether, given time, he would have achieved the same mastery of instrumental composition as he did of vocal composition must remain open to question, as the work was to be his last purely orchestral one, and beyond a note on the score that a hairpin crescendo and diminuendo should be added to all the parts, there is no evidence that it was ever played. Of the remaining movements he surely intended to write nothing survives, although it is by no means inconceivable that the March and Rondo for piano were originally intended as scherzo and finale. Not only are they in appropriate keys (C minor and C major), but the trio section of the former opens with a phrase evocative of a pair of horns and continues with mock timpani rolls.

In view of the words with which Wesley was to describe the 'position of a young musician who . . . joins a country Cathedral',[105] it is likely to have been with few regrets that he left Hereford. His stay in the city had, by the standards of the time, been brief—a mere three years—but not uneventful. It had, moreover, served to increase his reputation as an organist and church composer, but had also brought him face to face with the problems encountered by church musicians throughout the country. Clerical indifference, exemplified by the poor pay and lowly status enjoyed by organists and choirmen, and the necessity of submitting to the clerical control of the musical arrangements were to be two targets of the lifelong campaign for the comprehensive reform of cathedral music on which he was now to embark.

[105] *A Few Words*, 11.

3

Exeter

I ever regret leaving Devon.[1]

WITH its busy port and general air of prosperity the city of Exeter must have seemed a hive of activity after the rural seclusion of Hereford. But it was not only commercial activity that contributed to its vitality, as it also had a flourishing cultural life and was home to the Devon Madrigal Society and the Devon Glee Club; Wesley was doubtless most gratified to be invited to join the members of the former on 17 September 1835 for a dinner in honour of their president, the amateur composer Sir John Rogers (1780–1847). According to a newspaper report, 'The greatest cordiality was also expressed on the President proposing the health of the newly appointed Cathedral Organist, Mr. Wesley, who, much to the regret of the members, was unavoidably prevented from accepting the invitation of the Society on this occasion.'[2]

Within a short time (12 November) he had also been proposed as a member of the local Masonic lodge (which he attended sporadically until 1840) and, with a temporary respite from financial worries, the challenge of a new post and an initially harmonious working relationship with the Dean and Chapter, the omens were good and the first few years of Samuel Sebastian's and Mary Anne's stay in the city were to be among their happiest. For Wesley there was the additional satisfaction of knowing that his arrival was something of an event. Within a week of Paddon's death it had been announced that it was likely that the post would be 'thrown open to all England for competition',[3] and details of the new appointment were carefully reported in the local press; interestingly Wesley was still referred to as the 'son of the celebrated Mr. Wesley, of London'.[4]

Few details of his competitors for the post have survived, but we know that one of his rivals was the fifteen-year-old George Dixon, an erstwhile chorister of Norwich Cathedral and pupil of Zechariah Buck. Despite his lack of years Dixon had already been a candidate for the vacancy at Hereford, and in

---

[1] Letter dated 2 Aug. [1870] to Sarah Emmett (*Lbl* Add. MS 35019, fo. 167).
[2] *WEPG* (26 Sept. 1835), 3. [3] Ibid. (20 June 1835), 2.
[4] Ibid. (22 August 1835), 3.

some quarters was clearly considered a serious contender. Wesley, however, had a champion in the Dean, who noted the recent improvement of the boys at Hereford and offered a general endorsement: 'Everything I can learn confirms me in the opinion of Mr. Wesley's personal respectability'.[5] The Dean moreover had a poor opinion of the music at Norwich, making Dixon's connection with it no commendation; should there be a division of opinion between the two he would be 'decidedly favourable' to the former.[6]

Wesley's appointment was minuted at the chapter meeting on 15 August,[7] but despite his being allowed one half of the organist's salary for the quarter ending at Michaelmas—the other half being divided between Paddon's two apprentices, Hawke and Harding—he did not commence his duties until Wednesday 7 October. The Dean and Chapter had already made quite clear what they expected from the new incumbent:

> The Duties of the Organist are to conduct the Service in the Choir upon all occasions, and as Informator Puerorum to instruct the Choristers daily, and the Secondaries when required. In the discharge of this duty he is to attend regularly in the Music School from Seven to Nine A.M. in the Summer, and from eight to nine in the Winter, and to practise the Choir occasionally in the Organ Loft.
>
> As Organist, Sub-Chanter, and Informator Puerorum, he receives about One hundred Guineas Per Annum, and as Lay Vicar about Seventy pounds per Annum. He is allowed to take one or two Apprentices (with whom the late Organist received One hundred Guineas premium) and to employ his leisure in general Tuition.[8]

The thought of employing his leisure in the 'tiresome . . . occupation'[9] of teaching would have brought a wry smile to his lips although now, with a salary close on triple what he had received at Hereford, the need for such additional income was less pressing. The presence of two apprentices was a bonus, particularly when (as William Spark recalled) the daily boys' practice was at an inconveniently early hour. A full report of his first Sunday appeared in *Woolmer's Exeter and Plymouth Gazette*: 'On Sunday last, Mr. Wesley . . . commenced his duties. In the afternoon the anthem by Boyce, 'O! where shall wisdom be found,' was performed in such a masterly manner, as to prove this gentleman deserving all which report had said of him as to his professional talent.'[10]

Two weeks later a further account appeared from the pen of an anonymous but enthusiastic reader. Pointing out that the anthem on Sunday 25 October

[5] From a letter dated 5 Aug. 1835 to the Chapter Clerk (*EXc* MS D & C Exeter/7061/Wesley Papers/1).

[6] Ibid.   [7] See *EXc* MS D & C Exeter 3581, 280.

[8] Minutes of the meeting on 8 Aug. 1835 (ibid., 274).

[9] Letter to his father dated Oct. 1832 (*Lbl* Add. MS 35019, fo. 6).

[10] *WEPG* (17 Oct. 1835), 2.

('The Wilderness') was by the new organist himself, he eulogized it by saying
it 'would have done credit to the immortal Handel' (in those days the
inevitable touchstone of taste) and 'riveted the attention of all'. In view of the
composer's youth, what, he asked, might not be anticipated in future?[11]
Among those whose attention was riveted was the young William Spark, then
a twelve-year-old chorister but later one of Wesley's best-known and most
faithful pupils:

It was in 1835 that Wesley was appointed . . . organist and master of the choir of Exeter
Cathedral. He looked much older than he was, being then slightly bald; and in after
years he was denuded of all his black hair, and always wore a wig.

I had been a chorister for two years . . . but I was, though one of the youngest boys,
soon able to assist him by taking the pianoforte or the organ . . . at the choir boys'
practices, which generally took place at half-past six in the morning [or seven o'clock
according to his brother Frederick][12]—rather too early for Wesley, as a rule.

When I first heard him play on the organ, I was seized with reverential awe. It was
at the close of the afternoon service in the cathedral. The choir men and choir boys
were asked to remain in their stalls; and we all listened in rapt silence to Wesley's masterly playing—one or two pieces, but chiefly extemporaneous—for about forty minutes . . . [and] we now heard for the first time what organ playing was under the magic
touch of a master like Wesley.[13]

Even the passage of some sixty years could not erase the sense of excitement
and anticipation which Wesley's arrival had aroused. And, as the frequent references to the choir and organist in the local newspapers demonstrated, no one
was disappointed. January 1836 was particularly noteworthy for the excellence
of its musical performances, and an anonymous correspondent addressed a
sonnet to *The Western Luminary*, 'Written after hearing the Communion
Service very beautifully performed in Exeter Cathedral, on Sunday, Jan. 31,
1836':

> Oh! What a world of harmony was there!—
> Deep harmony in all or seen, or heard—
> In look, tone, feature, gesture, thought, or word,
> This Sabbath morn 'neath that high roof of prayer:
> Whilst from the 'Table of the Lord' the priest
> To the bow'd multitude, impressive, spake
> Those hests which erst the Almighty, 'mid the quake
> Of mountain tops, and flame and fear, address'd.

[11] *WEPG* (31 Oct. 1835), 2.
[12] See Frederick R. Spark, *Memories of my Life* (Leeds: Fred. R. Spark & Son, [1913]), 1–2.
[13] W. Spark, *Musical Memories*, 66–8.

No flame nor terror now!—the whiles the swell,
Soft, solemn, slow, of the deep organ rose,
And tongues and melted hearts, with one accord,
Or sang or pray'd response—'Have mercy, Lord!
"Incline,—O God, incline our hearts to keep thy Laws." '[14]

By now Wesley was thoroughly established at Exeter. The choir, unlike that at Hereford, was entirely lay in composition, with ten choristers, seven lay vicars, and five secondaries, while we also know far more about day-to-day events through the survival of the weekly manuscript music lists. Not only do they provide a complete record of the music sung, but they also give fascinating snippets of information about everyday events. In July 1836, for example, weekday choral services were discontinued for the best part of a month while the organ was cleaned and tuned, while in January 1837 the services were again being read, this time because 'The greater part of the choir [were] ill in the Influenza'.[15] The repertoire Wesley inherited, though large, was, as might have been expected, conservative with a centre of gravity in the eighteenth century. At first he did little to change this general pattern, although over the succeeding months he quietly dropped no fewer than fifty-one of the anthems formerly in use,[16] reserving his severest pruning for two Exeter musicians, his predecessor-but-one, William Jackson (1730–1803), whose tally of seventeen services and anthems dropped to seven, and Hugh Bond (c.1710–1792) whose eleven anthems were reduced to one. Neither, given his experience of the Gresham Prize, is it surprising that he chose to drop Kellow J. Pye's 'Turn thee unto me', winner of the 1832 competition. In place of these works he revived some thirty-four works, among them William Boyce's 'O where shall wisdom be found', Maurice Greene's 'Lord, let me know mine end', James Nares's 'The Souls of the Righteous', and John Travers's 'Ascribe unto the Lord'. No less interestingly, he also drew more freely than his predecessors on Elizabethan and early seventeenth-century music as reflected in Boyce's and Samuel Arnold's *Cathedral Music*. While the number of works was small—a total of eighteen services and anthems—several appeared frequently in the lists. Orlando Gibbons's Short Service and 'Almighty and Everlasting God' were especial favourites, but his 'Hosanna to the Son of David', 'Lift up your heads', and the two parts of 'O clap your hands together' also received occasional hearings. So, too, did Byrd's Short Service, 'O Lord, turn thy wrath away', and 'Bow down thine ear', Richard Farrant's 'Call to remembrance' and 'Hide

---

[14] *WL* (1 Feb. 1836), 3. The setting was William Jackson's Service in F.
[15] *EXc* MS D & C Exeter Mus Lists.
[16] While the selection of music was nominally the responsibility of the Precentor, it seems unlikely that Wesley's views on the subject would not have been heeded.

not thou thy face', and three anthems by (or attributed to) Tallis, 'All People that on Earth do Dwell', 'I call and cry', and 'Up, Lord, and help me'.[17]

Yet for all his considerable—and growing—achievement as a composer, Wesley performed remarkably few of his own compositions. Indeed, only the Responses to the Commandments and the Creed from the Service in E were sung with any regularity (with no fewer than fifty-seven performances of the latter between 17 April 1836 and 5 December 1841), while among the anthems even 'The Wilderness' (fifteen performances) was heard less often than Walmisley's 'O give thanks' (seventeen performances). Of the others, 'O God, whose Nature and Property' was heard nine times (but not after November 1837), 'Blessed be the God and Father' seven times, 'Trust ye in the Lord' three times, and 'O Lord, thou art my God' once. But it is not simply the paucity of performances which is so surprising, but the fact that the years between 1836 and 1840 saw Wesley embarking on the publication of a volume to be entitled *Six Anthems*, of which only two works, 'The Wilderness' and 'O Lord, thou art my God', were ever sung in the cathedral!

The first announcement appeared in *Woolmer's Exeter and Plymouth Gazette* on 6 February 1836:

> Under the Patronage of Her Majesty.
> Shortly will be Published,
> Six Anthems,
> Composed by Mr. S. S. Wesley.
> The Words selected from the Prophet Isaiah.

These Anthems are humbly designed for performance in the solemn and beautiful Service of our Cathedrals, and will be published in Score, with an Accompaniment of the usual kind for the Piano-Forte, or Organ, with an additional Organ Part for the use of those who have made much progress in the study of that Instrument.[18]

The Western Luminary carried an additional report that 'the highly talented Organist of our Cathedral, is about to publish . . . a set of Anthems, expressly designed for our solemn Cathedral Service . . . and we anticipate that these Anthems must, when known, become established favourites in our Cathedral choirs, and classic models of Ecclesiastical composition.'[19]

Although he had already started collecting the names of subscribers—one of his notebooks contains a list of 'Parties who ought to be got' (among them the Dean of Exeter and other Hereford and Exeter acquaintances, but not the Dean of Hereford)[20]—he had probably as yet only completed two of the works, 'The Wilderness' and 'O Lord, thou art my God'. Progress on the

---

[17] Neither 'All People that on Earth do Dwell' nor 'Up, Lord, and help me' is now attributed to Tallis.
[18] p. 2.   [19] *WL* (1 Feb. 1836), 2.   [20] *Lcm* MS 2141e, fo. 4ᵛ.

others must have been slow, and it is not until January 1840 and his enquiry to Vincent Novello about publishing 'two little anthems' that we learn any more about the project. 'I am', he continued, 'preparing some, I think, better things for publication, but wish the present things produced separately'.[21] The 'better things' were finally announced in September:

> To be Published,
> Six Anthems,
> By Samuel Sebastian Wesley.
> Subscription Price, One Guinea and a Half.

It is respectfully announced that the present Work has extended to a length which makes it impossible to publish it at the Price originally mentioned to Subscribers; it will contain about 200 Pages, which cannot be supplied at a less Subscription Price than One Guinea and a Half.

The Work will be prefaced by some remarks on the present state of Musical Art as connected with Divine Worship, and the sentiments of the Musical Profession and the Public on the subject.[22]

The first instalment of a review by Henry Smart (under the heading 'Anthems, by Samuel Sebastian Wesley') appeared in *The Musical World* on 8 October, and a week later the collection was advertised as 'Just Published'.[23] Smart's review continued in the next two issues but then, despite a conclusion being promised, mysteriously broke off—and this was the last that was heard of the *Anthems*.[24] Whilst it is impossible to know for certain what happened, the announcement 'Just Published' was clearly premature. All that had so far taken place was the printing of some incomplete proof copies (containing 'O Lord, thou art my God', 'The Wilderness', and the first two movements of 'To my Request and Earnest Cry') and it must have been from one of these that Smart had begun his review.[25] Fate then intervened, as Wesley recalled when he wrote of 'the loss experienced by the destruction of the plates of the work by a Fire at the Engraver's house, years ago',[26] bringing publication to an abrupt halt. Having lost money, he was in no position to continue and laid the volume aside until 1848; it finally appeared in 1853 (without 'To my Request and Earnest Cry') as the well-known *Anthems*, a collection of twelve works. Not least among the unanswered questions is that of the identity of the three anthems never printed in 1840. After 'Blessed be the God and Father' and

---

[21] Letter dated 29 Jan. 1840 (*Lbl* Add. MS 11730, fos. 227–8).   [22] *WEPG* (19 Sept. 1840), 2.

[23] *MW*, 14 (1840), 252.   [24] Ibid. 231–3, 242–4, 277–8.

[25] Only three copies of the collection, all equally incomplete, are known: at *LPC*, the Rowe Music Library, King's College, Cambridge, and *Ob* (Tenbury Collection).

[26] Letter dated 21 Jan. 1853 to the Chapter Clerk at Exeter (*EXc* MS D & C Exeter/7061/S. S. Wesley/7).

'Trust ye in the Lord' are excluded on the grounds that they were the 'two lit-tle anthems', three works emerge as strong candidates—'O give thanks unto the Lord', 'Let us lift up our heart', and 'Wash me throughly'. Stylistically all belong to the mid- or late 1830s and would also have filled the appropriate number of pages. But of the six only three—'The Wilderness', 'O Lord, thou art my God', and 'Let us lift up our heart'—set verses from Isaiah, suggesting that by 1840 the idea of 'Isaiah anthems' had been dropped: 'Trust ye in the Lord' and an unfinished fragment, 'All we Like Sheep',[27] both include verses from Isaiah and were perhaps originally intended for the volume.

Given their position at the centre of Wesley's output it is worthwhile to pause and look more closely at the works written since his arrival in the city. The earliest, 'O give thanks unto the Lord' (c.1835), is a medium-length full-with-verse anthem, possibly dating from his time at Hereford, which shares several features with 'Blessed be the God and Father' and 'Trust ye in the Lord': a common key (E flat), examples of Spohr-derived chromaticism, and a layout based around a central treble solo—though with its weighty first movement (including a well-developed fugato episode) it is closer to the tra-ditional three-movement full-with-verse anthem. One can also see the begin-ning of a gradual rapprochement between ancient and modern elements in Wesley's harmonic language as he began to distance himself from the early romantic lingua franca of his earliest works and, in the treble solo, an organ part invigorated by a profusion of contrapuntal devices. Passing-notes, appog-giaturas, brief snatches of imitation, and interrupted cadences not only impart forward momentum but, by keeping the music in a state of harmonic uncer-tainty, also allow one phrase to flow into the next and an expansive musical paragraph to unfold; the opening section also possesses a pleasing metrical irregularity, with its 33 bars divided into phrases of $6 + 3 + 4 + 5 + 7 + 8$ bars (see Ex. 3.1). The one departure from established practice is found in the short, quiet, homophonic final movement 'Blessed are they' (obviously inspired by 'And sorrow and sighing') in which a solo quartet alternates with the full choir; here too we find the first example of a II^6–V–I cadence approached via a diatonic ninth suspended over the mediant, familiar from Mozart's motet 'Ave verum corpus' (see Ex. 3.1b and c).

It is only a short step from 'O give thanks' to the second group of full-with-verse anthems, written between 1836 and 1840, 'O Lord, thou art my God', 'Let us lift up our heart', and 'To my Request and Earnest Cry'. They too have several features in common, calling for a double choir and containing extended arias for baritone soloist. But there any similarity ceases, as they each

---

[27] 5 bars only (collection of Robert Pascall).

Ex. 3.1. *a* 'O give thanks unto the Lord', second movement; *b* 'O give thanks unto the Lord', final cadence of third movement; *c* Mozart, 'Ave verum corpus'

represent a different solution to the challenge of large-scale anthem composition. 'O Lord, thou art my God' stresses massive choral writing, 'Let us lift up our heart' a quieter, more intimate style of expression, and 'To my Request and Earnest Cry' a new and closer relationship between choir and organ. It is not, however, merely the quality of the musical invention that makes these works stand out, but the fact that they possess such musical and emotional power, all within the confines of an essentially old-fashioned formal scheme. This was an achievement acknowledged by Dannreuther when he wrote of the 'persistent strength of this contrapuntal music'[28], and has been recognized more recently by William Gatens with his comment that the 'larger anthems have a remarkable coherence, for which a satisfactory explanation is elusive'.[29] Gatens himself offered a metaphysical interpretation, suggesting that the 'answer seems to lie more in the large-scale aesthetic gesture than in such conventional focuses of analytical attention'[30] as the character of the text, a plan of tonal relationships, or thematic development. But does it? The mid-1830s saw Wesley consolidating his grasp of tonal structure, and in these works he further developed his concept of the anthem in which the carefully chosen text helped to shape the finished work. Sometimes in the context of a preconceived formal scheme, sometimes in the course of an episodic through-composed movement, this resulted in a powerful amalgam of words and music, supported by his forceful harmonic idiom and underpinned by a carefully thought-out key scheme. Herein lies the secret of their success.

From 'The Wilderness' onwards Wesley adopted an individual approach towards the selection of anthem texts, usually taking verses from more than one source and invariably rearranging them to produce the perfect vehicle for his purpose. He also ranged more widely than was customary, and in addition to the Psalms—still the most commonly used source—took verses from the Old Testament prophets (Isaiah, Job, and Habbakuk), the books of Ecclesiasticus, Wisdom, and Ecclesiastes, the Gospels and Epistles, and the *Book of Common Prayer*. 'To my Request and Earnest Cry' sets verses from Tate's and Brady's 'New Version' of Psalm 119, while 'Let us lift up our heart' ends with verses from Wesley's grandfather's hymn 'Thou Judge of Quick and Dead' and 'By the Word of the Lord' includes lines from Milton's *Paradise Lost*. Only rarely, however, does he seem to have been influenced by an earlier composer, one of the few examples being 'Trust ye in the Lord', which sets the same unusual selection of verses from Isaiah and Habbakuk as an anthem by John Stafford Smith.[31] Wesley's text for 'O Lord, thou art my God' is one of his most inter-

[28] *The Romantic Period*, 290.   [29] *Victorian Cathedral Music*, 139.   [30] Ibid. 139–40.
[31] In his collection *Anthems Composed for the Choir-Service of the Church of England* (London: for the Author, [1793]) Stafford Smith ranged as widely as Wesley, frequently combining verses from several sources.

TABLE 3.1. *Internal structure of 'O Lord, thou art my God'*

Scoring	Text	Key
Full, SSAATTBB	Isaiah 25: 1. O Lord, thou art my God; I will exalt thee, I will praise thy Name; Thy counsels of old are faithfulness and truth; thou hast done wonderful things. Isaiah 25: 4. For thou hast been a strength to the poor, a strength to the needy in his distress[, a refuge from the storm, a shadow from the heat].[a]	E♭
Bass solo	Psalm 33: 21. For our heart shall rejoice in him; because we have trusted in his holy name. Psalm 33: 22. Let thy mercy, O Lord, be upon us, according as we hope in thee.	B♭
Full, SSAATTBB	Isaiah 25: 8. He will swallow up death in victory; and the Lord God will wipe tears from off all faces; the rebuke of his people shall he take away from off all the earth: for the Lord hath spoken it.	d D♭
Verse ssattb	1 Corinthians 15: 53. For this mortal must put on immortality. 1 Corinthians 15: 34. Awake to righteousness, and sin not; for some have not the knowledge of God. Wisdom 3: 9. They that put their trust in him shall understand the truth. 1 Corinthians 15: 51, 52. We shall not all sleep, but we shall all be changed, in a moment, in the twinkling of an eye, at the last trumpet.	B♭
Full, SSAATTBB	Isaiah 25: 9. And in that day it shall be said, Lo, this is our God; we have waited for him, and he will save us; This is the Lord; we have waited for him, we will be glad and rejoice in his salvation.	E♭

[a] Words set in the original 1840 version of the anthem but omitted from the revised score of 1853.
[b] Key of the original third movement in the 1840 version of the anthem.

esting compilations and an excellent illustration of his method (see Table 3.1). Drawing on no fewer than four sources—Isaiah 25, Psalm 33 (Authorized Version), Wisdom 3, and 1 Corinthians 15—it is so arranged that the verses from Isaiah (which look forward to the coming of Christ) are used in the three movements for full choir, with the verses from the other sources providing a gloss on the ideas they express. Note too the symmetrical tonal pattern, with the tonic reserved for the two outer movements.

It is, however, within the individual movements that Wesley's handling of his material is most distinctive. In the opening movement, for example, he used a combination of thematic, textural, and tonal means to give a sense of unity to an essentially through-composed structure, whose shape is largely dictated by its text. As Table 3.2 shows, each section of the text is initially associated with its own musical material, but certain phrases, notably the bold affirmation 'O Lord, thou art my God', are subsequently reintroduced with different music. Indeed, the last is used as a kind of verbal refrain, rounding off the opening section, introducing the vigorous new theme in the middle section (bar 100), and returning at the end (bar 144). To this verbal framework

Wesley added a musical dimension, treating the opening subject as a ritornello and bringing it back (in the dominant) at the opening of the middle section and again at the very end. At a more detailed level, he also used the progression to the mediant (V^7–III^6 or I^6–III^6) at the words 'thou art my God' (bar 54—see Ex. 3.2b) as a unifying factor, repeating it at the close of the middle section (bar 123) and again at the end of the work (bar 148). But underpinning everything is a clearly planned tonal scheme in which the first section is principally in the tonic (E flat) and the middle section opens in the dominant but moves quickly to its relative minor (G minor) and its own dominant major (D major) before a return to the tonic, via the subdominant (A flat), for the final section.

TABLE 3.2. *Internal structure of 'O Lord, thou art my God', first movement*

Bar	Theme	Text section	Text	Scoring	Key
1	I			Organ	Eb
17	I'	A	O Lord, thou art my God	Dec. TB	Eb
29	II	B	Thy counsels of old	Can. SATB	Eb–G
37	II'	B	Thy counsels of old	Dec. SATB	Eb
41	II"	A–B	O Lord, thou art my God, thy counsels of old	Dec. SATB	Eb–c
49	II'	B–A	Thy counsels of old. O Lord, thou art my God	SSAATTBB	Eb–Bb
61	I'			Organ	Bb
64	III	C	For thou hast been a strength	SATB	g–D
92	IV	C'	A strength to the needy	SSAATTBB	D–c
100	V	A	O Lord, thou art my God	SSAATTBB	Bb–g–D
112	V'	B–A	Thy counsels of old. O Lord, thou art my God	SSAATTBB	D–Ab
119	VI	D	I will exalt and praise thy name	SSAATTBB	Ab–Eb
134	VI'	E	For thou hast done wonderful things	Dec. SATB	Eb
144	II"	A	O Lord, thou art my God	SSAATTBB	Eb
156	I			Organ	Eb

Nowhere is the power of the freely dissonant contrapuntal textures to provide forward momentum and to give such a compelling sense of purpose better illustrated than at the very opening where the sinewy counterpoint—and indeed the whole anthem—grows from a single (tonic) Eb (see Ex. 3.2a). When the choir enters the very unobtrusiveness of its material—a solitary slow-moving cantus firmus-like phrase for the Decani basses—highlights the sense of expectation as voices and organ are combined in a closely knit texture, quickened by deftly placed chromatic harmonies. Contrapuntal development is cut short by the block harmony of the second subject ('Thy counsels of old', bar 29), and thereafter attention shifts to the interplay of Decani and Cantoris. Initially used antiphonally, they combine for the closing bars of this section as voice is piled upon voice, suspension upon suspension, and the whole passage crowned by two striking progressions—V^7–III^6 (= V^6 of c) and V^6–VII (= V of G)—III^{9-8} (= I of G)–vi–II^6_{43}–V (although the 9–8 appoggiatura in bar 59 was a product of Wesley's revisions between 1840 and 1853). Here indeed is a fine example of what he justifiably claimed to be one of his major achievements, 'the new use made of broad massive harmony' (see Ex. 3.2*b*).[32]

The angular, chromatic four-part fugal exposition in G minor ('For thou has been a strength to the poor in his distress') which opens the middle section also dates from the revisions Wesley made before the anthem's reissue in 1853, and is undoubtedly an improvement on his original development of the material first heard in bar 23 onwards.[33] Thereafter the texture reverts to eight parts with some wonderfully vigorous counterpoint as the music slowly builds up to another mighty climax, again crowned by an unexpected move to V^6 of c, before closing quietly. Whether in Bachian counterpoint, diatonically dissonant block harmony, or the interplay of Decani and Cantoris, or simply through constantly changing textures, Wesley handled his forces with skill and confidence and displayed a sure ear for vocal effect. No less importantly, he also demonstrated how his concept of an extended choral movement was steadily evolving from one dominated by a single *Affekt* to one in which various textures—fugue, free counterpoint, block harmony—are freely combined. It was perhaps his single most important contribution to the development of the anthem and is seen again in 'Let us lift up our heart', 'To my Request and Earnest Cry', and several of the shorter full anthems.

Passing over the bass solo 'For our heart shall rejoice in him'—a forthright movement in ternary form whose writing is envigorated by the free use of 7–6 and 9–8 suspensions—we reach the second of the anthem's three choral pillars, the short declamatory chorus 'He will swallow up death in victory'. This too dates from Wesley's revisions, when it replaced a comparable movement in D major, and is distinguished by an impressive fanfare-like opening with excellent word-setting (in irregular nine-bar phrases) and the fervour of its message, not least in the great unison outburst 'For the Lord hath spoken it' with which it concludes. It is at moments like this that Wesley's plea for greatly augmented cathedral choirs is most telling.[34]

Like the bass solo the six-part verse (also in B flat and in ternary form) serves as an interlude before the final movement, a triple fugue, 'And in that day it

[32] *Lbl* Add. MS 35019, fo. 125.

[33] As originally written this section developed the material first heard in bars 23 ff.: it assumed its current form some time between 1840 and 1853.

[34] See *A Few Words*, 24, 56–7.

Ex. 3.2. 'O Lord, thou art my God', 1853 version, first movement

Ex. 3.2. *cont.*

shall be said'. It was probably modelled on one of Wesley's favourite organ works—Bach's 'St Anne' Fugue (but with a slight accelerando rather than a change of time signature to mark the entry of each subject)—and provides a reminder that he later submitted the anthem as his exercise for the degree of D.Mus.; the combination of simple *stile antico* and florid counterpoint and an imaginative but sparing use of chromaticism provides one of the best examples of what Spohr described as the 'dignified and, frequently, antique style'[35] of his church music. Yet Wesley wore his learning so lightly and handled the material so effortlessly that the skill which went into its construction—and there is little thematic material which is not derived from one or other of the subjects—can all too easily be overlooked. As in other fugal works from this period he relied on the almost constant use of suspensions and other such contrapuntal devices to create harmonic tension, while a gradual accelerando, whereby the original tempo of ♩ = 96 increases to ♩ = 112 and then to ♩ = 152, further raises the emotional temperature. The final climactic statement 'This is our God; this is the Lord, we have waited for him' remains one of his

35 *Lcm* MS 3072.

finest utterances and, in its reversion to block harmony and modulation away from the tonic, makes an interesting comparison with the climax of 'The Wilderness'. If the latter is the inspired work of a youthful genius, this lengthy passage is the product of a more mature mind, able to take a transparently simple harmonic progression first used in 'The Smiling Spring' ((I^6, IV^7, I$^6_4$) and make it blaze incandescently (see Ex. 3.3). Here the transient modulations to keys on the flat side of the tonic are reserved for the short coda, whose composed rallentando and restatement of all three subjects in augmentation allow the music to move towards a relaxed close. As Nicholas Temperley has aptly suggested, the climax is indeed symptomatic of 'the Church of England's awakening from long slumber'.[36]

No less impressive but of a rather different character is 'Let us lift up our heart'. Although this is conceived on a similar scale, its choral writing is less massive (with more sparing use of double-choir textures), counterpoint is less prominent, and the harmony simpler and more mellow, albeit with a greater reliance on chromaticism. All these qualities are exemplified by the long through-composed first movement, which, unlike the equivalent movement in 'O Lord, thou art my God', includes neither musical nor verbal recapitulation. Closely following the text, with changes of mood, texture, and vocal scoring used to reflect the varying sentiments and again supported by a well-defined tonal structure, it provides another excellent example of Wesley's new practice in action. At its simplest it can be reduced to a move from the tonic (D minor) to the dominant major (A major) and back via the relative major (F major), with changes of key articulating the various sections (see Table 3.3).

TABLE 3.3. *Internal structure of 'Let us lift up our heart', (first movement*

Bar nos	Text	Texture and scoring	Key
1	Let us lift up our heart	Unison	d–c
20	Thy name is from everlasting	Double choir and imitative	C–c–A
67	Be not very sore	Varied texture and homophonic SSAATTBB	A–F
101	Oh that thou wouldst rend the heav'ns	Fugato SATB	F–d
136	That the mountains might flow down	Homophonic SATB	d reaffirmed

The movement opens quietly with an expansive unison melody for men's voices whose breadth of phrase and richness of harmony (with a liberal use of pedal-points and suspended sevenths) epitomize Wesley's mature harmonic style (see Ex. 3.4a). It also poses the question of which key the work is in: the D minor of the opening bar or the F major into which it immediately slips—

---

[36] *The Romantic Age*, 199.

Ex. 3.3. *a* 'The Smiling Spring'; *b* 'O Lord, thou art my God', 1853 version, last movement

an ambiguity which is not resolved until the end of the movement.[37] As more voices enter, the texture gradually builds up to the incisive block harmony of the powerful statement for double choir, 'Doubtless thou art our father' (bar 31), and a sudden—and unexpected—plunge into C minor for a striding imitative subject whose dissonant accented passing-notes and appoggiaturas maintain the harmonic and dramatic tension (see Ex. 3.4*b*). It is at moments like this, where long-held chords and pedal-points create a backcloth against which individual parts weave their own foreground texture, that the difficulty of placing Wesley's music in a wider context becomes most apparent. Who among his European contemporaries would have written anything quite like this? After a cadence in the dominant (cf. the similar pattern in 'O Lord, thou art my God'), a brief middle section introduces new material to the words 'See, we beseech thee', before the movement closes with an imitative, loosely fugal, development of two contrasted subjects which explores keys on the flat side of the tonic. Deriving its strength from the interplay of the melodic lines, it is characterized by restless sequential movement, and not until the final dominant pedal (bar 130) is any sense of tonal stability restored. Two arresting interpolations of Neapolitan harmony (bars 128 and 142) maintain the sense of flux, and only in the succeeding verse, which follows without a break, is the excitement thus generated allowed to dissipate. Scored for four-part verse ensemble and full (four-part) choir, the latter makes extensive use of solo voices, as well as exploiting the contrasts of scoring available, and serves in its turn as a prelude to the central bass solo.

With 'Thou, O Lord God' the emotional centre of the anthem is reached. The finest of all Wesley's arias, this opens with a sweeping melody in B minor spanning a rising tenth whose powerful affirmation 'Thou, O Lord God, art the thing that I long for' sets the tone of the whole movement. Like so much of his music from the later 1830s, it is driven forward by diatonic dissonance—appoggiaturas (especially over chords of the dominant thirteenth) and accented passing—and sequential movement through keys a third apart—G major, E flat major, C minor and later B minor, G major, E minor, C major. The calm middle section in the relative major provides a brief respite before a shortened, varied recapitulation leads to the most remarkable part of the whole anthem, the thrilling restatement of the opening theme in the Neapolitan key, C major. For the remainder of the movement the tonality fluctuates between this key and the tonic, B minor, before a characteristic tritone shift in the bass

---

[37] It can be argued that the movement actually opens in F major, but the fact that it closes in D minor and that the remaining movements are in D minor/major (or a related key) clearly implies that the tonic is D.

Ex. 3.4. 'Let us lift up our heart', first movement

a)

Ex. 3.4. *cont.*

accompanied by an enharmonic change (F♮ = E♯) leads back to a dominant pedal and extended cadence (see Ex. 3.5).

It is impossible to sustain such emotional intensity, and the final two movements are both calmer in mood. The first, an extended hymn tune scored largely for the three lower voices—the trebles enter only for the central climax and the poignant final cadence—sets the first two verses of Charles Wesley's hymn 'Thou Judge of Quick and Dead' and is one of the earliest examples of such a movement in one of Wesley's anthems. Its harmonic restraint, sparing use of chromaticism, and imaginative cadential scheme are wholly typical and achieve their effect almost entirely from the choice, spacing, and effect of the chords. The finale, an accompanied fugue setting the third verse of the hymn, follows without a break and forms a mellow conclusion to the anthem. But as in so much of Wesley's music, the effect of peaceful calm—as in the spacious (diatonic) writing of the last pages—is frequently the result of a sequence of individually dissonant passing-notes, a technique he surely learnt from Bach, whether directly or via his father (see Ex. 3.6). A coda, decorated by a chain of secondary sevenths and imparting a natural rallentando, brings the anthem to a quiet close.

Ex. 3.5. 'Let us lift up our heart', third movement

Ex. 3.6. *a* Samuel Wesley, 'Confitebor tibi, Domine', no. 15; *b* 'Let us lift up our heart', last movement

The third anthem, 'To my Request and Earnest Cry', is the most enigmatic. It was never published complete during Wesley's lifetime, and no complete source has survived: the first two movements are known from the incomplete 1840 proof copies, and the last from an isolated autograph score. A number of features are also decidedly unusual—the thematic links between the first and last movements, the elaborate obbligato organ part to the latter, the designation 'Pianoforte' prefixed to the accompaniment of the first two movements, and the entirely metrical text, taken from Tate's and Brady's *New Version* of Psalm 119. But most perplexing of all is the fact that, although it contains some of Wesley's finest music, there is no evidence that it was ever performed complete. It was not, however, quite forgotten, as the first two movements were later sung at Leeds Parish Church—but whether during or after Wesley's time is not clear—while the last movement contains alterations made with the blue ink he favoured in the late 1860s and early 1870s. Intriguingly, material from this reappeared in his late Andante in E minor for organ and would also feature in the 'extempore' fugue heard by Hubert Parry at Gloucester in 1865 (see Chapter 6).

Unlike its two companion works, which open with substantial movements for double choir, 'To my Request and Earnest Cry' begins with a comparatively short four-part chorus whose second phrase, 'Inspire my heart with heav'nly skill', contains strong echoes of Bach. The slowly descending bass-line, dissonant inner pedal, and ornamental chromatic auxiliaries all recall the aria 'Erbarme dich' (Have mercy, Lord) from the *St Matthew Passion*. Could Wesley have known the work, first published (in Germany) as recently as 1830? But the movement is of no less interest for the evidence it offers of his efforts to create a sense of unity by reintroducing both text ('Nor comfort knew but what thy sacred laws afford') and music—the opening subject—in the last movement.

Both the first and second movements—the latter an expansive bass aria in the dominant (B major) with relentless semiquaver figuration in the organ part—seem to be building towards the substantial finale. Framed by a slow hymn-like section and based on the contrapuntal development of three subjects—the first repeated from the opening movement (but now in 6/4 rather than 3/4 time)—it combines characteristics of sonata form with those of a triple fugue in a manner which defies easy analysis. Suffice it to say that only the second of the three expositions—in the dominant minor and to the words 'Like some lost sheep we've stray'd'—is rigorously fugal and that this also fulfils the role of second subject (but is never recapitulated). But the precise details of thematic or harmonic development or even the role of the important obbligato organ part ultimately matter little, for what the movement demonstrates is Wesley's ability to use these different elements to create a structure of great musical and emotional power. From the much-shortened recapitulation (bar 307) the music begins its inexorable progress towards the final climax, shifting kaleidoscopically from key to key until a typically Bachian chromatically rising bass-line introduces a note of stability. But then, with characteristic abandon, the music rapidly veers flatwards and the whole work is crowned by a triumphant dominant ninth in the Neapolitan key, F major. After the strenuous build-up its effect is overwhelming (see Ex. 3.7). The enharmonic transition back to the desolate E minor of the short coda is handled no less effectively. 'Like some lost sheep I've strayed', announces the choir, but with the return of the opening hymn tune melody to the words 'Now, therefore, Lord, thy servant seek' a sense of peace is restored and the work ends in a serene E major.

The note of personal anguish so prominent in 'Let us lift up our heart' and 'To my Request and Earnest Cry' is also found in 'Wash me throughly from my wickedness' (*c*.1840), probably Wesley's final work to be written at Exeter. A concise single-movement full anthem—a form he had not touched since his early *stile antico* setting of 'O God, whose Nature and Property'—it sets verses from Psalm 51 and vividly illustrates how far he had travelled during the intervening years. Although the use of a solo treble at the opening might suggest a link with the anthems of Attwood, they were products of the classical era, while 'Wash me throughly' is an example of full-blown romanticism. Nowhere is this better illustrated than in its harmonic idiom, which takes Wesley's individual style of chromaticism one stage further. The restless movement from key to key, deriving variously from enharmonic change and interrupted cadences, is entirely at one with the mood of the text. Take, for example, the opening phrase, whose D minor tonality is interrupted by an anticipated modulation to G minor, deflected towards E flat and abruptly turned towards the dominant, A major, by a seventh on the supertonic (see Ex. 3.8*a*). Yet despite its harmonic richness, often resulting from the use of higher dominant discords, economy is one of the anthem's chief virtues. Bairstow was to write of the 'lonely chords' which accompany the recapitulation of the arched main theme, and the final bars offer another instance of Wesley's ability to create a passage of great power and beauty from the simplest means—a rising unison melody supported by a series of diatonic triads.[38] No less memorable is the beautiful imitative subject 'For I acknowledge my faults' with which the second part opens; it returns later combined—in stretto—with the opening theme (Ex. 3.8*b*).

---

[38] Edward C. Bairstow, 'The Anthems of Samuel Sebastian Wesley', *MT*, 67 (1926), 309.

Ex. 3.7. 'To my Request and Earnest Cry', last movement

Ex. 3.7. cont.

Ex. 3.8. 'Wash me throughly from my wickedness'

Ex. 3.8. cont.

[Ped.]

Had the collection of *Anthems* been published in 1840 it would have stood as a memorial to Wesley's years at Exeter. And what a memorial. 'O give thanks' apart, the anthems bear comparison with any written during the nineteenth century, and it is small wonder that Henry Smart, even on incomplete evidence, considered the publication to be of such moment:

With this simple, unobtrusive title, comes forth the first part of a work, any one piece of which would furnish materials for half-a-dozen of the ordinary 'prize anthems' of the metropolis, and set up most of our cathedral organists with a stock of ideas for life . . . if grandeur of style, elevation of sentiment, beauty of materials, and perfect workmanship be looked for as essentials in music destined for the loftiest purpose to which human art can be applied, we can vouch that they will be found in these compositions.[39]

Yet most of these works were destined to remain unknown and unheard for at least a further thirteen years, and one is left pondering why Wesley, for whom the composition of church music had become a mission, should so comprehensively have hidden his light under a bushel. Was it merely that, as William Spark wrote, the cost of copying parts for the choir was too high, or were there other factors as well?[40] The death on 29 December 1838 of Whittington Landon, Dean since 1813, and his replacement by the Precentor, Thomas Hill Lowe, had certainly contributed to the souring of relations between organist and Chapter. Lowe, twenty-four years Landon's junior, was clearly concerned to maintain closer control over the daily business of the cathedral than his elderly predecessor had done, and it was surely no coincidence that in 1840 Wesley was sent a copy of the various 'Orders . . . concerning the Organ', one of which stipulated 'That no Anthems or Services for the use of the Church be pricked [i.e. copied] without an Order of Chapter'.[41] Was this, in effect, a veto on the introduction of new music? Given Wesley's later complaint that were a musician to 'offer his work as a present to *some* Cathedrals . . . *they would not go to the expense of copying out the parts for the Choir!*',[42] one can probably assume that such was its result. It should also be borne in mind that the number of performances of his music fell drastically from a peak of thirty-four in both 1836 and 1837 to a meagre ten in 1839—amounting to one work approximately every seventy services. Yet in spite of such increasingly unfavourable circumstances he continued to compose; one is left wondering whether, in true romantic fashion, he was writing not for his own time—or even for posterity—but simply because of a need to express himself musically.

[39] *MW*, 14 (1840), 231.
[41] *EXc* MS D & C Exeter/7061/Wesley Papers/4.
[40] See *Musical Memories*, 68.
[42] *A Few Words*, 52.

But while Wesley's music was slow to appear in the Exeter Cathedral repertoire—and thus to reach a wide audience—his fame as an organist spread
quickly through the West Country. Invitations to open new organs began to
arrive, one of the first being at the new church of St Mary, Penzance, where
a three-manual instrument by Henry Crabb of Exeter had been installed.
Wesley and four members of the choir travelled there by boat in readiness for
the opening of the church on 25 November 1835, an occasion which the indefatigable 'Red Rover' reported: 'The Service commenced with the Hundredth
Psalm, which was performed on the Organ by our Cathedral Organist,
Mr. S. S. Wesley, and accompanied by four of our Choristers. The skill of Mr.
Wesley is well known, and consequently this was the introduction of some of
the finest sacred music ever heard in the county of Cornwall . . .'[43]

The party remained until the following Sunday, as Wesley had also been
asked to select the first organist from four shortlisted candidates. His choice
was William Viner, who remained until his death in 1859. 'Red Rover' had
noted the 'boisterous state of the weather', and this doubtless lent credence to
a rumour that on their return journey 'the Vessel in which Mr. Wesley . . . and
other Professional Gentlemen belonging to the Cathedral, were returning to
this City from Penzance, had been run down by a steamer, and that all on
board were lost';[44] only the sound of Wesley playing the organ put paid to it!

The question of repairs to the organ now came up again. No major work
had been carried out since 1822, although at the time of Wesley's appointment
it had been reported that the Dean and Chapter intended putting aside several
thousand pounds for a 'thorough repair' and the inclusion of 'Every valuable
modern improvement' by J. C. Bishop.[45] All that resulted was a single visit by
Bishop to tune the organ in mid-December 1835, not minuted in the Chapter
act book and for which he was never paid.[46] In June 1836 Henry Crabb was
engaged to clean and tune it (with the proviso that this did not 'pledge . . . to
his being employed in any projected Improvements in the Instrument'),[47] but
following his decision to emigrate to America the contract passed to Messrs
Brooking and Son, who completed the work in early August.[48] Something
more fundamental than cleaning was, however, required, and questions about
the instrument's capabilities began to be asked. Wesley initially kept his own
counsel, but the publication of a letter from the Revd Abraham Vicary, Custos
of the College of Priest Vicars, listing all the improvements made during the

[43] *WEPG* (5 Dec. 1835), 2.   [44] *TEFP* (3 Dec. 1835), 2.
[45] *WEPG* (17 Oct. 1835), 2.
[46] See Laurence Elvin, *Bishop and Son, Organ Builders* (Lincoln: for the author, 1984), 172.
[47] Exeter Cathedral Chapter acts, minutes of the meeting of 4 June 1836 (*EXc* MS D & C Exeter 3581,
357.)
[48] Exeter Cathedral Chapter acts, minutes of the meeting of 23 July 1836 (ibid. 369).

previous quarter-century, was more than he could stomach. Not only had Vicary trespassed on his territory, but he had also cast doubt on his professional ability in so far as he had 'made an observation which is very disagreeable to myself and has left the public to infer . . . that I require the opinion of an Organ Builder to assist me in judging of an organ'. Writing a good deal more temperately than was his wont, he continued:

Now as it is a part of my professional duty to inspect organs, and control Organ Builders, I cannot allow such an idea to exist, particularly as I have lately drawn plans for the enlargement of the Organ at Crediton, and as the plans are to [be] effected in a few days hence by a London Builder . . .

I cannot but regret that Mr Vicary has written at all on this subject, excepting his allusions to the previous liberality of the Chapter, which I had wished to bear testimony to myself only I thought the subject better passed unnoticed altogether,—as he is manifestly uninformed on the subject of Organ Building, and I must observe to you, that the unfavourable opinion which has been expressed of the Organ in its present state did nor originate with myself, but with the professional musicians visiting Exeter. I have, excepting to the Dean and Canons, generally concealed my opinion of the organ, and took every possible means to prevent the insertion of the letter signed an Amateur in Woolmer's paper.[49]

The issue could no longer be evaded, and the London organ-builder John Gray was asked to inspect; he subsequently submitted an estimate for 'various Improvements', among them the downward extension of the Swell and the addition of pedal pipes.[50] Despite such encouraging progress, Wesley still harboured doubts: 'the Canons called to promise the repairs of the organ, and to assure me of their wishes to do every thing possible for the improvement of the Cathedral Music,' he noted, adding, 'I confess, I much doubt their ability to do either effectually. Prejudice and self love will carry the day, and I anticipate that no more than a very little good will ensue'.[51] As far as the organ was concerned, his fears proved unfounded, and after its reopening on 4 November, *The Musical World* commended the 'magnificent effect' of the new double diapason pedal pipes to GGG (24') and concluded that the instrument 'from being the worst, may now be reckoned one of the best in the kingdom'.[52]

The music chosen was all of a suitably festive nature—Benjamin Cooke's Service in G, Wesley's Responses to the Commandments and Creed, and Greene's anthem 'God is our hope and strength'—but appeared to strike less

---

[49] Letter dated 6 Jan. 1838 to the dean of Exeter (*EXc* MS D & C Exeter/7061/SSW/2).

[50] Exeter Cathedral Chapter acts, minutes of the meeting of 20–1 March 1838 (*EXc* MS D & C Exeter 3581, 528).

[51] *Lcm* MS 2141f, fo. 1.   [52] *MW*, 10 (1838), 152.

of a chord than the following Sunday's anthem, Mozart's 'Praise the Lord, O my soul' (adapted from the Kyrie of his 'Coronation' Mass, K. 317). Wesley, a correspondent wrote, 'had by his masterly performance, most completely *identified himself with* MOZART',[53] and only a few days later the press waxed enthusiastic about his improvisations on the new organ in Bath Abbey on 6 November. That before the morning service was considered masterly, while in the evening Wesley improvised 'three splendid voluntaries' based on Haydn's 'With verdure clad' (*The Creation*), John Travers's 'Ascribe unto the Lord', and the National Anthem.[54] Two years later, on 30 September and 1 October 1840, he enjoyed another notable triumph at the opening of the new instrument by William Hill in St Philip's Church, Sheffield. The *Sheffield Independent* declared:

Of Dr. Wesley, we scarcely know how to speak in terms sufficiently laudatory. We are at a loss whether most to admire his pedal playing, which appears to be executed by him with the greatest ease, or his playing on the keys; but certainly his mode of accompaniment, and the richness of his mixtures, are the finest we have heard . . . and we believe he is considered by the musical profession to be the finest organist of the English school.[55]

Among his contemporaries both Henry Smart and Thomas Attwood Walmisley were of a similar opinion. 'As an organ-player', Smart wrote, 'I may safely say . . . that Dr. Wesley has no rival in this country,' a view with which Walmisley concurred—'the finest organ-player that we have'.[56] The publication in 1836 of his Introduction and Fugue in C sharp minor (issued as the first number of a proposed series, Studio for the Organ) had also been well received. 'Here is a tough weather beaten fugue, constructed upon the most rigid orthodox principles',[57] declared *The Musical World*; the tightly argued work stands as a monument to Wesley's contrapuntal skill, not least the simultaneous entry of the subject in all four parts—in its normal form, inverted, augmented, and both augmented and inverted (see Ex. 3.9). While the fugue looks backwards to Bach, the introduction, which introduces the opening four notes of the fugue subject, is entirely modern in conception and exploits to the full the dramatic possibilities available from the juxtaposition of contrasted tone colours and harmonies. The work even had the honour of being pirated

---

[53] *WL* (12 Nov. 1838), 2.

[54] Ibid. 2. Given that the fugal section of Wesley's *Choral Song* takes for its subject the opening of the bass solo 'Tell it out among the heathen' from Travers's anthem, it is very possible that this performance was based on a preconceived model. Neither should it be forgotten that his first published organ work was a set of variations on the National Anthem.

[55] *WEPG* (10 Oct. 1840), 3.

[56] J. T. Lightwood, 'S. S. Wesley—A Sad Story', *CMJ*, 32 (1941), 102, 117.

[57] *MW*, 1 (1836), 143.

Ex. 3.9. Fugue in C sharp minor, original version

by the Leipzig organist C. F. Becker for the second volume of his collection of organ music entitled *Caecilia*, albeit with the misleading note 'Nach einer gestochenen Ausgaben, London 1800' (After an engraved edition, London 1800).[58] Although no other numbers of Studio for the Organ were issued, it is possible that the contemporary Larghetto in F minor was intended for it.

Still less than thirty and the foremost organist in the country, Wesley should have been able to look forward to a bright future. Yet with his working relationship with the Dean and Chapter starting to deteriorate, within a short time Exeter had become a place to be escaped from at all costs. There had been other changes too. On the morning of 17 June 1836 Wesley had become a father, and the births of John Sebastian and, eighteen months later on 28 December 1837, his brother Samuel Annesley must have imposed an additional burden on the family income.[59] Certainly worries about money (and later about setting his sons up in the world) were to beset him for the next thirty years, so it was perhaps for this reason that he made the otherwise unaccountable decision to take the additional post of organist at Holy Trinity Chapel, Exmouth, at Easter 1837. His appointment, of which the Dean and Chapter were surely in ignorance, was on the following terms:

That Mr. Wesley attend every Sunday evening, and that his assistant will attend the first & second services on every Sunday, and at other times when the Church Service has been usually accompanied with music. That Mr. Wesley himself is to devote one day in each week for the instruction of a Church Choir, & that the sum of £10, as voted by the Parish for the ensuing year, be paid to Mr. Wesley for his services.[60]

How enthusiastically he carried out his duties is open to question, but it is hard not to believe that, having pocketed the money, he lost interest in

[58] C. F. Becker (ed.), *Caecilia: Tonstücke für die Orgel*, vol. 2 (Leipzig: Friedlein & Hirsch, [c.1840]).

[59] While John Sebastian was named after Johann Sebastian Bach, Samuel Annesley perpetuates the names of Wesley's great-grandparents Samuel Wesley (1662–1735) and his wife, Susanna Annesley (1670–1742).

[60] Quoted (from the vestry book of Littleham Parish Church) by William Everitt in *Memorials of Exmouth* (Exmouth: T. Freeman, 1883).

Exmouth and its choir. Certainly no progress was made in his first six months: 'In most churches, where there is, as in Exmouth, an excellent organ and a first-rate organist (Mr. Wesley,), there is an efficient choir;—*in Exmouth, none!*'[61] Not surprisingly, he relinquished the post after a year.

1837 had also seen the death of this father on 11 October. Since 1832 they had seen little of each other, and of late the distance between London and Exeter had (as Samuel noted) made communication between them 'a lengthy and expensive Matter'.[62] The funeral took place in Old Marylebone Church on 17 October, and Samuel was laid to rest in the family vault alongside his parents, brother, and sister; James Turle, organist of Westminster Abbey, and a 'strong band of choralists' sang the burial sentences by Croft and Purcell.[63] Six months later in April 1838 Wesley recorded that he had been to London and 'ordered inscription on Father's Tomb Stone'.[64] One suspects that as both father and son had grown older and Samuel Sebastian had come to prize all that his father had achieved musically, so the bond between them had become stronger. Such feelings were reciprocated: one of Samuel's manuscripts, a prized volume containing fair copies of 'In exitu Israel', 'Omnia vanitas', and 'Tu es sacerdos', bears the touching inscription 'Samuel Sebastian Wesley. The Gift of his Father'. To this was added 'This Book and its exquisite contents are the property, by gift of his Father, of Saml. Sebn. Wesley. Exeter.'[65]

Bitter blow though it must have been, Samuel's death had no immediate effect on his son's career. Not so that of the Dean in December 1838, and, with fate also intervening, the late 1830s and early 1840s were an unhappy time for Wesley. On 9 December 1839 Mary Anne had given birth to her third child, a daughter baptized Mary; her death on 13 February 1840 came as a cruel blow:

Dear Mother.
I have this sad intelligence to give you our dear baby is no more. It left us last night at about twelve o'clock, I cannot tell you how we loved it, and what a dear infant it was, we are suffering the loss most heartily [?], and I am too weak to as yet discover any consolation, only that we hope and pray to have it again with us hereafter . . . I had never I confess given up hope of its recovery until yesterday when I saw that one of its eyes was dead, and towards the evening it got cold about the face, and the hands and feet swelled . . . we hope to learn of the doctor this morning more of the real cause of its complaint—I felt more proud of the dear child because it was very like myself, I cannot write more.[66]

[61] *WEPG* (7 Oct. 1837), 4.
[62] Letter dated 30 March 1836 (*Lbl* Add. MS 31764, fo. 32).
[63] See *GM*, 8 (1837), 545–6.   [64] See *Lcm* MS 2141f, fo. 1ᵛ.   [65] Now *Lcm* MS 4022.
[66] Letter dated 13 Feb. 1840 (*Lbl* Add. MS 35019, fo. 24).

Mary was buried in the New Cemetery, Exeter, where thirty-six years later her father would be laid at her side. Little could Wesley, who with the cathedral choir had been present at the consecration of the cemetery less than three years before, have realized under what tragic circumstances he would return.[67] Mary's death has also been linked to a number of sightings of Wesley's ghost in his bedroom, together with the sound of Mary Anne running along the landing at their home, 9 The Close. One cannot but suspect that the effects of her death further strained his already fragile relationship with the Dean and Chapter, and the next few months were marked by a string of reprimands. On 16 May he was informed that he was 'not to give Lessons on the Organ either to his Apprentice or to any other person'[68] and on 20 June 'that no private Engagement should interfere with his attendance on the Chapter on Saturday Mornings'.[69] He was also sent a copy of the various 'Orders of Chapter concerning the Organ', setting out what he was, and was not, permitted to do. With business carried out by diktat there was clearly no love lost between either party, but worse was to come. On Saturday 26 September Wesley entered the cathedral singing school and found two choristers there, John Holmyard and Robert Kitt:

Holmyard says
Last Saturday in the Singing School before the Morning Service . . . I was practising a glee with Kitt, singing it, without the organ. Dr Wesley came in—he asked if we had been practising with the Men—we said we had—Dr Wesley said who gave us orders to go—we said the Men had asked the Dean and had leave for us—Dr W said the Dean is not your Master—I am your Master—and he went over to the Window, and immediately turned round to us, and ran over, and said 'you shan't go without <u>my</u> leave['], and struck me several times hard blows with his fist on my back—I was holding down my head to avoid the blows, when I received a blow on my chin by a <u>Kick</u> of the Foot from Dr Wesley[.] A hard kick, and there was a mark on my chin for many days from it . . .
Kitt says—
Directly as Dr Wesley quitted Holmyard he struck me a blow on the side of my face, and knocked me down with one blow and then when I was on the floor kicked me on the floor.[70]

Realizing that he had overstepped the mark, Wesley immediately dispatched a most courteous and carefully worded letter to the Dean, setting out his principles *vis-à-vis* the attendance of the choristers at the Glee Club. Of the attack on the two boys, not a word.

[67] See *WEPG* (26 Aug. 1837), 3.   [68] *EXc* MS D & C Exeter 3582, 238.   [69] Ibid. 243.
[70] Account taken down on 3 Oct. 1840 (*EXc* MS D & C Exeter 7061/Wesley Papers/5).

Revd. and dear Sir

I beg to mention for your consideration the circumstances under which the application to you was made for the attendance of the Choristers at the Glee Club, first
observing that I have no wish whatever to prevent their singing at the Club, and that
it was my intention to have allowed their being present in the usual manner on my
having a request to that effect made to me as their master.—That request not having
been made I have prevented their attendance as yet at the practice meetings of the
Singers and in consequence Mr. Cole has waited on yourself to give leave for them,
as he believes in opposition to my wishes. I trust you will not think me to entertain
any intrusive or disrespectful feeling if I suggest that the Organist of the Cathedral has
always been here and is in every other Cathedral Town, the authority conferred with
on matters connected with the Musical Services of his pupils the Choristers and that
he will be placed very often in unpleasant situations if the public are allowed the use
of the boys' services without the sanction of the music-master, for they may often be
called upon to perform things of which they know nothing, and their ignorance vis-
ited upon him, besides which, the granting leave for their attendance at such engagements is a privelege [sic] connected with his office which serves to attach a little respect
to it, and to place the public under occasional obligations to him.

If however the Chapter intend to depart from Custom on this subject I shall be
happy to acquiesce in their determination, but believing that they have not such a wish
I take the liberty of making these observations in reference to the irregular interference of Mr. Cole, and if you have no objection that the authority of my office should
still have its weight, I shall take an opportunity of naming your intention to Mr. Cole.

I beg to add an apology for this hurried communication, being in the midst of
preparations for a long journey, but as the first meeting of the Glee Club takes place
before my return to Exeter I felt I should be suffering an injustice if I did not suggest
to you the terms on which Mr. Cole has submitted his application to you.

I am, Your very obedient Servant,
S. S. Wesley[71]

The two choristers gave their accounts to the chapter on 3 October, and
these were duly noted down by the Chapter Clerk, Ralph Barnes. Barnes and
Wesley were sworn enemies (the former later describing the latter as 'The
most to be avoided man I ever met with');[72] on a reading of the transcript the
suspicion arises that Barnes stirred the whole affair up in an attempt to blacken
Wesley's name. He certainly felt free to insert his own glosses, and on the fair
copy declared, 'I (RB) should say from the description that a more dastardly
low vulgar <~~and blackguardly~~> sort of attack considering the persons and in
such a place could not have been imagined'.[73] Wesley was now summoned
and on 20 October gave his version of events:

---

[71] Letter dated 26 Sept. 1840 (*EXc* MS D & C Exeter 7061/S. S.Wesley/3).

[72] From a wrapper around a bundle of Wesley's papers (*EXc* MS D & C Exeter 7061/Wesley Papers/10).

[73] *EXc* MS D & C Exeter 7061/Wesley Papers/6.

The Statement taken from the two Choristers . . . was read over to them in the presence of Dr. Wesley and they stated it to be true.

Dr. Wesley was asked what he had to say when he admitted that the Statement was in substance true insisting on his right to punish the Boys because they had not asked leave or mentioned the leave they had obtained to him and justified what he had done . . . although it was admitted that the Boys said at the time they had the Dean's leave, & in fact they had the Dean's leave.

The Dean & Canons present are of opinion that Dr Wesley was unjustified in inflicting any punishment much less in making the attack he did which was offering an indignity unworthy [of] his situation & degrading to the Boys.

They think that Dr. W. having betrayed such great want of temper and not now offering any excuse or apology that he ought to be suspended from the duties & emoluments of his Office of Instructor of the Choristers until the Meetg. of the Chapter at their next Christmas Audit when his whole conduct in this matter should be submitted for the judgment of the Chapter.[74]

Once again he had allowed his feelings to get the better of him, but on reflection he realized that an apology to the Dean was called for:

Dear Sir

I was not surprised to find . . . that the Chapter were much offended by the expressions used by me at the meeting you allude to, as I immediately became sensible of the extreme impropriety of my conduct, and if it can be received as an apology, I have no hesitation in expressing my great regret that my remarks should have induced me to show more warmth of manner than was becoming in me, or was consistent with the obligations I am under to the Chapter.

I am Dear Sir
yours Obediently
S. S. Wesley.[75]

The proposed suspension was not carried out, but relations with the dean and chapter were to remain on a precarious footing, not least because of Wesley's frequent absences. The rapid advance of William Spark, his most recent apprentice (taken on in 1839), must have helped, for the latter recorded that Wesley 'often left me for two or three days . . . to exercise his favourite pastime of fly-fishing'.[76] A rather longer absence in 1841 led to an official reprimand: 'Dr. Wesley having been absent since Thursday the 27th. May without previous communication to the Chapter, and having left the Organ to a young and inexperienced Pupil they directed the Chapter Clerk to inform Dr. Wesley that it is expected that the Organist should have leave of absence from

---

[74] *EXc* MS D & C Exeter 7061/Wesley Papers/3.
[75] *EXc* MS D & C Exeter 7061/S. S. Wesley/10.   [76] *Musical Memories*, 69.

the Chapter'.[77] By now it was perfectly clear that Exeter offered no chance of a secure, contented future, but the options open were limited and in practical terms were restricted to two—another cathedral post or one of the four university chairs of music. Given Wesley's recent experiences, the latter option must have seemed particularly tempting, and it was doubtless with this in mind that early in the previous year he had renewed enquiries about taking the degree of Bachelor of Music at the University of Oxford. Samuel Wesley had first raised the subject with William Crotch in March 1836:

My Son requests me to forward you a copy of a few of his Compositions, and a Manuscript which he submits to you as an Exercise for the Degree of Bachelor in Music. He has some fear that it is not precisely the Kind of Exercise which the Statutes require, but if it can be accepted, he would feel himself greatly indebted . . .

You have heard no Doubt that his Abilities (from a Child) were extraordinary . . . and I rely on your great Kindness that if you can serve him in any Way, you will.[78]

Nothing came of this approach, but now, through the offices of Dr John Bull (one of the Exeter canons), he made tentative enquiries of the Revd Dr Philip Bliss, the university registrar, about the possibility of taking the degrees of Bachelor of Music and Doctor of Music at the same time. Having received a favourable reply, he matriculated at Magdalen College, where the Vice-President's register records that on 3 June 1839 'Samuel Wesley organista Exoniensis admissus est'.[79] With memories of the Gresham Prize still fresh in his mind, he had already been in contact with Crotch, and his exercise, 'O Lord, thou art my God', was now submitted to the professor's scrutiny.[80] Crotch apparently at first refused to accept it unless Wesley would 'expunge or alter some passages which he affirmed were not in accordance with the laws of harmony and modulation',[81] but finally relented in the face of Wesley's refusal to give way. Of the anthem's performance in Magdalen College Chapel on 20 June *The Oxford University, City, and County Herald* reported that 'The introduction on the organ was exceedingly good, and did great credit to the author . . . but of the vocal [writing] we could not fairly judge, the singers, in many parts, being both out of time and out of tune'.[82]

With no immediate vacancy to apply for Wesley had perforce to return to the humdrum world of Exeter. But while the cathedral and its services formed

---

[77] Chapter minute of 7 June 1841 (*EXc* MS D & C Exeter 3582, 352).
[78] Letter dated 30 March 1836 (*Lbl* Add. MS 31764, fo. 32).
[79] *OM* MS 730 (c.), 224.
[80] An entry in Wesley's notebook records that in April 1839 he 'went twice to London, saw Dr Crotch' (*Lcm* MS 2141f., fo. 1ᵛ).
[81] Bumpus, *A History of English Cathedral Music*, 481.
[82] *The Oxford University, City, and County Herald* (22 June 1839), 3.

the focus of his professional life, he took full advantage of any opportunities to join in other more convivial activities and also undertook a certain amount of teaching. Even the latter brought some rewards: he numbered among his pupils Lady Acland, wife of one of the MPs for North Devon, Sir Thomas Dyke Acland. An acquaintance developed, and Wesley and his wife were regular visitors at the Aclands' Devon home, Killerton House, some eight miles north-west of Exeter. It was ostensibly for Lady Acland, too, that Wesley wrote his two sets of *Three Pieces for a Chamber Organ* (discussed in Chapter 4) although, the title and dedication notwithstanding, the first set is most definitely not suitable for a small instrument such as the one at Killerton. Not surprisingly it was found to be 'too difficult for her Ladyship' and Wesley responded by writing a less demanding second set.[83]

Practical music-making held much more appeal, and Wesley was a regular attender at the Devon Madrigal Society and the Devon Glee Club. Both societies met monthly during the winter months to combine gastronomic and musical pleasures, and he was first admitted to the former as a visitor (singing countertenor) on 7 November 1835, before being formally 'proposed by Mr. Moore seconded by Mr. Pye and elected by acclamation'.[84] That 'O God, whose Nature and Property' had been included in the evening's programme was a particularly nice touch.[85] Showing the versatility expected of a professional musician, he sang countertenor (most frequently), tenor, or bass as required and often took the chair at the monthly meetings. The Madrigal Society always met on the 'Evening preceding each Meeting of the Devon-Glee-Club',[86] no doubt because the country seat of their president, Sir John Rogers, was at Ivybridge, some distance from Exeter. While the activities of the Glee Club are less well documented, we know that Wesley was active in its affairs too. On 2 December 1836, for example, it was reported that the 'vocalists of the Devon Glee Club dined by invitation at Trehill, the hospitable mansion of J. H. Ley, Esq.' when the glees were 'relieved by the interspersion of songs . . . a duet on the harp and pianoforte . . . and an extemperaneous [*sic*] performance on the piano forte by Mr. S. S. Wesley'.[87]

By the late 1830s the members had transferred their patronage from the Subscription Rooms to Cockram's New London Inn (see Pl. 9), and it was here, in March 1838, that a new glee by Wesley enjoyed a minor triumph. Sir John Rogers had recently been appointed sheriff, and at a festive dinner of the

---

[83] See the note by Martin Cawood in his copy (now *Lbl* h.2733.w.(4)).

[84] *EXce* MS 41.

[85] The society's first performance of the anthem had been on 3 Nov. 1831, scarcely three months after its publication.

[86] *EXce* MS 41. [87] *WL* (5 Dec. 1836), 3.

club a glee composed in his honour by Wesley (to words by his friend W. H. Bellamy) was 'rapturously received'.[88] Wesley, who had received Bellamy's verses only on 28 February, was not present, as he mordantly recorded in his notebook: 'Three days ago I wrote a glee . . . in honour of Sir John Rogers's Shrivalty—badly sung I hear'.[89] The club was now under the musical direction of a rival professional, Kellow J. Pye, two years his junior, and this perhaps explains his lack of enthusiasm! But neither the Glee Club nor the Madrigal Society cultivated large-scale works or catered for more than a select audience, and to remedy this deficiency Wesley had announced a series of four subscription concerts for the winter months of 1836. Yet although his plans were warmly received, a shortage of subscribers led to the whole venture's being cancelled. Pye, however, took up the challenge the following year, advertising a series of five concerts for which Wesley was engaged as solo pianist (although his contribution probably did not extend beyond the first two concerts on 5 and 6 October). Playing second fiddle held little appeal, and the arrival of Pye on the scene as both conductor and composer (the first concert included his Septuor for piano, strings, and wind) also raises the question of Wesley's relations with other musicians.

It is unfortunate that he almost invariably viewed professional colleagues with suspicion and was always ready to believe that their actions were determined by ulterior motives—a trait which worsened as he got older. Whether Pye, who had offered the hand of friendship by proposing him for membership of the Madrigal Society, gave rise to such feelings of paranoia is not clear, but Wesley would surely have viewed the cancellation of his second series of concerts (1838–9 season) with the quiet satisfaction of one who had just seen off the threat to his own musical supremacy. At all events, relations appear to have remained cordial, with Pye's new anthem 'O Lord I will exalt Thee' introduced at the cathedral in March 1839 and Pye assisting Wesley with the correction of the proofs of his anthems a year later. But Pye was not the only rival. There was also Henry Haycraft, organist of St Petrock's Church. Haycraft, however, encroached rather too closely upon Wesley's chosen field, church music, and Wesley neither contributed nor subscribed to his two collections, A Selection of Sacred Music (1837) and Sacred Harmony (1851). Haycraft also had a second string to his bow and appeared in 1840 as 'conductor' of the 'Devon and Exeter Quartett Concerts'. Yet when in June 1837 Wesley had embarked on the organization of a 'musical society, for the practice of classical music',[90] Haycraft's name was notably absent.

    [88] WEPG (10 March 1838), 3.   [89] Lcm MS 2141f, fo. 1.   [90] WEPG (17 June 1837), 3.

This new venture, announced in September 1837, was clearly intended to ensure that Wesley kept a foothold in the city's musical life:

The Musical Association lately established in this city, for the performance of first-rate instrumental music, held its first meeting at Congdon's Rooms, on the 11ᵗʰ instant [September], when Beethoven's Symphonies, Nos. 1 and 2, were admirably gone through. This society is indebted for its existence to Mr. S. S. Wesley, organist of the Cathedral, who has been active in its success, and has accepted the post of its conductor; and to Mr. Rice, the talented violinist, who for a long period has kept together a clever party of instrumentalists.[91]

Yet its success was short-lived, and after this first meeting no more is heard of it. Was it purely coincidental that Pye's first concert, some three weeks later, also included Beethoven's Second Symphony? Wesley was not, however, one to admit defeat, and the following year he turned his attention to yet another musical undertaking, a new choral society. This would, he wrote, provide an 'opportunity, so long wished for . . . of performing in the city of Exeter, *those* noble works of the great writers which require a large choral body to make them really effective'.[92] Details of the potential—or actual—membership are preserved in one of his notebooks and reveal that cathedral colleagues and acquaintances formed the largest part, from the choristers (who were initially to supply the treble part) to one of the assistants in the Chapter Clerk's office. Needless to say his two articled pupils, Harding and Franklin, were also roped in, but what did he do with those he listed as 'Doubtful voices'?[93] Were they encouraged to take some singing lessons?

Mr. Wesley announces to persons desirous of joining the Society but who wish to attain previously a greater degree of proficiency in singing than they may now boast of, that, to them he will make a reduction in his usual terms for singing lessons, that they may in a short time, it is hoped, so far overcome the rudiments of vocal practice, as to sustain their respective parts with confidence and correctness.[94]

The choral society, too, apparently came to naught, and Wesley must surely have wondered whether everything he tried was doomed to failure. But what he still hankered after was a full-scale music festival, and as late as January 1840 he informed Vincent Novello that he had been 'striving hard to get a Festival in our fine roomy Cathedral but our Clergy are at present unfavourable to it'.[95] It was not to be, and the people of Exeter had to remain content with occasional visits by parties of touring musicians. Occasionally there were opportunities for their local colleagues to participate: in January 1839 Wesley

[91] *TEFP* (21 Sept. 1837), [3].   [92] *WL* (9 July 1838), 2.   [93] See *Lcm* MS 2141e.
[94] *WL* (9 July 1838), 2.   [95] Letter dated 29 Jan. 1840 (*Lbl* Add. MS 11730, fo. 228).

and the gentlemen of the cathedral choir joined the harpist Amelia Elouis and her party, Mlle Lanza (soprano), Henry Phillips (baritone), and Philip Ernst (flute). While the vicars choral provided three glees, Wesley presided at the piano—a new grand, 'one of Erard's patents . . . sent expressly from London'[96]—accompanying, among other things, his song 'There be none of beauty's daughters' and a duet for harp and piano by Bochsa and Herz.

Although the song had been published in 1835, with a dedication to the soprano Deborah Knyvett, this was its first recorded performance. It impressed Phillips sufficiently, however, for him to repeat it (perhaps in its alternative orchestral guise) at the forthcoming Worcester Three Choirs Festival, when *The Musical World* described it as 'a composition that none but a man of genius and a scientific musician like Dr. Wesley could produce'.[97]

Another visitor in 1839 was the pianist Thalberg; he was followed a year later by Franz Liszt, who was persuaded by Wesley to subscribe to his forthcoming *Anthems*. Yet even the attraction of so famous a name failed to draw the crowds. Small wonder then that Wesley was chary of entering into some proposal he had received from Hawes:

The success of such undertakings as the one you propose . . . is very uncertain I regret to inform you. Mori made them answer, and . . . Bochsa also had partial success, what he would never have again, perhaps. Some excellent concerts have entirely failed, Blagroves, and Madame Dulken's both were ruinous.

I once endeavoured to give concerts here by subscription but could not get enough subscribers. Another professor [Pye] made the attempt and certainly gave excellent concerts, but lost much money.

I do not think I should like to engage your party. And I am sure there is no one here who would, unless perhaps one of the little quartet parties of 'native talent' might like to avail themselves of your visit and partly engage with you . . .

If you intend to take Exeter in your way Westward, and wish me to take the piano forte and manage the affairs in Exeter I perhaps may, upon consideration, and learning the extent of your party, undertake such a charge but then I should wish you to engage me.

I regret to say, much as I should like our Devonshire gentry to hear Miss Maria Hawes and also Mr [Henry] Hayward who I am informed plays admirably, I cannot say I think your success would be of a nature satisfactory to all. I fear it would be far otherwise from what I know of our musical public . . . [but] if the matter is determined on [I] will make any effort to promote your views.[98]

[96] *MW*, 11 (1839), 120.   [97] *MW*, 12 (1839), 327.
[98] Letter to William Hawes, dated 26 July 1840 (*Lbl* Loan 79). The musicians referred to were Nicholas Mori (violin), Nicholas Bochsa (harp), Henry Blagrove (violin), Louise Dulcken (piano), Maria Hawes (contralto), and Henry Hayward (violin).

But Hawes never came, and within a few months Wesley would be embroiled with the Dean and Chapter over his treatment of Holmyard and Kitt. At this point, one suspects, any interest he might have had in furthering his own (or anyone else's) musical career in Exeter would have evaporated. With the death in May 1841 of John Thomson, Reid Professor of Music in the University of Edinburgh, however, came a chance to escape. His candidature was announced in *The Musical World* on 3 June and was supported by an impressive list of testimonials, including ones from Thomas Adams, Henry Smart, and Walmisley; an editorial in a later issue also came out in his favour and praised his compositions for showing 'evidence of a most gifted mind, and sedulous study'. It continued:

his theoretical learning is well known to be both extensive and profound, the peculiar bent of his fine intellect having led him more deeply into the mysteries of his art, than any other native student known to us, excepting, perhaps, Dr. Crotch—his secular compositions, and orchestral writings, display an intimate knowledge of the best and grandest examples, and a grasp of harmony, and exuberance of imagination, almost entirely without a rival.

. . . the Professor's duty is no restful one, and Dr. Wesley has youth and vigour, independent of other qualifications, which will enable him better to fulfil the design of the institution and should insure him the preference.[99]

The voters knew little of the candidates, so it is not surprising that their choice should have fallen on his better-known rival Henry Bishop. But for Wesley another opening had already appeared, and on 20 November, well before the Edinburgh result was announced, he informed the Chapter of his wish to resign.[100]

A month earlier, on 18 October, he had given the opening recital on the new organ in the recently consecrated parish church at Leeds and, according to Spark, was 'so much impressed with the wealth of Leeds, and delighted to be asked by two rich merchants to select grand Broadwood pianofortes for them, that bearing in mind his disagreement with Dean Lowe at Exeter, he . . . accepted from the vicar and churchwardens the offer of organist at £200 per annum, guaranteed for ten years'.[101] Yet despite having made known his wish to leave Exeter, it was not until the beginning of January that he wrote to the Chapter Clerk to announce that 'At March next I intend to give up all further attention to the duties of my offices at Exeter Cathedral'.[102] It was in fact in early February that Wesley quitted Exeter, but for close on two months he contrived to receive two salaries by dint of leaving the nineteen-year-old

[99] *MW*, 16 (1841), 290.
[100] See *EXc* MS 3582, 392.
[101] W. Spark, *Musical Reminiscences*, 166.
[102] *EXc* MS D & C Exeter 7061/S. S.Wesley/4.

Spark—who still had two years of his articles to serve—as nominal organist at Exeter while he took up his duties in Yorkshire! Because of a delay in the holding of the annual cathedral audit (at which his successor would be elected) the Dean and Chapter requested that Spark be allowed to remain longer. This did not go down well:

I cannot feel that the Chapter should ask a favor of me when I view the serious and most distressing consequences of my not having met with a more agreeable reception in my connection with Exeter Cathedral. I do deeply regret that at the present moment the Chapter should ask a favor [of] me, as it is only with the most extreme pain that I have been led to move myself and family from a place and neighbourhood to which I was so much attached as Exeter.

I have struggled much to write to you without making an expression of this nature but that has been impossible.[103]

But as at Hereford it was money which really soured his departure. A request on 11 March that the Chapter should settle its account with him up to the time of the expiry of his notice (25 March) elicited a reply that the matter would be settled 'in the course of a day or two'.[104] This, however, came to nothing and on 6 April he tried again, with a further letter on the 19th and, finally, a strongly worded protest to the canon in Residence:

Dr Wesley has had to make very many applications to get his account settled . . . and, strange to say, they have not met with what he considers to be due attention. Mr Sanders wrote promising in two days he would see into the matter, this was about a month since, but Dr Wesley has not yet got the Matter settled and therefore finds it necessary to trouble the Canon in residence with the subject, and he would be obliged by the money due to him being paid into the bank and transferred to him at Leeds without delay.[105]

Even this did not do the trick, and he was forced to write again on 22 August. While the letter has not survived, the Chapter Clerk's reply gives a good idea of its tone:

The Dean of Exeter received a Note apparently in your handwriting. Dated Leeds Aug 22 beginning Dr. S. S. Wesley &c. The Dean transmitted it to me to be submitted to the Chapter. I have so done.

The Insolence of the note is so surpassing, that you can expect, assuredly you will receive, no other answer that that announcement.

[103] *EXc* MS D & C Exeter 7061/S. S.Wesley/5.
[104] *EXc* MS D & C Exeter 7061/S. S.Wesley/15.
[105] Letter dated 20 April [1842] (*EXc* MS D & C Exeter 7061/S. S.Wesley/9).

No further communication addressed to the Dean will receive any reply whatever. If you have any to make to the Dean & Chapter, I beg it may be made to me, if in terms fit to be communicated.[106]

With this the correspondence ended, but by now Wesley was many miles away, once again enjoying the status of a local celebrity and as yet untroubled by such disputes as had marred his final years in Exeter. Yet it must have been with very mixed feelings that he left the city. He had arrived in 1835 newly married and full of high hopes for the future. He departed six and a half years later a sadder man, bitter about his treatment at the cathedral. While his reputation as an organist had undoubtedly been enhanced, he had made little progress in the public eye as a composer, for although the Introduction and Fugue in C sharp minor and the glees had been well received, what should have been his *chef d'œuvre*—the *Anthems* of 1840—had never been issued. Neither had his various attempts at concert-giving met with much success, while on a personal level there had been the tragic death of his infant daughter Mary. Not even the birth of another son, Francis Gwynne, on 29 January 1841 could, one suspects, erase that memory. But it was at the cathedral that fate had dealt him the poorest hand. Ever since the death of Dean Landon in December 1838 the odds had been stacked against him, and with each passing year the prospect of a harmonious working life had receded further. This, unfortunately, had only served to bring out some of the worst aspects of his character, and his actions and attitude after receiving the offer at Leeds show him in an undignified light, motivated by self-interest and not averse to double-dealing. All things considered, it was hardly surprising that the prospect of a post in which he would be untroubled either by an interfering chapter or by 'frequent disputes with the dean respecting the musical arrangements'[107] should have been so alluring. In some well-considered remarks *The Musical World* seems to have expressed the state of affairs with encouraging judgement. Referring first to his disappointment at Edinburgh, it stated

We need not condole with Dr. Wesley; he is a young and enterprising person, full of the vigour of manhood, and the enthusiasm of art; a long career is open before him, and a successful one it must be, whether pursued in the North or the South, as the founder of a Scottish school, or the perfecter of an English one.

It then proceeded to welcome his acceptance of the post at Leeds:

which will necessarily bring his eminent abilities out of their limited exercise in Exeter Cathedral to a wider, more appropriate, and every way more fertile field: we are sure

---

[106] Letter dated 26 Sept. 1842 (*EXc* MS D & C Exeter 7061/Wesley Papers/8).
[107] W. Spark, *Musical Memories*, 65.

of the musical benefit his presence will effect in the very populous district of central Yorkshire, and we anticipate nothing less than that his exertions will be gratefully received and adequately remunerated.[108]

[108] *MW*, 16 (1841), 370.

4

Leeds

A desire to do what was best for the Public rendered me miserable under such a Dean and Chapter Clerk as those in which Exeter did then & still rejoices. I was earning a fine income & loved the County of Devon but I packt up, I gave up <u>all</u>—& much it was—& went to <u>Leeds</u>.[1]

LEEDS . . . in 1841 [recalled William Spark] . . . was very different from the Leeds of to-day. Then it was one huge mass of dingy-looking mills, warehouses, poorly built houses, badly paved streets, uninviting shops, and huge chimneys that poured forth their miles of black smoke, begriming and blackening all that lay in its course. The generality of the inhabitants also at that time were brusque in their talk and manners, and were inclined to assert their independence, which Wesley often said meant impudence. He had not realised that under a rough exterior there often beats a soft and tender heart; he failed to give our 'Leeds loiners' credit for anything better than he saw upon the surface.[2]

It must indeed have been a shock to Samuel Sebastian and Mary Anne to exchange the fine buildings and rural surroundings of Hereford and Exeter for the 'dirt, smoke, and inhabitants'[3] of Leeds, for the contrast between Devon and industrial Yorkshire could not have been greater. Whereas Exeter had owed its prosperity to traditional industries based on the wool trade, Leeds, whose population had risen from 53,162 in 1801 to 123,393 in 1831 and was still increasing,[4] was very much a product of the industrial revolution, 'situated in the midst of one of the most thriving manufacturing districts in the kingdom'.[5] But for Wesley such things would have mattered little. 'I am going to live in Leeds in Yorkshire', he had written to Henry Phillips, 'Very cold I fear . . . but in musical matters they are much <u>warmer</u> than we are in Devon'.[6] Indeed, the warm reception he had enjoyed at the parish church must have

---

[1] Letter dated 19 Sept. [1858] to Henry Ford (*RSCM* Nicholson scrapbook, fo. 40).
[2] W. Spark, *Musical Memories*, 65–6. [3] Ibid.
[4] W. R. W. Stephens, 'Hook, Walter Farquhar (1798–1875)' in Leslie Stephen and Sidney Lee (eds.), *Dictionary of National Biography* (London: Smith, Elder, 1907), 9. 1171.
[5] James Bell, *A New and Comprehensive Gazetteer*, 4 vols. (Glasgow and Edinburgh: Fullarton & Co., 1836), 3, 38.
[6] Letter dated 14 Jan. [1842] (*CA*).

convinced him that here there was indeed a future for church music. But before we look at his work in the town a glance at the unique choral establishment at the church and the man responsible for it, Walter Farquhar Hook (1798–1875), will help to set the scene.[7]

Hook had been appointed Vicar of Leeds in 1837 and on arrival found himself in charge of a vast parish encompassing both the town and much of the suburbs, served by fifteen churches. The parish church was a much-altered medieval building, and his initial concern was to improve its internal arrangements, both to accord with his own moderate High-Church views and in response to an address from 640 parishioners requesting better seating arrangements.[8] Work started in 1838, but the whole structure was found to be unsafe and the obvious course was to demolish it and rebuild. Demolition began immediately and the new church, designed in the Gothic style by R. D. Chantrell, was consecrated on 2 September 1841 (see Pl. 10).

It was not only the building that Hook had found to be in poor condition. The choir (one of the earliest to be robed in the north of England) was equally run down, 'the surplices in rags, and the service books in tatters'.[9] Determined that this state of affairs should be improved, he campaigned for—and against vigorous opposition achieved—the increase in the church rate needed to maintain the choir. A far more important development, however, took place early in 1841 as the new church neared completion:

A number of Churchmen waited upon the Vicar . . . and requested that he would permit Choral Service to be daily performed after its consecration. This was gladly acceded to by the Vicar, who promised his utmost support, so long as funds could be provided to sustain the choir in such a state of efficiency that the services should be performed complete in all their perfection and beauty.[10]

Hook recorded his progress in February 1841: 'I am now fully occupied in preparing to form a choir, a subject on which I am profoundly ignorant; but John Jebb has kindly assisted me . . . How I shall raise the money I know not; but this I know, a good choir must be formed . . . My whole heart is set on this business'.[11]

---

[7] Bernarr Rainbow has provided a detailed account of Hook's work at Leeds in *The Choral Revival in the Anglican Church (1839–1872)* (London: Barrie and Jenkins, 1970), 26–36.

[8] Hook was to write in 1839, 'I am not, myself, one of the Oxford Divines, although they are among my dearest Friends. Engaged in the Duties of a large Parish . . . it would be imprudent for me to render myself answerable for publications over which I could have no direct control' (letter dated 3 April 1839 to J. W. Coker, *Ob* MS ENG LETT.d.368, fo. 35ᵛ).

[9] Stephens, 'Hook, Walter Farquhar', 1171. A body of professional singers had been recruited by the Vicar, Richard Fawcett, in 1815, and a surpliced choir of men and boys introduced three years later.

[10] 'Church Music in Leeds', *PC*, 3 (1850), 148.

[11] W. R. W Stephens, *The Life and Letters of Walter Farquhar Hook*, 2 vols. (London: Richard Bentley & Son, 1878), 2, 125.

The Revd John Jebb, to whom he had turned for advice, was one of the foremost advocates of the 'cathedral' service, and to prepare the ground he was also commissioned to give a series of lectures at the Leeds Church Institution. These were subsequently published in May 1841 as 'Three Lectures on the Cathedral Service of the Church of England' in the third number of *The Christian's Miscellany* and, according to *The Parish Choir*, circulated widely and 'greatly contributed to promote a strong feeling in favour of the Choral Service'.[12] On Jebb's advice Hook had appointed a new choirmaster, James Hill (an alto lay clerk from Westminster Abbey), to superintend the establishment of choral services, but the organist of the old church, Henry Smith, initially continued in office and played at the consecration. For the inauguration of the new organ, however, a better-known player had been wanted and, at the instigation of Martin Cawood (a wealthy brass founder and amateur musician and 'the vicar's right-hand man in matters musical'),[13] Wesley was engaged. The opening took the form of Evensong, at which Wesley introduced 'The Wilderness', followed by selections from Haydn's *Creation* and Handel's *Messiah*, interspersed with organ solos (among them Bach's 'St Anne' Fugue and an unspecified composition of his own) and created an immediate impression. '. . . there is a chasteness and delicacy of feeling in his accompaniment of the vocal parts rarely to be met with' declared *The Leeds Intelligencer*, 'whilst in bolder and more prominent performances, his mighty and herculean grasp of all the varied powers of the instrument displays the great vigour and power of his mind'.[14] Given that Henry Smith had by now resigned, it gave Cawood little trouble to persuade the Vicar to offer Wesley the post. Hook wrote:

My dear Cawood

I perfectly agree with you about Dr Wesley. And I will at once offer him the Situation and guarantee him £200 a year, if you will be responsible for half the Sum. What I mean is this that I will raise £100 a year, making up the deficiency myself if there be any deficiency, and making over to you the surplus, if there be a surplus, if you will do the same.

I will be answerable to him for £200 a year.

You will be answerable to me for £100.

When he is here we shall soon realise the money.

It is important that we should decide upon this at once.[15]

Hook had now achieved his ambition: not only had he succeeded in establishing a choir which was already the equal of those in most cathedrals, but he

[12] 'Church Music in Leeds', 148. [13] W. Spark, *Musical Reminiscences*, 166.

[14] *LI* (23 Oct. 1841, 2nd edn.), 5. [15] Letter from Hook dated 28 Oct. 1841 (author's collection).

had also attracted the country's leading organist and church musician. The general satisfaction felt at this achievement is evident from reports in the local press: 'We have hitherto abstained from mentioning that Samuel Sebastian Wesley, Esq., Mus. Doc. and now organist of the Cathedral, Exeter, had accepted the situation of organist and composer of this splendid Church . . . [and] we cannot but congratulate our readers on the high acquisition which music will receive from having so distinguished a professional gentleman to reside in our town'.[16]

On his arrival in February 1842 Wesley thus found a musical tradition and enthusiastic choir which, although as yet only a few months old, boded well for the future. Just as importantly, he found a church where the services were conducted with a degree of reverence almost unknown elsewhere. 'Dr. Wesley says that our service is most sublime: beyond anything he ever heard in any cathedral',[17] Hook confided to an acquaintance, and the atmosphere certainly produced a strong effect on a contemporary visitor:

The service was conducted according to the strict letter of the rubric, and with a fervor and solemnity of manner, which gave it a proud pre-eminence over those similar establishments where the pure and beautiful language and formularies of the Protestant church are sacrificed to the rapid and careless manner of the officiating priests . . . We had never previously seen or heard the services of the English Church so impressively conducted; and we left that house of God full impressed with the conviction that the example here set would rapidly effect wondrous changes in the manners, habits, and religious opinions of British society, from which manifold blessings, spiritual and temporal, will inevitably follow.[18]

Although music was only accorded a brief mention—'As we entered the porch, the rich swell of the organ fell on our ear, mingling with the full and clear tones of the choir, and our soul felt at once the divine influence of the sacred minstrelsy'[19]—it was clearly the combination of excellence in all the elements of worship, from the 'sacred utensils of the sacrament of the Holy Eucharist', the 'blazonry of painted glass' in the windows, and the grandeur of the internal decoration to the dignified celebration of the liturgy, the eloquent sermon, and the contribution of the choir and organ which so impressed. Their effect on Wesley himself was no less profound, and during the next few years his own vision of the ideal choral service as an art form combining liturgy, music, ceremony, and architecture took shape.

Once established he lost little time in arranging matters in a way more to his own liking. Immediately before his arrival Hill had been acting as both organ-

[16] LI (1 Jan. 1842), 5.   [17] Stephens, Walter Farquhar Hook, 2. 135.
[18] LI (14 Oct. 1843), 7.   [19] Ibid.

ist and choirmaster, and the direction of the choir had remained in his hands. It was to him, too, that applicants for vacancies had to apply in June 1842, but, as William Spark recalled, such an arrangement irked Wesley:

After a year or two the distinguished organist got across with Mr. Hill, the able and indefatigable choir-master—Wesley's object being to get the whole business into his own hands. After some months of wrangling with Hill and interviewing the vicar and wardens, Mr. Hill had notice to leave, and Wesley then took the entire direction of the choir and the training of the boys.[20]

These events presumably took place during 1843, as at the meeting of the parish church choir committee on 15 January 1844 it was proposed 'That Dr. Wesley be offered £30 per Annum to provide a proper & competent person to instruct the Boys & men—& whose duty shall be more strictly defined by the Vicar & the Secretaries'.[21] Spark, now out of his articles, was appointed and made an immediate impression. '. . . there was a wonderful amount of respect for him' recalled a former chorister, 'Dr. Wesley always treated him differently . . . His musical abilities . . . his gentlemanly carriage, his winning way to us boys . . . all marked the man'.[22] Spark was to retain his post until May 1845, when he received the 'cordial thanks' of the choir committee for the 'very efficient manner in which he discharged his duties'.[23] His successor, John Harding, had also been one of Wesley's pupils at Exeter and was appointed on 22 July at a salary of £60 per annum, twice what his predecessor had received. He in turn resigned in the summer of 1846 and was followed by Robert Senior Burton, of whom more anon.

While Wesley's desire to gain complete control of the choir was the primary cause of his dispute with Hill, disagreement over the selection of music may well have been a secondary factor. The choirmaster, it must be remembered, had been recommended by Jebb, himself an enthusiastic advocate of sixteenth-century music who had been invited back after the consecration 'to superintend . . . [the] performance [of the choral service] and aid its progress'.[24] His hand can surely be seen in the choice of Tallis's Short Service (of which he declared that 'no service . . . deserves deeper study')[25] for the first major

[20] *Musical Reminiscences*, 167.

[21] Leeds Parish Church Subscriber's, Choir, and Organ Fund minute book, Sept. 1833–Oct. 1847 (*LPC*).

[22] Samuel Dyer, *The Dialect of the West Riding of Yorkshire: A Short History of Leeds and other Towns* (Brighouse: J. Hartley, 1891), 119.

[23] Leeds Parish Church Subscriber's, Choir, and Organ Fund minute book, Sept. 1833–Oct. 1847 (*LPC*), minutes of the meeting of 29 May 1845 (in which Spark is referred to as the 'late Choir Master').

[24] *PC*, 3 (1850), 149.

[25] John Jebb, *The Choral Service of the United Church of England and Ireland: Being an Enquiry into the Liturgical System of the Cathedral and Collegiate Foundations of the Anglican Communion* (London: John W. Parker, 1843), 338.

festival, Christmas Day 1841. Wesley, however, thought otherwise and had no patience with those who uncritically praised all early music:

Such works [as services by Tallis, Aldrich, and Rogers] may very well be presumed to have escaped the attention of connoisseurs; but as their demerits . . . will not be found without advocates, or even professed admirers, the Writer does not venture to say all that might be said concerning a musical taste so defective as that which can sanction the almost general use of such music in the daily performance of the Cathedral Service . . . such Works . . . are as unworthy of the words to which they are set, as they are ill calculated to excite interest in any congregation acquainted with music at the present day.[26]

Given such strictures and the fact that Wesley was ideally placed to influence the development of the repertoire, it is interesting to find that whilst a number of sixteenth-century and early seventeenth-century works were sung regularly, these were markedly fewer than those sung at Exeter (owing, one suspects, to the absence of Boyce's and Arnold's *Cathedral Music*). Three works by Byrd were thus reduced to a solitary anthem ('Bow down thine ear'), six by Gibbons to two (the Short Service and 'Hosanna to the Son of David'), and four by Tallis to one—the Short Service, which still received occasional hearings; only Farrant's and Tye's contributions increased. Considerably more extracts from Handel's oratorios were performed, however, as well as works by the two best-known contemporary composers, Spohr and Mendelssohn and, more unusually, three adaptations from Hummel's masses. Of Wesley's English contemporaries only Walmisley was represented by his Magnificat and Nunc Dimittis in B flat (1845), which was sung once (13 September 1846). Among Wesley's own compositions it was again the Creed from the Service in E which received the most performances, being sung fifty-two times between September 1846 and September 1849.[27] It was an earlier performance—perhaps even the first—which was the most significant, however: '. . . a gentleman, Mr. Martin Cawood, of Leeds, on hearing the Creed performed, proposed to the Author the completion of the entire Service, undertaking to remunerate him for his work, and incur the sole risk and responsibility for its publication.'[28]

Here was generosity indeed, but it was exactly the sort of encouragement Wesley needed and it came at a propitious time. Not only had the move to a new and more promising appointment reinvigorated him, but it had already borne fruit in a flurry of composition and publication. Within a year of his

---

[26] *A Morning & Evening Cathedral Service*, [i].

[27] During the same period the newly composed Chant Service in F was sung no fewer than 67 times.

[28] Wesley, *A Morning & Evening Cathedral Service*, vi–vii.

arrival both sets of *Three Pieces for a Chamber Organ* had been issued, together with the only major piano work of his maturity, the March and Rondo (dedicated to another Devon pupil, Miss Caroline Newman of Mamhead), and the much-revised second edition of *A Selection of Psalm Tunes*, now preceded by a three-page preface in which for the first time he voiced his criticisms of the musical arrangements at cathedrals. The last, whose original issue had been blighted by misprints, was clearly undertaken with great care, with at least one of the new numbers—the 'giving-out' for 'St Anne'—sketched in open score to allow the part-writing to be more easily worked out (see Pl. 11). A few months later the pointed psalter with chants compiled for the use of the parish church was published to considerable critical acclaim, *The Musical World* declaring that it was 'beyond all comparison the most excellent work of its kind that ever came under our notice' and noting that it contained 'many original compositions [i.e. chants] from the distinguished pen of Dr. Wesley himself—some . . . of exceeding beauty and freshness'.[29]

As Nicholas Temperley has observed, cathedrals had managed without pointed psalters for nearly 300 years, and it was only the recent spread of congregational chanting that had made their provision necessary.[30] The first such publication, J. E. Dibb's *Key to Chanting*, had been issued as recently as 1831, but Dibb's example was soon followed by others, among them Robert Janes, organist of Ely Cathedral, whose psalter of 1837 doubtless acted as a spur to Wesley. The idea, however had been in his mind for many years, and now, with a new choir and choral tradition to be established, he put it into practice:

My pointing is founded on the Chant singing of the best master of Vocal Utterance this country ever had, probably one Tom Welsh . . . Welsh was a Chapel Royal man when I was a Boy there. I used ever to listen & admire his Chanting & it was at that time I resolved to <u>do</u> a pointed Psalter 'when I was a man'.[31]

While Dibb and Janes had done little more than regularize the well-tried 'rule of 3 and 5', whereby the last three (or five) syllables of each half-verse were allocated to the terminal portion of the chant, Wesley had no hesitation in allowing considerably more flexibility, should the sense demand it. In this, as in his omission of internal barring in his own chants (a practice adopted by *The Parish Choir* a few years later), he allied himself with the proponents of '*no time in chanting*'[32] who believed that the note values of the chant should be subordinate to the rhythm of the words. John Jebb was of a similar opinion,

---

[29] *MW*, 18 (1843), 205.
[30] See Temperley, *The Music of the English Parish Church*, 2 vols. (Cambridge: Cambridge University Press, 1979), I, 219–23.
[31] Undated letter to an unknown correspondent (*Lcm* MS 4001, fos. 1–2).
[32] 'Short Notes on Chanting.—No. 2.', *PC*, I (1846), 15.

writing that the 'transition from the reciting note to the melody should be as smooth and gentle as possible: and the best way to secure concord in the Choir . . . would be, to attend to the prosodial value of the syllables, or rather to the accents of the words.'[33] But there were others, among them Stephen Elvey, and Frederick Ouseley and E. G. Monk in their psalters of 1856 and 1862 respectively, who held the opposite position, maintaining that the chant should be sung in strict time, with a strong accent on the last important sylla-ble of the recitation to ensure that no undue stress fell on the (unaccented) first syllable of the terminal portion—the antithesis of Jebb's smooth transition. With the publication in 1875 of the influential *Cathedral Psalter* this view gained the ascendancy, and not until the appearance of the pioneering speech-rhythm psalter, *The Psalter Newly Pointed*, in 1926 were the principles of the 'no time in chanting' school finally endorsed (see Table 4.1).

TABLE 4.1. *Comparison of the Pointing in Wesley's* Psalter *(1843), Ouseley's and Monk's* Psalter *(1862),* The Cathedral Psalter *(1875), and* The Psalter Newly Pointed *(1926): Psalm 6: 8*

S. S. Wesley[a]	Ouseley and Monk	*Cathedral Psalter*	*Psalter Newly Pointed*
Away from me, all | ye that work vanity: for the Lord hath | heard the | voice of my weeping.	Away from me, all ye that work | vani | ty: for the Lord hath HEARD the | voice | of my | weeping.	Away from me, all YE that | work | vanity: for the Lord hath HEARD the | voice | of my | weeping.	Away from me all | ye that ' work | vanity: For the Lord hath | heard the | voice of ' my weeping.

Note: capitals indicate the accented syllables.
[a] Wesley did not indicate the full subdivision of the verse

Among the chants are six by his father and three by Wesley himself, includ-ing the very beautiful single chant in F sharp minor, assigned to Psalms 142 and 143 on the twenty-ninth evening. It combines the richness of mid-nineteenth-century harmony with contrapuntal rigour, and its second half could almost be described as a study in the use of suspensions.

Another work written for the parish church (where it was sung 'a few times')[34] was a setting of the Versicles and Responses, apparently of a festive character.[35] No longer extant, it would doubtless have been included in 'The Daily Choral Service Book', containing chants, Versicles, Responses, prayers, and Litany, which was described as 'Preparing for Publication' in December

[33] *The Choral Service*, 306.
[34] See the letter of 26 April 1899 from C. S. Rooke to F. G. Edwards (Novello & Co. private library).
[35] In his letter of 9 Feb. 1847 to Cawood, Hook wrote, 'I am sorry that I cannot comply with your request to have Dr Wesley's Responses used during Lent, as I consider them unfit for that Season' (author's collection).

1844 but was never issued.[36] But all these were only a prelude to the major work of Wesley's early Leeds years, the completion of the Service in E. Thanks to Cawood's generous backing he was able to add settings of the morning and evening canticles to those of the Communion service written at Hereford and Exeter, and in so doing discovered how demanding the task was:

To these [the general public and music critics] . . . he would suggest, how essentially unlike every other species of musical composition such a work must be; designed as it is for performance during the very brief space of time allotted to our daily Cathedral Worship; a period so brief,—while the subjects to be treated are so various, of such grand and universal application,—as necessarily to divest composition of its ordinary features; rendering almost every species of amplification of a particular subject either difficult or impossible; and this, too, in connection with words which seem, in the musician's judgement, to demand of him the most exalted efforts of which his art is capable.[37]

There, in a nutshell, lay the dilemma he faced. For well over a century composers had been content to write short full or full-with-verse services whose brevity and ease of performance masked any artistic shortcomings.[38] But Wesley was unable to accept such a purely functional view or to work within the confines of these restricted forms: the short service allowed little scope for musical development, while the full-with-verse service suffered from a fragmented structure in which every change of sentiment was marked by a new subject, new time signature, or new tempo (and sometimes all three). His solution was to take the sectional pattern of the latter, but to reduce greatly the number of subdivisions and to expand the overall timescale. The result is a work which largely overcomes the limitations of the form. Although movements are still divided, individual sections are considerably longer than was customary and, in a sensitive performance, coalesce into a remarkably coherent whole. Indeed, in the Te Deum he produced a more or less continuous structure in only four sections (the first containing 206 of its 303 bars), ranging over a wide tonal spectrum and responsive to every nuance of the text. The innovative nature of his approach is brought home by a comparison of the movement with his father's earlier setting in F (1808), which falls into eleven short sections, no fewer than nine of which close in the tonic.

Using deftly managed transitions (often to keys a third apart) and frequent slight changes of scoring Wesley created a kaleidoscopic work, shaped as much by the words as by any formal considerations. Tonality, modulation, and

---

[36] *LI* (7 Dec. 1844), 1.   [37] Wesley, *A Morning & Evening Cathedral Service*, [i].
[38] 'Full' and 'Full-with-verse' services are analogous to 'Full' and 'Full-with-verse' anthems, i.e. they are scored for full choir throughout, or alternate sections for full choir with ones for verse (solo) ensemble.

TABLE 4.2. *Comparison of the internal structures of Samuel Wesley's Te Deum in F (1808) and Wesley's Te Deum in E (1843)*

Samuel Wesley in F					Wesley in E				
Section	Text	Tempo	Scoring	Key	Section	Text	Tempo	Scoring	Key
1	We praise thee		SATB	F	1	We praise thee	♩ = 80	SSATB	E–B
						Holy, holy, holy			F#
2	Heav'n and earth	Slower–Faster	satb, SATB	F–C–d		Heav'n and earth			d#–B–D
3	The Father		SATB	d–F		The Father			D
4	Thou art		SATB	F–d		Thou art			A
5	When thou	Slow	satb	Bb–F		When thou			C#–F#
6	Thou sittest	Faster	SATB	F		Thou sittest			F#
7	We believe	Slow	satb	F		We believe			b–D–G
8	Make them	Lively	SATB	F		Make them			G–C
					2	O Lord, save	Slower	SSATB	Ab
9	Day by day		SATB	F					
10	Vouchsafe	Slow	satb	F	3	Vouchsafe	Slower	s, SSATB, ssatb	g#–e–G–b
11	O Lord	Faster	SATB	F	4	O Lord	Tempo primo	SSATB	E

harmony are all harnessed to the principle of expression, yet such was his skill that these primarily 'expressive' devices often take on an additional 'architectural' role. Take, for example, the totally unexpected G minor triad which not only throws the word 'martyrs' into relief, but also acts as a pivot around which the whole structure turns as the music modulates to D major (Ex. 4.1*a*). Elsewhere, as at the words 'the Father everlasting' a foreign chord (VI–#IV⁷–II) is used simply to underline the text (Ex. 4.1*b*).

Although he had used a closed ABA formal scheme for his setting of the Creed, Wesley chose not to develop this concept further. Only in the Te Deum, where the opening subject returns for the final phrase, 'O Lord, in thee have I trusted', is there any recapitulation of earlier material, although there are a number of small thematic links between different sections—perhaps entirely coincidental—which contribute further to a sense of musical unity (see the lines marked with brackets in Ex. 4.2).

In general, however, he relied upon a well-defined tonal plan to instil a sense of coherence, reinforced by changes of texture and scoring. The low

Ex. 4.1. Service in E, Te Deum

Ex. 4.1. *cont.*

Ex. 4.2. Service in E, Te Deum

tessitura of 'The goodly fellowship of the prophets' and 'The noble army of martyrs' is thus contrasted with the higher tessitura and more spacious texture of 'praise thee', or the change to ATB in unison for 'The holy church' (see Ex. 4.1). Such writing is crucially dependent on the organ, and throughout the service one is constantly aware of its essential role. In the movements originally written for boys' voices alone Wesley had, as Edward Holmes observed, made a virtue out of necessity and written a truly independent accompaniment 'to supply the interest and variety which his choir lacked'.[39] 'Effect once called in', Holmes continued, 'has been too powerful an auxiliary to be easily relinquished', and in the later movements the organ plays an equally important, if less prominent, part. Whether at such moments as the fanfare-like opening of the Magnificat, the brief interludes shown in Ex. 4.2, or when the voices join together in unison, it adds an extra dimension to the music, allowing Wesley to make much greater use of unison textures and to exploit the contrast between a single line and full four- or five-part harmony. The result, especially if it coincides with a change of harmony, can be electrifying. Take the very opening of the Te Deum, where the initial 'We praise thee, O God' is answered by the full choir in unison, or the phrase 'For behold, from henceforth' in the Magnificat, where octave writing gives way to the satisfying sound of the full choir (see Ex. 4.3a). Note too how a series of 'English' cadences is woven effortlessly into the organ part—an example, surely, of what Holmes meant when he noted Wesley's 'familiarity with our old cathedral writers'.[40] Another 'ancient' feature is the pair of pre-cadential consecutive-sevenths (V^7–iv^7–V^6_{43}–I), popular with composers of the late seventeenth and early eighteenth centuries, at the words 'this day without sin' in the Te Deum (Ex. 4.3b).

Paradoxically, while the longest movement—the Te Deum—is the most tightly organized, the shortest—the Jubilate—is both the most leisurely and the most sectional in form. It also shows Wesley at his most expansive, writing for double choir and double quartet and venturing into such exotic keys as A sharp major, D sharp major, and G sharp major. The most adventurous writing is at the end of the delicate eight-part verse 'For the Lord is gracious', where Wesley slips briefly from the prevailing F sharp major into D sharp minor and A sharp major, before presenting choir and congregation with a *coup de théâtre*—a Gloria which opens with the dominant chord of G sharp minor. Thereafter he casts aside all considerations of time and produces a fine contrapuntal setting for double choir which provides both a splendid climax and a further illustration of his structural use of tonality. Based on a series of

---

[39] *Sp*, 17 (1844), 235.   [40] Ibid.

Ex. 4.3. Service in E, *a* Magnificat; *b* Te Deum

modulations through keys a major third apart—E major, G sharp major, C major (cf. 'The Wilderness')—it steadily increases in tension and is crowned by a wholly unexpected lurch from C sharp minor to a root-position triad on D, the flat seventh. The preceding build-up is deceptively simple, but its subtle changes of direction reveal the depth of Wesley's harmonic insight. Notice, too, the unobtrusive entry of the 'Dresden' Amen in bar 119 (see Ex. 4.4).[41]

Both the Magnificat and the Nunc Dimittis are equally fine, and the latter is perhaps unique among contemporary settings in having no internal divisions; its Gloria is a much-shortened version of that of the Jubilate. The Magnificat also contains a rare example of word-painting: the jagged melody at the words 'He hath put down the mighty from their seat'. It was, however, a technique about which Wesley had serious misgivings, as his comments on settings of the Te Deum make clear:

> Purcell and Handel [were] wrong about to thee all angels. My Father also (to some little extent) about He hath put down the mighty; it is our business to sing of his praise of his having done these things, not to describe by music our own little notions of the means employed by God in doing them . . . Father's Service exalted the humble, (novel and charming).[42]

No less importantly, the opening of the Magnificat (whose fanfare-like introduction follows the harmonic outline of that of Mendelssohn's Octet) provides an excellent illustration of the distance separating Wesley's word-setting from that of his contemporaries. In comparison with the four-square settings by Attwood in C (1832), Walmisley in D (1843), Edward Hopkins in F (1849), and Henry Smart in F (1868) (see Ex. 4.5) his own brings a sense of breadth and shape to the words, not least from the inclusion of dynamic markings and avoidance of intermediate cadences; paradoxically, he also created an extended paragraph which makes perfect musical sense without the voices. Moreover, by scoring it for the lower voices in unison he demonstrated his awareness that (as Arthur Hutchings has written) certain 'sections of prose would be ill-served by counterpoint or ponderous choral harmony'.[43] Lastly, his sensitivity to words led him to avoid the repetition of small fragments of text or to indulge in such barbarisms as the unfortunate stress on 'doth' which mars Smart's Service in F. Even Walmisley, who brought to the service something of the elegance of his godfather Attwood managed to break free from

---

[41] The 'Dresden' Amen is derived from the threefold 'Amen' of the Chapel Royal in Dresden, said to have been written by J. G. Naumann. It was later used by Mendelssohn in his 'Reformation' Symphony and by Wagner in *Parsifal* (see Percy Scholes, *The Oxford Companion to Music*, 10th edn., ed. John Owen Ward (London: Oxford University Press, 1980), 28).

[42] *Lcm* MS 2041f, fo. 2.

[43] *Church Music in the Nineteenth Century* (London: Herbert Jenkins, 1967), 103.

Ex. 4.4. Service in E, Jubilate Deo

Ex. 4.4. *cont.*

Ex. 4.5. Openings of Magnificat settings: *a* Thomas Attwood, Service in C; *b* T. A. Walmisley, Service in D; *c* Edward Hopkins, Service in F; *d* Henry Smart, Service in F; *e* Wesley, Service in E

the old tradition only in his last work, the curiously archaic Evening Service in D minor (1855), whose forthright declamation and bold organ part surely owe much to Wesley's example.

Work on the service progressed quickly, and the morning canticles were completed by September 1843 (when a performance at St Bartholomew's, Leeds, was announced)[44] and the complete work engraved and ready for publication by February 1844.[45] At this point Wesley, who had been itching to set out at greater length his strongly held views on the general lack of support for music in cathedrals, the inadequacy of most choirs, and the poor quality of the music they were obliged to sing, added a lengthy preface and, as with the *Anthems* of 1840, distributed a few advance copies to the press. One of these reached Edward Holmes at *The Spectator*, and another Charles Gruneisen of *The Morning Post*. Their responses could not have been more different. To the former the service was 'a work of great dignity and beauty of harmony; which is especially remarkable . . . as giving a *carte blanche* admission into the English cathedral-service of the modulations and transitions of the modern school . . . [and] from the dependence of the work on the prominence and effect of the organ accompaniment'. 'In the application of the effects and peculiarities of modern music to the cathedral style', he continued, 'his work is entirely original'.[46] Gruneisen, in contrast, liked neither music nor preface. Wesley, he complained, wrote music in which there was 'no imitation—no use or paralldisms [*recte* parallelisms] of the harmonic ratios, none of the secret mingling of the ancient rhythm—no change of old church gamuts, no unity of feature but the composer makes way by a series of cadences, some strained, and others wanting in symmetry'.[47] He was, he continued, 'a grumbler and a Radical Reformer, a rater of the clergy, and particularly of the dignitaries of the Church; but, like most Radical reformers, has no reason that we can see for his discontent'.[48] Even the generosity of 'guileless Martin', the 'simple-minded Yorkshire amateur', was turned into a matter of mirth. Wesley, who was clearly stung by his words, was unwisely tempted to enter the fray and wrote to the editor of *The Morning Post*:

the preface so severely commented upon is not published, and was issued by the publisher in defiance of my express directions to the contrary. A few copies were printed, but on reconsideration they were suppressed.

The proofs were not even corrected, and I think I have a right to complain at having a composition alluded to in public which I had declined to submit to the public.[49]

---

[44] See *MW*, 18 (1843), 311. There is no evidence that this performance took place.
[45] The plate number used by Chappell's, 6697, implies a date *c*.June 1843.
[46] *Sp*, 17 (1844), 234.   [47] *MP* (26 Feb. 1844), 3.   [48] Ibid.
[49] *MP* (5 March 1844), 5.

To this the editor replied:

We should have been glad to publish Dr. Wesley's letter without comment, if it had been confined to the gratifying announcement of his repentance for the wanton attack he made on his benefactors—the dignatories of the Church; but as the ungrateful organist has indulged in two insinuations which are utterly at variance with truth, we must take the liberty of replying to him. In the first place, his work was left for notice at our office, addressed to the Editor in the usual manner, and *in a perfect form* . . . Dr. Wesley has adopted the stale trick of imputing personal motives to escape from a castigation, the justification of which is to be found in his own statement, that the disgraceful preface has been withdrawn, but whether *before* or *after* the publication of our review, we leave our readers to decide.[50]

Yet there was more to Gruneisen's review than meets the eye, for it appears that he had been assisted by Wesley's one-time ally (and now bitter enemy) H. J. Gauntlett. Wesley himself certainly thought so (and hinted as much in his letter to *The Morning Post*).[51] So, too, did *The Musical World*:

If a work is to be reviewed with any technical care (which is seldom the case in the *Post*, unless when something is to be abused)—a musical doctor, who at least knows what constitutes a common chord, is brought in to assist. In this manner were the Madrigal of Professor Taylor and the Services of Dr. Wesley analysed and cut to pieces.[52]

The precise cause of the rift between Wesley and Gauntlett remains a mystery. Suffice it to say that the latter's earlier enthusiasm for Wesley's music had by now completely evaporated and critic and composer viewed each other with mutual dislike and suspicion. When reminded of the warm testimonial he had supplied in 1835 and of his complimentary remarks about 'The Wilderness', Gauntlett excused himself on the grounds that a 'long course of study . . . has led . . . to a change of opinion'. Not content with refuting his own opinion, he also attempted to do the same for a generous testimonial from Spohr: 'It would apply as well to any Mr. Smith, or Mr. Browne, as to Dr. S. S. Wesley, and, I think, you may properly quote that testimonial in reference to any polka that has been published for these many years past'.[53]

But to return to the Service in E. The rebuff Wesley had received must have brought back bitter memories of the Gresham Prize controversy. To be told that 'Whatever in this composition is new is not good, and whatever is good

---

[50] Ibid.　　　　　　　　　　　　　　　[51] Ibid.

[52] *MW*, 19 (1844), 203. Edward Taylor had gained notoriety two years earlier when it was discovered that the madrigal which gained the Western Madrigal Society's prize in 1841 contained 15 bars 'borrowed' from Marenzio. While *MP* made much of the affair, *MW* merely noted 'how readily a molehill may be swoln [*sic*] to a mountain by the sophisticated breath of rumour' (vol. 18 (1843), 125).

[53] *MW*, 30 (1852), 679.

has been heard before in a better form and in better company',[54] when he was an established composer and Doctor of Music, smacked of public humiliation, and it is hardly surprising that he decided to delay publication for a further twelve months. A revised, slightly less forthright preface did nothing to satisfy Gruneisen, who continued his attack in *The Illustrated London News*:

This work contains a preface which . . . speaks contemptuously of the noblest church services in the world: the works of Tallis, Byrd, Tye, Gibbons, Purcell, and a hundred other worthies, cannot be set aside for the vain pretensions of a modern, who thinks he can excel them . . . This is not the work of a poetical musician. Mr. Wesley may be, and indeed is a wonderful executive organist; but he has no creative fancy beyond that of foolishly entering the ring with his betters. His work is coldly correct, and that is all. Our reverence for the ancients may have provoked us to severity; but we do not like to hear lake birds cawing at the nightingales of Elizabeth's reign.[55]

That a critic of German extraction, with a limited knowledge of music, should have thus leapt to the defence of so specialized a part of the repertoire is ironic, to say the least. But irony would have been far from Wesley's mind, for if the affair had done nothing else, it had demonstrated yet again how controversial a figure he remained. Not only did general recognition as a composer still elude him, but also he now found himself implacably opposed by a number of influential critics and writers—Gauntlett, Gruneisen, and J. W. Davison (to be joined later by Henry Chorley).

Gruneisen's demolition of the service had not, in fact, been the first occasion on which one of Wesley's works had been attacked in the press. A year earlier Davison had performed a similar task on the two sets of *Three Pieces for a Chamber Organ*, followed a few weeks later by a very grudging welcome for the March and Rondo which, despite displaying 'a fund of learning, and no small share of ingenuity', was blighted by an 'utter want of interest'.[56] The organ pieces he considered:

dull, from their want of character—monotonous, from their want of variety—uninteresting, from their want of subject—vague, and in many places ugly, from their want of all that rule and habit lead us to think necessary—and tedious, from the trite, hacknied, mawkish, meaningless phraseology of which they are composed . . . [while] they abound in the most harsh mismanagement of passing notes—the most stale and antiquated sequences—the most clashing false relations—and the most ugly, unaccountable and irregular, combinations and progressions, strung together with a provoking affectation of originality, and superiority to the 'unmeaning' laws by which the capabilities of music are confined, that we have met with in any publication of the present time.[57]

---

[54] *MP* (26 Feb. 1844), 3.   [55] *ILN*, 6 (1845), 229.   [56] *ME*, no. 13 (1843), 90.
[57] Ibid., no. 11 (1843), 74.

But what are they really like? Despite its title, *Three Pieces for a Chamber Organ* consists of three substantial pieces whose layout and content clearly demand the resources of a substantial two- or three-manual instrument. The most traditional is the well-known *Choral Song*, whose two-movement form of march-like prelude and concluding fugue could easily have earned it the title 'Voluntary'; it could possibly be one of the works Wesley told his mother he was writing at the end of December 1832.[58] Both the sparing use of the pedals (which play no part in the contrapuntal development of the fugue) and the frequent recourse to octaves in the left hand suggest an early date, but with its sheer energy and bold use of unexpected modulations at the climax—a device also used by Thomas Adams[59]—it remains one of the most colourful organ pieces of its time. Its companions, the Andante in E flat and Andante in F, represent a more radical break with the past. Both show Wesley developing the type of large-scale recital movement he had earlier essayed in the Andante in A and, in their sometimes pianistic style, point towards such works as Mendelssohn's organ sonatas, published three years later in 1845. Of the two, the Andante in F is the more ambitious work, a substantial 'orchestral' score which makes effective use of (unmarked) contrasts of scoring and was considered by George M. Garrett to be a 'complete illustration of Wesley's extraordinary technical power as a player', demanding 'clear, crisp, part-playing; the power of changing the position of the hand instantaneously and with certainty; and a touch of the closest and smoothest character'.[60] Based on rondo form (but with five statements of the main theme), it offers another demonstration of Wesley's ability to sustain a large structure. The gradual build-up in the third episode (from bar 82) is particularly effective, with some characteristic harmonic twists and virtuoso arpeggio writing for the manuals (see Ex. 4.6), but it is crowned by something as simple as a sequence of root-position chords. Placed after a series of chromatically rising triads, they impart a sense of stability and lead naturally into the final dominant and tonic pedals.

The *Second Set of Three Pieces for a Chamber Organ*, in contrast, is more truly domestic music, conceived on a scale appropriate for the small two-manual organ in Killerton House. Musically, the pieces build on the foundations of the organ 'miniature' developed by Wesley's father, but now clothed in contemporary harmonic language to produce the organ equivalent of the short romantic piano piece. Textures are mainly homophonic and the keyboard writing—like that in the earlier Andantes—frequently pianistic: only in the second number, the so-called Larghetto in F sharp minor, is there much

---

[58] Letter postmarked 1 Jan. 1833 (*Lbl* Add. MS 35019, fo. 14).

[59] See, for example, the fugue from the second piece in Adams's *Six Organ Pieces*.

[60] 'S. S. Wesley's Organ Compositions', *MT*, 35 (1894), 448.

Ex. 4.6. Andante in F

b)

exploitation of the different tone colours available on the manuals and pedals.[61] Consisting of no more than the theme, a central variation, short episode, recapitulation, and coda, this short piece is one of Wesley's best and succeeds by virtue of being concise and unpretentious. The haunting opening, based on a rising minor sixth (cf. 'Wash me throughly'), at once imparts a feeling of sadness, and the whole piece is pervaded by a sense of reticence and introspection. This is strongest in the hesitant bars which lead back to the recapitulation and in the coda (see Ex. 4.7), where the frequent breaks suggest a private, personal grief. Nowhere else did Wesley quite recapture this same spirit of intimacy, and the Larghetto remains a unique contribution to the native romantic literature for the organ. Despite containing many beauties— and some typically quixotic harmonies—the Andantes in E flat and G fail to maintain quite such a high standard, and both suffer from an over-emphasis on simple textures, presumably adopted for Lady Acland's benefit.

Although Wesley possessed a fine keyboard technique, writing that he had had 'the very highest advantages as to <u>Piano-forte</u> style & practice'[62] through his father having been the friend of Clementi, Cramer, Kalkbrenner, and Moscheles, he wrote little for the instrument, and the March and Rondo is the only substantial work of his maturity. Despite echoes of other composers— Spohr at the opening of the March, the finale of Mozart's Piano Concerto in C minor, K. 491, at the surging triplet accompaniment accompanying the return of its main theme, the composers of the London Piano School in the bravura passage-work (especially strings of parallel thirds and sixths), and the finale of Beethoven's Piano Sonata Op. 2 No. 1 in the Rondo—both movements are unmistakably his own and, using the disguise of arpeggio figuration, translate his naturally contrapuntal idiom into a new medium (see Ex. 4.8a). With the striking new theme in D minor introduced in the bass at the end of the development in the Rondo, however, one encounters a passage of simple diatonic harmony, as effective as it is unexpected. Driven forward by dotted rhythms (cf. the Symphony) and harmonized by a series of triads (ii, I, ♭III, ♭VII, ii, III, VI), it possesses a purity not unlike that of the phrase 'The darkness is no darkness with thee' in 'Thou wilt keep him in perfect peace'. Here, surely, is an example of Wesley's sacred music influencing his secular (see Ex. 4.8b).

Davison's curt dismissal of his most recent compositions must have been a bitter blow for Wesley, not least because the Rondo and the two large-scale Andantes show him at last coming to grips with the possibilities of thematic

[61] The title is Garrett's, added in his edn. of 1894. Wesley sometimes referred to it as an 'Air varied'.
[62] Letter dated 13 May 1861 to W. P. Aylward (*Eu* MS Dk.7.384).

Ex. 4.7. Larghetto in F sharp minor

Ex. 4.8. Rondo in C

a) **Allegro con spirito** ♩ = 120

b) 78

smorz.

p   smorz.

development. At a stroke all the encouragement he had received from more sympathetic pens had effectively been dissipated (and it is surely not coincidental that these were the last serious instrumental works he was to write for over twenty years). Of what value was Holmes's generous notice of the Service in E when placed alongside the review in *The Morning Post*? With the editorship of the hitherto supportive *The Musical World* passing in 1843 to Davison, who three years later became music critic at *The Times*, the future looked bleak. Swallowing his pride, he published nothing for the next three and a half years, and devoted what time he had to pursuing the subject which had so gripped his imagination—the reform of cathedral music. He did not have to wait long, as on 12 March 1844, less than two weeks after Gruneisen's onslaught, he embarked on a course of eight twice-weekly, illustrated lectures on church music at the Collegiate Institute, Liverpool (see Appendix I).[63] His aim was to provide a history of church music from the earliest times to the present and, as he had done in both the controversial preface and the introduction to *A Selection of Psalm Tunes*, to draw attention to the low standards of performance and the lack of support for choirs. Attracting audiences of up to 2000 people, they were extremely well received. (Spark's was the only dissenting voice, but as much of his time for the past four months had been spent 'copying out from old MSS. . . . [and] from the two celebrated Histories of Music by Burney and Hawkins, separate parts for the singers who were to illustrate the lectures',[64] it is less surprising that he took a more jaundiced view.) The secretary of the Collegiate Institution wrote:

The great delight which your lectures and performances occasioned to all . . . I cannot describe to you. Everyone is loud in their praise, and I have not heard a *single* objection of *any* kind. Indeed it is the only instance within my recollection of any public event of a like nature that has given universal satisfaction. Will you consent to reappear amongst us at the commencement of the year with a short course, say, of four lectures upon the organ and organ music? If you do consent, it will be doing much service to the organists of the town. One of them, of no mean reputation [W. T. Best?], told me, that your last performance did him more good than years of previous study.[65]

Like most musicians, Wesley subscribed to the generally held belief that music—in its secular branches—was steadily progressing towards a state of greater perfection. 'Perhaps no branch of Natural Philosophy can less reward

---

[63] Wesley's lectures had been preceded by a series by William Sturgeon on 'Electricity' and were followed by a series on 'Orators of Great Britain and Ireland' by Professor Greenbank.

[64] W. Spark, *Musical Memories*, 73.

[65] Letter dated 17 Aug. 1844 from J. Gregory Jones, quoted by Lightwood in 'S. S. Wesley—a Sad Story', 117.

Antiquarian research',[66] he told his audience, and it is clear from this and similar pronouncements that his would be no impartial account, but one coloured by both personal prejudice and contemporary opinion. His premise was that from the time of the Reformation sacred music had slipped further and further behind secular music in so far as its quality, standard of performance, and encouragement by the Church of England was concerned, and to support his argument he drew on the writings of Burney, Hawkins, and Hogarth and articles in *The Harmonicon* and *The Musical World*:

in the early religious Establishments the system of the provisions made in support of music were the . . . [most] judicious possible, the service being performed by those who practiced regularly together and that under the guidance of one who[se] knowledge was the most competent for the time, we then saw how at the reformation the musical system was neglected . . . and that the Clergy were no longer the conservators of the best and that no provision being made to supply the deficiency the service has proceeded ever since in a downward course . . .[67]

Wesley's own views on the music of the 'early religious Establishments'—plainsong—are unclear. On the one hand he could write enthusiastically of the 'Diatonic majesty of these old Melodies [which] in their simplest form harmonised must to the end of Time afford the true artist pleasure',[68] while at the same time scornfully dismiss the current fashion for its indiscriminate revival. 'Some would reject all Music but the unisonous Chants of a period of absolute barbarism,—which they term 'Gregorian' . . . These men would look a Michael Angelo in the face and tell him that Stonehenge was the perfection of architecture!'.[69] Gregorian chant was, however, more to his liking than the first attempts at counterpoint which 'were of the rudest nature': 'Ten centuries ago the drone of the bagpipes was the bass! To that there followed a system of extemporaneous descant in the singing of the church service, which was not only an offensive practice . . . but . . . caused disorder in the celebration of divine worship.'[70]

Turning to the English composers of the sixteenth century, Tallis, 'by many pronounced to be the Father of our Church harmony',[71] he considered overrated, and the canticles of his Short Service 'unpleasant not only on account of the peculiar, the Doric scale in which they are written but on account of their . . . monosyllabic tedium'.[72] Tye, in contrast, he thought a '<u>far</u> better artist'[73] and his compositions 'most pure and admirable'.[74] He also spoke

---

[66] *Lcm* MS 2141f, fo. 46ʳ: Wesley's lecture notes are preserved in this MS.
[67] Ibid., fos. 45ʳ, 44ᵛ.   [68] Ibid., fo. 15ᵛ.   [69] Wesley, *A Few Words*, 49.
[70] *LiM* (23 March 1844), 2.   [71] *Lcm* MS 2141f, fo. 24ʳ.   [72] Ibid.   [73] Ibid.
[74] Ibid., fo. 23ᵛ.

warmly of Robert White and included works by both among the musical illustrations (see Appendix 1). But for contemporary composers who attempted to imitate the sixteenth-century style he had no time, writing: 'I have been astounded to see how destitute specimens meant to be in this school, by the pupils of the Royal Academy of London, and the Cathedral and Deputy organists of the present time—how destitute such are of all the good qualities of this early but undying school of art . . .'[75]

Yet in his belief that the history of English church music had been characterized by a steady but relentless decline since the early years of the seventeenth century Wesley was paradoxically at one with Crotch, Horsley, Stevens, and others. There were, of course, exceptions, and works by Purcell, Croft, Handel, Greene, and Boyce figured among his examples; of later English composers there was only one—his father, whose music he considered as 'proof that talent in the highest order of Ecclesiastical Music can exist in modern times'.[76] But it was in his scheme for musical renewal that he disagreed so fundamentally with the admirers of the 'pure sublime'. This would come, he argued, not from a slavish imitation of the style of a past age, but from a vibrant musical tradition. It was, as his illustrations demonstrate, to Germany (in the persons of Bach, Mozart, Beethoven, Spohr, and Mendelssohn) that he looked, and as though to demonstrate the truth of his argument he had planned to conclude his survey with a performance of the Te Deum from his own newly completed service. Its omission (apparently because the singers from the Philharmonic Society had had insufficient time to learn the music) resulted in 'much disappointment . . . and a few tokens of disapprobation'.[77]

Concurrently with this historical survey, Wesley continued to emphasize the urgent need for musical reform, and it would soon have been apparent to his audience that his remarks were directed as much at the public at large as to them. Indeed, in his own mind he clearly regarded the lectures as but another stage in his continuing crusade for the reform of cathedral music, and in the final one—devoted to the 'resuscitation' of the choral service—he singled out the new 'model' choral foundations at Leeds Parish Church and St Mark's College, Chelsea, for particular mention.[78] We must therefore view them in

---

[75] Ibid., fos. 23^v, 26^r. [76] *A Few Words*, 77.

[77] *LiM* (13 April 1844), 3. Wesley's service was not, however, listed among the illustrations in the published syllabus.

[78] Founded in 1841 as the first Church of England training college for teachers, St Mark's College had already acquired a well-deserved reputation for the standard of the choral services in the college chapel. Under the direction of the Vice-Principal, the Revd Thomas Helmore, the whole student body and children from the adjoining 'model' school performed an ambitious repertoire of unaccompanied 16th- and 17th-cent. services and anthems to such effect that in 1848 it could be stated that 'perhaps no institution of

the context both of his other writings on the subject and of the wider movement for church—particularly cathedral—reform.

Two recent developments—the rise of the Oxford Movement and the
establishment of the Ecclesiastical Commissioners—had both served to bring
ecclesiastical matters before a wider public. Inspired by John Keble's sermon
'National Apostasy' at the University Church, Oxford, on 14 July 1833, the
Oxford Movement sought to reassert the identity of the Church of England
as part of the 'Holy Catholic Church' and to recover those ancient traditions
thrown overboard at the Reformation. John Henry Newman emerged as the
movement's leader, and by the end of the decade it was beginning to make its
mark nationally. During the early 1840s splits began to appear as several prominent members found themselves drawn towards the Roman Catholic Church,
and Newman's secession in October 1845 effectively marked its end. Its
continuing influence, however, was to be profound and a major factor in the
mid-nineteenth-century religious revival—not least through the rediscovery
of the hymnody of the early church. But if the Oxford Movement represented
a movement for church reform which grew from within, the establishment of
the Ecclesiastical Commissioners represented an official response to the unsatisfactory state of the established church. Set up in 1835 in the wake of the
Reform Bill, the Commissioners were instructed 'to consider the state of the
several Cathedral and Collegiate Churches in England and Wales with reference to ecclesiastical duties and revenues',[79] a task which naturally included a
review of their musical arrangements. They found that the relative positions
(and salaries) of the cathedral clergy and other officers had changed radically
since the time of their foundation. The Dean of St Paul's, for example, was
also Bishop of Llandaff and had a total income of £8624; the minor canons
and lay clerks who formed the choir received an average of £32 and £21
respectively, plus a share of the 'Cupola' money paid by the public to see the
building. St Paul's was by no means atypical. At many other cathedrals endowments originally intended for supporting the choir and music had been
diverted to the chapter coffers. Now, with reform in the air, such a state of
affairs was finally judged to be intolerable. Yet far from restoring the *status quo
ante* the commissioners proposed a general redistribution of income so that (as
Wesley was later to write) 'a very strong probability exists, that Cathedral
property will be taken away for objects in which Cathedral localities have but

modern times . . . has done so much for the choral music of the Church of England as St. Mark's Training
College' (*PC*, 2 (1847–9), 105). Although the music sung (including plainsong psalms) was largely the
antithesis of what Wesley would have chosen, he clearly approved of the encouragement of the choral service that St Mark's provided.

[79] [Edward Taylor], *The English Cathedral Service—its Glory, its Decline, and its Designex Extinction*
(London: Simpkin, Marshall & Co., 1845), 37.

a remote . . . interest, such as the building of Clergymen's houses, and the erection of school buildings'.[80]

The publication of the commissioners' first four reports in 1836 had prompted Gauntlett to enter the debate with a series of trenchant articles highlighting the poor treatment accorded to cathedral music and musicians, as well as the unsatisfactory nature of the proposals.[81] The time was clearly ripe for a concerted attack on the attitudes that had led to such a state of affairs, and several dozen articles, pamphlets, and books devoted to the subject appeared during the next decade and a half.

It was the prospect of legislation in 1840, however, that caused the greatest stir among musicians, galvanizing cathedral organists—not known for their radicalism—into some form of opposition. A memorial addressed to the deans and chapters of the cathedral and collegiate churches of England and Wales was drawn up and circulated, and twenty-three organists signed, together with a further thirty-one professional musicians and 115 beneficed clergy:

The Memorial of the underwritten . . . Showeth,

That your memorialists view with regret the imperfect manner in which the service is at present performed in our Cathedral Churches.

That the Choirs are inadequate to the due and solemn performance of Cathedral music; and that such improvements as the Chapters may be pleased to make in their respective Choirs will be hailed by your memorialists with gratitude.[82]

Wesley, who had received a copy in April 1840, was not happy. 'I have means of knowing that there are several portions of the Memorial wh. either <u>want force</u> or have really not that consequence wh. everything should possess . . . [while] there are also omissions which I consider more untoward', he replied, declining to add his name. 'My own conviction is that if ye matter is properly brought forward, something may be done—if <u>improperly</u> . . . nothing will be done and a good opportunity . . . thrown away'.[83] Henry Smart was of a similar opinion and considered that the inclusion of any clergy was a grave error, writing: 'Is it probable, then, that . . . having now an act of Parliament to justify all future speculations, [cathedral chapters] will be induced to act justly by such a submissive bit of memorializing as we have above quoted?'[84]

Yet with the subject of cathedral music now gracing the pages of several periodicals, some progress was certainly being made. No less importantly, ideas

[80] *A Few Words*, 76.

[81] See H. J. Gauntlett, 'The Musical Profession; and the Means of its Advancement Considered. No. 1.—Cathedrals and Collegiate Churches', *MW*, 3 (1836), 129–35.

[82] See *MW*, 14 (1840), 398.

[83] Letter dated 25 April [1840] to an unknown correspondent (*Lco*).   [84] *At*, 16 (1840), 841.

were also forming in Wesley's mind. He began cautiously with the preface to the revised edition of *A Selection of Psalm Tunes* (1842), which quickly developed into a critique of the musical shortcomings of cathedrals and drew attention to their inadequate choirs and organs and the shortage of first-rate music to sing. Inevitably it was to the subject closest to his heart—the lack of a fully qualified, well-paid musical director—that he particularly drew attention:

I refer to the endowment of some musical office in cathedrals, which may be considered . . . as an ample reward and provision for the entire services of the best musical talent, in the person of a professional superintendent of the music; to whom should be entrusted the selection and management of the singers; the care and improvement of the organs; and, above all . . . the provision of musical composition in connexion with the words of the service, of a more elevating and impressive character than that now in common use.[85]

Wesley's words found a sympathetic hearer in Smart, who shared his indignation that the authorities should treat organists as 'hired menials . . . subjecting them to dictation on the subject of their profession, always of an ignorant, and often of an offensive kind—in short, by robbing them of the feelings of gentlemen and the proud responsibility of artists'.[86] Similar sentiments were expressed in *The Leeds Intelligencer*: 'The heads of our Cathedral establishments would do well to make provision for some such distinguished composer as Dr. Wesley, and engage his herculean talents in cleaning out the Augean stable of their present collection of services and anthems, and selecting such works as are really worthy to be the standards of our Church music'.[87] How Wesley would have agreed!

With the preface to the Service in E he went much further, producing a lengthy analysis of the musical deficiencies of most early settings of the canticles before drawing on his own unhappy experiences to paint a melancholy picture of the sad state into which cathedral music had fallen. 'No musician', he declared, 'can attach himself to a cathedral without depriving himself of all self-respect':[88]

It is . . . no easy task for the musician wholly to abstain where the subject is so interesting to him, and while it calls loudly for investigation . . . Not only is the welfare and advancement of a portion of his very numerous Profession concerned, but . . . the decencies and interests of religion itself suffer from the general dearth of good musical principles, and their corresponding development in practice; for, there are numberless instances in which a few, slight but judicious, efforts in the cause for

---

[85] Preface to *A Selection of Psalm Tunes Adapted Expressly to the English Organ with pedals*, 2nd edn. (London: R. Cocks & Co., [1842]), 2.
[86] *At*, 18 (1843), 139.   [87] *LI* (1 April 1843), 7.
[88] From Wesley's original preface as quoted in *MP* (26 Feb. 1844), 3. No copy is known to survive.

improvement, would relieve the Choral Service from a condition which is absolutely unbearable to well-cultivated ears . . .

But another mischief is, that . . . from the deficiency of all accurate knowledge of the habits and feelings of the musical profession on the part of those in whom the right of election to musical offices in the Church is vested,—and from the absence of every species of information concerning the just requirements of the Art in its connection with public worship . . . it is more than probable that when a Professor of better standing *does* join a Cathedral in this capacity, after the efforts of a few years, he will feel himself compelled to choose between his interest and his duty; and, either to relinquish such connections as he may have there formed, and leave it again, or, incur the disrespect of his Profession by remaining in a position from whence nothing is seen to proceed for the advancement of his Art . . .[89]

Invitations to give a second course of lectures at Liverpool in April 1846 and to contribute a lecture at the Leeds Church Institution a month later provided further opportunities to return to the subject. Finally, prompted by the threat of further legislation 'by which it is . . . proposed to reduce the Cathedral Choirs to the "least possible state of efficiency"'[90] and in a desire to reach a wider audience, Wesley embarked on two ventures—the circulation of a brief 'Address' (written in collaboration with Edward Taylor) to cathedral organists and other 'friends of the Church', and the publication in June 1849 of his celebrated pamphlet *A Few Words on Cathedral Music*, which included a detailed 'Plan of Reform'.[91]

Although the 'Address', which was intended to stimulate interest through the calling of public meetings, leading to a petition to Parliament, made little impression, *A Few Words* caused a minor stir. Wesley's contribution to the debate—both here and elsewhere—is of particular interest in coming from the only cathedral musician to enter the fray, and whilst his grasp of the historical issues involved was not as great as that of either Jebb or Taylor,[92] his writings are imbued with a fervour borne of a determination to do his utmost for a cause in which he believed so strongly:

That I prefer the Choral Service of the church to any other public mode of worship . . . I do most [illegible] assert, I admire its pervading feature that of separating in its

---

[89] *A Morning & Evening Cathedral Service*, vi.   [90] Wesley, *A Few Words*, [5].

[91] The only know copy of the 'Address' was formerly among the papers of Gerald W. Spink, but does not appear to have been transferred with the remainder of his collection to *Eu*. It was addressed to R. A. Atkins and bore the postmark 21 March 1849. *A Few Words* is dated 24 May 1849.

[92] It is clear from his notes that Wesley was well acquainted with Jebb's *Three Lectures* (1841) and *The Choral Service* (1843). He no doubt also attended the lectures given by Taylor in Leeds in Nov. and Dec. 1843 (to which he referred in his own lectures), acknowledging that he knew less than Taylor of 'the Cathedral Customs' (*Lcm* MS 2141f, fo. 3ᵛ). Taylor's anonymously published *The English Cathedral Service* had first appeared in nos. 33 and 35 of *The British and Foreign Review* within a few months of the original preface to the Service in E, and perhaps in response to it.

offices everything which might tend to remind the Congregation of the earthiness of its ministering servants, all of whom appear in garments unlike those of their common use, almost everything uttered is unlike the ordinary language of mankind. Language, and that only of the most exalted character and connected with music of the most simple and I do not hesitate to say . . . of the most sublime character, [means that] the individuality of the ministering servants scarcely anywhere appears . . . The object of mans [sic] assembling thus was to address God, not to be addressed by man, to have their thoughts by the magnificent effects of architecture and music more effectively wrested from common pursuits bringing all heaven before their eyes to use the words of Milton.[93]

The root of the problem lay in the fact that ultimate responsibility for the music rested, as it had done since the Reformation, in the hands of the clergy: 'the musical Profession, as a body, can scarcely be said to have any voice in the matter, and its management is as completely in the hands of others, as it was at the period when the clergy knew and practised all *the little* which was known, and a musical Profession was not in existence.'[94]

What hope was there when, as he quaintly observed many years later, 'We are working Railways with the rolling stock of Henry 8ths reign!!'?[95] Yet neither the cathedral organists' Memorial nor the ensuing Dean and Chapter Act had addressed either this or the diversion of choir endowments to other purposes. The latter, of course, was reflected in the pitifully low salaries paid to lay clerks and was thus at least partly responsible for the inefficient state of most cathedral choirs. '. . . the very natural reflection must arise', he wrote, 'that to confide funds to the clergy, for the joint support of religion and *something else*, must be wrong, because religion being of paramount importance, the clergy may, on an emergency, be tempted to deprive the *something else* of its due portion for the benefit of the object in which they are professionally concerned'.[96] But all the act had done was to legalize existing abuses, among them the present non-choral role of most minor canons. Thus in those cathedrals in which they technically formed part of the choir they had generally ceased to take part in the singing, merely intoning the responses and collects. As a contemporary commentator observed, 'the Choirs, which before were accidentally inefficient "by lapse and neglect," would [now] . . . be made "necessarily inefficient by law." '[97] Such a situation inevitably led from bad to worse, and it was not unknown for totally unmusical persons to be appointed to vacancies. When the Bishop of London, introducing the bill in the House of Lords, announced '*It is not our intention to tax the musical powers of the Minor*

[93] *Lcm* MS 2141f, fos. 7–8.   [94] Wesley, *A Morning & Evening Cathedral Service*, vi.
[95] Letter dated 20 Feb. [1875] to Joseph Bennett (collection of the Revd Brian Findlay).
[96] *A Few Words*, 36.   [97] *ChR*, 18 (1849), 384.

Canons'[98] it seemed to Wesley as if the very fabric of the choral service was under threat:

When his Lordship said . . . that he did . . . not wish to tax the Musical abilities of the Minor Canons . . . he made an admission calculated to destroy the Ancient service of the Church of England because . . . the part sung by the Minor Canon is of equal importance musically considered as that sung by the choir and congregation. If the Priest is not to sing there will be an end of the Choral Service.[99]

Within four years it did indeed look as though this gloomy prophecy would be fulfilled. Following the appointment in 1848 of a 'titled but unmusical candidate'[100] to the office of minor canon at Bristol Cathedral, the Dean and Chapter 'shortly afterwards abolished the Choral mode of performing certain portions of the Service altogether'.[101] All was not lost, however, as the local outcry—taken up by *The Parish Choir*, *The Athenaeum*, and *The Illustrated London News*—forced the Dean and Chapter to reverse their decision. Yet if it had done nothing else the incident had provided Wesley with further ammunition:

for the musical members of a Cathedral thus to have placed over them, as rulers, those to whom Cathedral service is but as a sealed book, or a thing to be systematically disparaged, must be conclusive as to its fate in any instance. And may not the example thus furnished be viewed as suggestive of what Church music has to contend against *generally*; that its foundation is one of sand, and that some general and comprehensive system of reform is necessary, in order to place our Church musical affairs in a position which the public and the music profession can thoroughly approve?[102]

It was doubtless with this in mind that in his 'Plan of Reform' he proposed (as he had hinted in the Service in E) the removal of practical musical matters from the jurisdiction of the clergy. The election of lay singers at a cathedral or collegiate church would instead be placed in the hands of the organist and the organists of the two nearest cathedrals, while the election of the organist himself would be entrusted to a committee consisting of the organists of the seven nearest cathedrals. In each case the clergy would merely be allowed to pass judgement on the candidates' moral fitness. Other aspects were less controversial. Choirs should each have a complement of at least twelve adult members, with a further three—one of each voice—to be called upon as occasion demanded. Better singers would be attracted by more generous salaries—£85 per annum for regular members and £52 per annum for supernumeraries— while if it were not 'deemed desirable for them to occupy themselves in trade

---

[98] [Taylor], *The English Cathedral Service*, 60.   [99] *Lcm* MS 2141f, fo. 44ᵛ⁻ʳ.
[100] Bernarr Rainbow, *The Choral Revival in the Anglican Church*, 257.
[101] Wesley, *A Few Words*, 38.   [102] Ibid. 39.

. . . and that it is *not* desirable cannot be a question . . .'[103] they should receive from £100 to £150 per annum. Other aspects reveal the influence of his experience at Leeds. Rehearsals would be compulsory and choirmen 'should be required to give the degree of attention to *rehearsals* and every other musical duty exacted of all such persons at ordinary performances of music, and . . . should be subject to an early removal in cases of wilful inattention'.[104] Another proposal drawn from practical experience was that in large towns and cities up to six voluntary singers should be sought to augment the regular choir: 'At Leeds Parish Church . . . several gentlemen attend on this footing . . . with regularity and good effect'.[105]

The second element of Wesley's plan was for the establishment of a 'Musical College', 'for imparting a thorough and complete musical education to the musical professors employed by the Church'.[106] It should, he proposed, be attached to one of the cathedrals and under the jurisdiction of its Dean and Chapter, but supported financially by contributions from the other cathedrals. Undoubtedly the most interesting part is that relating to the organist, for here he gave free rein to his imagination and painted a picture of the ideal situation as he saw it. 'The Cathedral Organist should, in every instance, be a professor of the highest ability,—a master in the most elevated departments of composition,—and efficient in the conducting and superintendance of a Choral body'[107] and, 'if a man of eminence in his art, should hardly be teazed with the tuition of the singing boys'.[108] Nor should he be expected to resort to teaching to supplement his income, but 'prohibited from ever giving a single lesson of the popular kind . . . and be compelled to devote himself exclusively to the high objects of his calling [i.e. composition]'.[109] The salary he had in mind, from £500 to £800 per annum, he justified on the grounds that 'The artists pointed to are the *bishops* of their calling—men consecrated by their genius, and set apart for duties which only the best talent of the kind can adequately fulfil'.[110] 'A man with a genius for the higher branches of musical composition', he observed, 'will generally, no doubt, cancel every other occupation for the loved one of devoting himself to that end; and a comparatively

---

[103] Wesley, *A Few Words*, 57. Writing to R. A. Atkins, organist of St Asaph Cathedral, on 13 Sept. 1848 Wesley had asked for information on 'the number of your Choir & something of their incomes & abilities. Not, however, for any other purpose than to clarify my own Curiosity'. (*Eu* MS Dk.7.384).

[104] *A Few Words*, 57. A system of fines for non-attendance at services and practices was in operation at Leeds Parish Church. Under the 'New Choir Rules' drawn up on 1 March 1849 these ranged from 5s. for unauthorized absence from both Sunday services to 6d. for missing all or part of the Monday or Friday choir practices. The choristers were fined 2d. for missing a service, 1d. for missing a choir practice, and 1d. for 'carelessness or misbehaviour in church'.

[105] Ibid. 58.   [106] Ibid.   [107] Ibid. 58–9.   [108] Ibid. 73.   [109] Ibid. 60–1.
[110] Ibid. 61.

small income, which offers the desired facilities, be preferred to any other means of livelihood'.[111] Contrast this with his own experience:

Were the musician who should produce a work of the highest merit in eight days [as Landseer reputedly did with the picture of a horse], to ask, not a thousand guineas, but a thousand shillings, pence, farthings, the reply would be, invariably, 'No!' Let him study hard in his art, from the age of eight to thirty-five, sacrificing every interest to this one sole pursuit, let him offer his work as a present to *some* Cathedrals, and *they would not go to the expense of copying out the parts for the Choir!*[112]

To Wesley, the cathedral organist was no mere musician but an artist whose principal task was to compose music to the glory of God, 'to promote the solemnity of Divine worship, and give a larger emphasis to passages of Holy Scripture'.[113] But such a view was also a highly personal one. Who among his cathedral colleagues, most of whom he held in little regard, would have considered himself an artist?

It was inevitable that such idiosyncratic proposals would meet little sympathy in some quarters. One critic was the Revd C. A. Stevens, author of the anonymously published *Practical Remarks on Cathedral Music*. Regretting that in the attempt to raise musical standards 'the influence of the learning, and chastened judgement of the superior Clergy, has not been more apparent', he warned of the dangers of 'encouraging, or even aggravating, the musical mania of the organist'.[114] 'With a natural prepossession in favour of the (supposed) paramount importance of their own particular subject of interest' many organists, he claimed, 'have been led by an ardour, in many respects praiseworthy, to bring about, by their industry and energy, a state of things, in which, instead of music being considered merely *adjective*, it has become almost the *substantive*'.[115]

A pamphlet recently published, from the pen of a very energetic Cathedral organist, exhibits some amusing instances of this persuasion; which are not the less amusing, because the writer seems so innocently unconscious of a contrary possibility.

It intimates, too, what even in these musical days will be thought a rather high view of the aspirations which the profession may reasonably entertain. For instance, that organists can only be adequately paid by a salary in full, of from 500*l*. to 800*l*. a year . . .[116]

Having drawn attention to Wesley's proposal that lay clerks should earn up to £150 per annum, Stevens warmed to his theme:

---

[111] Ibid. 62.   [112] Ibid. 52.   [113] Ibid. 62.

[114] *Practical Remarks on the Reformation of Cathedral Music* (London: Francis and John Rivington, 1849), 59.

[115] Ibid. 59–60.   [116] Ibid. 59.

But the author of the pamphlet must be strangely unaware of the value of such incomes in these days in other professions. How many men of high talents and education . . . are unable to obtain the return of incomes of 150*l*. by the most industrious exertion of mind and body? . . . how many Curates or Incumbents of Livings . . . the manifold responsibilities, anxieties, annoyances, and labours of whose office are likely to result . . . in the utter destruction of health; who have no means . . . of increasing their income, nor prospect nor hope of obtaining preferment;—would rejoice to be assured of such a net receipt? . . .

It is no answer, that [the office of organist or lay clerk] . . . is in the sanctuary. So is the Curate's, who not only can be paid no more than £100 salary, but must . . . contrive to preserve an exterior befitting a Clergyman and gentleman . . . Remunerate, we say, organist and lay-clerks fairly. But not in a degree which bears no reasonable proportion to the real value of their personal services, relatively to all other professions . . .

The analysis of the plan recommended . . . cannot now be fully entered upon. We may say, however, that when it comes to be entertained by the State authorities, we shall begin to be seriously alarmed . . . We should indeed dread to see arise from his pamphlet bureau a vivacious embryo-Minister of Musical Instruction, with a draft of minutes of an irresponsible Committee of organists in his pocket for the establishment and encouragement of a class of musicians, similar to the arrogant turbulent class of men by some anticipated to spring from the system proposed in another office. We should fear to see such an one insinuating ostentatiously or unostentatiously Management Clauses for the Choirs of England, with special provisos for the exclusion of the Clergyman from directing the musical arrangements in his Church . . . or for nullifying the reasonable appellate authority of the Ordinary on the point, the desire of the founders of the Church, of the Congregation, or of all the Congregations in the country notwithstanding.

At present, however, we must candidly say we are not seriously alarmed.[117]

What Wesley would have thought of Stevens's proposal that 'the modern "Cathedral Service"' should be reduced to 'the Choral Service of the Church: to a unison or harmonized Chant or Chants; so ordered, that the People may join in it in all those portions in which it may be judged that it is their privilege, and therefore duty, to join'[118] can be left to the imagination. That it came from a clergyman who stressed that his colleagues were 'gentlemen' (and musicians by implication were not) would hardly have helped! By now, however, he had grown so wearily accustomed to such anti-musical prejudice that he wisely refrained from responding.

Elsewhere, however, Wesley's views fell on more fertile soil. In the course of a wide-ranging review of seven pamphlets devoted to cathedral reform, *The*

[117] *Practical Remarks on the Reformation of Cathedral Music* (London: Francis and John Rivington, 1849), 60.
[118] Ibid. 63.

Christian Remembrancer upheld the 'Plan of Reform' as a model of what might be achieved, and took exception only to the proposal that the organist should not be 'teased with the tuition of the singing-boys'. 'This general proposition', it declared, 'is falsified by universal experience; and the particular application of it is utterly unworthy of a professional organist, and augurs ill for the future of the Winchester Choir [to which Wesley had recently been appointed]; for an organist, however eminent, who can be "teased" with such duties, must have a very inadequate conception of the sacred nature both of his own office, and the Services in which the Choir is engaged'.[119] Yet it was precisely because Wesley felt such an emotional involvement with his subject matter that he was unable to distance himself and write in a disinterested, purely objective manner: he could see nothing wrong with an assistant teaching the choristers their notes if this allowed him time for composition. But such involvement also made it extremely difficult for his very personal proposals to be taken up by others, with the result that *A Few Words* made little immediate practical impact. During the ensuing two decades, however, much that he had campaigned for came to be realized, but by then his own active involvement had long since ceased. The *Reply to the Inquiries of the Cathedral Commissioners* (1854), which builds on the recommendations of *A Few Words*, was to be his last published contribution to the debate, and none of his later, decidedly hare-brained schemes either to promote himself as a composer of church music or to encourage the radical reform of cathedral chapters ever got off the ground (see Chapter 6).

By the time Wesley was taken to task he had left Leeds for the more peaceful surroundings of Winchester, and we must now turn back to discover what had prompted him to relinquish an appointment which had augured so well. In the event, relations with Hook, initially so cordial, had soon taken a turn for the worse. The first hints of trouble are found in his last-minute withdrawal from the opening of the new organ in Mosley Street Chapel, Manchester, on 24 December 1843:

subsequently it was discovered that some prohibitive authority had been exercised over Dr. Wesley, and the result was a missive, giving the information that he was unable, from imperative circumstances to fulfil his engagement. It is said that Dr. Hook, Vicar of Leeds, interfered in this affair. Whether this rumour be true we know not; but after the escapades of the Doctor, since he became possessed of the Vicarial dignities and emoluments of Leeds, we should be prepared to expect anything from him but liberality towards Dissenters.[120]

---

[119] *ChR*, 18 (1849), 384–5.   [120] *MW*, 18 (1843), 431. The organ was opened by Henry Smart.

Early the following year these suspicions were more or less confirmed when, as one of the conditions of a proposed new agreement between the church and the lay clerks, it was stated that the latter should 'decline Playing or singing in any Place of Worship or School Room, unconnected with the Church of England'.[121] To Wesley such narrow restrictions would have appeared petty and, notwithstanding that he had been in the town for less than two years, he was already on the lookout for an opportunity to leave.

But what had gone so profoundly wrong? After the initial euphoria had worn off both Wesley and Hook, one suspects, had found the prospect of working together less attractive than it had at first appeared. The Vicar, for his part, would have come to realize that, for all his brilliant musicianship, his new organist was an awkward character, jealous of his reputation, quick to take offence, and highly suspicious of any 'interference' in musical matters. Neither his early machinations to ensure the dismissal of Hill nor his increasingly frequent absences from duty on illicit fishing expeditions can have helped, and the latter surely lay behind a subsequent resolution of the choir committee (17 October 1847) 'That the Secy. do make arrangements to ensure that the whole of the Choral Music has Organ accompaniments'.[122] Even the choice of music was now subject to scrutiny, and at the same meeting it was resolved 'That the Committee in future meet every week, and appoint the whole of the Music, to be performed by the Choir during the ensuing Week'.[123] What particularly annoyed Hook were Wesley's forays into print. 'I wish you would prevent Dr Wesley from writing in the newspapers', he wrote wearily to Martin Cawood in 1847:

To have him as our Organist is a misfortune and has involved me in needless expense and difficulties, and it is very grievous, in addition to this to have disgrace brought upon the Parish Church by his Letters. People at a distance think that I ought to remove him from his Post, little knowing that I could only do so at a cost of £200 a year.

You will really oblige me if you will prevent his putting pen to paper except for the purpose of composing music, and you will confer, by so doing, a benefit upon himself for he sadly exposes his ignorance on points upon which he ought to be well-informed.[124]

The lack of sympathy was mutual, as Wesley soon discovered that it was no easier to work with Hook than it had been with any of his clerical superiors in the past. '. . . disappointed as I was with Dr Hook & his powers to either

[121] Leeds Parish Church Subscriber's Choir and Organ Fund minute book, Sept, 1833–Oct. 1847 (*LPC*), minutes of the meeting of 2 Jan. 1844.
[122] Ibid.   [123] Ibid.   [124] Letter dated 9 Feb. 1847 (author's collection).

aid his Church Music or me', he was later to write, 'I soon bitterly repented of leaving Exeter'.[125] Hook's interference at Mosley Street Chapel perhaps convinced him that Leeds offered no more certain or settled future than had either Hereford or Exeter, and within a matter of months he was looking for a chance to leave. The enforced resignation of Henry Bishop from the Reid Chair of Music at Edinburgh in early December 1843 seemed to provide just this, and he wrote to the authorities to offer his services: 'The office I should prize above every other in my profession, and . . . I beg . . . again to declare myself a Candidate, and to express my anxiety of being thought worthy of the high and valuable power of your support.'[126]

Two months later he wrote again, enclosing a 'few recommendatory letters',[127] including testimonials from Spohr, Moscheles, and Taylor. Spohr was especially enthusiastic in his praise:

Through the compositions which Mr. Wesley . . . has sent me . . . I have become acquainted with a composer who has already made happy and successful essays in a great variety of composition . . . His works of Sacred music especially distinguish themselves by their dignified and often antique style, by their rich and choice harmonies, as well as by the unexpected beauty of their modulations.[128]

Despite such generous support—and Moscheles and Taylor wrote equally warmly—Wesley inexplicably withdrew his name before the election was held in June, perhaps in response to the vigorous campaign on behalf of Sterndale Bennett waged by Davison in *The Musical Examiner* and *The Musical World*. While the claims of John Donaldson, Gauntlett, and Joseph Mainzer had been easily dispatched, Wesley he considered a 'much more dangerous opponent'.[129] A little disinformation, however, would do Bennett's cause no harm, and as early as 13 January, over three weeks before Wesley submitted his testimonials, the *Examiner* announced that he had, 'we are given to understand, resigned his claims'.[130] The eventual appointment of Henry Hugo Pierson, a rank outsider if ever there was one, left Davison muttering darkly: 'Such compositions as Mr. Pearson [*sic*] has published to the world show, not merely that he is no musician, but that he is a very uncultivated amateur—which, for the credit of the University and the satisfaction of the Professors, we shall take an opportunity of proving . . .'[131]

Undaunted by his lack of success, Wesley now applied for the post of organist at Worcester Cathedral, vacant after the death of Charles Clarke. *The*

---

[125] Letter dated 18 Sept. [1858] to Henry Ford (*RSCM* Nicholson scrapbook, fo. 40).
[126] Letter dated 8 Dec. 1843 to T. Henderson (*Eu* MS Da Reid).
[127] Letter dated 8 Feb. 1844 to T. Henderson (*Eu* MS Da Reid).
[128] Translation of a testimonial dated 30 Jan. 1844 (*Lcm* MS 3071).
[129] *MW*, 19 (1844), 2.   [130] *ME*, no. 63 (1844), 377.   [131] *MW*, 19 (1844), 187.

Musical World again took a keen interest, not least because it had been rumoured that 'some local interest is to be consulted, and a person on the spot 'unknown to fame,' is to be the successor of Mr. Clarke': 'We hate to see mediocrity successful, even when talent has not been opposed, but where the former is triumphant over the latter, the result is painful indeed.'[132]

'Local interest' was indeed consulted, and William Done, Clarke's assistant, appointed. For once commiseration from *The Musical World* was forthcoming: 'It is quite enough for any one who entertains the slightest respect for the interests of art, to see the name of Dr. Wesley among the rejected candidates, and own the justice of our strictures in the article which has elicited the *bilious* observations of our anonymous and impotent asperser . . . [in] the *Worcester Journal* . . .'[133]

For Wesley, however, the desire to get away from Leeds remained as strong as ever. When after a mere eight months Pierson in his turn resigned, he was quick to submit another letter of application: 'I much regret that a second Englishman should have received the honor of being appointed whose performance of its duties would be deemed unsatisfactory . . . I trust I may not be greatly in error when I picture to myself—in the event of success—a more fortunate result.'[134]

Success again eluded him, as this time the Scottish musician-turned-lawyer John Donaldson was chosen. Yet had Wesley been fortunate one wonders how the appointment would have turned out, for his main interest in the post— financial considerations apart—was the direction of the annual Reid concert, with the opportunities for composition and performance this entailed:

The emoluments attached to the Musical Professorship [£300 per annum] I esteem as ample, and as a more than adequate remuneration . . . I should feel myself called upon . . . to produce at every one of the College Concerts an original work of as much consideration as my humble abilities might allow. The College Concerts would command my utmost endeavours to render them profitable and of the best possible kind.[135]

As far as other duties were concerned, he made no more than vague references, writing that 'In respect to the course I should pursue . . . it may not be necessary for me now to attempt to occupy your attention'.[136] When Donaldson attempted to organize lectures the senate placed so many obstacles in his path that he was forced to resort to legal action which led ultimately to the building of the University Music Department (1861). Wesley, one suspects, would have given up the unequal struggle long before!

[132] *MW*, 19 (1844), 195.   [133] Ibid. 216.
[134] Letter dated 21 Feb. 1845 (*En* MS MS 3445, fo. 22).
[135] Letter dated 10 Nov. 1841 (*En* MS 3443, fo. 256).   [136] Ibid.

But it was to the south of England that he really wished to return, and the combination of Mary Anne's suffering a serious illness and the invitation to open a new organ at Tavistock Parish Church in 1846 almost induced him to accept the offer of the post of organist there. In April, two months before the opening, it had been confidently announced that his services 'had been secured', on account, it was said, of his 'predilection for Devonshire . . . preferring its salubrity to the dingy atmosphere of Leeds'.[137] His playing at the opening on 25 June was much appreciated, and as late as August (when he drew up an agreement with the choirmaster, Robert Burton, for the sale of the goodwill of his teaching practice for £500)[138] he still clearly envisaged leaving Yorkshire. Indeed, it appears that his departure was merely a matter of time:

Augt 7th. 1846
My Dear Madam . . .

Mrs. Wesley has been very seriously ill. She is now well enough to move about, and, before She goes to the South, for good, the Medical Man says She should go to Thorp Arch for a short time as the Change would give her strength to undergo the fatigue of the longer journey. It has occurred to me that if it suited your convenience—and I am sure you would at once say if it did not do so . . .—it would be far more pleasant to Mrs Wesley if she could stay a few days at your comfortable house and so see York, and be amongst friends.[139]

Whether Mary Anne made a better recovery than was hoped for, or Wesley had second thoughts about exchanging his position at Leeds for a far less prestigious one in rural Devon (which none the less attracted eighty applicants),[140] he chose not to accept the Tavistock appointment. The enthusiastic response to his performance—'such a musical treat in the way of an organ performance has never before been enjoyed in the West of England'[141]—however serves to remind us that regardless of the reception of his written works, no voices were raised against his organ playing. Even Davison was happy to acknowledge his skill—'decidedly, without disparagement to other men of genius, and before all, to Dr. Mendelssohn—the greatest organist now living'[142]—and it was as a player that he was most widely known. 'His fame and talents', William Spark recorded, 'were on the lips of all Yorkshire musicians; they flocked in scores to hear his extempore fugues, etc., after the evening service—performances which were often of the grandest, most beautiful and most elaborate

---

137 *PDSH* (11 April 1846), 3.

138 The date of Burton's appointment as choirmaster is not known. John Harding still held the post at the beginning of June, but his place was taken by Burton before 13 Nov.: see *LI* (6 June 1846), 3; (14 Nov. 1846), 1.

139 *Lgc* MS 10 189/2, fos. 359–60.

140 See *PDSH* (11 April 1843), 3.

141 *PDWJ* (2 July 1846), 3.

142 *ME*, no. 48 (1843), 362.

character'.[143] Autumn 1843 had found him in particularly good form, with a fine performance at the Leeds Music Hall in November. Bemoaning the inadequate nature of the instrument, the critic of *The Leeds Intelligencer* observed:

the Grand Fantasia in C, which, to do complete justice to, required an organ of the most varied powers . . . In turns the silvery-drawn tones of the oboe—the dying cadence of the swell stop diapason—the softest and most liquid tones of the flute—the massive trumpet-tongued ophiclyde are required—whilst to give due effect to the deep rolling fugue at the conclusion, and such as Dr. Wesley no doubt intended should be produced, none but one of the largest organs in the kingdom would have been capable of.[144]

What is particularly intriguing is that no 'Grand Fantasia in C' has survived, and it seems likely that it and similar pieces were 'preconceived' extemporizations. Indeed, Wesley's son Francis's comment that his father's 'facility of extemporization made him content, unless he was preparing a work for publication, with the merest sketch skeleton or suggestion'[145] suggests as much, and the whole question of the exact relationship between his extempore and written works is a fascinating one. What were the former, particularly the large-scale recital performances, really like? Most, like the one described above, probably fell into two parts, a fantasia-like section to show off the instrument's tonal resources and a concluding fugue. The latter, like the fugue in the *Choral Song*, were no doubt loosely constructed, with heavy reliance on sequential writing, brilliant passage-work for the manuals, and, at the climax, a shift from counterpoint to block harmony accompanied by a series of bold modulations away from the tonic. But apart from the *Choral Song*, the Variations on 'God save the King', and, to a lesser extent, the Andante in F, the major published works contain few examples of the 'brilliancy, clearness, and rapidity of execution' or 'truly extraordinary' performance on the pedals earlier praised by Gauntlett. There are, however, snatches of both in a most unlikely source, the recently published second edition of *A Selection of Psalm Tunes* (1842). One of the interludes to 'Old 100th', for example, contains rushing demisemiquaver scales, a brief flourish on the pedals, and concluding double trills: together they generate a remarkable sense of excitement and surely provide a hint of what it was that so thrilled contemporary audiences (see Ex. 4.9).[146]

Nationally, Wesley's reputation had been considerably enhanced by two solo performances during the 1843 Birmingham Triennial Festival. 'Dr.

[143] *Musical Memories*, 71.   [144] *LI* (25 Nov. 1843), 8.

[145] Letter dated 7 March 1917 from F. G. Wesley to Hubert Parry (*Lcm* Wesley Scholarship file).

[146] For a fuller discussion of Wesley's improvisations, see my article 'Samuel Sebastian Wesley: "One of the finest and most dignified extempore players of his day"', *The Organist* 1/1 (1990), [2]–[4].

Ex. 4.9. *A Selection of Psalm Tunes*, 2nd edition, third interlude for the 100th Psalm

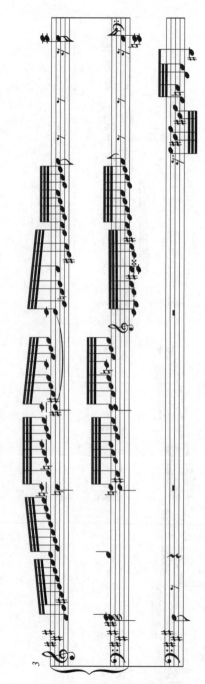

Ex. 4.9. cont.

Wesley's performance was magnificent, and created an immense sensation'
declared *The Musical World*, which considered that he had 'no rival now living, except Dr. Mendelssohn—and it would be difficult to decide between
them as to their respective merits'.[147]

Dr. Wesley's unrivalled performance on the organ, [was] one of the most extraordinary specimens of pedal playing we ever listened to. He chose the noble air, 'Ruddier
than the cherry,' for his theme, and rendered it admirably subservient to his purpose.
To those who had never heard the great organist, it was well worth the journey to
Birmingham to listen to his masterly performance.[148]

It was perhaps these performances which led to his being approached a few
months later for advice on the design of an organ for St George's Hall,
Liverpool, then in course of construction. Unlike several of his fellow organists—notably Gauntlett and Smart—he had little knowledge of the mechanics
of organ-building or practical experience of organ design, and he instinctively
turned for inspiration to William Hill's recently completed instrument at
Birmingham, with the result that the specification he eventually submitted for
a large four-manual organ is clearly based on the Birmingham one.[149] As such
it represents a further example of what Nicholas Thistlethwaite has dubbed the
'Insular Movement' of organ-building, which sought to meet the demands for
increased power and the inclusion of a full-compass pedal organ by developing the idiosyncratic English instrument, retaining its long-compass manuals
(descending to GG or FF), adding independent pedal pipes, duplicating diapason registers, and adopting extremely large pipe scales for the lower-pitched
registers.[150] Wesley incorporated all these characteristics in the St George's
Hall specification, which immediately pitched him into battle with the advocates of the rival 'German system', who drew their inspiration from the
German and Dutch traditions with their use of complete diapason choruses,
equal temperament, and shorter C compass (descending only to CC), in universal use on the Continent. Foremost among the latter was Gauntlett. On
learning of Wesley's involvement he fired the first shot, proposing to the
Liverpool authorities that he, Mendelssohn, Walmisley, and Wesley should
form a committee to consider the plans submitted. He also objected to
Wesley's specification, and in November 1845 the latter found himself

---

[147] *MW*, 18 (1843), 324.

[148] Ibid. 325. Wesley's improvisation was based upon the bass aria 'O ruddier than the cherry' from
Handel's *Acis and Galatea*.

[149] For a more detailed account of Wesley's involvement at St George's Hall see my article '"A Organ
should be *an Organ*": S. S. Wesley and the Organ in St George's Hall, Liverpool', *BIOSJ*, 22 (1998).

[150] For a comprehensive account of the subject see Nicholas Thistlethwaite's *The Making of the Victorian
Organ* (Cambridge: Cambridge University Press, 1990).

summoned to answer the 'objections raised by Dr Gauntlett'.[151] But it was not only this which irked him, but the fact that Gauntlett had been making free use of Mendelssohn's name to promote his own plan: '. . . just at the last minute I have become subject to the opposition of a person whom I by no means respect, who has made himself odious to the Musical Profession of this country . . . ,' he complained to Mendelssohn, 'The Person I allude to is Dr Gauntlett'.[152]

I have been officially appointed by the proper authorities at Liverpool to design and superintend the erection of an organ for their Hall . . . my plan had been approved of in committee and applications for estimate made to the two Builders whom I had recommended, viz, Gray of London & Bishop of the same place—that the estimate of Gray had been accepted and the sum of money voted by the Corporation of the Town—that nothing remained to be done but to sign the contract and begin the work, when—without any application having been made to him Dr G addressed a series of letters to the Gentlemen of Liverpool . . . assuring them that they were being imposed upon, that my Plan was 'incomplete ridiculous and radically bad'—that I was 'an inexperienced player,' that he and his friend Mr Hill, the organ Builder, would build as large an organ for half the money asked by Gray, and so has caused a most unpleasant hesitation in the proceedings. Dr Gauntlett having made use of your name as well as that of Dr Walmisley of Cambridge . . . I take the liberty of addressing you, for I feel sure that you will not sanction the interference of this unprincipled person . . .[153]

Mendelssohn, who scarcely knew Wesley and had no wish to become involved in the controversy, sought to distance himself from both parties, claiming to know 'too little of the technical part of the instrument' and to be 'too little experienced in the art of organ building'[154] to offer an opinion on Wesley's plan, and there the matter rested.

Despite Gauntlett's intervention, the Liverpool authorities remained unswayed. Yet doubts had been sown, and, unknown to him, they demanded that Wesley's plan (finally completed in April 1846) be scrutinized by four of his colleagues—Vincent Novello, James Turle, Walmisley, and Edward Hopkins—who recommended various minor additions. Having suffered the indignity of having his professional expertise publicly questioned—but to a large degree endorsed—Wesley might reasonably have expected work to begin. The committee, however, prevaricated and, despite having awarded the contract, invited new tenders in May 1847. Even now they proved inca-

---

[151] Minutes of the meeting of the Law Courts Committee of 25 Nov. 1845 (*LRO* MS 352 MIN/LAW 1/1, 250).
[152] Letter dated 3 Jan. 1846 to Mendelssohn (*Ob* Mendelssohn Green Books XXIII, 4).
[153] Ibid.   [154] Letter dated 15 Jan. 1846 (*Lcm* MS 3066).

pable of making a decision, and with the death of the architect, Harvey Elmes, in November, closely followed by a serious accident to Wesley (see below), all activity connected with the organ came to a halt, not to be resumed until December 1850. By then, however, he had had the satisfaction of seeing another scheme come to fruition.

The church of St Giles, Camberwell, where he had been organist from 1829 to 1832, had been destroyed by fire in 1841, and the foundation stone of its replacement (designed by Gilbert Scott and W. B. Moffett) laid the following year. Wesley had been invited to draw up the specification for a new organ and, with the exception of his accommodation of C-compass manuals and pedals, his design for a three-manual instrument of thirty-nine stops (built by J. C. Bishop) was very much in the insular tradition he was to espouse at Liverpool. Surviving virtually unchanged, it allows one to hear at first hand the particular sound he sought: while some have criticized its duplication of registers (including eight ranks of mixtures), others (most notably Gilbert Benham) have seen it as 'a church organ of classical design, leaving on one's mind a full sense of completeness . . . and [standing as] proof for all time that a large battery of mixtures, properly treated, spells cohesion, instead of overbalance and mere force'.[155]

Wesley had also been engaged to play at the consecration of the church by the Bishop of Salisbury on 21 November 1844, when a congregation of 'nearly 2,000 persons'[156] filled the building to capacity, and his concluding improvised fugue threatened to deny the Bishop and the other guests their chance to partake of a 'sumptuous repast' in the vicarage garden! 'Here', *The Times* reported, 'the company remained for some time, and it was dark before they retired'.[157]

Another memorable performance was to take place at the opening of the rebuilt organ in St Matthew's, Manchester, on 25 February 1847:

There is that happy combination of inventive and manipulative talent in the Doctor's effusions which separate him '*longo intervallo*' from all his contemporaries . . . Perhaps the Doctor's originality of invention is his predominating characteristic, rather than a

---

[155] Gilbert Benham, 'Interesting London Organs, XXV: St. Giles's Church, Camberwell', *Org*, 13 (1933–4), 46–7.

[156] *T* (22 Nov. 1844), 6.

[157] Ibid. According to Lawrence Elvin, the Bishop (who was expected to give the final blessing) intimated to J. C. Bishop that he was anxious to bring the proceedings to a close: 'Thereupon he went to the door of the blowing chamber . . . Holding up half a crown, he said in a loud whisper: "I am going now and I like to give the blower something before I leave." Both men rushed to get their tip but did not get back to the blowing levers in time; the wind failed for a second or two and the thread of the fugue snapped' (*Bishop and Son, Organ Builders* (Lincoln: for the author, 1984), 142). Elvin's statement that the Bishop was forced to act by fear of missing another engagement 'in about an hour's time' is not borne out by contemporary accounts.

compact and independent *obligato* style of pedalling. The Doctor's surprising resources of harmony, as exhibited in his compositions and in his execution, were strongly contrasted with the bold and masculine melody of Gregorian-like strains which formed part of the composition. The Doctor, with a munificence of talent, exhibits treasures old and new, neither despising the harmonic opulence revealed by the master-minds of successive generations; nor, on the other hand, insisting, with superstitious tenacity, on the retention of an antiquated style which degrades the eloquent handmaid of devotion into mediocral and barbarous vociferation.[158]

Other engagements included playing at St Mark's, Hull, on 4 November 1847,[159] but such occasions paled into insignificance in comparison with his re-engagement as solo organist for the 1849 Birmingham Triennial Festival (Gauntlett having been preferred in 1846):

After the *Athaliah* [on 5 September], Dr. Wesley . . . played a solo on the great organ . . . [which] began with a very long *fantasia*, the plan of which we cannot attempt to define after a single hearing. In the course of the *fantasia* almost every effect of which the resources of this enormous instrument are capable was developed by the learned musician with masterly skill. But by far the most interesting part . . . was the extemporaneous *fugue* with which it terminated. A more ingenious and extraordinary improvisation we never listened to. Dr. Wesley chose an unusually short theme, as though resolved to show how easily he could set contrapuntal difficulties at defiance. After working this with remarkable clearness, he introduced a second subject which he soon brought in conjunction with the first, and subsequently a third; ultimately combining the three, in the *stretto* of the fugue, with the facility of a profound and accomplished master. Dr. Wesley's performance was greeted with uproarious applause, and, while he was playing, it was interesting to observe the members of the orchestra and chorus crowding round the organ, anxious to obtain a view of his fingers or his feet, with which he manages the ponderous pedals with such dexterity.[160]

Wesley's performance on the 'ponderous pedals' was all the more remarkable because some twenty-one months earlier he had suffered a severe accident while returning from a fishing expedition to the river Rye. On the evening of Thursday 23 December 1847 he fell whilst leaping across a 'small brook' and sustained a 'compound fracture of the right leg below the knee'.[161] Discovered by some boys, he was conveyed to Helmsley, where for the next seven months he was laid up at the 'Black Swan'. For a few weeks domestic matters take centre stage, and for almost the only time in their married life

---

[158] *The Manchester Courier* (24 Feb. 1847), 125.

[159] See G. H. Smith, *A History of Hull Organs and Organists, together with an Account of the Hull Musical Festivals, and the Formation of the Various Musical Societies in the Town* (London: A. Brown & Sons, [n.d.]), 129.

[160] *MW*, 24 (1849), 564.   [161] *LI* (1 Jan. 1848), 5.

Mary Anne emerges from the background. She described the situation to Eliza Wesley:

Intelligence was sent me by Telegraph & I immediately came to him bringing with me Mr. Teale the very eminent Surgeon [and member of the Parish Church congregation]. We were detained 4 hours by an accident on the Rail but arrived in time for Mr. T. to do all that was necessary . . . he did not conceal from me that the danger was eminent [?] & for five days I was Sick with apprehension, since then, all bad symptoms have gradually disappeared, & for the last week there has been no fever, no swelling, no inflammation & the wound becoming every day more healthy. Mr. Teale knows the medical man of this place, Mr. Ness, & he assures me there is every probability of a perfect recovery but time of course will be required—& the greatest quiet. Mr. Ness sees our poor sufferer twice every day—You will be glad to hear he suffers scarcely any pain . . . but the confinement of course is very trying to him. His bad leg lies on a pillow with the knee bent & he must on no account move so as to disturb the leg. I have had no nurse, nor even any one to sit up with me, I have a little bed in the same room, & I trust your brother has every comfort and advantages, but it is a miserable little Inn, I scarcely can leave his room—the people in the neighbourhood are extremely attentive in calling, leaving game, & offering any service in their power & several of my own friends have offered to come to me if I wished—but he cannot bear the thought of anyone being near him but myself.

I can only wonder that I am able to go thro' what I do. It is a sad grief to me to be away from home with all five of the childn. at home, but I have an excellent person as nurse who has lived five years with me & whom I can trust implicitly. She or Johnny write to me almost every day & they all remain quite well.[162]

Looking after her husband was a lonely and exhausting task, particularly as (according to Wesley) Mary Anne had been 'constantly ill for these last two years'.[163] 'I am feeling very ill today' she wrote to Eliza at the end of January, 'It is a long time to have gone thro' when I have . . . no one to comfort or assist me, & never knowing an hour's uninterrupted rest'.[164] She also bore the burden of being separated from their children, of whom Charles Alexander and William Ken had been born (on 4 February 1843 and 8 July 1845 respectively) since their arrival in Leeds: one letter to Eliza ends with the touching words 'My little Charley's birthday. 5 yrs. old. He is to dine with nurse and baby at his Godmamma's'.[165] Wesley's recovery was slow, but by early February there had been further gradual improvement:

You would be surprized at the little absolute pain in the leg that he has suffered, but his sufferings have been & are very great notwithstanding—you may imagine it must

[162] Letter dated 8 Jan. 1848 (*Lbl* Add. MS 35019, fos. 192ᵛ–94).
[163] Letter dated 17 March [1848] to his mother (ibid., fo. 27).
[164] Letter postmarked 30 Jan. 1848 (ibid., fo. 199ᵛ).
[165] Letter dated 20 Feb. 1848 (ibid., fo. 201).

be a dreadful thing to lie day after day & night after night in the same position, besides the constant fear of moving the leg and so doing mischief—for the <u>wound</u> has hitherto been too large to allow of any <u>stay</u> being applied to the limb—but the worst trouble is <u>dreadful starts</u>, so violent that they shake his whole frame, whenever he becomes at all drowsy, so that, poor fellow, he is afraid to go to sleep even when he feels sleepy—this is from the irritability of the nerves—a usual circumstance in such cases, I am told, & to quiet this in some measure he takes every night a very strong opiate, which has had effects in other ways—still it cannot be dispensed with.

Thank you for offering to send anything, but we get everything from York with great ease.—Port wine & all sorts of nourishment are ordered. A friend at Leeds sent a hamper of remarkably fine old Port as a present. I make Bla'mange & Calves foot jelly which the poor Invalid takes at all odd times in the day when he can. Altho' he is much reduced I do not much fear keeping up his strength.—You will imagine him to be <u>a difficult</u> patient to manage, but no one unless they saw him could think <u>how difficult</u>. There is no doubt the relapse is brought on by his irritability.[166]

In the same letter Mary Anne had written of the necessity of opening all Wesley's correspondence, and one thing of which he had been kept in ignorance was that his name had been put forward for the Heather Chair of Music in the University of Oxford, vacant after the death of Crotch on 29 December 1847. Martin Cawood had solicited support, obtaining promises from, among others, Walmisley (who considered that Wesley stood 'a very fair chance of succeeding')[167] and Edward Taylor. The latter was decidedly less confident:

I should think our friend, with all his fine talents, would not stand a <u>good</u> chance. The opinion of those persons here who are likely to be informed . . . is that the contest will be between Bishop & [Stephen] Elvey, both of whom have claims, tho' of a different kind—the former having taken Crotch's place as Choragus for the 2 last Festivals at Oxford, the latter being a resident there—Organist of New College, & known to be a skilful Organist as well as a sound Musician.

Unquestionably if the Electors were to say 'We will have the best man' they would offer the situation to Dr. Wesley, but this would not be much in accordance with the mode in which patronage in our art is given. I think if I were in his place I would do no more than merely notify that if elected, I would accept the office.[168]

'I tell him nothing at present', Mary Anne had confided to Eliza, and one suspects that Wesley did not learn the full story until some weeks after he had again been a runner-up to Bishop. By mid-March he was finally out of dan-

---

[166] Undated letter (probably early Feb. 1848) (ibid., fos. 203ᵛ–204ᵛ). The gift of port was probably from Walker Joy, a Leeds businessman, who provided valuable financial support for the parish church choir and, according to Stanford, 'nursed' Wesley during his illness (see C. V. Stanford, *Pages from an Unwritten Diary* (London: Edward Arnold, 1914), 254).

[167] Letter dated 29 Jan. 1848 to Martin Cawood (author's collection).

[168] Letter dated 3 Feb. 1848 to Martin Cawood (ibid.).

ger (and able to inform his mother that he was 'going on well' and had 'been on . . . my back three months. You may guess my trouble').[169] Mary Anne now relinquished her role as nurse in favour of his sister Rosalind. Games of chess helped to pass the time, but Wesley was a bad loser, and 'if it appeared that the game was going against him, he would pull the bedclothes, groan about his wounded leg and contrive at the same time to upset the chess board'.[170] Yet such pastimes can have done little to compensate him for his long separation from musical activity, and, given his temperamental inability to see fellow musicians other than as rivals, it is not surprising that he should have been concerned about what was going on at the parish church. 'I have, in the newspapers, seen the announcement of very difficult music for the Sunday [services]' he wrote to William Bower, organist of Holy Trinity Church, who had been standing in for him, 'Should it occur again . . . I hope you will have it altered, as I am sure it can be altered'.[171] How it must have irked him to have had to remain an observer for so long! But his long convalescence had one compensation in that it allowed time for composition (of which he had done very little since the completion of the Service in E in 1843), for further reflection on the reform of cathedral music, and for thinking again about his long-delayed *Anthems*. During the latter part of his stay in Helmsley he was thus able to start work on a planned series of sacred songs (settings of his old friend W. H. Bellamy's anonymously published *The Collects for the Sundays and Holydays throughout the Year . . . Rendered into Verse*), to compose a further 'sacred song' for baritone and orchestra, 'I have been young and now am old', and to complete two new anthems, 'Cast me not away' and 'The Face of the Lord'.[172]

The idea of setting Bellamy's verses had been in Wesley's mind for some time, and well before their publication in January 1848 he had seized upon them 'as the "long desired" materials for a continuous "series of Church Anthems"'.[173] Such enthusiasm had not, however, been matched by an equal determination to begin work, and it is unlikely that he had put pen to paper when, on 14 December 1847, Bellamy reported on his enquiries to Messrs Leader & Cock about 'your setting the Collects, in the two fold way in which

---

[169] Letter dated 17 March [1848] (*Lbl* Add. MS 35019, fo. 27).

[170] G. W. Spink, 'Samuel Sebastian Wesley: A Biography', *MT*, 78 (1937), 240 (quoting Rosalind's daughter, Mrs Florence Dean).

[171] Letter dated 14 April [1848] (collection of the late Sir John Dykes Bower).

[172] The earliest reference to 'I have been young and now am old' is to be found in a letter of 27 July 1848 to Henry Phillips (*Cfm*). Phillips it was who finally gave the first performance at the 1850 Gloucester Three Choirs Festival (see Chap. 5).

[173] [W. H. Bellamy], *The Collects for the Sundays and Holydays throughout the Year, in the Order in which they Occur in the Book of Common Prayer, Rendered into Verse* (London: Hatchard & Son, 1848), vi.

you suggest . . . [which] they seem to like . . . very much'.[174] '. . . they of
course would like to see specimens of the two sorts', he added, but Wesley's
accident nine days later put paid to any hopes of early progress. During June
1848, however, settings for solo voice and piano of the collects for the first
three Sundays in Advent were completed and published by Charles Coventry
in August;[175] of the remaining works and the alternative versions (presumably
for choir) originally envisaged we hear no more, although the third collect,
'Lord Jesu Christ' was copied into the choir books at Leeds and sung as an
anthem at Winchester in 1850.[176] The sacred song was a form in which he had
hitherto shown little interest, contributing a single specimen ('The Bruised
Reed' of 1834, also with words by Bellamy) to Charles Hackett's *The National
Psalmist* (1839) but, with his views on what was stylistically appropriate in
church now changing, he perhaps saw it as a possible alternative to the
anthem—and in *The Collects* simply transferred his 'church' style, replete with
diatonic dissonance and suspensions, from the chancel to the home. A more
fundamental reappraisal of his church music style was, however, taking place,
and as a prelude to this we must turn to an anthem probably written some
three years earlier, 'Man that is Born of a Woman'.[177] Setting part of the burial sentences, it was 'intended to precede the Verse 'Thou knowest, Lord' by
Purcell',[178] whose simple dignity and word setting (with frequent use of
Scotch snap rhythms) it successfully emulates. Indeed, its concentrated, almost
entirely syllabic, writing in which harmonic colour, modulation, and dissonance carry the burden, provides a vivid illustration of the changes which had
taken place in his music since leaving Exeter. The final page contains some
particularly moving writing, with the harsh dissonance of a simultaneous false
relation used to depict the 'bitter pains of eternal death' (see Ex. 4.10); here,
and throughout the final phrase, he drew on the organ to enrich the vocal texture, which enabled him to write five- or six-part chords without the necessity of dividing the voice parts—a technique later favoured by Stanford. This
process of simplification, of baring the music to its bones, was taken a stage
further in the two anthems written at Helmsley ('Cast me not away' and 'The
Face of the Lord'), which show Wesley not only experimenting with a novel
musical style but also setting texts of a deeply personal nature.

[174] Letter dated 14 Dec. 1847 (author's collection).
[175] See the note in Martin Cawood's copy (now *Lbl* H.1185.n.(23.)): 'Martin Cawood from Dr. Wesley
August 1848 These Collects were written at Helmsley. June 1848'.
[176] Versions of all three collects for soloist and four-part choir were published by Sir Frederick Bridge in
1908, but the first appearance of one in a collection of words of anthems appears to have been in 1859, when
'Lord Jesu Christ' was included in the 4th edn. of the book used at Leeds Parish Church.
[177] Of all Wesley's anthems 'Man that is Born of a Woman' is one of the hardest to date: on purely stylistic grounds it appears to date from the mid-1840s.
[178] S. S. Wesley, *Anthems* (1853), 246.

Ex. 4.10. 'Man that is Born of a Woman'

Words, as we have seen, meant a great deal to Wesley, and 'Cast me not away' is no exception. Its selection of verses from Psalm 51—changed from the Prayer Book version to the Biblical version during the course of composition—clearly reflects both his troubled state of mind and, at the harsh discords accompanying the words 'That the bones which thou hast broken may rejoice', the physical reality of his injury:

Cast me not away from thy presence; and take not thy holy spirit from me.
Restore unto me the joy of thy salvation; and uphold me with thy spirit.
The sacrifices of God are a broken spirit; a broken and a contrite heart thou wilt not despise, O God.
Make me to hear joy and gladness; that the bones which thou hast broken may rejoice.

'The Face of the Lord' conveys a similar message:

The face of the Lord is against them that do evil, to cut off the remembrance of them from the earth.
The Lord is nigh unto them that are of a broken heart; and saveth them such as be of a contrite spirit.
Many are the afflictions of the righteous: but the Lord delivereth him out of all.
The righteous cry, and the Lord heareth, and delivereth them out of all their troubles.
He keepeth all his bones: not one of them is broken.
Evil shall slay the wicked: and they that hate the righteous shall be desolate.
The righteous cry, and the Lord heareth, and delivereth them out of all their troubles.
The Lord redeemeth the soul of his servants: and they that trust in him shall not be desolate.

To express these sentiments Wesley adopted a restrained, deliberately archaic style. Endowed with a real understanding of how counterpoint works, he was ideally placed to infuse genuine life into such music and with 'Cast me not away' produced a wonderfully successful fusion of the sixteenth and nineteenth centuries. Unlike the mock-historical works of such Gresham Prize winners as W. H. Havergal or Charles Hart, or the skilled but often inert pastiches of Ouseley, it is genuinely a work of its own time. The *stile antico* counterpoint may observe the rules of sixteenth-century part-writing, but the harmonic daring proclaims it a work of the romantic era. Like the other anthems of the Leeds period it is through-composed and falls into the same bipartite form as 'Wash me throughly'. But there any similarity ceases. Eschewing chromaticism for a serene diatonicism, it is one of Wesley's most completely vocal works, whose organ part can easily be dispensed with, and owes its effect entirely to his masterly handling of the six-part (SSATTB) choir. Textures constantly fluctuate as imitative passages alternate with sections of block harmony, lightly scored phrases with ones for full choir. But the outstanding feature of the vocal writing is its suppleness. Phrase lengths are variable, rhythms lively, and the verbal accentuation invariably sympathetic, so that even within his self-imposed constraints Wesley was able to create a work of considerable emotional power and strong constrasts. Compare, for instance, the calm opening (for SSAT, see Ex. 4.11*a*)—which paradoxically uses the same progression as the chorus 'God of our Fathers' from Spohr's *The Fall of Babylon (Der Fall Babylons)*—with the incisive statement for full choir 'that the bones which thou hast broken may rejoice', centred on a striking dissonance ($\flat$III imposed on its own V^9; see Ex. 4.11*b*).

While these words clearly had a special significance, so did those of 'The Face of the Lord', with its allusions to the 'afflictions of the righteous' and expression of hope, 'He keepeth all his bones; not one of them is broken'. Although the first of its three movements opens in a similar vein (and the same key), it differs in one important respect: while 'Cast me not away' is a largely contrapuntal work, 'The Face of the Lord' is primarily harmonic in conception, with the part-writing determined as much by harmonic as by melodic considerations. A good example is to be found in the first movement, where a long dominant pedal in the organ part underpins the imitative entries of the impassioned drooping figure 'Many are the afflictions of the righteous'. Indeed, the dissonant sevenths and ninths between the upper parts and the pedal provide the whole *raison d'être* of the passage, and it clearly made an impression on Walmisley who included something remarkably similar in his anthem 'Blessed is he that considereth the poor and needy', composed for a choir benevolent fund service in Cambridge in May 1854. He too was in poor

Ex. 4.11. 'Cast me not away'

health, and the Psalmist's words 'When he lieth sick upon his bed: make thou all his bed in his sickness' doubtless carried particular meaning.

In the second and third movements—a double quartet and brief chorus respectively—Wesley reverted to a more purely nineteenth-century idiom. The former rises to a powerful climax at the words 'The righteous cry', with a stabbing motif in the Decani treble part and harshly dissonant harmony (see Ex. 4.12), before closing with a prolonged and expressive cadence based on material from the end of 'To my Request and Earnest Cry'. But the final chorus lacks the substance to form a wholly satisfactory conclusion and highlights the anthem's main weakness—a lack of unity between its constituent parts. Indeed, the gradual change of mood from the austere opening to the more contemporary mode of expression in the later movements suggests that Wesley himself was not entirely certain of the direction in which his music was moving.

A similar blend of ancient and modern is found in the last works to date from his time in Leeds, the brief introits 'Blessed is the man that feareth the Lord', 'Hear thou in Heaven', and 'I will wash my hands in innocency' (c.1849), written (by tradition) for use in the very short processions from the vestry to the chancel at the parish church. Although not published until 1908, they quickly began to circulate and by 1856 were already in use at St Andrew's, Wells Street, London, and Manchester Parish Church.[179] After leaving the town Wesley himself seems never to have performed them again.

What prompted Wesley to make such a radical break with his own past? Both his notes and published writings bear witness to a real—if limited—interest in the vocal music of the sixteenth and seventeenth centuries. At Exeter he had not only performed some of the finest sacred works of the period, but had also encountered many secular pieces at the meetings of the Devon Madrigal Society. At Liverpool, compositions from this period (both English and continental) were among those examples Spark had had to copy out. Knowing such music from within, he may have been motivated by no more than a desire to try his hand at something similar himself. But whatever the reason, it was symptomatic of a broader change of emphasis in his church music taking place at this time, linked to his experience at Leeds Parish Church and foreshadowed in his lectures.

Hitherto he had concentrated almost exclusively on verse and full-with-verse anthems, consisting of a succession of separate movements (or sections) scored for full choir, various combinations of verse ensemble, and solo voices.

---

[179] See William Mulready Terrott (ed.), *Anthem Book* and John Joseph Harris (ed.), *A Collection of those portions of the Psalms of David, Bible and Liturgy which have been Set to Music, and are Sung as Anthems in the Cathedral and Parish Church of Manchester*, 3rd edn. (Manchester: sold at the Depository of the SPCK, 1856).

Ex. 4.12. 'The Face of the Lord', second movement

Ex. 4.12. cont.

All had included substantial solo arias (and in many cases obbligato organ parts as well), and each had been written in a thoroughly contemporary idiom. He had used the same technique in the Service in E (though with less use of solo voices), but from this date onwards arias are most notable by their absence, while organ parts do little more than double the voices; when these facts are taken in conjunction with his own words it is obvious that a significant change had taken place:

Solo singing in the Church, I confess, I do [not] think should be much encouraged. I do not think it should be absolutely prohibited, but the portions of the service set apart for music are meant to be the voice of the people, and altho' perhaps our music should not altogether be restricted to Chorus, still I think the Solo should be a rare exception, and in almost every instance so mixed with chorus that the individuality of the Singer may [not] attract that attention to himself which belongs solely to the sense of the words, and for a higher purpose.[180]

---

[180] *Lcm* MS 2141f, fos. 18ᵛ, 25ʳ. On both occasions Wesley's omission of 'not' is accidental, as his original wording was 'Solo singing in the Church I confess, I am not desirous to see promoted' and '. . . the Singer does not attract that attention'.

Given his dependence upon Jebb's writings and the latter's influence at Leeds it is surely not coincidental that they held similar views:

And besides, [in the performance of full anthems] . . . there is less room for that personal exhibition to which the more modern compositions so largely administer. Disregard of self is one of the chief moral characteristics of Catholic Christianity: and the sinking of the individual in the ministerial office should always be borne in mind in Christian worship.[181]

Nor can it be coincidental that the whole ethos of the traditional High-Church worship to which both Jebb and Hook subscribed maintained a clear distinction between the sacred and the secular, as much in music as elsewhere. In Nicholas Temperley's words, 'the notion of a special style of music for the Church, deliberately distinguished from secular music, was precisely opposite . . . to the low-church cultivation of the fashionable styles of art music.'[182] Wesley, as we have seen, had already drawn on this argument in his apology for the choral service; he now proceeded to put it into practice.

It was in fact some two years before the composition of 'Cast me not away' that Wesley had made his first venture into the realm of 'historical composition' with the Magnificat and Nunc Dimittis of his Chant Service in F (published as *Magnificat and Nunc Dimittis, A Chant*). Conscious that the Service in E was likely to prove too long for everyday use, he had proposed the revival of the chant service form in which chanted and fully harmonized sections alternate:

The object of saving time could have been more readily attained, and a far better effect produced, by reserving certain portions . . . to be sung in harmony; and chanting, either in unison or harmony, the rest. Such a course would . . . [be] more in accordance with the primitive model; and would also afford great opportunity for the development of modern genius . . . It had often occurred to the Writer, before he was made aware that some such idea had been acted upon by the late Precentor Creighton [1636 or 1637–1734], of Wells . . .[183]

Here, too, as Wesley noted, he and Jebb were of a remarkably similar mind:

'Several eminent musicians of old time, and of the unreformed Churches,' observes the Rev. Mr. Jebb . . . 'have adapted the Canticles to the ⟨descant, as it is called, upon the⟩ plain song or Gregorian chant' (meaning a unisonous unmetrical chant, it is presumed) 'making variations somewhat after the manner of our Services, though less free in their departure from the original structure of the melody.'[184]

---

[181] Jebb, *Three Lectures*, 27.   [182] *The Music of the English Parish Church*, 1. 249.
[183] *A Morning & Evening Cathedral Service*, iii.
[184] Ibid. Whether by accident or design Wesley omitted part of his quotation from Jebb's *The Choral Service*, 349.

Within a year he had embarked on just such a setting himself, noting later that it was 'an attempt to attain the utmost brevity, without sacrificing *Expression* in setting *Te Deum* &c. to Music'.[185] The evening canticles were completed by summer 1846 but, unlike the harmonized eighteenth-century settings, alternate unbarred plainsong-like sections for men's voices in unison with passages for full choir, rather in the manner of the *alternatim* settings of some two to three centuries earlier. But despite possessing a superficial similarity to early *fauxbourdon* settings the music makes few concessions to antiquity.

In retrospect it matters little whether Wesley's revival of the chant service form was inspired by Jebb or not. Of far more interest is the fact that by the mid-1840s he was no longer fully satisfied with the style and form of his earlier works. His enforced stay at Helmsley thus came at an opportune moment, providing him with a breathing space, a time to consider in practical terms the direction in which his own music should move. 'Cast me not away' and the sacred songs may thus be seen to represent a parting of the ways, a breakdown—albeit temporary—of the marriage of 'sacred' and 'secular' elements he had effected so triumphantly some fifteen years earlier. Yet having demonstrated so eloquently that he could produce a masterpiece of restrained, purely vocal writing, Wesley evidently found that the discipline placed too great a limit on his imagination. Likewise his failure to complete the series of sacred songs (assuming it was not merely due to lethargy) suggests an awareness that his future as a composer lay in the chancel rather than the drawing-room. Indeed, as 'The Face of the Lord' demonstrates, the 'sacred' and 'secular' strands almost immediately began to draw together again. It was such an idiom, shorn of the more extreme features of his earlier works, and with diatonic dissonance replacing the fluid chromatic harmony of a decade earlier, that Wesley would pursue after his move to the more traditional surroundings of Winchester Cathedral a year later.

Whilst he was convalescing Wesley's thoughts had also turned again to the *Anthems* he had abandoned in 1840. Writing in August 1848 to R. A. Atkins, organist of St Asaph Cathedral, he informed him that he was 'completing a set of Anthems for Cathedral Service', adding that 'If two thirds of the Cathedrals favour me with their subscriptions I shall publish'.[186] Six weeks later he wrote again, enclosing some 'Announcements of my forthcoming work'[187] which he hoped that Atkins would distribute, but not until 14 October did he make his plans public with an advertisement in *The Leeds Intelligencer*: 'Dr. Wesley has the honor to announce that he has nearly ready for Publication, a

---

[185] *A Chant Service*, 1.   [186] Letter dated 5 Aug. 1848 (*Eu* MS Dk.7.384).
[187] Letter dated 13 Sept. 1848 (ibid.).

Collection Of Anthems, For Cathedral Service, Composed by Himself.'[188] A week later he wrote again to Atkins:

With regard to the chapters of Asaph & Bangor subscribing for only 3 copies, it appears to me that the work would be of no use to them. They cannot perform the Anthems from three copies. To copy in writing would be most dishonest as by so doing they avail themselves of my labours without affording me the stated reward . . .[189]

He also enclosed a letter for the Dean:

I am obliged by your kindness & by the compliment of your Chapter's subscription to my intended publication.

Allow me to remind you that I expected and hoped that each Chapter would sub-scribe for what I called a Set of Copies. Eight Copies. The Anthems cannot be per-formed with less than 8 copies for the Quire . . . and I do not see how works of this kind are to be brought out if the Cathedral Chapters will not purchase copies . . .

This begging is far from pleasant, but so little is known of Musical affairs by the Clergy that it seems proper to inform Parties interested as to how we stand in propos-ing a new work for Cathedral use. The painter & the Sculptor fixes his price & there is <u>no mistake</u> as to his profits.

The poor Musician has to beg for Subscribers & as to <u>living</u> comfortably by his talents, the man who expects to <u>live</u> by writing for the Church must be stark mad.[190]

Despite tight-fistedness on the part of chapters (of whom no fewer than thirteen subscribed for fewer than eight copies), subscriptions quickly mounted up so that by the time of the publication of *A Few Words* on 9 June 1849 Wesley could announce that 'About 400 Copies are subscribed for'.[191] But then, as so often before, there was a hiatus, and no more is heard of the projected collection until January 1853, with publication finally taking place in the autumn (see Chapter 5).

We must now turn back to the summer of 1848 and pick up the threads of Wesley's career at the parish church. Periodic accounts of his convalescence had appeared in *The Leeds Intelligencer*, which on 1 July announced his return to the town, although a further two months were to elapse before he was able to resume his duties, when a contemporary remembered him 'wobbling onto the organ Pew'.[192] The first of the new anthems, 'Cast me not away', was heard on 29 July, to be followed on 14 September by 'The Face of the Lord'.

---

[188] p. 4.   [189] Letter dated 20 Oct. 1848 (*Eu* MS Dk.7.384).   [190] Ibid.

[191] *A Few Words*, back endpaper.

[192] Letter dated 1[?] Oct. 1907 from Charles R. Chorley to Morris Hodson, Precentor of Leeds Parish (Letters Relating to the Wesley Memorial in Leeds Parish Church, *LPC*).

Returning to the church after such a long absence cannot have been easy. Responsibility for the music had been shared by William Bower and the choirmaster, Robert Burton, and one can be sure that the latter—a local man from Dewsbury with considerable ambitions of his own—would have been reluctant to resume a secondary role. Unlike his predecessors he had not been one of Wesley's pupils, and doubtless for this reason never enjoyed such a close relationship with him. He had, moreover, already shown himself a professional rival, both as conductor of the 'old' Leeds Choral Society (when Wesley directed the markedly less successful 'new' society) and as a music teacher. For Wesley to find himself ignored in a report which expressed 'approbation at the manner in which the difficult services and anthems are now performed by the boys of the parish church' and declared that 'the taste and expression they give to the solos do the greatest credit to our talented townsman and able choirmaster, Mr. R. S. Burton'[193] cannot have helped matters. Indeed, given that it was found necessary to introduce a new set of choir rules which laid particular stress on attendance in March 1849, it seems likely that the lack of sympathy between the two contributed to a more general malaise afflicting the choir. Fortunately for all concerned, the death on 23 May 1849 of William Chard, organist of Winchester Cathedral, offered a way of escaping the 'dirt, smoke, and inhabitants' of Leeds which (according to Spark) had left Wesley 'eternally grumbling and craving to go somewhere else'.[194] Although he moved quickly to seek support from professional colleagues, it was not until 17 July that he sumitted a letter of application to the Dean and Chapter, who, despite some justifiable suspicion of such an outspoken character, decided to offer him the post (see Chapter 5). At the end of the summer he was thus able to return to a more peaceful environment, free of the hectic bustle of the industrial north, but before following him southwards we must glance at those aspects of his career not concerned with church music.

While Wesley's duties at the parish church had formed the centre of his professional life, they had precluded him neither from participating in a broader range of musical activities nor, in March 1842, from 'informing his Friends and the Public in general, that he will be prepared . . . to attend a Select Number of Pupils in Leeds and Neighbourhood';[195] a further advertisement appeared a month later:

Dr. S. Wesley begs to announce that he Receives Pupils at his Residence, 25, Albion-Street, Leeds, on Wednesdays and Saturdays, on the usual School Terms.

Pianoforte   8 Guineas Per Annum
Singing   8 Guineas Per Annum

---

[193] LI (4 Nov. 1848), 5.   [194] W. Spark, Musical Memories, 66.   [195] LI (26 March 1842), 1.

Applications for Private Lessons, Addressed to 25, Albion-Street, will receive attention.[196]

Among his pupils the most promising was undoubtedly Emily Hudson, whose piano playing drew praise from Thalberg (who also 'passed a warm compliment on her master'),[197] and whose 'vocal abilities' also gave rise to 'great expectations'.[198] Yet despite being (as *The Musical World* put it) 'thronged with private pupils',[199] Wesley rarely saw teaching as anything but drudgery, and one suspects that Spark's comment that 'he could have made plenty of money, had he not been so erratic and uncertain in his professional ways and doings' had a particular relevance![200] Much more to his liking was practical music-making, and it was doubtless due to his initiative that the Leeds Parochial Choral Society began meeting on a more formal basis:

Formation of a Choral and Instrumental Society.

. . . for some time past an assemblage of nearly 200 musical performers, vocal and instrumental, has taken place at St. John's School-room, under the direction of Dr. Wesley, at which many compositions of established reputation and beauty have been very creditably performed. The meetings were first proposed by Dr. Wesley with a view . . . of calling forth and testing the musical taste and talent which has been generally supposed to exist in the North of England, and more especially in this district; and it is with much gratification we announce that so satisfactory has been the result, that there appears every probability of a Choral and Instrumental Society being established on a more extended and judicious plan than has ever been effected in Leeds.

. . . the Music Hall has been engaged for a term of years as the future place of meeting, and an extensive orchestra [i.e. platform] . . . is now being erected.[201]

Wesley had become president of the society in April 1842,[202] and within seven months it had grown to such an extent (besides dropping the word 'Parochial' from its title) that it was already a serious rival of the 'old' Leeds Choral Society, established in 1838. The first concert, a performance of Handel's *Messiah* ('Under the Patronage of the Rev. the Vicar and the Parochial Clergy'), took place on 29 December and was well received. 'The manner in which the performance was conducted by Dr. Wesley augurs well for musical taste in this town', declared *The Leeds Intelligencer*, 'and the thanks of the public are eminently due to him for his invaluable exertions'.[203]

---

[196] *LI* (30 April 1842), 4.   [197] *MW*, 20 (1845), 78.   [198] Ibid. 490.
[199] Ibid.   [200] W. Spark, *Musical Memories*, 71.   [201] *LI* (12 Nov. 1842), 5.
[202] Writing to F. G. Edwards on 24 Jan. 1906, Morris Hodson quoted from the minute book of the society (no longer extant): 'On April 14 1842 Dr. Wesley was asked to be president' (Novello & Co. private library).
[203] *LI* (31 Dec. 1842), 5.

Haydn's *Creation* followed on 16 January, and the season closed with a selection from Handel's *Israel in Egypt* and Spohr's *Die Letzten Dinge* on 28 February. With the Music Hall now required to house the Leeds Public Exhibition, rehearsals were suspended until February 1844, when *Messiah* was again put into practice for a performance on 15 April. The season continued with Haydn's *The Seasons* (16 December) and *Creation* (17 February 1845), but the society was now in serious financial difficulties and this concert was its last. Perhaps the most extraordinary aspect of its demise, however, was the fact that Wesley was 'unavoidably prevented from being present' at the final concert.[204] Was there another, unpublicized, reason—perhaps a rift between conductor and committee—which contributed to its collapse? With this in mind it should not pass unnoticed that a few months earlier, when the society's future was far from assured, he had transferred his allegiance to Manchester, taking part in a 'Soirée Musicale' organized by the Lancashire and Cheshire Working Men's Singing Classes on 12 November 1844 and, from September 1844, acting as organist for the Manchester Choral Society; his presence in the town even gave rise to a rumour that he was going to settle there.[205] Described in the press as 'a powerful magnet of attraction',[206] he played for all six concerts of the 1844–5 season, but brought the society no luck as it too was dissolved after the concert on 22 May 1845.

Concurrently with his work with the Leeds Choral Society Wesley had also taken part in a number of individual concerts. In April 1843, for example, he acted as conductor at the farewell concert given by Mr Suffrein, 'Flutist, and Master of the Band of the 17th Lancers', whose services he had earlier called upon for the choral concerts. The programme included Beethoven's Symphony No. 2, the overtures to *Guillaume Tell* by Rossini and *Ahnenshatz* by Karl Reissiger, and his own glee 'I wish to tune my quiv'ring lyre'. Two months later, on 21 and 22 June, he 'presided at the piano forte' while his old acquaintance J. D. Loder led the orchestra at the thirty-fifth annual meeting of the Yorkshire Amateur Musical Society (held in rotation in York, Hull, Leeds, and Sheffield). As no conductor is specified one can only assume that they adopted the old-fashioned practice of sharing responsibility for the performances between them, with Loder directing the orchestral works from the leader's desk and Wesley playing 'continuo' from the score and accompanying the solo items. One of the works performed was Beethoven's Symphony No.

---

[204] *LI* (22 Feb. 1845), 5.   [205] See *The Manchester Guardian* (20 Nov. 1844), 4.
[206] Ibid. The concerts for which Wesley played were the following. 26 Sept. 1844: Haydn, Mass No. 3; Handel, selection from *Solomon*; extempore performance by Wesley. 14 Nov. 1844: works by Beethoven, Croft, Handel, Leo, Rinck, Romberg; Handel, selection from *Joshua*. 19 Dec. 1844: Handel, selection from *Messiah*. 27 Feb. 1845: Spohr, 'How excellent'; Handel, selection from *Solomon*. 10 April 1845: Haydn, *Creation*. 22 May 1845: Handel: selection from *Alexander's Feast*.

9, which was receiving its first performance outside London. 'The performance this morning', Loder observed at the society's annual dinner, 'it would be absurd to call perfect; but I must say that the orchestra gave a very fine outline of that great work . . .'. 'To say the performance was excellent', he continued, 'would not be enough—it was wonderfully performed, considering that the band was composed of amateurs, and I have no hesitation in saying that out of London it could not have so much justice done to it'.[207]

The first day's programme also included Spohr's Symphony No. 2, extracts from Weber's *Euryanthe*, and 'I wish to tune my quiv'ring lyre', while the overture to Spohr's *Jessonda* and extracts from Weber's *Oberon* were to be heard at the concluding concert, together with a 'Grand Symphony' by Reissiger. All in all the performances passed off very satisfactorily and contributed to 'as brilliant and satisfactory an anniversary of the Yorkshire Amateur Musical Meetings as is perhaps remembered'.[208]

During the course of the dinner it fell to Loder to propose a toast to Wesley. Recounting how he had first known him as a child, he recalled that he was then 'a talented singer, and his genius grew with him every year'. 'No man', he believed, 'was more admired and esteemed in the profession, both for his talents and general good conduct, than his friend Samuel Wesley, whose health he begged to propose'.[209]

Yet for all Loder's generous words, Wesley seems to have withdrawn from the forefront of public music-making during the next eighteen months and, after the collapse of the Choral Society, confined himself almost solely to organ playing and his work at the parish church. Two of his rare later appearances were in 1849, when he returned to Manchester to accompany a performance of Haydn's *Creation* at the Mechanics' Institution (28 April) and both 'presided at the pianoforte and conducted' at a concert at the Leeds Mechanics' Institution (20 June); the latter programme included Mozart's overtures to *Idomeneo* and *La clemenza di Tito*, an overture by Reissiger, and miscellaneous vocal and choral pieces. One of the highlights, however, was his performance with a local violinist of one of Beethoven's sonatas, for which the press complimented him for 'giving *gratuitously* his invaluable aid for the gratification and improvement of the public taste in the elevating and refining art of music'.[210]

---

[207] *LI* (24 June 1843), 8. The symphony had received its second performance in the country as recently as 1837, when Moscheles conducted it at the Philharmonic Society. But by 1852, when it was played at the Birmingham Triennial Festival, the Leeds performance had been forgotten and it was described as 'never before performed at a provincial concert' (*Sp*, 25 (1852), 870).

[208] *LI* (24 June 1843), 8.   [209] Ibid.

[210] *LM* (23 June 1849), 5. Wesley had been listed as sharing the conducting of two similar concerts earlier in the season with Burton, but the comment that 'We are glad to find that Dr. Wesley has been able to resume his direction of the musical department' implies that this was his first appearance: see *LI* (16 June 1849), 5.

Disenchantment with musical life in general, and with the Choral Society in particular, had doubtless contributed to his withdrawal, and was reinforced by the furore over the Service in E and the deterioration in his relationship with Hook.[211] In severing his links with secular musical activity, however, Wesley brought to an end an era which had begun at the English Opera House, and tacitly acknowledged that his attempts to fashion a career beyond the confines of church or organ loft had come to naught. With a few isolated exceptions, he was not to return to this field until his appointment to Gloucester Cathedral twenty years later.

In retrospect the mid-1840s can be seen to form another watershed in Wesley's musical life. The burst of creative activity which resulted in the two sets of *Three Pieces for a Chamber Organ*, the March and Rondo, the *Selection of Psalm Tunes*, and the Service in E was soon spent, and it was not until his confinement at Helmsley that the urge—or opportunity—to compose returned. One of the few pieces completed during the intervening period was an appropriately satirical one, a set of 'Quadrilles á la Herz' entitled *Jeux d'esprit*. Their composition was the result of a dinner-table conversation at the home of Martin Cawood when 'One of the Company told the Dr. that he could not understand his learned Church music, Could he not compose some light music?', to which Wesley replied that 'he would compose a set of Quadrilles if Mrs. Martin Cawood (then present) would allow him to dedicate the music to her—& in a short time they appeared'.[212] The quadrilles represent Wesley's last contribution to the solo piano repertoire and contain some charming music. They were available in versions for both piano solo and duet (even running to a second edition) and provide a rare example of Wesley writing in a lighter vein: the third number, 'La Poule', is particularly graceful (see Ex. 4.13).

That we should take our leave of Wesley and Leeds at the Cawood household is apposite. Not only had Martin Cawood been responsible for bringing him to Yorkshire, but he had also commissioned the remaining movements of the Service in E and had generously acted on his behalf at the election for the chair of music at the University of Oxford. As a member of the parish church choir committee (and secretary in 1844 and 1845) he had also, one suspects, served as a buffer between Wesley and Hook and was certainly seen by the latter as a channel through which influence might be brought to bear upon his recalcitrant organist.

[211] William Spark observed that Wesley's 'great musical genius was [generally] fully recognised and encouraged, though strange to say less perhaps in Leeds than anywhere else' (*Musical Memories*, 65).

[212] The story as recalled by C. S. Rooke in a letter of 26 April 1899 to F. G. Edwards (Novello & Co. private library); Rooke was one of those present at the farewell dinner given for Wesley on 12 Feb. 1850.

Ex. 4.13. *Jeux d'esprit*, 'La Poule'

It was, of course, the breakdown of trust between vicar and organist that had played the principal part in persuading Wesley that his future lay elsewhere, and it was with feelings of disappointment and disillusion that he left Leeds. He had arrived seven and a half years earlier with high hopes for the future, convinced that he had found as near ideal conditions for the performance (and support) of the choral service as he ever would. He was fêted and deferred to on his arrival, and his first two or three years were (as Spark wrote) 'tolerably happy and successful'.[213] But once he realized that Hook had little interest in his crusade to revive church music, the downward spiral began. In the context of what he conceived to be a betrayal of trust he felt under little obligation to honour his side of the bargain and became increasingly

---

[213] W. Spark, *Musical Memories*, 71.

neglectful of his duty, so much so that (according to Spark) he and the organ-builder [Thomas?] Greenwood would 'sally forth . . . and give themselves up for days to the exercise of the gentle art' of fishing.[214] Such conduct merely exacerbated the situation, and had Hook not guaranteed his salary for ten years he would, as he had hinted to Martin Cawood, have taken steps to terminate his employment rather sooner.

But it was not only at the parish church that Wesley had encountered setbacks. The Leeds Choral Society had survived barely three seasons, while his most ambitious work, the Service in E, had received a mauling at the hands of the press. Indeed, the one thing he prized above all else—universal recognition as a composer—had continued to elude him. For someone of his sensitivity (and despite an abrasive exterior he was a very private individual plagued by feelings of insecurity) it was a bruising experience, and it led to his withdrawal from most musical activity beyond the confines of the church. Only as an organist, in which capacity he was acknowledged to have no peer, did he regularly continue to appear in public, and it is thus fitting that his departure from Leeds should have coincided with his second (and final) appearance as solo organist at the Birmingham Triennial Festival.

Within a month of his triumph Wesley had left Yorkshire, but his departure was fortunately not marred by the personal bitterness which had so soured his leaving Devon, and took place almost unnoticed. Of the local newspapers only *The Leeds Intelligencer* (which had always taken a close interest in his doings) referred to it, besides urging its readers to attend the farewell concert he planned to give. But the great cholera epidemic had (as he wrote to one prospective performer, Henry Phillips) 'driven so many Families Away that it would be useless for me to give my Farewell Concert now',[215] and although he made a brief return in November to try out the new 'relief pallets' fitted to the parish church organ by William Holt,[216] no concert materialized. At the church, however, it had been different, and after his acceptance of the post at Winchester the congregations were treated to a near-complete performance of *Messiah*, with excerpts being performed as anthems for close on two weeks (26 August to 8 September).[217] Past differences at the parish church were quickly forgotten: when he was invited back for a farewell dinner at the Scarborough Hotel on 12 February 1850 to be presented with his portrait by the local artist W. K. Briggs and an illuminated scroll signed by members of the clergy, choir and choir committee 'as a mark of our Friendship and high

---

[214] Ibid.   [215] Letter dated 11 Sept. 1849 (*Mr* MS MAM P 12 C, fo. 28).
[216] See *LM* (17 Nov. 1849), 8.
[217] Allowing for the omission of some intermediate headings, no fewer than 35 numbers appear to have been sung during this period.

appreciation of your Musical Genius',[218] there was goodwill on both sides, as the vicar's toast demonstrated:

I have been requested by the committee of gentlemen who have subscribed for this portrait to present it to you as a mark of their high admiration of your musical genius and of their recollection of the ability, kindness, and courtesy with which you invariably conducted the choral services during the several years you were organist at the Parish church of this town. (Applause.) They have selected this form of testimonial . . . not only as a means of expressing their own regard for you, but also of their feelings of respect for and their recollection of the kindness of Mrs. Wesley. (Applause.) I am sure, Sir, to Mrs. Wesley and family, as well as to yourself, this mark of the estimation in which you are held in Leeds must afford very high gratification. (Applause.) Allow me, gentlemen, to conclude by proposing the health of Dr. Wesley. (Cheers.)[219]

The only sour note was struck by the apparently 'unavoidable' absence of Burton (whom Wesley was to take to court in 1852 over his refusal to honour their 1846 agreement over the sale of Wesley's teaching practice).[220]

Wesley had achieved much during his stay in the town. He had established a choral tradition at the parish church which has survived to the present day.[221] His Service in E was to be a landmark in the history of the genre and an inspiration to other composers. *A Few Words* was a valuable—if idiosyncratic—contribution to the debate about the reform of cathedrals and their music. Any one of these would have kept his name alive, but it was to the first that he chose to look back when he found himself addressing his former colleagues for the last time:

Gentlemen, it is now my duty to express my thanks for the very kind compliment which has been paid to me, and I assure you that the kindness shewn me in Leeds has been, and through life will be, a source of high gratification. No one could be insensible to the good opinions of his fellow-men; I am not, and I receive with great satisfaction and pleasure the present to my family so kindly bestowed. I belong to a profession which confers, perhaps, no real and substantial benefits on society. I am not like the surgeon, the engineer, or the divine. At the same time it must not be thought that my profession needs no encouragement, or that encouragement would be of no use. Although the profession of music may confer no solid advantages, a mastery in musical art is not attained with less natural ability and less industry than are essential in

---

[218] *Lcm* MS 4040.   [219] *LI* (16 Feb. 1850), 5.

[220] See *T* (16 July 1852), 7. When Wesley left Leeds Burton had agreed to buy his teaching practice on the terms set in 1846—£500. When he refused to pay more than £350 Wesley took legal action and was awarded £100 damages.

[221] Of the other choral foundations established at this time (among them the Temple Church, All Saints', Margaret Street, St Andrew's, Wells Street, and St Michael's College, Tenbury), only Leeds Parish Church has maintained daily choral services.

other walks of life, and so long as music is connected with our acts of public worship, you will, I am sure, agree that what is done should be done well. But it is not from private individuals that the necessary encouragement should be expected, but from the highest authorities in the church. Perhaps, at the present time, church music is not appreciated in this country as it ought to be . . . I think that church music must be encouraged before it and its professors are placed in a proper position. (Hear, hear.) In Leeds you have made a noble effort. I do not know where church music has made such progress as in this town. The expense of the Parish Church choir is as large as any unendowed choir I know of, if not larger. It originated with the Vicar, who has often incurred great responsibility connected with it, but the way in which it has been supported is such as I know not to be equalled in any other town. I do not mean to say that it was prompted by my labours—(Yes, yes)—but I did my best in the situation I occupied. I beg to assure you that my coming to Leeds has been a source of great gratification, and I feel deeply the kindness which I always met with from the choir committee. I beg to offer my sincere thanks for the handsome present—handsome on account of the cost, and not on account of the subject—(Laughter and applause)—I beg to return my warmest thanks for the great kindness and liberality which you have shewn me in presenting me with that portrait. (Applause.)[222]

At the end of the evening, the health of the secretary of the choir committee (R. L. Rooke) having been proposed, 'coffee was served, and after much pleasant conversation the party separated, all delighted with the proceedings'.[223]

---

[222] *LI* (16 Feb. 1850), 5. The portrait is now in the Department of Portraits at the Royal College of Music, London.
[223] Ibid.

5

Winchester

I soon bitterly repented of leaving Exeter & when <u>this</u> place was vacant I
offered for it & was elected.[1]

My dear Wesley,
   . . . I have written <u>this post</u>, to the Bishop & Dean of Winchester . . . having taken
every possible shape <u>in abusing your</u> detestable talent & your unaccountable pre-
sumption in offering yourself as a Candidate [wrote Charles Knyvett]. I now wish you
my dear Friend all success, but I much fear the result proving as I would wish, for there
is a person nam'd <u>Long</u>, not only so nam'd, but measuring 6 ft without his night Cap,
who has servd as Dr Chards Deputy for many years, & therefore may stand in your
way. I had not heard of the Vacancy till your letter came, which I judge has taken
place by the death of Chard, unless by his usual & universally condemn'd neglect, He
has precipitated the situation—altho possessing a very nice feel for music, He was
much more attach'd to fly fishing & hunting, for frequently, when on his journies to
Scholars, of which He had as many as time could occupy, if per chance He heard the
hounds, '<u>Tally ho</u> 'tis the merry ton'd horn' says He 'have at ye,' go it my Pippins,
over hill & dale into the adjoining County, and with or without the brush of the fox,
wd brush into the first Public house, handy for brandy Pipes & Backie, till sometimes,
breakfast was next morng awaiting his return, besides the many pupils that had been
<u>hard</u> practising (during his absence) the <u>Battle of Prague</u> . . .
   Of all Cathedral stations in England I should prefer Winchester, not only on
account of its matchless locality, but for teaching which is, of the first class, with also
no mean appendage in the neighbourhood (Trout fishing <u>very good</u>).[2]

Unlike Leeds, which had been transformed by the Industrial Revolution,
Winchester had remained a small country town, dependent upon agriculture
and old-fashioned in both outlook and character. Indeed, while Leeds looked
to the future, Winchester remained wedded to the past, and both Wesley's
predecessor, William Chard (b. 1765), and the Dean, Thomas Garnier (b.
1776), epitomized this survival of the eighteenth century into the nineteenth.
During the latter's long term of office (1840–72) there was little evidence of

---

[1] Letter dated 19 Sept. [1858] to Henry Ford (*RSCM* Nicholson scrapbook, fo. 40).
[2] Letter dated 22 June 1849 (*Lcm* MS 3063).

the upheavals and reforms taking place elsewhere, but to Wesley, who had had his fill of energetic, reform-minded clergy at Leeds, this would have been no disadvantage, particularly as Winchester also offered the prospect of good fishing and, at Winchester College, the opportunity of a sound education for his sons.

Some knowledge of Wesley's reputation had clearly preceded him to Winchester, and in the reply to his application Dr David Williams set out the duties of the post so that he could see 'whether the Office is such as you could undertake with satisfaction to yourself, & with a determination to fulfil all it's [sic] requirements'. But this was not all. 'There are points on which, after the experience of past years, you will not be surprized to hear that they [the Dean and Chapter] would be glad to have proper security', he continued, noting that the organist should not only conduct himself 'in a spirit of respectful & courteous attention' to the wishes of the Dean and Chapter but, in a phrase which suggests an acquaintance with *A Few Words*, should also give proper attention to the 'laborious & sometimes unavoidably irksome . . . training & preparation of the Choristers'. Lastly, he suggested that 'it might possibly be considered prudent to guard against the unpleasant consequences of failure . . . by a written undertaking on your part to resign your Office if at any time the D. & C. should signify to you their opinion that such a step was advisable'.[3] A satisfactory reply presumably having been received, Wesley was now invited to appear before the Chapter on 21 August, when the 'statutes of the Cathedral affecting the organist, and account of the Duties and conduct required of him' were read to him before his admission:

Duties of the Organist.

1. That the Organist accompany on the Organ the daily morning and evening Services, except such occasional absences as the Dean and Chapter may judge reasonable.

2. That he be also the Master of the Choristers, giving them the benefit of his peronal instruction in music & singing and being responsible to the Dean and Chapter for their due progress and improvement.

3. That he preside twice a week at Rehearsals of the Choir.

4. That the above Duties be carried out in a spirit of respectful and courteous attention to the wishes of the Dean and Canons and with due regard to the authority of the Precentor, and with kind and conciliatory demeanour towards the subordinate Members of the Choir.

5. That steady and uniform attention shall be paid to the performance of the Choral Service, and to that careful training and preparation of the Choristers which is essential to their proper effect.

[3] Letter dated 30 July 1849 (*WC*).

Pl. 1. Interior of the Chapel Royal, St James's Palace, 1816, by R. B. Schnebbelie (reproduced by kind permission of the Guildhall Library, City of London).

Pl. 2. St James's Chapel, Hampstead Road, London, c.1825, by J. C. Deeley (reproduced by kind permission of the Guildhall Library, City of London).

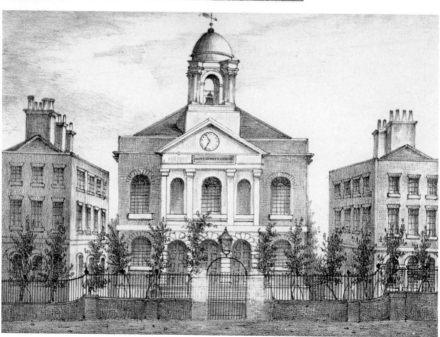

Pl. 3. St Giles' Church, Camberwell, *c.*1825, by G. F. Prosser (reproduced by kind permission of the Guildhall Library, City of London).

Pl. 4. St John's Church, Waterloo Road, London, *c.*1830, by T. H. Shepherd.

Pl. 5. Hampton, Middlesex, *c.*1840, by N. E. Green (reproduced by kind permission of the Guildhall Library, City of London).

Pl. 7. S. S. Wesley's fishing ticket for the Surrey Commercial Docks, 1830 (Add. MS 35019, fo. 185, reproduced by kind permission of the British Library, London).

Pl. 8. Olympic Theatre, Westminster, 1830, by T. H. Shepherd (reproduced by kind permission of the Guildhall Library, City of London).

Pl. 6. Playbill for *The Dilosk Gatherer* at the Olympic Theatre, 30 July 1832 (reproduced by kind permission of the Victoria & Albert Museum, London).

Pl. 9. Subscription Rooms and New London Inn, Exeter, *c.*1830, by W. H. Bartlett.

Pl. 10. Parish Church, Leeds, 1841, engraved by J. & E. Harwood.

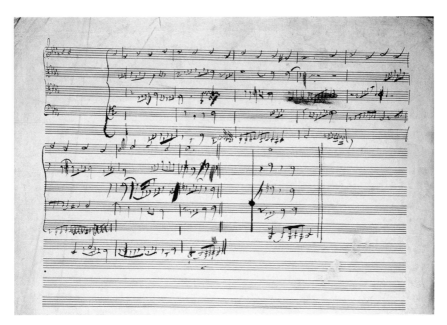

Pl. 11. S. S. Wesley, sketch of 'giving-out' for 'St Anne' (MS 4031, fo. 5ᵛ, reproduced by kind permission of the Royal College of Music, London).

Pl. 12. S. S. Wesley, opening of 'By the Word of the Lord' (MS 4030, fo. 81, reproduced by kind permission of the Royal College of Music, London).

Pl. 14. S. S. Wesley, photograph by H. N. King, Bath, c.1865.

Pl. 13. S. S. Wesley, anonymous portrait in oils, c.1835 (reproduced by kind permission of the Royal College of Music, London).

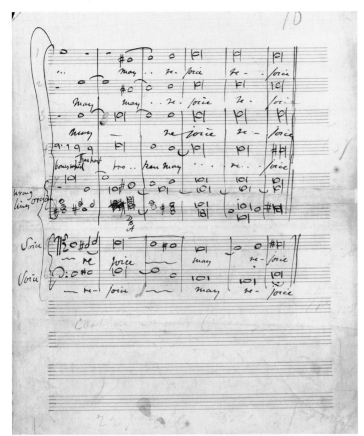

Pl. 15. S. S. Wesley, revised ending to 'Cast me not away', c.1868.

Pl. 16. S. S. Wesley, arrangement of the old ballad 'Light o' Love' (reproduced by kind permission of Robert Pascall).

<u>Salary &c</u>

1. That the Salary of the Organist shall be one hundred and fifty pounds per Annum.

2. That he be at liberty, if he judge it necessary to employ an assistant, to be approved by the Dean and Chapter: in which case the Dean and Chapter will allow twenty Pounds per Annum towards the remuneration of such Person.[4]

His attention had again been drawn to the fact that if he was 'negligent or indolent' in teaching the choristers he would be 'put out of his office, after being thrice warned',[5] and he was likewise reminded of the necessity of showing 'due obedience' to the Dean and canons.

With business matters still to be settled at Leeds it was not until Friday 5 October that Wesley was sworn in as 'Organist and Master of the Choristers'.[6] Immediately, however, he made a point of introducing his own compositions, and the music sung on his first Sunday included the Creed from the Service in E (to which Winchester had not subscribed) and the Magnificat and Nunc Dimittis from his recent Chant Service. 'The Wilderness' was heard on 2 December, 'Blessed be the God and Father' on 31 March 1850, 'Lord Jesu Christ'—the third setting in *Sacred Songs: The Collects for the First Three Sundays in Advent* (1848)—on 14 April 1850, and the Kyrie and Sanctus from the Service in E on 30 June 1850, with the Magnificat and Nunc Dimittis following a week later; the Te Deum and Jubilate, rarely sung at Leeds, seem never to have been performed.[7] In other respects the rather old-fashioned repertoire he inherited from Chard (with its emphasis on music by eighteenth-century composers) continued with little change. Perhaps the most revealing feature was Wesley's continuing refusal to include works by other contemporary composers, none of whom (as he was to write to Sir Frederick Ouseley in 1858) did he consider capable of writing 'a <u>single</u> high and fine specimen of the finest Church Music'.[8]

Despite Wesley's fame, his arrival in Winchester had aroused little public interest, and he seems to have made few attempts to venture beyond the confines of the cathedral. The relative proximity of London, however, prompted him to advertise in December 'his intention of giving Lessons on the Organ, in London',[9] while eight months later he had the satisfaction of being appointed the first professor of the organ at the Royal Academy of Music.[10]

---

[4] Winchester Cathedral Chapter Acts, 1824–50, pp. 430–1 (*WC*).   [5] Ibid. 430.   [6] Ibid. 432.

[7] Information on the repertoire is taken from *HA*, but as this printed only the Sunday service music it is possible that some works received earlier, unrecorded performances.

[8] Letter dated 3 Feb. 1858 (collection of the late Sir John Dykes Bower).

[9] *MT*, 3 (1849–50), 249.

[10] Royal Academy of Music, minutes of the committee of management (*Lam*). On 15 March 1850 it was minuted that Sir Henry Bishop had recommended Wesley's appointment as professor of organ, and on

Not until May 1851, however, was it minuted that an organ class had been arranged at seven shillings per hour,[11] and he did not receive his first payment—a cheque for £22 8s. 0d.—until January 1853.[12] Information on his pupils and subsequent years at the academy is sparse, but the fact that Charles Steggall was teaching the organ by 1862 implies that he had resigned before then.

As in the past a new post and surroundings proved invigorating, and it was with renewed enthusiasm that he embarked on his duties and indeed on life in general. Not only did his first few years in the town see the completion of two much-delayed projects—the publication of the *Anthems* (1853) and the building of the organ in St George's Hall, Liverpool (finished in 1855)—but they also saw him embark on a third: a large collection of psalm and hymn tunes, eventually published in 1872 under the title *The European Psalmist*. Even being again subject to the jurisdiction of a dean and chapter and, at least nominally, answerable to a precentor initially caused no problems, and rarely can he have written so warmly of a clergyman (who had moreover publicly endorsed his *Psalter*):[13]

Now . . . altho' the Precentor claimed, & had conceded to him an absolute power here, I found him desirous to consult me in every way. He urged me to always express my views to him & whatever I said was attended to.

His views & my own were similar on all subjects. Hence, I found his absolute power a very great advantage as he did all I wanted & I was saved all trouble as regards Chapter or Choir. I have had nothing to annoy me at all. I have not minded the Precentors appearing to be the head of the Music when in fact I was & ought to have been acknowledged as such, in strict justice.[14]

In such circumstances his thoughts again turned to composition, and during his first two years at the cathedral he produced three new anthems, 'Thou wilt keep him in perfect peace' (c.1850), 'O Lord, my God' (c.1850), and 'Ascribe unto the Lord' (1851). Whilst they all retain two of the Leeds features—the avoidance of solo voices and of independent material in the organ part—they none the less differ significantly from 'Cast me not away'. No less importantly, they also represent a further development of his concept of the form. 'O Lord, my God' is a short homophonic single-movement full anthem, wholly reliant on a harmonically inspired partsong-like idiom. 'Thou wilt

10 Aug. it was resolved that 'Mr. Samuel Sebastian Wesley, Mus. Doc., to be placed upon the List of the Professors of the Academy, for the Organ,—a letter to be forwarded to Dr. Wesley, communicating to him this appointment'.

[11] Ibid.

[12] Ibid., minutes of the meeting of 14 Jan. 1853; payment was for tuition up to 7 July 1852.

[13] *MT*, 5 (1852–4), 100.

[14] Letter dated 19 Sept. [1858] to Henry Ford (*RSCM* Nicholson scrapbook, fo. 40).

keep him', in contrast, is laid out in rondo form and combines both contrapuntal and homophonic textures within its single movement, while 'Ascribe unto the Lord' is an extended full-with-verse anthem, a form he had not touched for over a decade.

'Thou wilt keep him in perfect peace' is a short, full, five-part setting of verses from a typically wide range of sources (Isaiah 26, Psalms 119 and 129, Matthew 6, and 1 John 1) whose unashamedly modern idiom reveals it to be a true successor to 'Wash me throughly'. Like many of Wesley's works from the 1840s and 1850s it includes both contrapuntal and homophonic textures—ranging from the simple arioso-like writing of the first expisode ('The darkness is no darkness with thee') to the dissonant sequential counterpoint of the second ('For thine is the kingdom')—within a single movement. Dominating all, however, is the spacious eight-bar theme (first heard in 'The Face of the Lord') whose arching melody and beautifully balanced part-writing, weaving a contrapuntal pattern around an underlying harmonic framework, make it one of Wesley's most perfect achievements. Repeated almost note for note in the centre of the movement (to the words 'God is light, and in him is no darkness at all'), it returns at the end before the anthem closes with a brief four-bar codetta. Based on a prolonged plagal cadence, ornamented by some characteristically dissonant close position suspensions, it forms an expressive and peaceful conclusion. Only once does the dynamic level rise to forte, and the whole work possesses a chamber-music-like delicacy.

Although contemporary with 'Thou wilt keep him', 'O Lord, my God' could not be more different. A short homophonic and largely syllabic setting of Solomon's prayer at the dedication of the Temple (1 Kings 8), part of whose text Wesley had already set in the introit 'Hear thou in Heaven', it is his only anthem to include an alternative (high) ending for use when the treble part is sung by sopranos (whose voices he considered of 'vastly superior quality and power').[15]

The third new work, 'Ascribe unto the Lord', sets a selection of verses from Psalms 96 and 115 and was written 'expressly for a service in aid of Church missions'[16] (almost certainly the Church Missionary Society's annual service on 22 May 1851; its first performance on a Sunday was on 21 December 1851). It forms the first of a series of four similar works written at Winchester—the others being 'By the Word of the Lord' (1854), 'Praise the Lord, O my soul' (1861), and 'Give the King thy judgements' (1863)—which, although outwardly comparable with the large-scale anthems of the 1830s, differ in several important respects. Rarely scored for more than four voices, they never

---

[15] Wesley, *A Few Words*, 72.   [16] *T* (8 Sept. 1865), 5.

achieve the same sheer, massive power. It was as though the setbacks Wesley had encountered in Exeter and Leeds had so dented his confidence that he no longer had the determination to succeed, come what may. One can sense this in the absence of sustained development of thematic material and the increasing number of self-borrowings: three of the first four anthems written in Winchester include ideas already heard elsewhere.[17]

In its broad lineaments—a succession of six fairly short movements culminating in a more extended final chorus—'Ascribe unto the Lord' comes closer to the eighteenth-century pattern of full-with-verse anthems than had Wesley's earlier works. Yet within this layout he displayed considerable ingenuity, and few anthems have opened so impressively with a simple choral recitative for men's voices in unison. Dignified, measured declamation, and sustained diatonic harmony (with a generous use of dissonant suspensions) all combine to create an impression of absolute strength. No less striking is the juxtaposition of this passage with a short, richly harmonized phrase for full choir, 'Let the whole earth stand in awe of him', which returns in the dominant, pianissimo, to close the movement. Thereafter movements for verse ensemble and full choir alternate—a delicate quartet for high voices ('O worship the Lord in the beauty of holiness'), a vigorous fugato ('As for the Gods of the heathen') and choral recitative ('Their idols are silver and gold') in E minor, a brief verse for men's voices ('They that make them'), a powerfully confident chorale 'As for our God', and an extended finale, 'The Lord hath been mindful of us'. As in earlier anthems it is the movements for full choir that provide the structural pillars, while the whole work is again shaped by Wesley's instinctive response to the text—and demands an equally instinctive response from the performer(s). But when the conditions are right—particularly in the matter of the tempo, where any lingering over the sumptuous harmonies can destroy the flow of the musical argument—the cumulative effect of such an apparently disjointed and episodic work can be electrifying. In such circumstances the first six movements coalesce into a single structure culminating in the mighty chorale, to which the finale provides a satisfying conclusion. The relaxed mood, simple textures (though with some typically astringent suspended minor ninths in the second subject), diatonicism, and grateful melodic writing of this expansive sonata form movement epitomize the style of Wesley's later works (see Ex. 5.1), but one cannot but agree with a contemporary critic (Joseph Bennett?) when he commented on the lack of development:

[17] 'Thou will keep him' 'borrows' from 'The Face of the Lord' and the Magnificat in E, 'Ascribe unto the Lord' from the Magnificat in E, and 'I am thine, O save me' from 'Ascribe unto the Lord'.

Ex. 5.1. 'Ascribe unto the Lord', final movement

We must own to a certain disappointment on finding that Dr. Wesley had contented himself with a simple answer, 'in the octave,' for the first [subject], with a couple of simple answers, 'in the octave,' for the second ('Ye are the blessed of the Lord'), and, on the recurrence of the first, where the ear longs for at least a *fugato*, with merely giving out the theme unanswered.[18]

The three new works formed the final additions to the long-delayed *Anthems*, which, although announced as 'now being engraved'[19] in August 1849, had still not appeared. By November 1852, however, publication was at last in sight, prompting Wesley to write to the Dean and Chapter of Exeter to enquire whether they still wished to subscribe to the much-enlarged work at the higher price now being asked. Not having received a reply he wrote again in January, explaining why progress had been so slow, complaining of the conditions under which church musicians had to work, and provocatively reopening old scores:

It would have been quite agreeable to myself to have removed the name of the Chapter from my list of Subscribers, without any enquiry . . .

I dare say one or two Members of the Chapter would wish to discourage my work—judging from [the] line of conduct which I experienced from them when resident in Exeter—but I did not feel inclined to notice anything of this kind . . . [and] to avoid an altercation, as to the right of a claim of my Publishers for the Chapter's Subscription, I ventured on troubling yourself on the point, and I am still desirous to hear about it . . .

That the book has not appeared sooner arises from the difficulty I have felt in giving attention to what are called the higher departments of the Art, I mean composition for the Church Musician is not so much an Artist as a Mill-horse, I regret to have found . . . I have however persevered & am by no means displeased with the subject matter I am about to issue.[20]

A week later he wrote again:

I thought from the Dean's having given me what opposition he could (to speak plainly—and of what I can prove) since my leaving Exeter, that a difficulty might arise about this subscription & I really wished it (the difficulty) to be as little open to observation as might be . . .

I should perhaps submit to you that the Musician—unlike the Sculptor or Painter—reaps but little profit from his labors. The purchaser obtains his work at the mere cost of Paper & printing in most cases. If all my subscribers pay for their copies (which is very seldom done, I learn) a profit would accrue in this case, but it would not have done so had the enlarged work been issued at the original terms . . . Many of the

[18] *T* (8 Sept. 1865), 5.   [19] Wesley, *A Few Words*, endpaper.
[20] Letter dated 21 Jan. 1853 to the Chapter Clerk of Exeter Cathedral (*EXc* MS 7061/S. S. Wesley/7).

Subscribers, you will observe, have long since ceased to feel interested in earthly music.[21]

Finally, having received a positive reply, he gave brief details of the enlargement, explaining that he had added 'Four or perhaps five' anthems which would increase the size by some seventy pages and bring the total cost up to 2 guineas.[22] But even at this late stage the collection had apparently not received its final form, as the additional anthems ultimately numbered six. A letter dated 22 May about the insertion of an advertisement in *The Times*, however, listed all twelve; notwithstanding Wesley's belief that nothing could be achieved without some consideration on his part, no advertisement appeared:

If what I wanted can be managed I should like to repeat the advertisement at least 3 times, making four in all, or, if <u>you</u> thought it of use, I would have it in <u>for Six successive days</u> . . .

I have little doubt the Times office does nothing without due <u>remuneration</u> and I think you might make up your friend at Court a little parcel of your nice spices, mustard, &c. which might be useful to him. I would go to half a guinea or put what you thought best . . .

I would not lose an hour in the appearance of the advertisement as my work is now printing and the subscribers' list has to be printed with it.[23]

An advertisement in the June issue of *The Musical Times* described the volume as 'Now publishing',[24] and publication (by Addison & Hollier) had clearly taken place before 2 November, when Wesley wrote to Sir Frederick Ouseley enclosing a complimentary copy in addition to the four for which he had subscribed: 'I rather wish you to look at the things for some of them do not wholly displease me, for altho' I have unfortunately been long out of the Musical world, & might do better, <u>with notice</u>, I cannot quite forget my early predilections and use up so much paper to only the very meanest purpose, I trust.'[25]

Well might Wesley write that some of the works did not 'wholly displease' him, for by combining an up-to-date harmonic palette with a refusal to be bound by tradition, he had not only demonstrated that the established forms of verse, full-with-verse, and full anthem could be rejuvenated, but had also produced the finest collection of church music to be published during the nineteenth century. From the youthful vigour and dramatic excitement of

---

[21] Letter dated 29 Jan. 1853 (*EXc* MS 7061/S. S. Wesley/8).

[22] Letter dated 31 Jan. 1853 (*EXc* MS 7061/S. S. Wesley/11).

[23] Letter dated 22 May [1853] to an unknown correspondent (*Lbl* Add. MS 35019, fos. 177–8).

[24] *MT*, 5 (1853), 208. Wesley's draft is to be found in *Lbl* Add. MS 35019, fo. 123. The published order of the anthems takes no account of chronology and appears to be purely arbitrary.

[25] *Lcm* RSCM loan.

'The Wilderness' and 'Blessed be the God and Father', through the massive grandeur of 'O Lord, thou art my God' and 'Let us lift up our heart', and the pathos of 'Wash me throughly' and 'Cast me not away' to the resolute warmth of 'Ascribe unto the Lord', the anthems embrace—and complement musically—the whole gamut of religious emotion.[26] They also reflect a creative genius of no mean order, and it is this which so distinguishes them from the work of other composers: of his contemporaries only Walmisley had shown a similar—but less inspired—breadth of vision.[27] Wesley himself recognized their worth, writing many years later: 'My published 12 Anthems is my most important work . . . I think the style of my Anthems should have notice. I think they may claim notice for the manner in which the words are expressed & for the new use made of broad massive harmony combined with serious devotional effects.'[28]

Something of his stature as a church musician can be gauged from the fact that the list of subscribers (which ran to 341 entries) includes the organists or statutory bodies of all but nine of the thirty-four cathedral and collegiate churches in England and Wales. Even George Elvey subscribed, although neither John Goss (St Paul's) and James Turle (Westminster Abbey) nor their respective chapters did so—and the refusal of St Paul's led to Goss's own setting of 'The Wilderness' (see Chapter 2). The most unusual name, however, is 'LISTZ, Monsieur F.' [sic], presumably obtained on his visit to Exeter in 1840. Yet despite the scale and nature of Wesley's achievement, publication passed almost unnoticed. Henry Chorley in *The Athenaeum* eventually gave the collection a grudging welcome, praising the 'considerable science' it displayed, but criticizing 'needless, and perilous' modulations and complaining that in the inspired bass solo 'Thou, O Lord God' (from 'Let us lift up our heart') 'the resolution to produce and the power to write are unaccompanied by the requisite idea'.[29] Not until August 1855 did *The Musical World* even refer to the collection: erroneously ascribing it to a 'clergyman', it promised a review alongside one for *Fifteen Anthems* by George B. Allen (1822–1897). In the

---

[26] Of the anthems written since his arrival in Hereford only 'Trust ye in the Lord' and 'To my Request and Earnest Cry' are missing. He presumably deemed the former to be too 'secular', but what led him to omit the latter, which he had intended to publish in 1840? Did he no longer care for the verses by Tate and Brady it sets? It is intriguing, however, to find that the MS of the last movement contains corrections in the blue ink he favoured in the late 1860s and 1870s, a time when he returned to several works conceived—if not completed—many years before.

[27] It is worth noting that of Wesley's contemporaries who adopted a more modern style, both John Goss and Henry Smart completed the majority of their anthems in or after the mid-1850s, and the same is true of the more characteristic works of Edward Hopkins; the anthems of George Elvey (and several others) are written in an unashamedly conservative idiom.

[28] Biographical notes intended for G. J. Stevenson (author of *Memorials of the Wesley Family*) in a letter to his sister Eliza, dated 10 Dec. 1875 (*Lbl* Add. MS 35019, fos. 124–5).

[29] *Ath* (15 July 1854), 884.

event, after an introductory essay and two instalments devoted to Allen's anthems the review broke off without once mentioning Wesley's work! Already, however, the reviewer's remarks about the favoured positions occupied by cathedral organists would have brought a wry smile to Wesley's face; they also reveal a woeful ignorance of the reality of life as a cathedral organist:

it is worth remarking that they have temptations and facilities for writing not enjoyed by secular musicians. Not the least of these is the certainty that their compositions will—or at least may, if they so please—have public performance. With their choirs always at hand, they need never have to complain that a single page of their writing lies inglorious and neglected in their portfolios. Furthermore, the respectable, and in some cases handsome, amount of their stipend, and the great professional advantages conferred by their position, forbid all necessity for that struggle with the grosser ills of poverty which so many secular composers have to endure, and which, of all conceivable things, acts most depressingly on the imaginative faculties.[30]

Yet a dignified silence was perhaps better than the storm provoked by the first performances of two recent works—the 'sacred song' with orchestra, 'I have been young and now am old', and an orchestral version of 'The Wilderness'. The former, which had been written (or started) at Helmsley in 1848, is a setting of words from a variety of Old Testament sources—the Psalms, Lamentations, Micah, and Habakkuk—and captures so well the sense of resignation, even despair, found in the two contemporary anthems. Like them it is sturdily diatonic and, in the rhapsodic first movement in particular, shows Wesley at his best. Shaped as much by the text as by any formal considerations, it is dominated by the eloquent main theme, which emerges from a moment of sudden stillness at the end of the orchestral introduction. As rapid harmonic movement gives way to long-sustained harmonies its effect, in imitative dialogue with a solo cello, is magical (see Ex. 5.2). And this in a work condemned for an 'absolute want . . . of melody' after its first performance at the 1850 Gloucester Three Choirs Festival: 'Mr Phillips did his utmost for the voice-part, which is awkward and ungrateful . . . [but] its absolute want of phrase or melody, from first to last, is ill atoned for by strange harmonies and excessive modulation'.[31]

The short Larghetto second movement opens with a delicately scored passage for woodwind and solo cello, much of whose material is shared with the Jubilate of the Service in E. Suspended sevenths and ninths impart a characteristically Wesleyan flavour, and the reflective character of the music provides a moment of relief between the sombre opening and the joyful conclusion. The latter takes for its main subject the rondo theme from Samuel Wesley's

---

Ex. 5.2. 'I have been young and now am old'

Piano Sonata in D minor, but suffers from the rigid rhythm of the original, with its persistent pattern of a minim and two crotchets in each bar. Where the music is able to break free it truly comes to life, and the resulting mood of joyous optimism (rare in Wesley's mature works) is sustained by some florid— and rather old-fashioned—vocal and instrumental writing, driven forward by an almost obsessive use of the rhythmic figure [♪|♫♪♪♫] in the string parts. Although Wesley initially resisted Phillips's suggestions for some cuts, the presence of several in the last movement implies that he later relented. He was also very insistent that it should not be described as an anthem. '. . . pray do not call the Song <u>Anthem</u>', he told Phillips, 'It is not an Anthem. I shall be hauled over the coals if it gets called <u>Anthem</u>'.[32]

If Wesley (who conducted the first performance) had hoped for a better reception, worse was to follow when 'The Wilderness' was given at the Birmingham Festival two years later. Having been invited to submit several works for approval, he had chosen to orchestrate the anthem, which was first heard in its new guise on 8 September 1852. One of the intriguing aspects of the work's transformation is its demonstration of how implicitly orchestral his original conception had been. Only rarely did he need to expand or modify the texture for the new medium, although in the aria 'Say to them of a fearful heart' he successfully translated long-held organ chords into more idiomatic string textures (with pizzicato cellos and double basses taking the stalking bass-line). But perhaps the biggest gain was the opportunity an orchestral palette provided for adding colour and detail and for creating an impression of space. Take, for example, the use of the trombones to add weight to the Neapolitan harmony at the words 'will come and save you' (bar 91) or the ethereal sound of flutes, clarinets, and horns that accompanies 'but the redeemed shall walk there'. He also took full advantage of the forces available, scoring the work for double woodwind, four horns, four trumpets, three trombones, serpent, ophicleide, timpani, organ, and strings, but husbanding his resources carefully. At such moments as 'And a highway shall be there' and the end of 'And the ransomed of the Lord', however, he used the full panoply of instruments to produce a majestic blaze of sound.

On its first hearing 'The Wilderness' signally failed to impress. Opinion was almost uniformly negative and, with memories of the harsh reviews he had earlier received from Davison, Chorley, and Gruneisen, Wesley could have been forgiven for believing himself to be the victim of a concerted campaign. In comparison with the invective now heaped upon the anthem, Stevens's earlier comment, 'a clever thing, but not Cathedral Music', had been mild

[32] Letter dated 9 July [1849] (*ATu* John Wesley Collection, BV 2, no. 95).

indeed. Davison, writing in *The Times*, described the work (in language redo-
lent of that he employed against the 'New German School' of Schumann, Liszt
and Wagner) as 'not a very successful effort': 'Deficient in melody, confused
in harmony and partwriting, full of intricate combinations and 'modulation
run mad,' it by no means gives a true expression to the text which it is
intended to illustrate'.[33] *The Spectator* was equally unenthusiastic: Wesley displayed 'little genius as a composer', and the anthem was 'entirely conventional
and exhibits no inventive power'.[34] Chorley, who on its publication two years
later described it as 'brilliant and vigorous',[35] simply dismissed it as 'a weak,
tiresome, and pedantic exercise, not likely to be again heard of'.[36]

As on previous occasions Wesley rose to the bait, this time writing to both
The Hampshire Chronicle and *Aris's Birmingham Gazette*:

The writer of the Musical articles [in *The Times*] is Mr. Davison, and his acquirements
may be estimated by the fact of his having asserted that *Sebastian Bach knew nothing of
Counterpoint*. His criticism is as objectionable from its mongrel phraseology as from the
instrinsic worthlessness of the subject matter; and it may be likened to a glass of very
bad porter, the larger and better portion of which is the undrinkable froth . . . [and]
Sir, if I may be believed, I would assert that for some years past I have never read a
Musical article in that paper, or in a paper called 'The Musical World,' of which the
Critic of the *Times* is proprietor and editor, which did not fill me with annoyance.[37]

Spark rallied to his old master's cause and a lengthy and virulent correspondence ensued in *The Musical World*. The anthem's poor reception was, he
believed, the result of the performance, which 'was on the whole certainly
unsteady and unsatisfactory', owing in large measure to the 'want of spirit and
decision in the doctor's conducting of his own work, occasioned, I have no
doubt, by extreme nervousness'.[38] Gauntlett, too, was drawn into the debate,
opining that Wesley's failure at Birmingham 'might reasonably have been
expected' and publicly disowning his earlier enthusiasm for both composer
and anthem.[39] The last word, however, should rest with 'A Subscriber of
Sixteen Year's Standing', who advised 'the learned, but very thin-skinned
Doctor, to eschew Festivals and keep himself secure in the cloisters of
Winchester Cathedral, where perhaps the critics would not trouble him, and
where he may live and die *unheard*, and *almost unseen*'.[40]

---

[33] *T* (9 Sept. 1852), 6. See the leading article in *MW* in which he wrote of a 'class of critics, whose *beau
idéal* is concentrated in a certain modern school of composition which might be properly styled the Music-
run-mad School' (*MW*, 32 (1854), 252).

[34] *Sp*, 25 (1852), 870.   [35] *Ath* (15 July 1854), 884.   [36] *Ath* (11 Sept. 1852), 976.
[37] *ABG* (4 Oct. 1852), 1.   [38] *MW*, 30 (1852), 620.   [39] Ibid. 679.
[40] Ibid. 700.

Yet the musical profession and the general public embraced Wesley's music enthusiastically. Within a year of publication of the *Anthems* he was able to announce that 'From the reception this work has met with, a *Second Edition* will be issued at *Subscriber's* terms',[41] followed in December 1854 by complete sets of the individual voice parts and a year later by separate issues of 'The Wilderness', 'Blessed be the God and Father', and 'O Lord, my God'.[42] Ever suspicious of music publishers and their motives, he issued the parts himself and turned to the literary publishing firm of Arthur Hall, Virtue & Co. for the reissues of the individual anthems. Inevitably, however, his decision to retain the copyrights resulted in a considerable burden of business matters, not least the tiresome task of collecting subscriptions. Never one to shirk a conflict, he threatened one recalcitrant subscriber with legal action (as he described to R. A. Atkins):

I told Mrs Jones that if She did not pay by yesterday I would proceed against her. She has not paid & will hear very shortly from a Solicitor who will carry the matter through for me.

Such conduct is really past all excuse & people who so act deserve severe punishment. Had <u>all</u> behaved so I must have been in prison now.[43]

But it was not merely a desire to obtain his money which led Wesley to pursue his creditors with such determination: 'The truth is I cannot go on at all with my new book until the old accounts are in for I have such sad losses in various ways that money flies away like smoke. This Psalmody may perhaps be a profit to me.'[44]

The 'Psalmody' to which he referred was *The European Psalmist*, a collection of hymn and psalm tunes on which he had been working for several years and which would occupy him for close on another twenty. Its origin lay in 'a request made to the Editor . . . that he would form a Collection of Psalm and Hymn Tunes, including those most commonly used in public Worship'.[45] We do not know whence the request came, but once Wesley started investigating other collections of tunes he clearly became smitten. 'I have been looking through a vast number of Foreign works', he wrote to S. N. Barber in May 1854, 'from which I have extracted many charming specimens & I add a Collection of . . . our standard tunes newly harmonised & publish a Book of the kind at a no[t] very remote date'.[46]

[41] *MT*, 6 (1854), 124.

[42] The first ref. to the voice parts is in a letter of 23 Dec. 1854 to Zechariah Buck (*NWr* MS 11090/57).

[43] Letter dated 11 July [1854] (*Eu* MS Dk.7.384). Atkins had acted as an unofficial agent in north Wales and had been sent no fewer than 56 copies of the *Anthems* in Jan. 1854!

[44] Letter dated 24 June [1854] to R. A. Atkins (*Eu Eu* MS Dk.7.384).

[45] *The European Psalmist*, [3].

[46] Letter dated 2 May 1854 to S. N. Barber (Drew University Library, Madison, New Jersey).

Exactly what had attracted him is not clear, as hitherto he had shown little interest in psalmody, and one of the complaints levelled against him by Joshua Doane (see Chapter 1) had been that 'his psalmody was played in a style that would preclude the possibility of any children singing to it'.[47] Likewise his compositions in the genre had been few and far between—three early tunes (including 'Hereford') copied into his wife's manuscript album in 1834 and two tunes ('Hampton' and 'Harewood') contributed to Charles Hackett's *The National Psalmist* in 1839. He had, of course, made the organ arrangements in *A Selection of Psalm Tunes*, and also harmonized six tunes (in a more sober style) for John Hullah's *Psalter* (1843). But it was clearly not deep practical involvement that had led to his sudden—and wholehearted—plunge into the subject. That Gauntlett had begun to make a name for himself in this field, first in collaboration with his old acquaintance Kearns in *The Comprehensive Tune Book* (1st series 1846, 2nd series 1851), and second with the Revd J. J. Waite in *The Hallelujah* (part 1 1849) may, however, have spurred him on, as no doubt did the conviction that he could produce as good a book as anyone else. He also believed that there was money to be made: 'I think I might ultimately profit by it' he wrote to a potential subscriber, adding disingenuously '& having Sons to place out in business I am acting chiefly in their behalf'.[48] But whatever the reason, his conversion to the cause of hymnody took place at an apposite time, just as hymns were poised to oust metrical psalms from their pre-eminent position in Anglican parochial worship.

It was, indeed, as recently as 1820 that a book containing hymns had received even unofficial approval for use in the Church of England, as a direct result of a legal challenge to the introduction of the eighth edition of Thomas Cotterill's *Selection of Psalms and Hymns* in his church, St Paul's, Sheffield. After a detailed investigation the chancellor of the diocese of York concluded that there was no legal bar to the use of hymns before and after services, whereupon the Archbishop of York prepared a revised version of a *Selection of Psalms and Hymns* (as *A Selection of Psalms and Hymns for Public Worship*) and the way was opened for the flood of nineteenth-century hymn books.[49] Cotterill's contemporary Reginald Heber had been less fortunate: his manuscript collection was refused authorization, and was issued as *Hymns Written and Adapted to the Weekly Church Service of the Year* only in 1827, a year after his death. Its significance lies in the fact that it was (as W. H. Frere has written) the first

---

[47] See Lucas, 'Samuel Sebastian Wesley', 245.

[48] Letter dated 19 May 1854 (collection of the late Betty Matthews).

[49] The first edn. of Cotterill's book had been issued in 1810. For a more detailed account of the development of Anglican hymnody during the early 19th cent., see Temperley, *The Music of the English Parish Church*, 1. 208–9.

'definitely Church hymnal'[50] and thus represents the final stage in the gradual evolution from metrical psalter to 'modern church hymn-book'.

Neither Heber's book nor the other early hymnals provided any tunes, and for the next two decades the growth of Anglican hymnody was more literary than musical. Gradually, however, the published collections of tunes began to reflect the increasing popularity of hymns. Among the first was a musical edition of Cotterill's work (entitled *Christian Psalmody*), edited by Samuel Mather and issued in 1831.[51] Another early work was J. B. Sale's *Psalms and Hymns*, published six years later to accompany H. H. Milman's *A Selection of Psalms and Hymns* and containing 117 psalms and 46 hymns, while three other collections of tunes—Vincent Novello's *The Psalmist* (1839–44), Gauntlett's and Kearns's *The Comprehensive Tune Book* (1846), and Charles Steggall's *Church Psalmody* (1849)—all contain a considerable number of tunes in metres uncalled for by metrical psalmody. 'A book . . . containing tunes of a sound church-like character, and sufficient variety of these to suit our modern Hymn Books has long been wanting',[52] Steggall had observed, and it was in such an environment, and at a time when the idea of a standard—and comprehensive—collection of hymns had yet to become established, that *The European Psalmist* was conceived.

As an early draft of the contents reveals, it began life as a conservative collection very much along the lines of Steggall's or of W. H. Havergal's *Old Church Psalmody* (1847)—a selection of psalm tunes of the sixteenth, seventeenth, and eighteenth centuries with a substantial minority of German chorales (including about a dozen in J. S. Bach's arrangements, then little known in England).[53] Progress was initially swift, with Wesley able to write in 1854 that 'between 4 & 5 hundred pages have been engraved these three years & I now am hastening the completion of the work',[54] and a year later the first advertisements for subscribers appeared.[55] Within a short time, however, proceedings had inexplicably come to a halt; the lack of news and the appearance in 1859 of a prospectus for William Horsley's *Psalmody of the British Empire*[56]

[50] W. K. Lowther Clarke, *A Hundred Years of Hymns Ancient & Modern* (London: William Clowes & Sons, 1960), 17

[51] By the time of its publication both Cotterill and Mather had died, in Dec. 1823 and 1824 respectively.

[52] *Church Psalmody* (London: Addison and Holler, [1849]), viii.

[53] As the only information on the original contents is a list of tunes in one of Wesley's notebooks (*Lcm* MS 2141f), it is impossible to be certain of their precise identity, especially when a tune subsequently appears in more than one version.

[54] Letter dated 2 May 1854 to S. N. Barber (Drew University Library, Madison, New Jersey).

[55] See *MW*, 33 (1855), 191.

[56] Compiled not by the celebrated glee composer but by his namesake from Manchester. A full-page advertisement for the collection (which seems never to have been published) appeared in Jan. 1864 (*MT*, 11 (1864), 211).

prompted one disgruntled subscriber to complain to *The Musical World* that 'the matter had seemed to have been given up in disgust':[57] 'Now, Mr. Editor, will you be kind enough to enlighten us subscribers in the country whether Dr. Wesley intends to publish his work? or whether this work of Horsley's is the same, bought from Wesley?'

In a typically evasive reply Wesley admitted that the book had been delayed 'longer than was absolutely necessary', adding that he hoped 'soon to place what remains to be done in the hands of the engraver'[58] (on whom he had tried to put some of the blame). But there the matter rested until the invitation to prepare a musical edition of the Revd Charles Kemble's *A Selection of Psalms and Hymns*, issued with words only in 1864, drew him back.[59] During the intervening years the hymnological landscape had changed considerably, and while he was able to draw largely on *The European Psalmist*, he also found himself having to provide tunes for a number of hymns newly set in the recently published and phenomenally successful *Hymns Ancient and Modern* (1861). Under the musical editorship of William Henry Monk (1823–1889) this had brought to the fore a new generation of composers, among them Monk himself and the Revd J. B. Dykes, for whose work Wesley had little regard (as he explained in the preface to Kemble's book): 'From the frequent occurrence of unusual metres, much new composition seemed necessary, unless I accepted the alternative of inserting Tunes apparently quite devoid of merit.'[60]

In all Wesley wrote no fewer than thirty-three tunes for Kemble's book, including settings of 'Abide with me', 'Brightest and best of the sons of the morning', 'Holy, holy, holy' and 'Just as I am without one plea', attributing them all to *The European Psalmist*. With his interest now revived and further boosted by the reception it received—'We can . . . strongly recommend the musical portion of the work'[61] pronounced *The Musical Standard*—he returned to hymnody with a vengeance and over the next eight years proceeded to enlarge the collection. However, with publication not taking place until 1872, we must temporarily take our leave of it and return to that other unfinished business of the early 1850s—the organ for St George's Hall, Liverpool.

Not until December 1850, with the building nearing completion under the supervision of C. R. Cockerell, was this matter again taken up, but events now moved forward quickly. In February 1851 the organ-builders Frederick

---

[57] *MW*, 37 (1859), 392.   [58] Ibid. 484.

[59] It is worth noting that advertisements for *The European Psalmist* reappeared in *MT* at this time (1 April 1863) after a gap of almost nine years (see *MT*, 11 (1863), 38).

[60] Wesley, *A Selection of Psalms and Hymns . . . by the Rev. Charles Kemble*, [3].

[61] *MS*, 3 (1864–5), 178.

Davison and Henry Willis were invited to tender for the contract, while William Hill also submitted a specification and estimate.[62] The three estimates were considered in April, and in September ibid Wesley was requested to meet the committee and Walmisley—to whom they had recently turned for advice—at the Great Exhibition in London.[63] Instruments by all three builders were among the fourteen on display, but pride of place went to one of seventy stops by the young (and relatively unknown) Willis. Wesley already knew both Willis (whom he had first met at Novello's showroom in the early 1840s)[64] and his instrument, which he had played at the opening of the exhibition on 1 May,[65] and must also have been acquainted with Willis's favoured organist, W. T. Best, who had dedicated his Op. 1, *A Fantasia for the Organ*, to him. Many years later Willis recalled that September morning:

At six o'clock the Liverpool committee . . . in addition to S. S. Wesley and T. A. Walmisley, their musical advisers, duly appeared. Messrs. X. and Messrs. Z. [Hill and Gray & Davison] had specially engaged two eminent organists to play for them. I retained nobody. But I had previously said to [W. T.] Best, who had given several recitals on my organ at the Exhibition, 'It would not be half a bad plan if you would attend to-morrow morning at six o'clock, as you usually do for practice.' Best was there. After the two other organs had been tried, the Town Clerk . . . said: 'We have come to hear your organ, Mr. Willis. Are you going to play it yourself?' 'Do you expect an organ builder to play his own instrument?' I replied. 'If I had known that the other builders had specially engaged two organists to play their instruments, I might have done the same. Why don't you ask Wesley or Walmisley? They should be made to play, unless one is frightened of the other.' As Wesley and Walmisley declined to perform, I said to Mr. Shuttleworth, 'There's one of your own townsmen standing there (that was Best), ask him.' . . . The matter was arranged, and I said to Best: 'Now, in order that everything shall be quite fair and square, would you mind playing the same piece on all three organs?' 'What shall it be?' asked W. T. B. 'The overture to "Jessonda"' . . . While Best was playing the overture on the two other instruments, the specially engaged organists stood on each side of him to manipulate the stops, &c. . . . When Best came to play on my organ, he politely declined the similar kind help . . . as he was perfectly familiar with my pistons, stop arrangements, &c. It was a splendid performance, and I was told that the organ was quite a revelation to those Liverpudlians. The committee retired to deliberate in private, but only for twenty

[62] Minutes of the meeting of 11 Feb. 1851 (*LRO* MS 352 MIN/LAW 1/2, 59).

[63] See the minutes of the meeting of 8 Sept. 1851 (ibid. 101).

[64] See W. L. Sumner, *Father Henry Willis, Organ Builder, and his Successors* (London: Musical Opinion, [1955]), 13.

[65] The instrument by Gray & Davison was used to accompany the massed singing of the National Anthem and the 'Hallelujah' chorus (played as duets by John Goss and James Turle, and by George Elvey and Henry Wylde respectively), and those by Walker, Hill, Ducroquet, and Schultze demonstrated by Edward Hopkins, George Cooper, Felix Danjou, and Henry Smart respectively.

minutes, when Wesley came up to me and said: 'I am very happy to tell you that the delegates of the Corporation have decided to recommend you to build their organ.'[66]

Confirmation of the decision to employ Willis is to be found in the minutes of the Law Courts and St George's Hall Committee meeting of 24 September; his 'plan, Specification and Estimate' (merely a revised version of Wesley's original scheme of 1845 as modified by Novello, Turle, and Hopkins) were finally approved on 29 October.[67] The question of Wesley's further involvement had now to be addressed, and in January 1852 the committee tried to reach agreement over his 'professional services in superintending the construction of the Organ'.[68] With the committee arguing that he should not receive a 5 per cent fee as originally agreed because the order had been secured without his aid, and threatening to suspend his services, agreement proved hard to reach. Eventually they gave way, and on 11 September it was resolved that 'Dr. Wesley be paid the sum of Five per Cent on the Contract price of the Organ . . . and in addition such travelling expences as the Committee may from time to time sanction'.[69]

The organ was meanwhile making steady progress, but by summer 1854 it was clear that it would never be finished by the date fixed for the opening, 18 September—and this doubtless explains what *The Athenaeum* described as the 'curious indecision'[70] concerning the plans for the occasion. In the event it was celebrated by three oratorio performances under the direction of Sir Henry Bishop, with Wesley as solo organist: with only about one third of the stops usable it was reported that he 'wisely refrained from anything like *solo performance*'.[71] The committee were invited to hear the organ in February 1855,[72] and three months later, on 1 May, Best gave a further 'trial' performance. The formal opening took place on 29 and 30 May, when Wesley gave two recitals which revealed both the 'grand and forcible' and the 'lighter and more delicate and brilliant properties of the instrument'.[73] His programmes included both original works and transcriptions, among them the 'St Anne' and 'Giant' fugues by Bach, a two-movement fantasia of his own, and two overtures by Spohr, and each concluded with a number of solo and concerted vocal items.

Although it had been widely expected that Wesley would be appointed organist, the salary of £300 for being 'in attendance' (i.e. to perform) for two

---

[66] 'Henry Willis', *MT*, 39 (1898), 300.

[67] See the minutes of the meeting of 29 Oct. 1851 (*LRO* MS 352 MIN/LAW 1/2, 123)

[68] Minutes of the meeting of 27 Jan. 1852 (ibid. 144).

[69] Minutes of the meeting of 11 Sept. 1852 (ibid. 185). No explanation was given for the change of heart.

[70] *Ath* (9 Sept. 1854), 1094.   [71] *Ath* (23 Sept. 1854), 1149.

[72] Minutes of the meeting of 3 Feb. 1855 (*LRO* MS 352 MIN/LAW 1/2, 382).

[73] *The Liverpool Mail* (2 June 1855), 5.

hours on three mornings and one evening each week, as well as on any other occasions when his services were needed, was not sufficient to tempt him to remain a candidate, and on 20 July Best was appointed.[74] In withdrawing Wesley, who regularly played the same handful of pieces, undoubtedly made the right decision (as Henry Heathcote Statham observed):

In thinking that Wesley represented a higher plane of musical genius than Best we were perfectly right; what would have been the success of his appointment as organist to St. George's Hall is another question. There would certainly have been no sort of concession to popular taste; the programmes would probably have consisted mainly of organ music of the classical school (though . . . at the opening of the organ he did relax so far as to play 'Adelaïda' as an organ piece). But . . . his range of choice, even within the limits of classical music, would have been much more limited than Best's, and his powers of execution were unquestionably far inferior . . . I do not think he could have kept the performances going for long with any such varied interest as would have kept the audiences together; and I am inclined to think that he was much more in his right sphere as a cathedral organist.[75]

Willis, meanwhile, had been making final adjustments, and it was only on 17 October that Wesley certified that the instrument had been completed to his satisfaction;[76] Best gave his first recital three days later. For the next five years, however, the unsatisfactory matter of Wesley's commission and expenses hovered in the background, as he maintained that he was owed more for his travelling and attendance costs and stubbornly refused to accept any payment at all. In September 1856 the committee informed him that they were ready to settle the account 'whenever he applies for it',[77] but not until January 1860 did he finally consent to receive the sum in question (£392 6s. od.), a figure well in excess of two years' salary at Winchester!

Concurrently with his work at Liverpool Willis had been engaged on a further major scheme in conjunction with Wesley—a new instrument, based on the Great Exhibition organ, for Winchester Cathedral.[78] On his appointment Wesley had found himself with an old-fashioned instrument, completed by John Avery in 1799. Piecemeal additions had subsequently been made, but it retained its eighteenth-century character and was far removed from his conception of what a modern organ should be. It would be surprising if he had

---

[74] Minutes of the meeting of 20 July 1855 (*LRO* MS 352 MIN/LAW 1/2, 422).

[75] *The Organ and its Position in Musical Art: A Book for Musicians and Amateurs* (London: Chapman and Hall, 1909), 218.

[76] Minutes of the meeting of 17 Oct. 1855 (*LRO* MS 352 MIN/LAW 1/2, 437).

[77] Minutes of the meeting of 25 Sept. 1856 (*LRO* MS 352 MIN/LAW 1/3, 48).

[78] Willis's simultaneous work on both instruments has hitherto passed without comment. There can be no doubt, however, that by embarking on the two largest organs he had yet built he seriously overstretched his business, with the result that neither was finished on time.

not soon started agitating for its improvement or replacement, but nothing seems to have happened until 1853, when we find him thanking Sir Frederick Ouseley for 'writing about our Organ' and complaining about the opposition he had encountered from Canon Pretyman.[79] Already, however, money had been promised, and on 26 November the Chapter resolved to allow £500 towards 'the improvement of the present Organ or . . . the purchase of a new Organ'.[80] With 'the defects of the present Organ rendering it inexpedient . . . to make any further outlay of Money upon it', the latter option was immediately chosen,[81] and in December it was announced that a new organ would be installed at a cost of £2500,[82] with a public subscription being set up to help defray the cost.

Early in the new year the Dean revealed that he had 'concluded arrangements with Mr. Willis for the purchase and erection of the noble Instrument which attracted so much attention at the Great Exhibition of 1851',[83] although limitations of space necessitated a reduction in the number of stops from seventy to forty-eight, to be distributed over four manuals rather than three; curiously Wesley was happy to accept C-compass manuals and pedals (as he had done at Camberwell), notwithstanding his insistence on the G compass at Liverpool. Dismantling of the old organ began on 1 March.

With Willis and his men fully committed at Liverpool it seems amazing that it was seriously considered that the new organ could be finished in a matter of weeks. Yet preliminary notices referred to its being ready by the 'first week in Easter'[84] (16 April), and it must have been with some embarrassment that the opening was first deferred to 6 May and then postponed until 3 June. But even now the Pedal and Choir organs and the Great Organ reed stops were not ready, and (as *The Hampshire Advertiser* reported) 'the ceremony realised the old joke of the performance of the play of Hamlet with the part of Hamlet omitted . . . the grand organ . . . *was not half finished!*'[85] For the occasion members of the choirs of Chichester, Durham, Ely, St Paul's, and Salisbury cathedrals and Westminster Abbey had been invited to join their Winchester colleagues: among them was a thirteen-year-old chorister from St Paul's, John Stainer, who many years later recalled the performance of 'Ascribe unto the Lord':

At the rehearsal in the Cathedral, Wesley could not get the combined choirs . . . to take the movement 'As for the Gods of the heathen' rapidly enough. So he came

---

[79] Letter dated 2 Nov. 1853 (*Lcm* RSCM loan).

[80] Winchester Cathedral Chapter Acts, 1850–76, 52 (*WC*).

[81] Ibid. Ouseley was no doubt one of the 'professional . . . judges' whose opinions had been sought.

[82] See *HC* (3 Dec. 1853), 8. By the end of Jan. sufficient subscriptions had been obtained for it to be announced that the sum still required was 'upwards of £350', but presumably less than £400: see *HC* (28 Jan. 1854), 4.

[83] *HC* (21 Jan. 1854), 4.   [84] *HA* (25 Feb. 1854), 6.   [85] *HA* (10 June 1854), 6.

down into the body of the church, leaving one one of his assistants to play . . . and beat time with a stick on the side of a choirbook, a device which left no doubt as to the position of the down-beats! We all thought it a great scramble at the pace he took it, but of course he was right, and I have always kept it up to his pace.[86]

The other works sung were the Magnificat and Nunc Dimittis from Samuel Wesley's Service in F, Purcell's 'O give thanks unto the Lord', 'The Wilderness', and a new large-scale anthem, 'By the Word of the Lord'. Although *The Hampshire Advertiser* recorded that the last was 'very effectively sung', it was never heard again, apparently because Wesley was dissatisfied with it.[87] In consequence he never bothered to finish what was clearly intended to be an expansive obbligato organ part, laid out on three staves throughout and his first example of such writing for well over a decade (see Pl. 12). Given that long sections of the vocal parts are thinly scored and marked 'florid organ', this is a major loss, and all that survives are some brief sketches for triplet figuration similar to that later used in 'Give the King thy judgements'. What remains is a mixed work, ranging from the bold diatonic opening to the bizarre interpolation in the third movement of the Gavotte from his father's *Twelve Short Pieces* for organ. The third movement, which is a clear forerunner of 'Thus shall the man be blessed' in 'Give the King thy judgements', is based on a lyrical sequential theme built around a series of suspensions over a slowly rising bass-line; its climax obviously made a deep impression on the youthful Stainer, who later recalled it in *The Crucifixion* (see Ex. 5.3). A second 'opening' of the completed organ was arranged for 28 November when, in the course of a two-hour recital, Wesley gave a varied programme of works by Bach, Beethoven, Handel, Mendelssohn, Mozart, Spohr, and himself.

With the instruments at Winchester and Liverpool Willis had firmly staked his claim to be considered among the leading British organ-builders, but the combination of his youthful self-confidence and strong character had done little to endear him to certains sections of the musical press. With Wesley also *persona non grata* in some quarters the two men found themselves the victims of several barbed attacks. Henry Smart was particularly forthright:

Dr. Wesley and Mr. Willis . . . *did* furnish the description of their organ which we have quoted; and, by so doing, they certainly are entitled to the credit of having published the most unintelligible, unmechanical, and ungrammatical account of a work of

---

[86] Letter dated 12 April 1900 to F. G. Edwards (Novello & Co. private library).

[87] Information from a letter dated 30 April 1900 from the Revd W. R. W. Stephens (Dean of Winchester) to F. G. Edwards: 'I have asked Dr. Arnold . . . about the anthem 'By the word of the Lord'. He says that Dr. Garrett, who was at the opening of the Organ in 1854, told him that Wesley was not satisfied with the effect of the anthem and did not send it to be printed' (Novello & Co. private library).

Ex. 5.3. *a* 'By the word of the Lord'; *b* John Stainer, *The Crucifixion*, 'Fling wide the gates'

art, we have ever had the evil fortune to peruse . . . how Dr. Wesley, an artist and man of education, could lend his name to this insufferable hodge-podge of vulgar puff and bad English, surpasses our comprehension . . .[88]

Tiresome though it might be, such pernickety criticism was only a minor irritation. Of rather more substance was Smart's denunciation of the instrument's perceived deficiencies, and with this one enters a minefield of musical politics and conflicting ideas of organ design. As we saw in Chapter 4 (and as Nicholas Thistlethwaite has lucidly described),[89] opinion was sharply divided betwen the supporters of the 'Insular Movement' and those of the 'German system'. Wesley belonged in the former camp and so, at this stage of his career, did Willis. The specification thus contains many of the hallmarks of 'Insular' thinking, with duplication of registers, large pipe scales, and little innovation in the choice of stops—though the provision of an orchestrally conceived Solo division points towards later nineteenth-century practice. Wesley's insistence on both the G compass for the manuals (though with a C-compass pedalboard) and unequal temperament was particularly backward-looking, and for some years he was involved in an intermittent but acrimonious public debate on the merits—or failings—of the Liverpool instrument. Yet although with hindsight one can see that many of his ideas were indeed misguided, this was by no means so apparent at the time. Only a small number of native organists or organ-builders had had direct experience of continental instruments, and when he drew up the specification for St George's Hall in the mid-1840s there were still only a handful of instruments on the 'German system' in the country, many designed by his arch-enemy Gauntlett. Thus J. C. Bishop, one of the more conservative builders, had nothing but praise for Wesley's scheme, believing that 'it would be the most magnificient Instrument that has hitherto been attempted in this Country'.[90] But to a supporter of the 'German system' like Smart the design was nothing but reprehensible:

the Liverpool instrument is merely a *large* organ as to number of pipes. In all its manuals the same features are discoverable. Magnitude is attained, and effect . . . sought, by simple re-duplications of old and known qualities. There is no evidence of able design in its scheme, no bold attempt at original invention, no frank and resolute adoption of any of the real novelties which the best men in England, France, and Germany, have in late years turned to such capital account.[91]

---

[88] *MW*, 32 (1854), 566. [89] See *The Making of the Victorian Organ*.

[90] Letter dated 18 Sept. 1847, quoted in the minutes of the meeting of the Liverpool Law Courts and St George's Hall Committee of 28 Sept. 1847 (*LRO* MS 352 MIN/LAW 1/1, 410).

[91] *MW*, 32 (1854), 567. Given his strong links with the firm of Gray & Davison (from whose grasp the St George's Hall contract had twice slipped), Smart had more than a purely professional interest in the subject.

When the instrument was finally completed *The Musical World* gave it a grudging welcome, claiming with evident self-satisfaction that its earlier gloomy predictions had been 'confirmed almost to the letter'.[92] Chorley, writing in *The Athenaeum*, was initially of like mind, but greater familiarity led him to revise his opinion, and by January 1857 he was praising the 'pompous, sweet, and delicate' quality of the fundamental and solo stops.[93] But perhaps the last word should lie with Best, who, even before it was finished, wrote that 'In my opinion, as well as that of some others . . . it must be considered a masterpiece, both musically and mechanically'.[94]

It was Wesley's retention of the G compass and unequal temperament, however, that was most fiercely seized upon as an example of outdated and irrational thinking and that returned to haunt him when he hoped to be involved in a third project—an organ for the new Town Hall in Leeds. Since Wesley had left the town Spark had become the leading authority there on organ matters, and he it was, in collaboration with Smart, who had been pressing for the installation of an instrument in the new hall. Wesley, learning of their involvement (and in a manner worthy of Gauntlett), immediately wrote to William Bower in the hope of exerting some influence:

Can it be that Leeds is going to allow Henry Smart to plan—in connection with your neighbour Mr. Spark—the great Organ for the Hall.

I see that you have a Relative on the Council, your Father perhaps?

I wish you would tell me what you know. There was some idea of leaving the Organ Business to myself. I hear that Spark has been working to prevent my being consulted.

This is not grateful of him as I have been of much use to him.[95]

Coincidentally, a certain W. Lyndon Smith had written to *The Leeds Mercury* about the instrument in St George's Hall. He had found much to praise—'The grandeur of the diapasons, never degenerating into coarseness, the sonorous reeds, and silvery brilliancy of the mixtures produce an *ensemble* perhaps

---

[92] *MW*, 33 (1855), 361. A degree of defensiveness can be seen in the journal's subsequent coverage of the new instrument, not least in its decision not to publish a 'long communication' from George Lake 'in which he bears some, though not a very extraordinary, testimony to the merits of the organ'. (*MW*, 33 (1855), 597–8). Lake had apparently been motivated by a belief that 'we [i.e. *MW*] have done the Liverpool organ wrong by "adverse criticism,"' while the decision to exclude his letter was made on the grounds that editorial policy was not to print 'anything in the shape of professional criticism on subjects which we personally undertake to discuss'. Claiming that it had 'not the slightest wish to check controversy about this or any matter', it promised a full and impartial account in due course—which never materialized. With his assumption of the editor's chair at the newly founded *The Musical Gazette* (1856) Lake was able to return to the subject and for three weeks (14 Feb.–7 March 1857) included both editorial comment and correspondence on the instrument, its compass, and its tuning (including the letter from W. Lyndon Smith quoted below and Wesley's response to it).

[93] *Ath* (24 Jan. 1857), 121.   [94] Letter dated 9 Aug. 1855, *MW*, 32 (1855), 522.

[95] Letter dated 9 Nov. 1856 (collection of the late Sir John Dykes Bower).

unequalled'⁹⁶—but his criticisms of the 'imperfect and unsuitable specification' and the 'disagreeable effect . . . of the system of "unequal temperament"'
and his observation that 'the employment of professional men in the construction of organs is not only perfectly unnecessary but undesirable'⁹⁷ hit a
raw nerve. Coming on top of what Wesley considered as Spark's interference,
it was all too much, and he unburdened himself in a long letter to Bower:

It will be a pity that Mr. Spark's activity in the Organ subject should interfere with the
engagement of a suitable person to advise the authorities . . . No costly or even cheap
musical Instrument can be safely purchased without sound professional advice. The
Organ builders try to dispense with our services, of course. I have no doubt that in a
short time one single suggestion of mine at Liverpool—that of blowing the Organ by
steam—which I was the first to introduce—will save the amount of my commission.
That great work, for it is a great work . . . must, of course, open one's views, extensively, for the future, and wonders might be done at Leeds for 5000. Smith's letter in
the Mercury is most injust to me. I did not suggest the few things which he objects to
. . . The equal temperament both Willis and I are of opinion will not do for Organs.
This was ascertained by the last generation but one. At Liverpool, to test the matter,
once more, we had two open Diapasons tuned in two ways as an experiment one on
the usual mode, the other by equal temperament. The latter was vastly inferior, indeed
destructive, as I have always considered it to be, as regards an Organ. We must be content to have some good keys and others bad and avoid the bad in writing and playing
as much as possible. The Liverpool Organ is to be used in a variety of ways and I did
not choose to plan a mere imitation of a Military Band, for that is what they now try
to make an Organ.⁹⁸

I will not sacrifice the great features of the Instrument. A Organ should be an
Organ. By all means have the finest Solo stops possible but don't sacrifice your Organ
to them. At L'pool I was pretty interfered with through the jealousy and opposition
of Musicians and people who wanted to ruin the Organ for the sake of the
Architecture. Willis had the Plan to study and wrote saying it would be the finest
Organ in the world which I have no doubt it really is. I laboured hard to get that
Organ for England and think I deserve well of the musical world for my efforts but
never having taken one solitary step to bring the nature of my services under public
notice nothing seems to be known on the subject and as yet I have seen no justice
done by the Press.⁹⁹

Somewhat disingenuously Wesley later claimed to have been 'unable to pay
any attention'¹⁰⁰ to Smith's letter, and not until February 1857 did he respond
with his first public comments on his involvement at St George's Hall.

⁹⁶ Letter dated 13 Nov. 1856, *LM* (18 Nov. 1856), 4.   ⁹⁷ Ibid.
⁹⁸ Two British organ-builders had recently labelled the organ by Cavaillé-Coll in the church of the
Madeleine, Paris, 'a big brass band and nothing more' (see *MW*, 31 (1853), 595).
⁹⁹ Letter dated 26 Nov. [1856] (collection of the late Sir John Dykes Bower).
¹⁰⁰ Letter dated 4 Feb. 1857 to F. G. S., *LI* (7 Feb. 1857), 8.

Disavowing any 'unworthy motives' on the part of musicians when offering professional advice, he proceeded to defend his insistence on the G compass and unequal temperament and in so doing offered a valuable insight into his playing technique and conception of the instrument.

For close on thirty years Wesley had been among the foremost pedal players in the country, yet at the same time he had retained one of the characteristic traits of earlier generations—the practice of playing the bass-line in octaves with the left hand (see, for example, the last movement of 'To my Request and Earnest Cry'). Likewise, despite the success of Best's early recitals, he refused to accept that the primary function of an organ was other than as an accompanying instrument. The combination of these two strongly held beliefs provided the foundation for his devotion to the G compass:

I adhere to my opinion that it is absolutely necessary . . . to prepare our large Concert Hall Organ for vocal performances, and I feel sure that the next century will show such performances to have been the most frequent and the most remunerative. I do not refer to any ill-advised and misconducted efforts, but to those sublime ones to which a superlatively grand instrument and vast chorus might conduce when wielded by a master who shall contruct new music expressly for their development . . .[101]

I considered that Liverpool might desire to have a Handel or Mozart at their organ, who should compose oratorios, and assemble the vast choral force of Lancashire for their performance, and I wished the instrument to be efficient for the accompaniment of every vocal effort which could possibly occur in that building: for that of a single voice, a quartet, a semi-chorus, or chorus: for a body of vocalists filling the hall, or for maintaining its dignity as an organ when joined both with these and the largest orchestral force ever to be there assembled.[102]

From this it followed that the G compass, whose lower range most nearly matched that of the bass voice, would be the most suitable:

For this species of requirement I consider . . . that our established, extended, English compass, GG, is indispensable. FF is better. I declare that, for the accompaniment of voices, the limited CC manual is so inefficient that almost every passage the player attempts in octaves with his left hand has to be transposed; to be constantly buzzing with pedal scales would be intolerable. Even in the music of public worship at a cathedral this deficiency is serious, and how much more important are the five lower semitones where an organist has to play through an oratorio, publicly, on his instrument . . .[103]

I ask, are we to play no octaves in the bass at all? The CC compass almost prevents our so doing. We have been previously told we were to play no full chords, in support of which prohibition Bach is again erroneously quoted. Bach left his counter

---

[101] Letter to the editor, *LI* (7 March 1857), 7.   [102] Letter dated 4 Feb. 1857, *LI* (7 Febr. 1857), 8.
[103] Ibid.

point at times <u>thin</u>, as a means of producing that essential feature in good composition, <u>contrast</u>.[104]

Yet despite possessing a certain logic, Wesley's point of view was very much a minority one, as the critic of *The Manchester Courier* observed:

Had I been Dr. Wesley I would not have let the secret escape that I wanted an extended compass in order to play the bass with the left hand in octaves, a style of organ playing in vogue with pianoforte players, and once necessary, perhaps, through the deficiency of the pedal department in English organs, but one which is not now, and on the continent never was, adopted by first-class performers.[105]

When one turns to Wesley's arguments in favour of unequal temperament, however, any trace of logic flies to the winds. From 'The Wilderness' onwards his church and organ music had been characterized by a freedom of modulation and a fondness for both chromatic harmony and sudden plunges into remote keys. All of these demanded the equality of key inherent to equal temperament, yet ignoring the evidence of his eyes and ears he now attempted to argue that some keys should be 'tuned as nearly perfect as possible . . . even at the expense of rendering other keys so out of tune as to require peculiar treatment from the performer'.[106] 'I think Dr. Wesley's accuracy of ear may not only be doubted but denied, after writing such passages as constantly occur in his service and anthems', observed one commentator, 'for the sake of rendering his own compositions endurable, one would have supposed the Doctor would have been the first to advocate the equal temperament'.[107]

There remains a suspicion, however, that certain parties felt that something could be gained from prolonging the controversy. Although the decision by George Lake, editor of the newly established *The Musical Gazette*, to revive it in 1857 may merely have been prompted by the refusal of *The Musical World* to publish his letter (see n. 102), it none the less suggests an awareness of the value, in terms of publicity and circulation, of taking such a step. Likewise, *The Musical Standard* would surely have known what a hornets' nest it would stir up when, some half dozen years later, it reprinted a letter from Wesley to *Trewman's Exeter Flying Post* on the vexed subject of organ tuning. His dogmatic response, 'Equal temperament will not do for organs',[108] inevitably

---

[104] *LI* (7 March 1857), 7.
[105] Letter dated 18 Feb. 1857 to the editor of *LI*, printed in *MG*, 2 (1857), 114. This letter was apparently never published in *LI*, which on 21 Feb. announced that it would not print unsigned letters on 'The Organ Question'. Doubt is cast on Wesley's claim that it was his own 'constant practice to use the lowest keys of an organ with my fingers' by a statement from the organ-builder who maintained the instrument in Leeds Parish Church that 'the dust on the half-dozen lowest keys on the GG manuals remained undisturbed for months, clearly proving that those parts of the keyboards were almost altogether in disuse as regards the fingers' (quoted by W. Lyndon Smith in a letter to *LI*: see *MG*, 2 (1857), 89).
[106] *LI* (7 March 1857), 7.   [107] *MG*, 2 (1857), 114.

embroiled him in a further public debate during which he was forced to admit that the evidence of his own compositions flew in the face of his arguments:

'A Constant Reader' points to *my* having written church music in the key of E major. I really do not see how such trifles affect the matter. I confess that the key is a very bad one, and that the way in which I have written is very bad for the key. My thoughts, I recollect, were influenced by the voice parts. The treble had to go very high and the bass very low, and so I disregarded the organ tuning; but the course taken is open to great objection, I allow.[109]

Among those drawn into the discussion was Edward Hopkins, organist of the Temple Church and co-author (with E. F. Rimbault) of *The Organ, its History and Construction* (1855). Wesley, who had objected both to Hopkins's arguments in favour of equal temperament and his assertion that J. S. Bach had been one of its early advocates, now found his case politely but effectively demolished:

The fact is,—and this is the point that Dr. Wesley seems wholly to have failed to perceive,—the advocates of equal temperament have grasped the question *as a whole*. By making a certain concession, the use of twenty-four practicable scales could be obtained in place of nine only. They willingly incurred the consequence of that concession, and found themselves, on the whole, much better off. The unequal temperament advocates 'went in' for the nine scales, that were found insufficient 186 years ago, to the neglect of the remaining fifteen; and having done so, have *not* kept to them. Four of the Doctor's most admirable compositions—the Service, in E major; the 'Wilderness' Anthem, also in E major; 'Blessed be the God and Father,' in E flat; and the Fugue in C sharp minor,—are written in such scales that their 'initial keys' even are beyond the *boundaries* of the good keys as set by unequal temperament, and of course many of their attendant keys are so also. It has not been proved then, that 'equal temperament will *not* do for organs,' still less has it been shown that unequal *will*.[110]

And with this the matter was finally laid to rest. It had brought little credit to Wesley, showing him to be impervious to rational argument and obstinately attached to an old-fashioned and, in the context of his own works, hopelessly inadequate system of tuning. Indeed, he emerges as a rather sad figure, increasingly out of sympathy with the world in which he found himself and, as he confided to Sarah Emett, isolated from his fellow musicians:

This [Winchester] is a very quiet place. Not <u>one</u> person have I had to speak to on

---

[108] *MS*, 1 (1862–3), 243. That this debate should also have taken place in vol. 1 of a new journal is perhaps not coincidental.

[109] Ibid. 338.   [110] *MS*, 2 (1863–4), 223.

Musical matters for many many years . . . All of the very few friends of my youth are gone. The last, I fear, died lately, Wm. Knyvett. He resided at Ryde & [I] used to see him and correspond, but he left us only a month or two ago. I am now quite unlike a Musician. I have lost all desire to do anything except as to <u>writing</u> which I may cultivate yet a little perhaps.[111]

Further distraction from musical matters had been caused by preparations for moving house from Kingsgate Street to 5 The Close.[112] 'Planting fruit trees, laying on gas and various things of the sort absorb my spare time', he wrote in November 1856,[113] and it must have been with a profound sense of relief that he was able to report some four months later that 'I am now in . . . & excepting <u>Carpets</u> to a few rooms am nearly <u>settled</u>. Here I shall remain, I suppose, & I feel thankful to be so quietly & respectably stationed'.[114] The sense of weary resignation in that last sentence conveys only too well Wesley's despondent state of mind, and one need not look far to discover some of the reasons for his discontent. Of his recent endeavours only two—the publication of the *Anthems* and the completion of the Liverpool organ—had been more than qualified successes, while others—notably the fiasco of 'The Wilderness' at Birmingham—had been little short of disasters. Indeed, at a time when his reputation should have been secure he had still not achieved a major triumph as a composer. Likewise, the recent press attacks had demonstrated how his former allies among the critical fraternity had either, like Gauntlett, deserted him or chosen to remain silent. One shred of comfort was provided by Herbert Oakeley's warm notice of the *Anthems* in *The Guardian* in 1859: 'there exists in this country, and in these times, talent of the highest order', he observed, 'let us appreciate the genius of [its author] . . . while he is yet with us!'.[115] For someone of Wesley's sensibility this lack of recognition was deeply discouraging, and it is surely no coincidence that during the later 1850s even the desire to compose seems to have deserted him: during the six years following the publication of the morning canticles from the Chant Service in F (1855) not only did work on *The European Psalmist* come to a halt, but he also completed only four works—an arrangement of the Hundredth Psalm ('Old 100th') written for performance by the Winchester choir at the laying of the foundation stone of the Royal Victoria (military) Hospital at Netley by the Queen (19 May 1856), the brief anthem 'I am thine, O save me', contributed to the first number of the newly established *The Musical*

[111] Letter dated 11 March 1857 (*Lbl* Add. MS 35019, fo. 153).

[112] The Dean and Chapter had granted him the lease at the Chapter meeting of 29 Sept. 1856, setting the rent at £52 10s. 0d. per annum: see Winchester Cathedral Chapter Acts, 1850–76, 104 (*WC*).

[113] Letter dated 26 Nov. [1856] to William Bower (collection of the late Sir John Dykes Bower).

[114] Letter dated 11 March 1857 to Sarah Emett (*Lbl* Add. MS 35019, fo. 152).

[115] 'Cathedral Music', *The Guardian* (12 Oct. 1859), 873.

Remembrancer (1857), the accompaniment to Edward Stephen's oratorio *Ystorm Tiberias* (The Storm of Tiberias, 1857), and an isolated setting of the Deus Misereatur (1858). Even a request from Sir Frederick Ouseley for a contribution to *A Collection of Anthems for Certain Seasons and Festivals* elicited only a frosty response:

I regret to have to submit to you that I feel opposed to taking any part in your projected work. I should be always inclined to keep myself separate from the persons who will, no doubt, act in this matter.

I fear the publication will do some harm. Your specimens ought all to be <u>great</u>. If they were so their authors, of course, would remain unpaid. Unpaid, that is, if works of the kind are to be viewed in the same light as other works of Art. Where you are to get but a <u>single</u> high and fine specimen of the first Church Music I don't know . . .

It vexes me to resist your bidding thus. I am looking to a time when the subject of Church composition will be fully and formally considered, but, if such a works as yours could be produced <u>at present</u>, my view of the subject are [*sic*] all erroneous and we need no reform.

If you should come to the determination to publish nothing but what is truly <u>great</u>, of the highest mark, perhaps the work will be some time in making its appearance.[116]

Yet fewer than three years earlier he had actively been developing a scheme whereby he could devote himself wholly to composition, spurred on, no doubt, by the receipt in 1853 of a brief circular letter from Richard Jones, secretary to the Cathedral Commissioners. Addressed to the precentors and organists of the cathedral and collegiate churches of England and Wales, this had asked three questions:

I. Are you of opinion that it is desirable to give greater musical power to the Choir of the Church with which you are connected, for the more effective performance of Divine Service?

II. Are you of opinion that Laymen of approved piety and zeal for the worship of Almighty God, and with adequate qualifications for taking part in its celebration, might be found in your Cathedral city, and would be desirous of being connected with the Cathedral, and who would offer their services (particularly on Sundays), gratuitously, as Honorary Lay Clerks, or Vicars Choral, in addition to the present body of Singing Men and Choristers?

III. If such a plan appears to you to be practicable, would you oblige the Commissioners with a statement of your opinion, as to the mode of carrying it into effect?

1. In ascertaining the qualification of such additional Members of the Choir.

2. In securing regularity of attendance.[117]

---

[116] Letter dated 3 Feb. 1858 (collection of the late Sir John Dykes Bower).

And with any other suggestions that you may think desirable, on this subject?

The invitation to put down his thoughts on a subject so dear to him must have seemed like a heaven-sent opportunity, and he responded with a long and discursive reply which quite overshadowed those of his fellow organists. Taking as his starting point the quality of the music sung—'the impressiveness, solemnity, and artistic propriety of the manner in which the words of Scripture or the Prayer Book are set to music'[118]—he developed the arguments he had employed in *A Few Words* and, while not ignoring the replies requested by the commissioners, took full advantage of the invitation to add 'any other suggestions'. 'The singing of Choirs and the playing of Organists, however good', he observed, 'can give no dignity and force to bad musical composition'.[119] From this he enlarged upon the role of the organist as composer, extending it to include the concept of a musician (himself) whose sole job was to write for the church, 'the result of which would be the providing not only Cathedrals with unexceptionable musical composition for their daily services, but all churches and all congregations'.[120] But as with his earlier forays into print, his plea that church composers should be more adequately remunerated was not well received. Thus while acknowledging that he had 'sense on his side' in his proposals for the organisation of choirs, *The Athenaeum* (presumably Chorley) argued that 'like many other artitsts and critics, he seems somewhat to misconceive the uses and functions of religious Art', concluding that composers of sacred music should never expect to receive the full value—in monetary terms—of their work.[121] To Wesley this would merely have been another example of the way in which the world at large misunderstood the reality of life as a cathedral musician, and in no way deflected him from pursuing his ideas further. Indeed, it was but a small step from this proposal to a situation in which one composer was employed jointly by a number of cathedrals, and in November 1855, no doubt encouraged by the success of the *Anthems*, he addressed a circular letter to the Dean of Windsor and the Dean and Chapter of Durham (and probably to other choral foundations as well) in which he enquired whether, in return for his producing a dozen new works each year, they would each award him an annual stipend of £20 or £25.[122]

Not surprisingly his appeal fell on deaf ears, with no response being minuted at Windsor and a polite refusal at Durham. Six years later he tried a different tactic, writing to the Ecclesiastical Commissioners to reiterate how poorly cathedral musicians were remunerated in comparison with those in the

---

[117] Reprinted by Wesley in *Reply to the Inquiries of the Cathedral Commissioners Relative to the Improvement in the Music of Divine Worship in Cathedrals* (London: Piper, Stephenson, and Spence, [1854]).

[118] Ibid.   [119] Ibid.   [120] Ibid. 11.   [121] *Ath* (1854), 404–5.

[122] Holograph letter entitled 'Circular', dated 28 Nov. 1855 (*WRch* Win XVII.14.24).

'secular branches of my Art' and 'to solicit the great favour of having my stipend raised to something which may approach an average payment for time devoted to the public service'. Reminding them that their earlier report had recommended 'adequate' salaries and that a figure of £500 had been suggested, he concluded that 'if any addition of money and the advantage of the house rent free and kept in repair could be allowed me on the score of my incessant duty I should be pretty favoured and obliged'.[123] We can only assume that no positive response was forthcoming, but the idea of looking beyond Winchester for some form of additional payment had not died, and in 1862 Wesley made an attempt to interest the Revd W. E. Dickson, Precentor of Ely Cathedral, in a different scheme.[124] Would Dickson feel able to recommend its adoption?

You are, no doubt, aware that Cathedrals do buy new music. They can apply money to this end. In some cases, I hear that a sum is voted yearly to buy new things.

And what are the things bought?

I know that Novello has raked up from its hiding place all the discarded trash of former times & published it as novelty & the Choirs have spent their money thus. And what are the new things[?] Sir F Ouseley's Services &c. The money all goes into Novello's pocket.

Now, if I wrote constantly for the Church, do the things I have done warrant the idea that I shd. be of use. That I shd. leave behind me things which will pay for some little outlay on my behalf during the few years I may possibly live.

I say nothing about the years I have wasted. I might have done much but the Church pays so ill that I could not neglect my Family to devote my mind to the absorbing pursuit of writing . . .

What I wish to effect is this. I wish each Cathl. to vote a small stipend for me to write new music instead of their laying out the money over Novello's Counter.

If Cathedrals will do this I will produce a new thing monthly & live, to do this, expressly. This business would make me the reverse of discontented & disappointed & uncomfortable. I could enjoy working & forget the bitter annoyance the state of Cathl. Music has ever been to me.[125]

We can infer that Dickson's response was less than wholehearted as Wesley's next letter included a long list of arguments in favour of his proposal. Among these were:

---

[123] Letter dated 29 June 1861 to the Ecclesiastical Commissioners: see David Gedge, 'The Reforms of S. S. Wesley', *Org*, 68 (1969), 45.

[124] Dickson appears to have introduced himself to Wesley in 1860 when he sent him a pamphlet on church music, presumably *A Letter to the Lord Bishop of Salisbury, on Congregational Singing in Parish Churches* (Oxford: J. H. & H. Parker, 1857).

[125] Letter dated 16 Aug. [1862] (*Lbl* Add. MS 45498, fos. 100–01).

The improbability of any <u>great</u> composer ever taking up this subject Voluntary from its want of remuneration.

The necessity of a writer's having great experience in Cathedral details.

The passé nature of so much of the music written before the advent of the great modern Germans.

The trashy nature of the revivals of long discarded specimens by Novello & Co.

The immediate appreciation by the Public of anything really good.

As though to show the seriousness of his intentions he concluded: 'I would give up every professional engagement, Cathedral & all to <u>write</u> for the Church. I was getting 12 hundred a year at Exeter.'[126]

With the response from Ely (where the Dean had now been consulted) still unenthusiastic, Wesley was forced to admit the likelihood of defeat: 'I dont know, Dear Sir, whether it may be agreeable to you to go further in the matter. I certainly <u>cannot</u> come forward to ask anything. But I can give intelligence that wd. enable a friend to bring in various Cathedrals.'[127]

And with that the subject was laid to rest. But what was it that, only a few years earlier, had led him almost to stop composing? The cumulative effects of discouragement and dissatisfaction with his professional lot had undoubtedly played a large part, but there were other factors as well. The burden of bringing up five sons and establishing each of them in business or a profession was certainly taking its toll and was, by his own admission, at least partially responsible for the relatively small number of works completed during the last twenty years of his life. But none of these seems quite sufficient to account for the level of dejection evident from his letters, and there remains a possibility that he, like his father, suffered from some form of clinical depression. While there is no direct evidence, both the hereditary nature of the illness and the later manifestation of mental instability in his eldest son, John Sebastian (see Chapter 6), support this theory. The lack of challenge in his professional life could also have contributed to his musical apathy and general lethargy. By 1857 he had already been at Winchester for longer than at any of his previous appointments and, as we have seen earlier, he needed the regular stimulus of a new position to reinvigorate himself. Not only was this missing but, with John Sebastian, Francis Gwynne, and Charles Alexander enjoying a good and economical education at Winchester College, he had little incentive to move: even when he did apply for the chair of music in the University of Cambridge (vacant after the untimely death of Walmisley in January 1856) it was with little obvious enthusiasm and apparently at the prompting of his sister-in-

---

[126] Letter dated 28 Sept. 1862 (ibid., fo. 102).
[127] Letter dated 25 Oct. 1862 (ibid., fo. 109).

law.[128] In the event he withdrew at the last minute, 'not because I underval-
ued the honour of the appointment, but because, having omitted to take any
steps to obtain it until a very recent period, I found too many of my friends
had already yielded to the numerous solicitations of other candidates to leave
me any likelihood of success',[129] and Sterndale Bennett swept to victory.
Although still only forty-five Wesley had effectively resigned himself to
remaining a provincial cathedral organist. What he did not know, however,
was that the free hand he had been allowed at the cathedral by an aged
Precentor and Dean would shortly come to an end:

the Dean is a most amiable man. Beloved by everyone. The Canons, too, are superior
men, but it is greatly to the qualities of the Precentor that things have been as they
have been here & I need not say that after Exeter I fully appreciate them. Now, I
regret to say our Precentor is unable to attend. I have been transacting his business in
the Music list way for some time.

We have a new man from Ely who is, I believe, to be Precentor in Novr. How
things will go on I dont know. Our Dean is 82 or 3 years of Age, & if I lose him &
the new Precentor is disagreeable of course I may find things less pleasant . . .[130]

What Wesley had perhaps forgotten was that as recently as 1854 the Dean
and Chapter had had to insist on the resolution of a long-running dispute
between him and the Precentor,[131] but his fears about Henry Wray, the latter's successor, proved well founded. At Wray's first Chapter meeting in
November 1858 a number of points relating to the music were raised: 'the
instruction of the Choristers in the rudiments of Musical Services and in the
practice of singing should be more effectually secured', supplementary chants
and additional services should be introduced, and the publication of the
anthem book expedited.[132] Finally, Wesley was reminded that his rent had
been unpaid for two years and 'that unless it be paid before the 1st. of Feby.
next his monthly stipend be stopped until the matter is settled'.[133] As he had
been unable to move into his new home immediately and had for some reason been continuing to pay rent for his old one, it was agreed that one quarter's rent would be waived and with that the business was settled—though it

---

[128] When writing to solicit the support of the Archbishop of York Wesley referred to his 'kind Friend
Mrs Merewether . . . having submitted my name to your grace': letter dated 22 Jan. 1856 (McMaster
University, Hamilton, Ontario, English Composers' Collection).

[129] Letter dated 5 March 1856, *MW*, 34 (1856), 147.

[130] Letter dated 19 Sept. [1858] (*RSCM* Nicholson scrapbook, fo. 40).

[131] See Chapter Acts, 1850–76, 104 (*WC*).

[132] Wray's successor at Ely was Wesley's correspondent W. E. Dickson, from whose comments it is clear
that full responsibility for the musical arrangement rested with the Precentor (see W. E. Dickson, *Fifty Years
of Church Music* (Ely: T. A. Hills & Son, 1894), 58–9). Wray would no doubt have liked to effect similar
changes at Winchester.

[133] Winchester Cathedral Chapter Acts, 1850–76, 148 (*WC*).

may be that that the Dean's generous offer to pay half of Wesley's annual rent (£52) dates from this time.[134] Other matters were less easily resolved, and twelve months later it was minuted that Wesley should be asked 'whether . . . he is prepared to introduce for immediate use a selection of new Chants . . . and that in failure of such a selection, the Precentor be requested to take immediate steps to execute the order of Chapter'.[135] More seriously, he was also admonished for the neglect of his duties and for his conduct towards the Dean and Chapter. During the year ending 30 November 1859 he had claimed to have been present at 397 out of a total of 780 services: he had only actually attended 383:

making every possible allowance for the claims of private teaching on Dr. W's time, the absences bear an undue proportion to his attendces.

But this ground of dissatisfaction is increased by the insufficiency of the Substitutes employed by Dr. W—saying nothing of the 2 recently gone it is not consistent with that due attention which shd. be paid to the Service, that the Cathedral Organ shd. be left entirely as it has often been to the care of a lad however talented of only 14 years of age.[136]

Neither had he been personally supervising the instruction of the choristers, and, with only two competent to sing solos and a lack of proficiency in the remainder, there was 'proof that this provision has been sadly neglected'. But the most disturbing charge concerned his relations with the Dean and Chapter:

The third provision enjoins on Dr. W. a spirit of respectful & courteous attention to the wishes of the Dean & Chapter &c. The Dean & Chapter regret that this has been lamentably lost sight of in Dr. W's position & the correspondence which has recently taken place [with] both the Dean & one of the Canons, when reminded by them of his duty without entering into the particulars—the Dean & Chapter wd. remind Dr. W. that a kind of threat that he might put the note addressed to him by a Member of the Capitular Body, into the hands of his Solicitor was utterly at variance with both the letter & the spirit of Dr. W's engagement.

The Dean & Chapter having thus expressed their view of Dr. W's neglect of his duties . . . as well as of his deficiency in proper courtesy & respect towards those to whom it is due would further express their hope that this monition may be the means of convincing Dr. W. of his error & of inducing him in future to pay that proper & steady attention to his duties which is indispensable to the efficiency of the Choir & to the performance of the Cathedral Services.[137]

---

[134] See the letter dated 29 June 1861 from Wesley to the Ecclesiastical Commissioners quoted by Gedge in 'The Reforms of S. S. Wesley', 45.

[135] Minutes of the Nov. 1859 Chapter meeting, Winchester Cathedral Chapter Acts, 1850–76, 166 (*WC*).

[136] Ibid. 169.　　　　　[137] Ibid. 169–70.

History seemed to be repeating itself with a vengeance. Although 1860 passed without incident (the only criticism concerned Wesley's continuing delegation of his responsibility for instructing the choristers), matters again came to a head in September 1861 when the Dean and Chapter found themselves 'constrained by a painful sense of obligation formally to admonish Dr. Wesley a second time of his violation of duty as an Officer of the Cathedral'.[138] Once again the complaints concerned his neglect of the choristers and his behaviour towards the clergy. Not only had he been absent without leave in July, 'to the great detriment to, & proper performance of divine Service',[139] but he had also refused to be present at a voice trial for a vacant lay vicar's place, arguing that it was not part of his duty. When finally prevailed upon to attend, he 'contumaciously' refused to give his opinion, 'after the request had been repeatedly made replying—first that if he gave his Opinion in favor of a Candidate it wd. be most probably to the injury of that Candidate & further that he wd. give his opinion if he thought it would be acted upon in a just & straightforward manner'.[140]

The causes of Wesley's annoyance were probably twofold: that it was to Wray (and not to himself) that candidates for the vacancy had had to apply, and that the advertisement had asked for a 'Tenor Singer, who is also qualified to act as Assistant to the Organist in teaching the choristers music'.[141] Under the terms of his engagement the Dean and Chapter had agreed to contribute £20 towards the cost of providing an assistant. Was the remainder of the advertised salary of £50 to be deducted from his own? Wray's hand is seen more explicitly in his next reprimand when he made formal complaints about Wesley's irregular attendance at the weekly full choir practice and his habit of leaving the choir for the organ loft during services. Although he disputed the first charge, Wesley agreed to undertake the full instruction of the men and boys and in general to leave the organ playing to his pupils. Experience had perhaps shown him that an occasional willingness to submit—at least in public—to a demand from above was more profitable than continual confrontation. His patience must, however, have been sorely tested by Wray's ventures into the realm of composition. His pupil Kendrick Pyne has left a graphic portrait of one encounter:

The Cathedral precentor was an unusually zealous officer. In a moment of musical enthusiasm he had written an anthem, 'Come unto Me,' which composition interested us all very much. This gentleman had the temerity, in the presence of Wesley,

---

[138] Minutes of the Chapter meeting of 28 Sept. 1861 (ibid. 196).   [139] Ibid.   [140] Ibid. 197.
[141] *MT*, 10 (1861), [65]. That the notice was drafted by Wray is proved by its appearance in his memorandum book, 'De Precentore' (*WC*).

to conduct the rehearsals. It was indeed a wonderful sight to see him directing affairs, Wesley grimly standing by his side. I am bound to say the precentor was *not* a favourite with the Winchester choir.[142]

Clashes with the Precentor, however, seem to have provided that stimulus to Wesley's creativity which the incident-free years under his predecessor had lacked. During the early 1860s he completed three new anthems, the first an extended full-with-verse anthem, 'Praise the Lord, O my soul', written for the cathedral choir to sing at the opening of the new organ by Willis in Holy Trinity Church, Winchester, on 10 September 1861. Divided into four movements (of which the first two are the most substantial), it is typical of Wesley's late works in having a profusion of musical ideas but little development. But most indicative of his changed conception of the genre, however, is the almost total absence of counterpoint and the reliance instead on a ready flow of melody and changes of texture and scoring. The first movement, which opens with a characteristic wide-ranging melody for men's voices in unison, provides a good illustration of this approach. A string of short phrases, each matched to the words they set, is held together and given a sense of continuity by the frequent use of feminine and interrupted cadences, and is provided with an overall framework by its ternary formal scheme.

The most outstanding part, however, is the second movement. Taking as its basis the idea of a dialogue between soloists and full choir, to which the obbligato organ part (obviously designed to show off the new instrument) contributes a decorative counterpoint, it represents Wesley's ultimate development of the integrated full-with-verse movement. The central section in B minor ('Let all them that trust in thee') is particularly effective, with constant fluctuations of vocal colour and timbre as first one voice and then another rises to the forefront of the texture (see Ex. 5.4). The movement also offers a good example of how Wesley's imagination was becoming increasingly dependent upon a half-remembered idea, with the opening subject bearing an uncanny likeness to Mendelssohn's part-song 'Im Walde': a contemporary reviewer perceptively remarked (presumably in ignorance) that 'the learned composer has set a prayer to strains, in our opinion, of scarcely a sufficient degree of solemnity'.[143] Throughout the work Wesley uses harmony and tonal relationships to provide a sense of coherence, with the four movements in D minor, A major, F sharp minor, and D major respectively. But the most interesting section is at the end of the second movement, where a prominent flat seventh (G♮) and plagal cadence prepare the ear for a return to D major, which even the interpolation of a movement in F sharp minor cannot disrupt. The final

---

[142] 'Wesleyana', *MT*, 40 (1899), 378.   [143] *MS*, 1 (1862–3), 11.

Ex. 5.4. 'Praise the Lord, O my soul', second movement

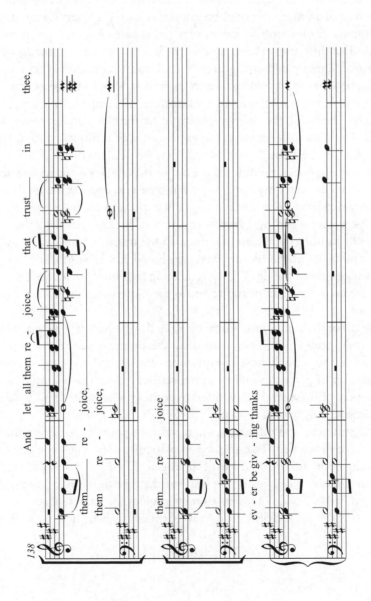

two short movements, the austerely harmonized chorale 'As for me' and the well-known 'Lead me Lord', are in fact so closely linked that the latter gains immeasurably from being heard in its intended context.

The death of the Prince Consort on 14 December 1861 came as a profound shock to the whole country, and at the suggestion of the Dean, Wesley composed an anthem 'All go unto one place', which was sung at a commemorative service on the day of the funeral (23 December) and published in January 1862. Economy is its most obvious feature, and both organ and choral parts are devoid of all unnecessary elaboration, yet such is his sensitivity to the text and command of harmony that its very understatement emerges as a positive virtue. The first movement, a sombre funeral march, is among his most expressive. Largely eschewing harmonized vocal writing, it is scored mainly for single voice parts whose static, narrow-ranging melodies, and subtle changes of harmony succeed in highlighting the text in a remarkable way. Take, for example, the telling chromatic harmonies which accompany the words 'The dust shall return to the earth as it was', with its contrast between 'dust' (flat keys) and the 'spirit' (sharp keys) (see Ex. 5.5).

The sparing use of the full choir ensures that its three entries—twice with the brief refrain 'truly my hope is even in thee' and again at the final climax—gain an added force. The last is particularly impressive and is crowned by a dramatic progression through successive triads of A major, B flat major, and C major which brings a sudden brightness to the music, entirely at one with the new confidence of the words, 'that we should not trust in ourselves, but in God which raiseth the dead'. The remaining two movements are both scored for four voices throughout and revert to the more conventional style of 'Lead me Lord'.

The last of these anthems, 'Give the King thy judgements', is a further large-scale work, composed to commemorate the marriage of the Prince of Wales (10 March 1863), for whose composition Wesley had been led to expect an honorarium of £70: the money, however, was spent on 'a somewhat third-rate display of fireworks!'[144] Written over thirty years after 'The Wilderness', it is a fascinating work, showing him still grappling with the challenges of musical structure and offering some tantalizing pointers as to how his music might have developed. Two features in particular stand out—the great variety of vocal colour and the bold use of the organ. The latter is not only entrusted with an important obbligato part but, for the first time since 'Blessed be the God and Father', is also allowed to remain silent for an extended period (bars 1–17). It is the second and third movements, however, that show Wesley at

---

[144] 'Wesleyana', 378.

Ex. 5.5. 'All go unto one place', first movement

his most imaginative. The former, like the opening movement of 'Praise the Lord, O my soul', is built up from a succession of short phrases, held together by a well-planned tonal scheme (F major, D major, G minor, D minor, F major) and the use of the opening subject (or its first two bars) as a unifying device. Never, perhaps, had Wesley sought to marry verbal and musical sentiment so closely, with the combination of voices used changing no fewer than fourteen times in the course of seventy-one bars.[145] The most dramatic and forward-looking writing is found at 'And break in pieces the oppressor' (marked 'accelerando con anima'), where dramatic organ flourishes separate the choir's vehement repetition of words which seem almost to have held a personal significance (see Ex. 5.6a). The third movement is no less effective and provides a good illustration of the harmonic warmth of Wesley's late style. Scored for full choir and verse ensemble and laid out in rondo form, it has a main theme which initially sounds Mendelssohnian, but subsequently demonstrates a characteristic astringency as appogiaturas and accented passing-notes clash with the underlying harmony, over a typical slowly rising bass-line (see Ex. 5.6b). Its tonal structure is exemplary (see Table 5.1).

TABLE 5.1. *Internal structure of 'Give the King thy judgements', third movement*

Bar	Text and thematic structure	Scoring	Keys
110	Thus shall the man be blessed I	Full	A
129	The Lord from out of Sion II	Verse	f#–C#–G#–E
146	Thus shall the man be blessed I	Full	A
153	Thy wife shall be as the fruitful vine III	Verse	D–A–E
170	Thus shall the man be blessed I	Full	A–C#–A

For all its beauties the anthem is an uneven and unbalanced work, with a preponderance of tonic harmony in the last three movements and all the verse passages concentrated near the beginning. It also poses a number of intriguing questions about its thematic material and overall style. Given his well-known antipathy towards the use of plainsong why did Wesley base the opening movement on a Gregorian theme (tone 8, first ending)? Why did he conclude with an 'Amen' whose 'classical' harmonic language and 'orchestral' accompaniment—brilliant scale passages and tremolandos—is far removed from that of the earlier movements and quite probably based on old sketches? Why did he choose to include a fugue (the penultimate movement), a form he had last used in 'Ascribe unto the Lord' and, contrary to his overall move towards a simpler mode of expression, revert to an obbligato role for the organ? Yet it

---

[145] attb, ATTB, at, bb, attb, SATB, sat, SATB, satb, AT, sattb, SATB, satb, SATBB.

Ex. 5.6. 'Give the King thy judgements', *a* second movement; *b* third movement

was clearly a work he held in some affection as it was one of those published (or reissued) by Novello, Ewer & Co. after he had sold his copyrights to them in 1868.

Even while writing 'Give the King thy judgements' Wesley's thoughts had moved ahead to two further projects, advertised in *The Musical Times* for April 1863, but with fuller details provided in a printed circular:

Twelve Anthems
By Samuel Sebastian Wesley, Mus. Doc.

never published

Composed for the Service of Cathedral, Collegiate, and all Choirs, but designed more especially for Parochial and newly-formed Choirs, many of which have applied to the Author for Anthems of a short and simple character, presenting no kind of difficulty in performance. The work has been revised with great care. Some of the Anthems are for special occasions.

To be handsomely Engraved and Published in Score, with Organ, Piano forte, or Harmonium Accompaniments.

A Small Volume of
Easy Organ Pieces.

The subjects selected from the best Authors, and partly composed for this Work . . . The Work is intended for Performers of moderate ability.[146]

A little further information can be gleaned from a letter to Marie, sister of his pupil David Parkes:

The trouble is to get the subject noticed by the <u>hundreds</u> of persons who would give their names if <u>cleverly</u> consulted. Now—Can you advise me as to the employment of one or more agents in Sheffield who would collect me names. Of course I should remunerate them . . .

I assure you that were I to put these works into a Music Seller's hands in London I should lose everything. By working myself, through friends, I may make <u>something considerable</u> by the undertaking. It is <u>time</u> I <u>did</u> make something, as from <u>leaving London</u> I have thrown my chance of fortune <u>away</u> . . .[147]

Given the prolonged and frequently interrupted gestation of his other publications, it should come as no surprise to discover that neither volume was ever issued! Nor, to judge from the shortage of possible candidates for inclusion, was either anywhere near completion, although as late as 1872 he was still referring to the set of organ pieces 'long promised to the subscribers'.[148] Apart

---

[146] The only know copy is in the Methodist Archives, Manchester (*Mr* MS MAM P 12 C, no.1).

[147] Letter dated 19 March [1863] to Miss Marie Parkes (collection of Mrs Angela Parkes).

[148] Letter dated 25 March 1872 to Henry Littleton (?), pasted into a copy of *The Hymnary* (*Lcm* RSCM loan).

from two isolated (final) advertisements in June and July 1870,[149] the only further references are some deliberately vague comments in a letter to H. T. Freemantle:

At this moment I cannot say when the Organ Book of mine will come out. I hope to get the Engraver to work shortly. Still, I can be certain of nothing, as to dates . . .

My 12 Anthems will be good, & are not a mere catchpenny publication. But I Cannot Puff & go on as some do. I must let my character have its due weight, whatever it may be.[150]

But what, apart from a desire to obtain subscriptions as soon as possible, led Wesley to make such a premature announcement? A clue may be found in his dismissal of self-advertisement, as the pages of the musical press currently contained numerous announcements for *Parochial Anthems by the Cathedral Composers of 1863*, compiled by his near-neighbour in Winchester Thomas Lloyd Fowle. Fowle, who had made a name for himself as a composer of simple anthems (for which he was dubbed 'The People's Musician'), had succeeded in obtaining contributions from eighteen composers, among them Ouseley, Macfarren, Elvey, Gauntlett, Stainer, Barnby, and Spark, and would assuredly have welcomed one from Wesley (who did at some point offer him the rights to 'I am thine, O save me').[151] It is not hard, however, to imagine the latter, stung by the effrontery of a self-taught local musician who styled himself 'Doctor of Music' (but refused to divulge the origin of his degree), deciding to announce his own rival collection—and hoping to benefit from the current demand for easy anthems into the bargain.[152]

There does remain one contemporary organ piece, however, the Andante Cantabile in G, written for the opening of the organ in the Agricultural Hall, Islington. The instrument had been exhibited by Willis at the International Exhibition in 1862 and was first heard in its new home on 3 November 1863. Wesley contributed a 'Fantasia—"Andante Cantabile" (and by request) "Extemperaneous Fugue"' between the two parts of *Messiah*, conducted by his brother Robert, and the former was published early the following year. As

---

[149] See *MT*, 14 (1870), 511, 516. Both advertisements were appended to ones for *The European Psalmist*.

[150] Letter dated 2 June 1863 to H. T. Freemantle (*Mr* MS MAM P 12 C, no. 11). None of the few unpublished anthems could be described as 'short and simple', although some of the works issued a decade later may have been conceived at this time; we also know that at his death Wesley left a quantity of unfinished organ music (since lost).

[151] There is no evidence as to when the transaction took place, but it was revoked on 13 Dec. 1870 by a memorandum from Fowle to Henry Littleton of Novello, Ewer & Co., Wesley having agreed to supply a new composition in place of 'I am thine' (formerly in the private library of Novello & Co.).

[152] It is worth noticing that a year earlier Fowle had written a fulsome letter to *MW* extolling the merits of 'All go unto one place' (*MW*, 40 (1862), 124). Some years later he was involved in a controversy with Stainer over his right to style himself 'Mus.Doc.' (see *MT*, 17 (1875), 10, 55–7, 74). His degree, it eventually transpired, was a Ph.D. from the University of Giessen.

the only example of the type of fantasia that he used to demonstrate the solo stops (cf. his performance at Birmingham in 1849) it is of considerable interest, not least for the obviously orchestral thinking behind its four-stave layout and the detailed registration and dynamic markings (see Ex. 5.7). How much the audience heard is another matter, as the performance was marred by excessive noise: 'When Dr. Wesley commenced there was a little lull in the talking, but only for a short time, when it started off again with much vigour and with a good 'crescendo,' and as the organ became louder so did the talking, until it became a perfect hubbub':

After this had gone on for some time, and the people who went out had returned, the audience became impatient for the second part of the 'Messiah,' and commenced to hammer on the floor with their walking-sticks and umbrellas in a most energetic manner. This continued for some time, and at last it became so bad that Dr. Wesley left the organ and went off the platform, evidently very much disappointed with the reception he had received.[153]

'It was like casting pearls before swine', observed *The Musical Standard*, ' "Nancy in the strand" would have been much more to their taste.'[154] On its publication the 'exquisite Andante' was warmly welcomed by the *Standard*, which approved in particular of Wesley's use of the 'resources and specialities of the instrument . . . in the production of effects . . . peculiar to itself'. 'This', it continued, 'we shall consider a great step in advance of the present frequently clumsy adaptations of Orchestral Music, often wholly unsuited to the organ, and the performance of which on that noble instrument, neither serves to enhance the reputation of the composer, the taste and judgment of the arranger, or the skill of the performer'.[155]

Wesley was to return to the Agricultural Hall the following year for the first performance of the only substantial non-church work of his maturity, the *Ode to Labour*, written for the opening of the North London Working Men's Industrial Exhibition in October 1864. Given that he had never before attempted a work on such a scale—its seven movements are scored for five soloists and chorus and organ (or orchestra)—it immediately raises the question as to what had prompted him to invest so much time and effort in setting a rather pedestrian text by W. H. Bellamy. The answer may again lie in professional rivalry. Sterndale Bennett had written an *Ode*—a 'wretched thing' as he termed it—for the opening of the International Exhibition in 1862.[156] Did Wesley perhaps see this as an opportunity to demonstrate that he could do better? At its first performance it was sung with organ accompaniment, but for its

[153] Letter from George Shinn, *MN*, 29 (1910), 42.   [154] *MS*, 2 (1863–4), 117.
[155] Ibid. 201–2.   [156] Letter dated 31 May [1862] to R. A. Atkins (*Eu* MS Dk.7.384).

Ex. 5.7. Andante Cantabile in G

repeat at the closure of the exhibition on 7 November 1865 (when it was sung by a choir of 1000) he scored it for large orchestra.[157] Although it is too occasional a piece to gain a foothold in the repertoire, several numbers possess great charm. The opening bass aria 'When from the great creator's hand', with its bold rising melody and rushing violin scales, is particularly effective (see Ex. 5.8), and both this and the following tenor solo 'And strong in heart', show that Wesley had lost none of his gift for melody, or for writing emotionally charged music. The delicate trio for two sopranos and alto, 'The wise, the wealthy and the great', carries echoes of 'O worship the Lord' from 'Ascribe unto the Lord' and is unusual in allowing the voices to remain unaccompanied (or supported by solitary pedal notes) for much of its length. In its concluding lines we also see the moralizing side of Bellamy's text, 'Learn this at least if nothing more, That work enobles man', and a similar sentiment is expressed in the following chorale and fugue: 'Each man 'tis writ, must stand or fall, As he his work has done'. In many ways these two movements—the first in which the choir is heard—form the heart of the work. The former is a quiet, gravely beautiful movement in C minor, unaccompanied save for the entry of the brass at the cadences of the second and final lines and linked to the fugue by a remarkable ad lib cadenza for solo soprano (rising to c''), which prefigures the opening of the latter. Here Wesley was surely taking advantage of one of his two soprano soloists, Louisa Pyne, a cousin of his pupil Kendrick Pyne and one of the leading operatic singers of her time. The final two movements exemplify a lighter, more popular, side of his output—a soprano ballad, 'Silently, silently' (which ran to a second edition) and a light-hearted chorus, 'All honor to the working man'. The latter possesses a raw vigour—almost vulgarity—enhanced by its sometimes brash scoring, with such typical devices as off-beat chords for the brass. The *Ode* forms an unusual epitaph both to that autumnal flowering of Wesley's art in the early 1860s and to that small group of choral works which thirty years earlier had promised so much but had since yielded so little. It was also his last work to be finished at Winchester, but before following him to Gloucester we must draw together the remaining strands of his life and career in the city.

In addition to his work on Kemble's *A Selection of Psalms and Hymns* Wesley had made several other ventures into the field of musical editing. The first, a collaboration with Bellamy (who provided new words) on an edition of

---

[157] The programme for the closing ceremony consisted of Wesley's arrangement of the 100th Psalm, his *Ode*, the 'Hallelujah' chorus, and the National Anthem; he also played the organ while the chairman (W. E. Gladstone) was conducted around the exhibition. It is not clear where his setting of Bellamy's 'The Song of the Seamstress' (whose words were provided in the programme) fitted in, unless it served as an additional movement for the *Ode*.

Ex. 5.8. *Ode to Labour*, first movement

thirty-six of Mozart's operatic arias and duets for Chappell's, had been started before he left Leeds and was completed by September 1851, while the second was a foray into highly unusual territory—Welsh sacred music. Its fruits are to be seen in the accompaniments he provided (or revised) for two works by self-taught musicians—'Wrth Afonydd Babilon' (By the Streams of Babylon) by William Owen (1854) and the first oratorio in Welsh, *Ystorm Tiberias* (The Storm of Tiberias) by the Revd Edward Stephen ('Tanymarian') (1857). In the absence of any other obvious motive, one can only assume that these were purely business arrangements for, as Ouseley had noted, Wesley would never do anything for nothing!

It had long been customary for the cathedral organist to serve also at the adjacent Winchester College and, had it not been for the Dean and Chapter's dilatory action in filling the vacancy, it is probable that Wesley would have followed directly in his predecessor's footsteps. Instead the college appointed Chard's deputy, Benjamin Long, and it was only with Long's premature death in December 1850 that Wesley was offered the post. For a salary of £80 (which he had succeeded in having raised from the £50 paid since the end of the seventeenth century) he was responsible for instructing the sixteen 'quiristers'—a task frequently delegated to one of his pupils—and playing at the weekly Sunday Evensong. With the latter following close on the afternoon service at the cathedral, the sermon was placed first to allow time for Wesley and the three lay clerks (who comprised the adult portion of the choir) to arrive. Someone with strong memories of these occasions was Wesley's youngest pupil, Kendrick Pyne:

He had a keen sense of sly humour. He carried in wet weather an enormous gig umbrella of a vivid green colour. Now after my being articled to him, when I was about thirteen, he used to go to the afternoon service at Winchester College, held on Sundays after the Cathedral service. We waited in the ante-chapel until Dr. Moberley had finished his sermon, and then walked up between the boys to the organ . . . at the North-East end. He frequently used to make me carry this enormous green gingham through the rows of boys, to my great discomfiture, and I can see the sly twinkle in his eye as he turned round to me when we arrived at our destination.[158]

Although the headmaster, Dr George Moberly, was a man of wide culture and a keen singer he, like most of his generation, regarded music as being an 'undesirable distraction for the pupils under his care',[159] and it had no official place in the life of the school. Not so within his family circle. His daughter Caroline recalled:

[158] Pyne, 'Wesleyana', 377.
[159] Alan Rannie, *The Story of Music at Winchester College, 1394–1969* (Winchester: P. and G. Wells, 1970), 29.

Open-air singing was a very special characteristic of those days. Dr. Samuel Sebastian Wesley . . . for ten years . . . came regularly twice a week and taught each each one of us when old enough to join the singing class. We were all musical, and had good voices, and were so many that we possessed not only a first and a second quartet, but a chorus as well, and reading music became no difficulty to any of us. Dr. Wesley could be fierce occasionally, and charming at other times, and would come of an evening to accompany our home singing. He once made us sing all through Rossini's opera of the 'Cenerentola' at sight, and sometimes brought his own compositions to try over.[160]

On another occasion, according to Edith Moberly, Wesley revealed with disarming simplicity his remoteness from the affairs of the world:

Dr. Wesley came unexpectedly this morning, and Kitty was in a dreadful fright because she had not practised her fugues; but Mary sang with them, and they went on with that much longer than usual. Arthur came up in the middle with the news of the taking of Lucknow, upon which Dr. Wesley remarked that he did not see why the English should want to take Lucknow at all! 'How should we like an enemy to come and take one of our towns in that way?'—showing that he had heard nothing at all about the circumstances [i.e. the events of the Indian Mutiny]![161]

Beyond these few glimpses we know very little of Wesley's life away from the cathedral and even the death of his mother on 12 September 1863 passed unrecorded. He had, however, continued to make appearances as an organist, playing at the opening of new instruments in St George's, Leeds (Spark's church), and St Margaret's, Lee, Kent, in 1850, and in St Jude's, Southsea, a year later, in addition to those already mentioned.[162] But with the passing years such occasions became considerably less frequent as, disappointed and discouraged, he lost the pioneering zeal he had displayed in Exeter and Leeds. A further consequence of this was that he only rarely involved himself in local musical activity, although for several years he undertook the arrangements for the annual dinners of the Charitable Society of Natives and Citizens and the Charitable Society of Aliens, 'presiding at the piano' while the lay vicars and choristers of the cathedral and college performed a selection of glees and other vocal music.[163] During the early 1850s he and his pupil George Arnold also gave tuition in vocal music to the students of the Diocesan Training School; that Wesley was absent from the half-yearly examination in June 1853 is per-

---

[160] C. A. E. Moberly, *Dulce domum: George Moberly, his Family and Friends* (London: John Murray, 1911), 119.

[161] Ibid. 134–5 (quoting a letter from her sister Edith to her sister Alice).

[162] Lee is now part of the London Borough of Lewisham. For a complete list of organs opened by Wesley see App. 2.

[163] Both societies were devoted to the apprenticing of poor children.

haps a reflection on his commitment![164] But apart from these isolated occasions and infrequent appearances at private concerts with the Moberly family or at the deanery, he showed little inclination to participate in such events and left concert-giving to his pupils or the local music-seller J. Conduit. His attendance at a recital by the pianist Arabella Goddard in January 1865 was considered sufficiently noteworthy for it to be reported in *The Musical World*.[165] It was as though he had taken literally the advice to 'keep himself secure in the cloisters of Winchester Cathedral'. There was surely more than a grain of truth in Florence Marryat's description in her novel *Nelly Brooke* of 'Dr Nesbitt', the organist of Hilstone (as she called Winchester): her account of his capricious playing rings particularly true:

He was a man of powerful intellect, and great musical ability, but with an uncertain and violent temper, and a reserved disposition which forbid his opening his heart to anyone. He was very much courted and deferred to . . . but everybody was more or less afraid of him. On his part, he treated the townspeople with politeness because it was his good will and pleasure to retain his appointment as organist . . . but there was ever a cynical look to be discerned lurking behind his readiest smile, and in his heart he hated and despised them all.

. . . a first rate musician himself, and with the capability of making the splendid organ under his charge sound in such a manner that all England would have been glad to crowd to hear him, he would yet on occasions mount the loft stairs in so bad a humour, that neither choristers nor canons could by any possibility follow the chords struck by his wayward fingers. And then Dr. Nesbitt would be delighted at the public failure, and before he had given the cathedral authorities time to reprimand him, would lull their anger by such exquisite music as is seldom heard upon this lower earth.[166]

Whether or not there was any foundation for her account of Dr Nesbitt's singular way of making amends for his erratic behaviour, there is ample anecdotal evidence to support her impression of a difficult, truculent individual. The American organist Samuel Tuckerman was one who encountered his quixotic behaviour. Arriving in Winchester armed with a letter of introduction from George Elvey, he was greeted with the words 'Elvey! Who is Elvey?'[167] and saw his letter thrown into the fire before being shown to the door. A fortnight later, however, he was summoned by a telegram to his host: 'Send down your friend Tuckerman; I have put up 'The wilderness' for him to hear to-morrow'.[168] After meeting Tuckerman at Winchester station, Wesley entertained him and, after dinner, played to him (largely extempore)

---

[164] See *HC* (25 June 1853), 4. [165] See *MW*, 43 (1865), 11.
[166] *Nelly Brooke: A Homely Story*, 3 vols. (London: Richard Bentley, 1868), 2, 185–6.
[167] Elvey, *Life and Reminiscences of George J. Elvey*, 102. [168] Ibid. 103.

for two hours. Yet this ill-mannered side of his character was rarely, if ever, encountered by his pupils. 'I had an absolute admiration and veneration for him, shared by many', wrote Kendrick Pyne, 'The most apocryphal tales are told as to his eccentricities. I lived with him for some time and do not share in the view. He was moody, often absent-minded, nervous, and irritable; but not more than one would expect from an artist, who is usually not accustomed to hide his feelings.'[169] Pyne was also present when one of Wesley's best-known works—the hymn tune 'Aurelia'—was first heard:

I was in his drawing-room in the Close, Winchester, as a lad of thirteen . . . when Dr. Wesley came rushing up the stairs from below with a scrap of MS. in his hand, a psalm tune just that instant finished. Placing it on the instrument he said: 'I think this will be popular.' My mother was the first to sing it to the words, 'Jerusalem the Golden.' The company liked it, and Mrs. Wesley on the spot christened it 'Aurelia'.[170]

Such glimpses of family life are all too rare and, as in Mary Anne's account of a holiday on the Isle of Wight, make one long to know more:

Ventnor is certainly an extremely pretty place, but it has great drawbacks—there are scarcely any houses *near* the sea and the beach is *all shingle*. I thought them so great when I was there last autumn that I and one of my sons settled ourselves about four miles to the west of Ventnor, at Milton, in a house *on* the beach, where we could walk down a few steps out of the garden on to very good sands . . .

A lady and gentleman are staying with me besides another friend, and my younger boys are at home, so I can with difficulty get a quiet moment *for writing*. So pray excuse this almost illegible scrawl . . .[171]

Wesley, too, left one tantalizingly brief reference to a part of his life which otherwise remains shrouded in mystery:

I have very often sailed down the Southn. Water & have also put in at Hamble, once with two of my Boys in the little Vessel with the object of sleeping at one of the Inns but they seemed very shy of strangers & they gave me the idea of being rather deep in the smuggling line & I have little doubt that such is the case.[172]

Was sailing, like fishing and shooting, a regular activity and another example of that love of nature which, as Spark noted, brought him 'calmness of mind, and tranquility of spirit'?[173] The only other hint is a sketch of a yacht

---

[169] Pyne, 'Wesleyana', 377.

[170] 'Dr. Samuel Sebastian Wesley', *ECM*, 5 (1935), 5–6. Another of Wesley's pupils, Francis Gladstone, recalled Wesley playing the tune to him before he left Winchester in 1864: see *MN*, 28 (1910), 670.

[171] Letter quoted by Paul Chappell in *Dr. S. S. Wesley, Portrait of a Victorian Musician* (Great Wakering: Mayhew-McCrimmon, 1977), 96.

[172] Letter dated 11 March 1857 to Sarah Emett (*Lbl* Add. MS 35019, fo. 152).

[173] W. Spark, *Musical Memories*, 72.

on the manuscript of his arrangement of the old ballad 'Light o' Love' (see Pl. 16). Be that as it may, with relations at the cathedral remaining strained and Winchester having lost any attraction it had formerly held—as early as 1855 he had described it as a 'little stagnant hole of a town'[174]—one suspects that by the early 1860s he would have welcomed any opportunity to move elsewhere. The invitation to advise the Dean and Chapter of Gloucester on the appointment of a successor to John Amott, who had died on 3 February 1865, offered just such a chance, but he none the less surprised everyone when he announced that he would be happy to take the position himself. The terms were little different from what he enjoyed—a salary of £150 per annum (the same as at Winchester) and a house, with an additional sum of £25 available should he wish to engage an assistant for the 'daily instruction' of the choristers.[175] His formal appointment was minuted on 18 February 1865 (with the proviso that the Dean was 'to receive in writing his consent to all the terms of the Act under which he is appointed'), and this having presumably been received he was sworn in six days later, although he did not commence his duties until 24 June. He immediately offered his resignation at Winchester, however, where the Chapter, to judge from the speed with which they appointed his former pupil George Arnold, were equally anxious to forestall any change of heart! Wray was no less eager to make certain alterations and on 22 February, the day before Arnold was appointed, wrote to the Vice-Dean proposing that the organist's personal attention at the choristers' morning practice should be required, that a short voluntary should be played before and after every service, and that access to the organ loft during services should be restricted. Finally, he warned that he could not be 'expected to make the same concession to a younger man . . . waiving the statutable duties of my office, [as] I did to the greater experience & acknowledged genius of Dr Wesley'.[176] And with this, Wesley's name made its final appearance in the cathedral records at Winchester.

As with each of his previous appointments, Wesley's time in the town had been characterized by what might be termed a gradual decrescendo. The bulk of his most important work—the publication of the *Anthems* and the *Reply to the Inquiries of the Cathedral Commissioners*, and the completion of the organs for St George's Hall and Winchester Cathedral—had been accomplished by 1855, and for the remainder of his time he had been content—or felt resigned—to remain in the background. With four of his sons enjoying the educational advantages of Winchester College and himself one of the professors at the

---

[174] Letter dated 14 March [1855] to Sarah Emett (*Lbl* Add. MS 35019, fo. 150).
[175] See Gloucester Cathedral Chapter acts 1863–92, 18 Feb. 1865, 84–5 (*GL*).
[176] MS 'De precentore', 33–4 (*WC*).

Royal Academy of Music, there had also been little incentive to move. Yet for someone who had not completely lost the urge either to compose or to leave his mark as a player, such a state of affairs must have been intensely frustrating, and when the opportunity to make a new start at Gloucester arose it was doubtless one he felt he could not refuse.

6

Gloucester

> I have moved from cathedral to cathedral because I found <u>musical troubles</u> at each.[1]

With his appointment to Gloucester Cathedral Wesley's career had turned almost full circle, and it must have been with mixed feelings that he returned so close to where he had embarked on the life of a cathedral organist nearly thirty-three years earlier. As if to emphasize how little had changed, he found himself succeeding Amott, who had been appointed in April 1832, some five months before his own arrival in Hereford, and whose long tenure was in such contrast to his own restless movement from place to place. In other respects, however, things were very different, and by the 1860s the relatively small city he had known had grown into an important port and centre of manufacturing, making such physical isolation as he had experienced in Hereford a thing of the past.

Although he had immediately offered his resignation to the Dean and Chapter, Wesley did not finally leave Winchester until June 1865 and on Midsummer Day took up his duties at Gloucester. Yet even now not everything was quite ready (as he reported to his son Francis):

> The day has been so fine that <u>everything</u> looks well. Still, I think my house is really improved. I have been unable to find out when I might expect it to be finished but I think it may be more than a month first . . .
>
> I played the service. Called on the Dean. He was napping. He came to the service & waited for me coming out to be the first to wish me all good.
>
> I called on the Powers. Mrs P went with me to see the Lodgings. They are <u>very good</u>. What do you say to lodging in Gloucester before the house is ready[?][2]

Already, however, he had begun to make his presence felt in the city, accompanying the Bishop's music-loving wife to Evensong in March and

---

[1] Letter dated 25 Nov. 1874 to W. H. Blanch (repr. in the *South London Press*: see *Lbl* Add MS 35020, fo. 32).

[2] Letter dated 1 July 1865 (*Lcm* MS 3076).

taking part in a concert at the bishop's palace a month later.[3] The latter was a noteworthy occasion as it included the first local performance of the newly published *Ode to Labour*, Sterndale Bennett's *The May Queen*, Mendelssohn's *Die Lorelei*, and a selection of partsongs. Wesley and Bennett conducted their respective works, and the evening made a strong impression on a seventeen-year-old schoolboy, Hubert Parry. Parry had first met Wesley at Winchester while a pupil at Twyford School, and now, with Parry back home at Highnam Court, a few miles from Gloucester, their paths again crossed:

Some parts of Wesley's ode are quite magnificent, especially the first bass solo, which is as fine as anything I ever heard of the kind . . . The fugue is good . . . The last chorus is rather strange, with some very novel ideas in it. Very fast. Wesley takes it all <u>very</u> fast . . . My little part song went very badly, through not having had enough rehearsal . . . Dr Wesley postively sang bass in it: it went better the second time . . .[4]

Of far more significance, however, was his appointment as conductor of the forthcoming Gloucester Three Choirs Festival. Despite the tradition that the festival conductor was always the resident organist, dissatisfaction with Amott's performance three years earlier had led one of the festival stewards to propose that this would be a good opportunity to ask the Dean and Chapter whether a London conductor might not be engaged instead.[5] Whether Wesley was aware of this is not recorded, but at their meeting on 19 April the stewards had read to them a letter from him which 'Stated that Dr Wesley was expected to be engaged as the Conductor of the Festival', and it was minuted that after 'much discussion, it was thought desirable to offer to Dr. S. S. Wesley the Conductorship, on the terms paid to Mr. Amott . . . viz. £130 for Conducting and £21 for travelling Expenses'.[6]

Although it was thirty years since he had last been involved with the festival, little had changed. Proceedings now always spanned four days, with the opening service (sung by the combined cathedral choirs) on a Tuesday morning and the concluding performance of Handel's *Messiah* and evening ball on the following Friday. The orchestra was still largely composed of professionals from London, while the chorus included the choral societies from the three cathedral cities, as well as contingents from elsewhere in the country. With his appointment confirmed, Wesley found himself responsible for organizing a body of over 300 instrumentalists and singers, and three weeks later he

---

[3] Mrs Constantia Ellicott was a keen amateur singer, and her daughter Rosalind (b. 1857) later became a successful composer.

[4] Parry's diary entry for 18 April 1865 (*ShP*); he sang the opening bass solo from Wesley's *Ode* at a concert at Eton in 1867.

[5] Letter from W. Price: see Anthony Boden, *Three Choirs*, 55.

[6] Minutes of the stewards' meeting of 19 April 1865 (*ThCh*).

returned, armed with a list of fourteen singers (from which ten names were
selected) and suggestions for the programme. Then, as now, the fees com-
manded by the most popular soloists dwarfed those of lesser beings; while the
stewards were content to pay the principal soprano Therese Tietjens the £350
she had asked for (with £25 being returned to the charity), they balked at the
£315 demanded by the tenor Sims Reeves. On his refusal to accept £200—
the amount he had received in 1862—the operatic singer Gustav Gunz was
engaged instead; as Wesley found to his cost, it was assumed that the omission
of the famous tenor was his doing and any shortcomings of the replacement
(who had never before sung in English) were placed firmly at his door. In contrast to these inflated figures the leader of the orchestra received £40 and the
rank-and-file string players between £6 and £16. The full list of singers, with
their respective fees, makes interesting reading (see Pl. 17):[7]

Therese Tietjens	soprano	£367 10s. 0d.
Louisa Pyne	soprano	£150 00s. 0d.
Hermine Rudersdorff	contralto	£105 00s. 0d.
Julia Elton	contralto	£31 10s. 0d.
Eleanora Wilkinson	contralto	£35 00s. 0d.
Gustav Gunz	tenor	£100 00s. 0d.
W. H. Cummings	tenor	£52 10s. 0d.
Charles Santley	bass	£136 10s. 0d.
Lewis Thomas	bass	£42 00s. 0d.
Sigr. Bossi	bass	£21 00s. 0d.

Arabella Goddard's piano playing in Winchester had clearly impressed
Wesley, and it was agreed that she could be engaged to provide an additional
attraction at the evening concert; of rather more moment was his suggestion
that the experiment of placing the orchestra and chorus at the west end instead
of under the tower, tried out at Hereford the previous year, should be
repeated, and this was agreed on the understanding that Willis could provide
a satisfactory temporary organ for 50 guineas.[8] Programming hardly featured
in the discussions, and apart from various references to Rudolf Schachner's
oratorio *Israel's Return from Babylon*, given two years before at Worcester and
benefiting from influential champions, the only further mention was on 26
July when Wesley presented a proof copy of his programme.[9] By now, one

---

[7] See Wesley's account book (*Lcm* MS 2141d). Four local singers were also engaged, Mrs J. K. Pyne, Mrs
St Brody, Mr Brandon, and Mr Thomas: the ladies were each paid £10, the gentlemen 7 guineas.

[8] See the minutes of the stewards' meeting of 31 May 1865 (*ThCh*).

[9] At the meeting of 28 June the oratorio was 'referred' to Wesley, who was later asked whether he could
include a continuous sequence rather than extracts. C. J. Monk, Chancellor of the Diocese and MP for
Gloucester, later wrote in support of it, while Tietjens (who had sung in the Worcester performance) had

suspects, the new conductor had begun to test the stewards' patience, as one of a series of memoranda written after the festival had closed opens with the ominous words 'The Conductor should be kept in due subordination' and notes that 'this important point was only secured after a series of struggles which threatened more than once to imperil the Festival'.[10] Wesley certainly appears to have used his disrection in reshaping what little had been agreed about the programmes, dropping among other things Schachner's oratorio in favour of a work he had conducted at Hereford in 1834, Spohr's *Die letzten Dinge*.

If Wesley's choice of works was unadventurous—the morning concerts consisted of Mendelssohn's *St Paul* (part 1) and *Die letzten Dinge* (Tuesday 5 September), Mozart's *Requiem*, extracts from Mendelssohn's *Lobgesang* (Hymn of Praise) and Beethoven's *Christus am Oelberge* (Christ at the Mount of Olives) (Wednesday 6 September), *Elijah* (Thursday), and *Messiah* (Friday)—this was only to be expected, in view of his long absence from the concert platform and the lack of rehearsal time. Neither, given his fondness for the music of Spohr, is it surprising to find that he included further works in the evening concerts—the Violin Concerto No. 8, 'in modo di scena cantante' (with the leader, Henry Blagrove, as soloist), the overtures to *Faust* and *Jessonda*, and a selection from *Azor und Zemira*. With a few exceptions, living composers were represented only by short vocal numbers at the evening concerts, and the sole novelty was Wesley's newly orchestrated version of 'Ascribe unto the Lord'. As the score reveals, he had lost none of his feel for the medium: it contains many happy touches, among them the impressive opening for strings and full brass, the mournful sound of horns and low woodwind at the words 'they have mouths and speak not', and the delicate figuration in the string parts in the last movement. Only rarely did he employ the full panoply of instruments, but at such moments as the conclusion of 'As for the gods of the heathen' or the final pages of the last movement they produce a gloriously rich sound which makes one wish he had tried his hand at more orchestral composition.[11]

Packed as it was into a lengthy programme on Wednesday morning, 'Ascribe unto the Lord' failed to make a great impression and also suffered

---

expressed 'her admiration of the Oratorio . . . and her willingness to sing . . . had it been desired'. See the minutes of the 5th–8th meetings of the stewards (*ThCh*). Constantia Ellicott was another prominent admirer of Schachner, and Hubert Parry encountered both the composer and his music in her company (see C. L. Graves, *Hubert Parry: His Life and Works* (London: Macmillan & Co., 1926), 1. 59, 104).

[10] F. T. Bayly, 'Memoranda for the Next Festival to Supplement the Shortcomings of that in 1865' (copied into the stewards' minute book, *ThCh*).

[11] One can trace several stages in the development of the work, from Wesley's original draft to the much-revised fair copy; the scoring of the opening was one example of a later revision.

from members of the audience leaving early for lunch! Indeed, one of the more notable features of the festival was the preponderance of inordinately long concerts in which, either for its own sake or to accommodate the soloists, Wesley had tried to cram too much music. Inevitably this exacerbated the lack of rehearsal time, with his father's motet 'In exitu Israel' being the most prominent casualty, but Beethoven's Choral Fantasia and Mendelssohn's *Die erste Walpurgisnacht* also suffering. The last brought a particularly epic day (Wednesday 6 September) to a close. Proceedings had begun at 11.30 with a performance of the orchestral movements and first solo and chorus from *Lobgesang*, followed by a string of vocal items, among them 'In exitu Israel' and 'Ascribe unto the Lord'. After a thirty-minute lunch interval Wesley played Bach's 'St Anne' Fugue (to the accompaniment of the audience retaking their seats) before returning to the platform for Mozart's Requiem, two further vocal items, and the final three numbers from *Christus am Oelberge*! Even after a 'morning' performance which finished at 4 o'clock there was no respite, with the evening programme beginning with 'Spring' from Haydn's *The Seasons*, followed by Mendelssohn's Piano Concerto No. 1 (with Arabella Goddard as soloist), a series of vocal items, the overture to Spohr's *Jessonda*, extracts from Rossini's *Guillaume Tell*, further vocal items, and, finally, Mendelssohn's *Die erste Walpurgisnacht*. As *The Times* noted:

The last piece in the concert . . . should properly have been the first. The audience were fairly worn out by the day's labor of listening, as the players and singers were fairly worn out by the day's labor of singing and playing. Think what had been heard at the Cathedral in the morning, and then to wind up a miscellaneous concert in the evening with such an elaborate and exciting work as the *Walpurgis Night*.[12]

Critical comment on Wesley's programming and conducting was mixed, although there were few favourable comments on the former. 'I must protest against the treatment Mendelssohn has received at this festival' wrote Davison:

Surely it was bad enough to cut *St. Paul* in half and ruthlessly dismember the *Lobgesang* without putting a work like the *Walpurgis Night* at *the end of a long concert!* I do not know who has the arrangement of these matters, but certainly the conductor ought to have *some* voice in it, and I can hardly think that a musician of Dr. Wesley's great and unquestioned ability can voluntarily have consented to the shameful usage to which Mendelssohn has been subjected.[13]

Why, it was asked, place *St Paul* before *Die letzten Dinge* to the clear detriment of the latter, or try to include such a mass of music?[14] The critic of *The Queen* also considered that the evening concerts were 'too heavy and preten-

---

[12] Quoted in *MW*, 43 (1865), 591.   [13] Ibid.   [14] Ibid.

tious to suit the taste of an auditory which had had a morning of sacred music'.[15] But there were good points too, and Henry Lunn considered that he had rarely heard *Die letzten Dinge* 'go better'.[16] There was also general agreement that *St Paul* and *Elijah* had received more than adequate performances, while Wesley must have been agreeably surprised to find *The Times* devoting so much space to 'Ascribe unto the Lord' (a 'work of such merit') and even more so at Davison's reprinting the notice in *The Musical World*—perhaps the first occasion on which a work of his had received unqualified praise in the national press.[17] Could this have been linked to his engagement of Arabella Goddard (Mrs Davison), whose performance of Mendelssohn's Piano Concerto No. 1 was described by her husband as 'the feature of the festival'?[18] Wesley was clearly less comfortable at the orchestral concerts, where the performances of Beethoven's Choral Fantasia and Symphony No. 8 left much to be desired. Not so Rossini's overture to *Guillaume Tell*, although the comment that the orchestra were up to the mark 'especially when they ran away from the conductor'[19] suggests that his presence contributed little. The same was true of the Mendelssohn concerto, when Wesley effectively relinquished direction to the leader, Henry Blagrove:

The music went on well enough in such accustomed hands as those of the pianist and the 'leader,' the Doctor's beat being little regarded—a circumstance which did not appear to trouble him. Gradually Wesley's face lightened and beamed. The music having hold of him, presently took entire possession. He swayed from side to side; he put down the baton, treated himself to a pinch of snuff with an air of exquisite enjoyment, and then sat motionless, listening. Meanwhile Blagrove conducted with his violin-bow.[20]

Once a successful performance of *Messiah* and a particularly brilliant ball (at which Mr Stanton Jones and his orchestra kept the dancing going until after 4 a.m.) had brought the week's proceedings to a close, it was generally agreed that, despite some shortcomings, Wesley had (to quote *The Times*) 'passed with credit through this first ordeal'.[21] Davison even went so far as to declare that

Those who condemn him for any occasional lapsus, should reflect that it is no easy task for any one who has been playing a Cathedral Organ all his life to be called upon suddenly to assume the bâton and conduct an orchestra of some 300 persons, and I have little doubt but that with further experience Dr. Wesley will show himself fully equal to a future occasion.[22]

[15] Quoted in *MW*, 43 (1865), 607.   [16] *MT*, 12 (1865), 142.   [17] Ibid.
[18] *MW*, 43 (1865), 567.   [19] Ibid. 606.
[20] Joseph Bennett, *Forty Years of Music, 1865–1905* (London: Methuen, 1908), 35.
[21] Quoted in *MW*, 43 (1865), 606.   [22] Ibid. 580.

Approval, albeit of a private nature, also came from another quarter. Hubert Parry had been an enthusiastic member of the audience and recorded his impressions in his diary. *St Paul*, *Lobgesang*, and *Die erste Walpurgisnacht* all pleased him greatly, but the two highlights of the week were *Elijah* and *Messiah*: 'I never hear[d] the "Baal" chorus so splendidly done as it was today; Wesley got <u>exactly</u> the right time in the first part; and as they did the last part I think it was about the finest chorus in the whole *Elijah*'.[23] Of *Messiah* he noted that the 'performance was, in my opinion, nothing inferior to any of the other performances' he had heard, although the breakneck speeds in which Wesley was prone to indulge spoilt the massive effect of 'For unto us' and the 'Hallelujah' chorus. Other choruses, however, 'could scarcely in any possibility have been done better', while both solo singers and chorus acquitted themselves splendidly.

All in all, Wesley could have felt content. Yet, as he might have expected, there was still sniping from some parts of the press . The *Saturday Review*, for example, observed that he was 'remarkable, if report was to be relied upon, no less for eccentricity than for talent', adding that 'from a recluse since thirty years, who now came forward with an inexperienced baton, at the caprice of an obstinate will, nothing very good was to be expected', although it was forced to admit that his conducting was 'fairer than had been anticipated'.[24] The critic of *The Queen* also indulged in an unwarranted personal attack, arguing that 'What a festival requires is . . . above all, a first-rate conductor. A narrow-minded local organist without experience—a mere dreaming theorist, full of prejudice and bigotry, is not the artist to be trusted with the engagements of the execution, nor with the the making up of the programmes.'[25]

Financially the festival had been an undoubted success, with receipts higher than in any year since 1853. But the costs were also higher, and there was criticism of the increase in the miscellaneous expenses, which was largely due to too many arrangements having been made at the last minute, without 'the usual supervision'.[26] Of no less concern was the relatively poor attendance at the evening concerts, Wednesday excepted, when Arabella Goddard's performance had attracted a capacity audience and more than paid for the cost of her engagement. Arguing that there was insufficient demand for a daily concert in the Shire Hall, the auditors proposed that in future years only two evenings— Tuesday and Thursday—should be devoted to music, with a ball on each of the other two nights. The only other comments on the artistic events are to be found in the 'Memoranda' compiled by the Revd F. T. Bayly in which he

[23] Parry's diary entry for 7 Sept. 1865 (*ShP*).   [24] Quoted in *MW*, 43 (1865), 621–2.
[25] Ibid. 606.   [26] Minutes of the stewards' meeting of 11 Oct. 1865 (*ThCh*).

took Wesley to task for appropriating too many decisions to himself and for incurring additional expense by placing the chorus and orchestra at the west end: in subsequent years they returned to their accustomed position adjoining the organ loft.

By the time these matters were being discussed the festival had long been over. Instead of such pleasurable diversions as hosting lunches for the principal singers there was simply the daily routine of services at the cathedral and the growing realization that, in so far as music was concerned, out of the festival season Gloucester was little different from Winchester. During Amott's long tenure musical standards had slipped, as *The Gloucester Journal* acknowledged when it hoped that Wesley's appointment would be 'the crowning point to raise our Cathedral Choir to rank among the most distinguished in the country'.[27] Neither was the organ in good shape. Rebuilt by the young Henry Willis in 1847, it was a smaller and much more old-fashioned instrument than the one he had left behind, with an odd mixture of compasses (Great CC to f''', Swell C to f''', Choir G to f''', and Pedal CC to f) and only a single pedal stop, added by Bishop in 1831. As Parry noted in 1864, it possessed a 'sort of glorious richness', but was 'rather in a bad state at present',[28] and its condition was a recurrent theme during Wesley's time at the cathedral. With a Dean and Bishop who had no interest in music (and had pointedly absented themselves from the recent festival) it was likely to be a struggle to get anything done, and a request to the chapter in 1869 for money for indispensable repairs fell on deaf ears. Wesley's reply makes melancholy reading:

I am ready to appeal to any competent organist as to the propriety and absolute necessity of what has been suggested. We cannot go on playing the organ without some change.

We are liable at any moment to get into trouble with the choir, and this is most painful, for when a difference arises the members of the chapter do not know who is right and who is wrong.

My nerves are too feeble to bear this. I am ready to give up all desire to win approbation, but what I point to is insupportable.[29]

Six years later nothing had been done, but with the Bishop's wife now showing interest, Wesley proposed the setting-up of a subscription to which he offered to contribute 10 guineas. But this too came to naught and Wesley ended his days with an instrument which, he told C. E. Miller, was 'not fit to play upon'.[30]

---

[27] *GJ* (18 Feb. 1865), 5. [28] Parry's diary entry for 31 Aug. 1864 (*ShP*).
[29] Letter dated 29 June 1869, quoted in Bennett, *Forty Years of Music*, 43–4.
[30] See C. E. Miller, 'Some Organists I have Known', *MO*, 57 (1934), 342. Miller had tried the instrument in 1875.

Parry had also borne testimony to the indifferent state of the choir when, on the Sunday after the 1865 festival, he had gone to hear Walter Farquhar Hook (now Dean of Chichester) preach. 'The Music was bad, and the sermon very good',[31] he recorded, but not until a further sixteen months had passed did he note that the 'Choir was worked up to something for the first time since Dr Wesley came'.[32] Some compensation for the poor singing in September 1865 had been provided by a 'most marvellous extemporaneous fugue' at the end of the service. Given that the subject he noted down is the phrase 'Like some poor sheep I've strayed' from the final movement of 'To my Request and Earnest Cry' and that his description of a gradually more complex accompaniment also fits the anthem, it was probably not quite as spontaneous as he imagined: 'He began the accompaniment in crotchets alone, and then gradually worked into quavers then triplets and lastly semiquavers. It was quite marvellous. The powerful old subject came stalking in right and left, with the running accompaniment entwined with it; all in the style of old Bach.'[33]

As in his previous appointments Wesley had made a point of introducing his own music soon after his arrival. The Chant Service in F—the only one known to have been sung in Gloucester before[34]—was put down for his first Sunday (25 June), with 'Thou wilt keep him in perfect peace' following on 21 July and 'The Wilderness' and 'Blessed be the God and Father' a few weeks later. The festival week saw the introduction of the morning canticles from the Service in E, 'Praise the Lord, O my soul' and 'O Lord, my God' but, with the exception of the opening day's service—when the Te Deum and Jubilate and Samuel Wesley's 'Thou O God, art praised in Sion' were sung—these performances were not (as *The Musical Standard* tactfully reported) 'of a most successful order'.[35] Perhaps for this reason no further new works were heard until the Communion Service in E made an appearance in December.

Of no less interest is the fact that for the first time Wesley found himself with a repertoire containing a number of works by his contemporaries. Although several anthems by Goss had been sung during his later years at Winchester, he had never performed the music of George Elvey, Edward Hopkins, Frederick Ouseley, or George Garrett (none of whom he held in particular esteem), and when it was proposed that further compositions by Hopkins and Garrett should be introduced, he lost his temper and said that

---

[31] Parry's diary entry for 10 Sept. 1865 (*ShP*).   [32] Parry's diary entry for 1 Jan. 1867 (*ShP*).

[33] Parry's diary entry for 10 Sept. 1865 (*ShP*).

[34] Although Amott had personally susbscribed to both Wesley's Service in E and *Anthems*, the Dean and Chapter had not, with the result that no copies would have been available. In contrast the morning canticles from the Chant Service in F had been sung no fewer than five times between his appointment and his swearing-in four months later.

[35] *MS*, 4 (1865–6), 98.

while he had no objection to 'your Hopkinses and your Popkinses',[36] he would countenance nothing more by his former pupil. Significantly, of the two services by Garrett in use before his arrival (in D major and F major, from a volume of three dedicated to the Bishop's wife) only the former continued to appear in the service lists.[37] On another occasion he wrote that he found the music of Goss less 'secular'[38] than the works of Hopkins and Garrett; there is a delightful irony in hearing such a statement from the composer of 'Blessed be the God and Father' or the Creed in the Service in E.

In other respects the repertoire was not so different from that at his previous appointments. The backbone consisted of late seventeenth-century, eighteenth-century and a few early nineteenth-century works, with a good selection from the anthems of Croft, Greene, and Boyce, and a number of extracts from compositions by Handel, Haydn, Mozart, and Mendelssohn, but almost nothing written before the mid-seventeenth century. An interesting name is that of Sir John Stevenson (see Chapter 2), whose music Wesley had apparently not encountered before, but nine of whose anthems he included in his collection *Words of Anthems*, published in 1869 and based largely on the Gloucester repertoire. Particular interest again attaches to his choice of con-temporary works: in addition to fourteen anthems by Goss, there are eight by Walmisley, and others by Elvey, Edward Hodges, Hopkins, Ouseley, Turle, and the young Herbert Oakeley. Perhaps the most unusual inclusions are Gresham Prize compositions by Alfred Angel, Edward Dearle, Elvey, Goss, Pye, and James Kendrick Pyne (senior).

To modern eyes one of the most surprising features is the very small number of services in regular use—no more than thirty, most of them respectable but uninspired late seventeenth-century and eighteenth-century settings. Such works as Rogers in D, Aldrich in G, King in C and F, Kent in D, Travers in F, Nares in F, and Arnold in A usually appeared at least once every three weeks and sometimes in two weeks in succession. Wesley's Chant Service in F belonged to this category as, in due course, did his dull *Short, Full, Cathedral Service in F* and Chant Service 'Letter B' (both published in 1869) and Chant Service in G (published in *The European Psalmist* in 1872). Parry heard the first in October 1867, 'Sung (or rather played) like the slowest and most mournful dirge that one could conceive', although as on an earlier occasion Wesley made amends by embarking on a 'fine extemporaneous hullabaloo' after the service.[39]

[36] *M* (July 1896), 152.

[37] George Garrett, *Cathedral Services in Score . . . Composed & Dedicated to Mrs. C. J. Ellicott* (London: Novello & Co., [1864]). The Service in F reappeared in the repertoire in the 1870s.

[38] Letter dated 4 May 1873 quoted in Donald Tovey and Geoffrey Parratt, *Walter Parratt: Master of the Music* (London: Oxford University Press, 1941), 159.

[39] Parry's diary entry for 6 Oct. 1867 (*ShP*).

It should not, of course, be forgotten that responsibility for drawing up the music lists officially lay with the precentor, but it is inconceivable that he would not have consulted someone of Wesley's eminence. Indeed, the latter's comment that for the first time he had a precentor with whom he was able to get on suggests this,[40] as do the disappearance of Garrett's Service in F, the frequency with which certain of his own works were sung, and, in an oblique way, the very defensive attitude he adopted when in 1875 Joseph Bennett requested details of the Sunday service lists for publication in the new journal *Concordia*. Claiming that they were made out by 'young Clerical Precentors', that the music in question was 'chiefly bad trash', that there was no 'professional knowledge amongst the parties concerned', and that the 'selections inflict a Martyrdom on true artists', he concluded: '<u>Do</u> let me say I am very very Sorry you are going to patronise Precentors by accepting their <u>Vile</u> (I do say) lists of music which are chiefly an <u>affront</u> to everything traditionally good. If you <u>will</u> have the lists I will tell a Pupil to send them [to] you "For this", amongst the rest, "am I ordained".'[41]

Even then he would not let the subject drop and in a second letter expressed amazement that a periodical would 'descend to put its stamp & seal to that which is so intrinsically wrong . . . as regards the most vital interests of a <u>Church Musician</u> . . . [who] may be even . . . more deserving than <u>the Dean</u>, but who yet has but a Lazarus position'.[42] As Bennett commented, the picture of Wesley 'sitting in rags at the gate of the Deanery, with the very reverend gentleman's dogs in suspicious proximity, is almost too funny'.[43] But he had not heard the last word: the unwanted arrival of a copy of *Concordia* unleashed a further diatribe against the efforts of some London critics to injure Wesley's reputation and position, making it impossible to believe that he did not feel personally responsible for the hated lists with their damning evidence of musical mediocrity.[44]

Unsurprisingly in view of Wesley's growing disillusion with church music, the taking up of a new post had not this time sparked off a bout of composition, and the only work completed within eighteen months of his arrival was an anthem, 'God be merciful unto us', written for the marriage of Parry's friend George Watson on New Year's Day 1867. Although Parry considered it 'Peaceful and graceful; and . . . very suitable for the Occasion',[45] even he

[40] See *M* (July 1896), 151.

[41] Letter dated 8 April 1875 (collection of the Revd Brian Findlay).

[42] Letter dated 26 April [1875] (collection of the Revd Brian Findlay). The Gloucester music list was first published on Saturday 1 May: see *Concordia*, 1 (1875), 18.

[43] Bennett, *Forty Years of Music*, 38.

[44] Letter dated 25 Sept. [1875] (collection of the Revd Brian Findlay).

[45] Parry's diary entry for 1 Jan. 1867 (*ShP*).

must have felt that its four short sections completely lack the breadth—or musical interest—of Wesley's earlier works. In one respect, however, it formed a landmark in his career, in that it was the first of his anthems to have been originally issued bearing the imprint of Novello, Ewer & Co.

Despite their position as the leading publishers of sacred music, Wesley had hitherto shown little inclination to be associated with the firm he had earlier accused of raking up and publishing 'all the discarded trash of former times'.[46] Publication of the *Anthems* had, as we saw, been entrusted to Messrs Addison & Hollier and reprints of individual items to Hall, Virtue & Co., who subsequently brought out 'Praise the Lord, O my soul' and 'All go unto one place'. Only in 1864, with the issue of his arrangement of the *Hundredth Psalm*, did his connection with Novello's begin.[47] It was they who published new editions of the Service in E, 'Ascribe unto the Lord', and Samuel Wesley's 'Thou, O God, art praised in Sion' for the Gloucester Three Choirs Festival the following year, and it was hardly surprising that Wesley should have turned to them for his new anthem. Of considerably more significance, however, is the fact that this transaction served as a prelude to a much greater one some fifteen months later.

With his suspicions of music publishers and their motives, Wesley had, with the solitary exception of the Service in E, always chosen to retain his copyrights. In March 1868, however, he overcame his scruples and sold the majority to Novello's for the princely sum of £750. Tradition has it that the transaction took several days, Wesley 'silently sitting on a stool, afraid to commit himself lest he might name too small a sum, and the then head of the firm . . . Henry Littleton, quietly writing his letters while waiting for the composer to proceed'.[48] When he received the cheque he is said to have remarked 'When I get home they'll think that I have been robbing somebody'![49] For his part he undertook to compose a Christmas anthem and a Morning, Communion, and Evening Service (published as his *Short, Full Cathedral Service in F*) for parish choirs, and to revise as necessary his other works before their reissue. The anthem, 'Blessed be the Lord God of Israel', was ready for publication in December and a year later received a generous review in *The Musical World*: what would Wesley not have given to have had some of his earlier anthems described as being of 'sterling quality' or containing 'masterly writing'?[50] Yet despite such lavish praise it can hardly be classed as one of his

---

[46] Letter dated 16 Aug. [1862] to W. E. Dickson (*Lbl* Add. MS 45489Q, fo. 100).

[47] Novello's had earlier taken over three other works—the two sets of *Three Pieces for a Chamber Organ* (originally issued by Cramer, Addison & Beale, reissued by Novello's in 1853) and *Sacred Songs: The Collects for the First Three Sundays in Advent* (originally issued by Coventry, reissued by Novello's in 1851).

[48] E[dwards], 'Samuel Sebastian Wesley', 455.   [49] Ibid.

[50] See *MW*, 47 (1869), 851, 864.

better works, and the same is even more true of the service. Written in the short service style, it suffers from the same 'jog-trot emphasis'[51] he had once so derided and contains considerably less musical interest than a similar work sung regularly at Gloucester—the Evening Service in E by John Goss. Even more mundane is a second chant service ('Letter B') published at his own expense in 1869. 'Just the thing for rustics',[52] he wrote to his sister Eliza, and it is depressing to discover with what regularity it was foisted on the Sunday congregation at Gloucester.

While the revision of most of the works sold to Novello's proved a straight-forward task (Pl. 15), Wesley took the opportunity to make more substantial alterations to three pieces dating from the late 1820s and early 1830s, the Variations on 'God save the King' (reissued as *The National Anthem, with Variations*), 'O God, whose Nature and Property', and the Introduction and Fugue in C sharp minor. In each case he sought to curb his youthful harmonic exuberance, but in doing so produced more finished but sometimes tamer and less idiosyncratic works. Thus the Introduction was considerably developed and received a beautiful new ending but lost the dramatic juxtaposition of unrelated chords which preceded it, while the effect of the *minore* movement from the Variations was softened by the removal of Neapolitan sixths; in compensation the final fugue was considerably extended and improved. In both works textures were simplified, and it is interesting to find Wesley doing the same, even to the extent of removing suspensions, in a much more recent work now published for the first time, 'Give the King thy judgements'.

By autumn 1869, with revisions to the anthems and other works almost complete, he was free once more to return to his final long-delayed project, *The European Psalmist*, and immediately summoned Eliza to help:

Can you give me a list of most of the new Hymns to which new Tunes have had to be put during the last few Years, or can you introduce someone who will make such a list, (sending me the words) & who I will refresh with a consideration[?]

I am very anxious to finish my European Psalmist & this is in the way.[53]

As he had discovered when preparing the music for Kemble's *A Selection of Psalms and Hymns*, the large number of hymns in unusual metres meant that he either had to include tunes 'quite devoid of merit'[54] or write new ones himself. The situation had not improved during the intervening years and an idea of the scale of the problem can be gauged from a simple statistic: *The*

---

[51] Wesley, *A Morning & Evening Cathedral Service*, iv.
[52] Letter dated 3 Sept. [1869] (*Lbl* Add. MS 35019, fo. 45).
[53] Letter dated 10 Nov. [1869] (ibid., fo. 61).
[54] Kemble, *A Selection of Psalms and Hymns*, [3].

Catalogue of Printed Music in the British Library to 1980 (London: K. G. Saur, 1981) lists no fewer than 584 hymn books with tunes published in England between 1850 and 1872, with forty appearing in 1865 alone. With men like J. B. Dykes, W. H. Monk, John Stainer, and Joseph Barnby writing tunes by the dozen and Gauntlett producing them by the hundred (if not thousand) the challenge was considerable. An invitation to contribute to the 1868 appendix to *Hymns Ancient and Modern* brought to the surface all Wesley's prejudices and objections to the work of such 'hack writers'[55] whose musical gifts were no match for his own:

I trust I fully appreciate the compliment I receive by your requiring my services in behalf of so esteemed a work as the one under notice.

I feel that if I am to give my humble assistance I should first have some little idea given me of your opinion as to the merits of [the] musical part of the work Hymns A & M already done, and also with respect to my own efforts of a similar kind. To compose a new good Tune would seem to be very difficult, and I have not had my name placed amongst ordinary contributors to many Hymnals.[56]

What especially irked him was the necessity of allowing his name to appear in the company of those amateur composers he so despised, of being 'asked to stand on a level with the writers of your music':[57]

when you speak of 'Many of our best Composers' I really do feel that 'bad is the best' & that I never have seen one first-rate Hymn Tune, the production of an Englishman, during the last 30 years. Most of those persons who practise such composition have not even attempted—publicly—any other kind but Church pieces & some of those who have done so have no made no effect at all. It is very unpleasant to me to have thus to express my mind . . . In my opinion the best that can be said of modern Hymn Tunes is that about Two new Tunes (all I ever noticed as being so) are pretty good. Not one is fine & great & the majority are contemptible & unworthy of being used in any Service of public worship from their love-song affectations (and this even in Tunes, by Clergymen, to the most solemn words) & even faulty writing, for their writers had evidently never been taught counterpoint.[58]

There was also a matter of principle. Unlike many contributors, Wesley was a professional composer of standing who had long campaigned for the better remuneration of church musicians. For him writing music was a matter of both art and business, and to this end he offered ten tunes for the considerable sum of 130 guineas (rather than 'furnishing a Tune or two at the ordinary

---

55 Letter dated 15 Feb. 1868 to Sir Henry Baker (*HA&M*).
56 Letter dated 22 Jan. 1868 to Sir Henry Baker (*HA&M*).
57 Letter dated 18 Feb. [1868] to Sir Henry Baker (*HA&M*).
58 Letter dated 15 Feb. 1868 to Sir Henry Baker (*HA&M*).

terms of hack writers')[59] and settled for the inclusion of two—'Aurelia' and 'Alleluia' (here first published)—for £25. Seven years later 'Harewood' was included in the new edition of 1875, but with the part-writing revised, against his better judgement, 'to better suit Rustics'.[60]

With dealings over the 1868 appendix out of the way and the prospect of finishing *The European Psalmist* at last in sight, Wesley set to work with a will and completed a further 104 tunes, bringing the number of his own contributions to 142—or over 20 per cent of the total. Although over one-third (39) were written for hymns from *Hymns Ancient and Modern*, he ranged widely, with a further twelve for verses by his grandfather and others for hymns from the *Sarum Hymnal* and Kemble's *Selection*. It is the tunes for such well-known hymns as 'Abide with me', 'Fierce raged the tempest o'er the deep', 'Just as I am, without one plea', 'Lead kindly light', 'Nearer, my God, to thee', 'Onward Christian soldiers', and 'Sun of my soul, Thou Saviour dear', however, that have aroused particular interest as all had been set elsewhere by his despised contemporaries, prompting Erik Routley to suggest that he was making a 'dead set' against the most prolific of these, J. B. Dykes.[61]

Certain texts clearly gripped his imagination, and he provided five tunes (three of his own) for John Keble's 'Sun of my soul' and three (two of his own) for Henry Lyte's 'Abide with me'. Doubtless aware that he had entered the last chapter of his own life, his empathy with verses which declare

> When the soft dews of kindly sleep
> My wearied eyelids gently steep,
> Be my last thought, how sweet to rest
> For ever on my Saviour's breast
>
> ('Sun of my soul')

or

> Hold Thou thy Cross before my closing eyes;
> Shine through the gloom, and point me to the skies;
> Heaven's morning breaks, and earth's vain shadows flee;
> In life, in death, O Lord, abide with me.
>
> ('Abide with me')

[59] Letter dated 15 Feb. 1868 to Sir Henry Baker (*HA&M*). Wesley was fully aware of the danger of being misunderstood when business was transacted by letter and would have much preferred to have put his views on hymn tune composition and remuneration in person: 'I must add, once again, that I feel flattered by your obliging proposal & that I am willing to do just what you desire & no more. I have felt the greatest objection to writing on this subject & have endeavoured to obtain the advantage & honor of an interview. I could not but forsee what may likely be the consequences of my opening my mind to you on this business'.

[60] Letter dated 18 Sept. 1873 to Sir Henry Baker (*HA&M*).

[61] See *The Musical Wesleys* (London: Herbert Jenkins, 1968), 217, which includes a detailed discussion of Wesley's hymn tunes.

becomes readily apparent. So too does his decision to print the second verse of Edward Dayman's burial hymn 'Sleep thy last sleep' with his tune 'Shillingstone':

> Life's dream is past,
> All its sin, its sadness;
> Brightly at last
> Dawns a day of gladness.
> Under thy sod,
> Earth, receive our treasure,
> To rest in God,
> Waiting all His pleasure.

('Sleep thy last sleep')

Without reading too much of a valedictory character into the work, one suspects that he knew it would be his last important publication. It must therefore have been with a particular sense of achievement that he wrote to Eliza in March 1870 to declare that 'My European Psalmist is done'.[62] But with the process of publication only now beginning there was still much to do, and in May 1871 he approached the organist and composer Ann Bartholomew (1811–1891) for assistance with the tedious and time-consuming business of proofreading. 'I have gone through my work carefully & consider it <u>correct</u> but am not contented, and wish for further examination',[63] he explained, and ten days later enlarged upon what was needed:

By your questions I see you are not aware that my work is already considered <u>correct</u> by <u>me</u>.

All proofs have been most carefully corrected (excepting a few new pages in cases where new Tunes have replaced canceld. ones) and the Book wd. come to you as ready for printing.

But I reflect how liable the Author is to overlook things, & especially when he has been poring over a thing for years.

Hence, I wished a fresh eye to come to bear on my pages.[64]

With his notoriously irascible nature Wesley cannot have been an easy person to work with, and on more than one occasion Mrs Bartholomew found herself the recipient of a decidedly tetchy letter. What particularly irked him was her inability (as he put it) to 'quite see my meaning',[65] and matters became even more complicated when she was asked to help with revisions to 'The

[62] Letter dated 4 March [1870] (*Lbl* Add. MS 35019, fo. 79ᵛ).
[63] Letter dated 29 April 1871 (*Lcm* MS 3077).
[64] Letter dated 8 May [1871] (*Lcm* MS 3078).
[65] Letter dated 13 May [1871] (*Lcm* MS 3080).

Wilderness' and 'Praise the Lord, O my soul'. With Henry Littleton of Novello's also getting on his nerves, he finally lost patience in January 1872 (see Pl. 18):

My dear Madam.

You ask me to approve of your remarks on my proofs. I regret to say I do not do so. On the contrary, your marking 5ths when there are none, so often as you have, would have been more promptly dealt with (as was, I see, necessary) had I not feared I might do you harm in Littletons sight.

I suspect your Harmony exercises were confined to 4 parts.

You seem to make no allowance for the motion of the parts but if it happens that they furnish 5ths for the organ part you straightway call out 5ths.

Mr. L, it seems expects me to take immense trouble but I cannot do it again. If my Anthems are altered I must call public attention to the fact in my own way. If I wished to charge heavily for revising my Anthems I might be very wrong but Mr Littleton will allow nothing and as my time is valuable I am in a difficulty. Excellent as your remarks are they are by no means invariably correct. And you see 5ths where they have been carefully avoided.

If I am to overlook your revisions there must be something new arranged as my te[m]per will not stand the annoyance of seeing my music misunderstood both as to defects & that which is meritorious.[66]

As he explained in a contrite apology, he had been especially annoyed by Littleton's complaint about 'disgraceful mistakes'[67] in 'Praise the Lord, O my soul'. To judge from his letters, the whole business had become a tiresome chore. 'I regret selling you my things',[68] he told Littleton bluntly, and constant demands for extra payment run like a refrain through their correspondence:

To revise the new edition & Mrs B.s remarks will certainly take me 4 hours.

I wish to know if it is the rule for Authors thus to give their time.

My bargain with you was—originally—for what you took. Were I to ask you to vary that bargain in my favor I know the sort of letter I should have to put up with from you. You say you pay Mrs. B. True. But Mrs Bs revision is not all that is wanted . . . for she does not quite comprehend my harmonies & sees errors where none exist & where I considered I had been most original & meritorious . . .

If my works are wrongly issued in your new copies of course I shall make a public statement to the effect that you wished me to give you my time for nothing.[69]

At length, with the revisions to the anthems complete and *The European Psalmist* engraved and corrected, he was able to write to Eliza in February

---

[66] Letter dated 19 Jan. [1872] (*Lcm* MS 3098).
[67] Letter dated 2 Feb. 1872 (*Lcm* MS 3099).
[68] Undated letter [?Jan. 1872] to Henry Littleton (formerly in the private library of Novello & Co.).
[69] Ibid.

1872—and assuredly with a profound sense of relief—to tell her that 'My European is all but ready. Dont name it to me tho!!'.[70] All that remained was to finish obtaining new subscribers or chasing up old ones: some had either asked for their money back or never paid, others had lost interest, and a few had died. 'I want 5000 at least, to pay me anything worth having', he had informed Eliza,[71] but the subscription list runs to barely one-sixth of that number and one would love to know how much, if anything, he did make. As he had done when issuing the *Anthems*, he persuaded various long-suffering acquaintances to assist, with the result that there were little pockets of subscribers in various areas, including a clutch in Lancashire and Yorkshire and others in Bath, Devon, Gloucester, the Isle of Wight, Winchester, and north Wales. R. A. Atkins was presumably responsible for the last, while a new friend, Dr Linnington Ash of Holsworthy, provided those from Devon. It was to him that Wesley wrote on 20 June to say that the copies were ready for dispatch and, with only the task of collecting any outstanding subscriptions remaining, more than twenty years' toil had finally come to an end. Yet, as with the organ in St George's Hall, the delay had cost Wesley dear. When he had started work the practice of using separate books for words and tunes was still common, but by now it was decidedly old-fashioned and three of the collections which were to dominate Anglican hymnody at the end of the century were already established—Kemble's *A Selection of Psalms and Hymns* (1864), *Hymns Ancient and Modern* (1861, new edition with appendix 1868) and the *Hymnal Companion to the Book of Common Prayer* (1870). In comparison with the last two *The European Psalmist* looked hopelessly out of date and, as a vehicle for practical use, was already obsolete. It was also, as Wesley was well aware, too large and, with the exception of his own contributions, it completely ignored the most popular ingredient of most contemporary hymnals—new tunes. 'There is <u>one tune</u> by a living writer ['Lucknow' by his friend James Kendrick Pyne]' he had told Mrs Bartholomew, adding 'I dont care for such stuff as I see now-a-days'.[72] But such high-brow views were not shared by the world at large, who preferred the works of Dykes, Monk, and others to his own, more old-fashioned tunes with their characteristic quirks of melody and harmony. Like his anthems, they take their models from the past: the eighteenth- or early nineteenth-century English psalm tune, the chorale, and, occasionally, the sixteenth- or early seventeenth-century psalm tune. Only rarely did he attempt anything outside these broad categories, and he largely ignored one highly influential form, the partsong. Yet he was not afraid

---

[70] Letter dated 13 Feb. 1872 (*Lbl* MS Add. 35019, fo. 72).
[71] Letter dated 4 March [1870] (ibid., fo. 79).   [72] Letter dated 19 May [1871] (*Lcm* MS 3083).

to experiment harmonically, and his tunes thus fall between the overtly conservative works of such composers as W. H. Havergal and Charles Steggall and those of Dykes and Monk. One finds the same striding melodies and independent bass-lines, suspensions and diatonic dissonance as in his larger works, but also the same skilful handling of key relationships and cadences; given his traditional outlook it is not surprising to discover that he rarely harmonized a melodic note as a (dissonant) unprepared seventh.[73] Paradoxically too the particular demands of the form—a restricted time-scale and a simple musical idiom—were ideally suited to his late style, and the tunes written during the 1860s constitute what is in many ways the most characteristic group of works to date from his final years, many of them as defiantly his own as the great works of earlier decades for cathedral use.

In addition to his original tunes Wesley reharmonized a majority of the older tunes and in these, as in his earlier arrangements for Hullah's *Psalter*, responded sympathetically to their different styles; several of his arrangements remain in use today.[74] It was the same with German chorales, in which, despite his veneration for Bach, he rarely sought to emulate the latter's complex part-writing. 'The Counterpoint of English Psalmody is more simple than that of the German',[75] he had written earlier, and he produced some admirably forthright settings of which 'Wachet auf' is an excellent example. One exception is the highly expressive Bach-inspired cadence to his otherwise severe harmonization of 'Da Jesus an dem Kreuze stund', misleadingly entitled 'Dordrecht' (see Ex. 6.1). What he would certainly not have countenanced was the simplification—or in some cases bowdlerization—of Bach's harmonies found in the 1861 and 1868 editions of *Hymns Ancient and Modern*.

It is only a short step from Wesley's chorale harmonizations to his own chorale-inspired tunes, of which 'Wigan', written for Matthew Bridges's 'Behold the Lamb of God!', and 'Brecknock', a setting of John Wesley's 'Thou hidden love of God', are outstanding. Both eschew contrapuntal elaboration and chromatic harmony, and achieve a sense of dignity and grandeur which makes no concession to popular taste; indeed, only the augmented sixth in the final line of the latter suggests a nineteenth- rather than a seventeenth- or eighteenth-century origin. Such tunes, however, only form a small part of his output, and a much larger number are ultimately derived from such lyrical,

---

[73] Wesley's practice contrasts with that of Stainer in such tunes as 'Charity' or 'St Francis Xavier'.

[74] See the versions of 'Halton Holgate' (William Boyce) and 'St Ephraim' (Benjamin Milgrove) in *Hymns Ancient & Modern Revised* (London: William Clowes and Sons, [1951]). Wesley's identification with the rugged simplicity of the dour Scottish psalm tune 'Coupar' in Hullah's *Psalter* was sufficient for him to allow it to end on an open fifth (John Hullah (ed.), *The Psalter or Psalms of David in Metre* (London: J. W. Parker, 1843), 79).

[75] Preface to *A Selection of Psalm Tunes*, 2nd edn., [1].

Ex. 6.1. Wesley's harmonizations, *a* 'Wachet auf'; *b* 'Da Jesus an dem Kreuze stund'

a)

'Wachet auf'

b)

'Da Jesus an dem Kreuze stund'

frequently triple-time, late eighteenth-century psalm tunes as 'Abridge', 'Richmond', or 'Rockingham'. 'Hereford', one of his earliest but most perfect creations, is a splendid example of pure eighteenth-century lyricism. Although written in 1832, it remained unpublished until its appearance—slightly revised—in *The European Psalmist* forty years later, where it was set to the 'New Version' of Psalm 103; its current association with Charles Wesley's 'O Thou who camest from above' dates from the 1904 edition of *Hymns Ancient and Modern*. With its flowing melody and part-writing, enhanced by the frequent slight dissonances on the down-beats, it provides a fine example of a tune that 'sings itself'. The subsequent metamorphosis of this style to produce such an idiosyncratic tune as 'Kerry' ('Sun of my soul, thou saviour dear') is a fascinating process, not least because two earlier stages of its existence survive in the form of different versions of the related tune 'Winscott'. In place of the seeming melodic inevitability of 'Hereford' one finds a tune shaped as much by harmonic as by melodic considerations. Take, for example, the two unexpected G♯ (bars 3 and 12), both the result of Wesley's penchant for darting off at a harmonic tangent. Yet, as the emergence of 'Kerry' from 'Winscott' shows, it is in such details that the character of a tune lies. Could anyone, having heard the radiant D major harmony in the last line of 'Kerry', not consider the original D minor of 'Winscott' drab and colourless in comparison?

Erik Routley has drawn attention to Wesley's handling of key relationships.[76] As in his larger-scale compositions it is to the keys a third above and below the tonic—the mediant and submediant, both major and minor—that he often moves in his hymns, preferring these to the dominant or subdominant. Together with a considerable variety of cadential patterns in which imperfect or interrupted cadences frequently predominate, this results in music which is original, unpredictable, and never complacent. It is not, however, always user-friendly and, as Routley observed, Wesley's tunes frequently appeal more to musicians than to the hymn-singing public.[77] Intellectual rather than emotional, they only rarely, as in 'Hereford' and 'Aurelia' ('The church's one foundation'), possess the 'common touch' so essential if a hymn tune is to be successful.

There are also a few tunes which fall into none of these categories. 'Celestia' ('Hark! Hark, my soul! Angelic songs are swelling') unashamedly adopts the idiom of the partsong and, with its rather sentimental chromaticism and evocative long crescendo in the first line ('swelling'), shows that when he chose to, he could easily compete with Dykes or Barnby on their own terms. 'Nazareth' ('Christ is born! exalt his name!') and 'Haverhill' ('The sun is

---

[76] See *The Musical Wesleys*, 207–11.   [77] Ibid. 223.

Ex. 6.2. *a* 'Winscott'; *b* 'Kerry'

sinking fast') adopt another of their innovations, a change of time signature or key part-way through (cf. Dykes's 'Christus consolator'). In 'Haverhill' the changes of mood are so abrupt that they almost defeat their original purpose, yet within this tune's dozen bars Wesley managed to pack so many fingerprints of his work—a central modulation to the mediant major, a typical rising arpeggiated melody, and a double $\frac{9}{8}\frac{7}{6}$ suspension over the mediant—as to make it irrefutably his own.

'Triumph', a setting of Thomas Hankison's 'Who shall ascend the holy place?' which concludes with an extended anthem-like setting of the last line, is another idiosyncratic tune, but the most original is undoubtedly 'Orisons', written for 'Abide with me'. One of Wesley's two settings of these words, it was first published in both unison and four-part versions in Kemble's *Psalms and Hymns*, and reveals a typically fascinating marriage of ancient and modern, mid-nineteenth-century chromatic harmony and classical treatment of dissonance. Who else would have been so 'modern' as to use augmented triads and juxtapose a B major triad and a dominant seventh on G, but conclude the second and third lines with impeccably prepared and resolved suspensions? But like so many of his tunes it is too personal a statement ever to have the universal appeal of Monk's 'Eventide'.

Before leaving *The European Psalmist* it is worth noting that it included sixty-five of Bach's little-known chorale harmonisations—the largest number so far published in Britain, two of which, settings of 'Vom Himmel hoch' (no. 7) and 'Es ist das Heil uns kommen her' (no. 378), cannot be traced elsewhere. Although Wesley had originally set out to produce a collection of psalm and hymn tunes, the book eventually expanded to include Anglican chants, settings of the Responses to the Commandments and the Sanctus, a handful of brief anthems (by Wesley and his father), and a new Morning and Evening Chant Service in G, soon to enter the repertoire at Gloucester. Yet despite its considerable musical interest it has remained a white elephant, serving as a repository to be drawn upon by later editors but sadly providing yet another example of Wesley's unfortunate capacity for self-defeat. One suspects that his comment to Mrs Bartholomew 'I wait to make my fortune by the book' remained a vain hope.[78]

For a few years in the late 1860s and early 1870s hymnody almost took over Wesley's life. He also contributed tunes to *The Sarum Hymnal* (1869), *The Hymnary* (1872), *Church Hymns with Tunes* (1874), and *The Song of Praise* (1875), while his final offering was as musical editor of *The Welburn Appendix* (1875), a collection of hymns and tunes compiled by the Revd James Gabb,

---

[78] Letter dated 22 May [1871] (*Lcm* MS 3085).

Rector of the parishes of Bulmer and Welburn, where his son Charles was assistant curate. Of all these ventures, his association with *The Hymnary* (musical editor Joseph Barnby) seems at first sight the most unlikely. Was it not Barnby who had recently written such a spirited defence of 'modern' hymn tunes and whose own works exemplify the prevailing fashion for secular-sounding church music?[79] Did not contributing to a book which in many ways stood for all he objected to represent an abandonment of his principles?

While we cannot know for certain how Wesley viewed the subject, we can be fairly confident that he considered it primarily as a business transaction with someone whose work as a choral conductor he knew and admired. As his dealings with *Hymns Ancient and Modern* had shown, it was precisely because he regarded himself as a professional composer that he drove such hard bargains: if there was now a demand for his music why should he not profit by it? Although the terms he accepted from Novello's, publishers of *The Hymnary*—£68 5s. 0d. for twelve new tunes—were considerably less steep than those he had put to Sir Henry Baker, they were still almost double the going rate of 2 to 3 guineas per tune; he also agreed to provide a thirteenth—not ultimately asked for—in exchange for a piano by Collard & Collard! Yet with a degree of wilfulness which borders on the perverse, his immediate response to requests to use his tunes was, as he admitted to Walter Parratt, almost calculated to offend:

My course has been . . . to print this letter & it offends all. Not one has even paid me the humble guinea I ask. It is not the value of the guinea they mind but they dont like finding I despise their attempts to compliment me by their improper request.[80]

Sir,

I can but be flattered by your wish to adopt my tune ( ) but I must inform you that I do not compose Music for pleasure solely.

My profession being that of a Musician, I can no more *give away* my compositons than can a Painter his pictures or a Merchant his merchandise.

For the privilege of printing one of my hymn tunes, for this special occasion, I require . . .

Here indeed was Florence Marryatt's Dr Nesbitt with a 'cynical look . . . lurking behind his readiest smile . . .'.[81] Profoundly disillusioned and with an ever-heavier chip on his shoulder, Wesley was only too ready both to impugn the motives and belittle the achievements of others. Thus in the same letter to

---

[79] See the preface to Barnby's *Original Tunes to Popular Hymns for use in Church and Home* (London: Novello, Ewer & Co., 1869).

[80] Undated letter [8 Jan. 1870] enclosing a standard printed reply (*Lco* Parratt papers). Parratt had asked to reprint 'Aurelia'.

[81] *Nelly Brooke*, 2. 185.

Parratt he witheringly dismissed the works of 'London Professors' who, he claimed, were 'so delighted at being asked for their wretched trash that people can get what they want by just asking . . . [while] those who look for a fair remuneration are tricked by such men as Goss & Hopkins'.[82] Even the placing of his name after Goss's on advertisements for *The Hymnary* roused him to ire: 'I would not say a word if I liked his music at all. But I dont like it at all'.[83] That he should now find himself the victim of petty jealousy is particularly ironic, but Gauntlett, piqued by the selection of 'Aurelia' for the thanksgiving service for the recovery of the Prince of Wales in February 1872, issued a circular denouncing it as 'secular twaddle . . . inartistic and not fulfilling the conditions of a hymn tune',[84] and also advertised his own 'New Thanksgiving Hymn'.[85] 'Aurelia', he claimed, was based on 'Auld Robin Gray', although it was pointed out that it bore more than a passing resemblance to Robert Pearsall's partsong 'O who will o'er the downs so free'—a work Wesley claimed never to have heard.

A variety of factors had contributed to Wesley's low state, but foremost among them was a sense of isolation, both social and musical, which he had already encountered in Winchester. That this was largely due to his own rebarbative nature would have done nothing to lessen the feelings of ill will he bore towards those who, he considered, enjoyed more than their fair share of the good things of life. 'I ever regret leaving Devon and Gloster is very objectionable',[86] he wrote in 1870, and dissatisfaction with the city and his lot, and worries about his sons and his health, run like a refrain through his letters. Eliza was the recipient of many of these complaints:

I am sadly depressed in spirits. No amusement of any kind & very many cares from the unsettled position of my Sons. This change of weather, too, has given me much pain in the knee belonging to my broken leg . . .

I have been alone here this 3 weeks. Mrs. W. in Yorkshire with my medical Son [John Sebastian] who is worried by having to make a new agreement with his assistant who is trying for a large sum. Never mind . . .

Dear me. What a dull life I lead. Not one object here of interest.

You ridiculed my enquiry about Dead organists. I might—old as I am [—] be very glad—under peculiar circumstances—to get away from here. Besides, my Son

---

[82] Undated letter [8 Jan. 1870] (*Lco* Parratt papers).

[83] Letter dated 2 Aug. 1870 to Henry Littleton (formerly in the private library of Novello & Co.).

[84] Although no copies of Gauntlett's circular are known, the end was quoted in *The Choir* and reprinted in *MT*, 47 (1906), 678. Gauntlett's accusation led several correpondents to write to *MS* to point out that similar charges could be laid against his tunes 'St Alphege' and 'Houghton', and no more was heard of the matter (see *MS*, new ser., 2 (1872), 112, 129).

[85] See *MS*, new ser. 2 (1872), 107.

[86] Letter dated 2 Aug. [1870] to Sarah Emett (*Lbl* Add. MS 35019, fo. 167).

[William] in London wants a place much. There is <u>no</u> business for me here. No gentry. All mean grasping Tradesmen who send in bills twice & you had need keep receipts.[87]

'I am so out of spirits that I really need companionship',[88] he wrote three months later, and even a recuperative holiday in the Lake District in July was brought to a premature end by his recall on 'family business' which, as he gloomily observed, 'is not always favourable to Musical business & with the Anxieties attendant on the placing [of] five Sons out in the world, Music is not always a welcome subject'.[89] Indeed, for close on thirty-five years the burden of bringing up five sons and establishing them in the world had lain heavily upon his shoulders. By the late 1860s the two eldest, John Sebastian and Samuel Annesley, were already making their own way. John, who had studied medicine at King's College Hospital after leaving Winchester College in 1855, was now established as a general practitioner in Wetherby, while Samuel, who had spent a year at Lancing College in 1853, initially went to sea but by late 1862 had settled in Australia. Here he remained, working as a carrier and later as a publican and hotel owner and, in 1866, fathering an illegitimate daughter, Fanny, of whose existence one suspects her grandparents remained in ignorance; his unexpected suicide in 1893 was surely another manifestation of the line of depression running through the family.[90] Francis, a commoner at Winchester from 1855 to 1859, had gone up to All Souls College, Oxford (1861–65), and subsequently taught at his old school (1865–8) before being ordained deacon by the Bishop of Manchester (1869) and priest by the Bishop of Gloucester and Bristol (1871). After serving his second curacy at St Michael's, Gloucester, he was appointed Vicar of Hamsteels, a new mining parish in County Durham (1874), for the consecration of whose church (6 July 1875) his father wrote two hymn tunes. Here he remained until he retired in 1911 to Winchester, where he died on 21 November 1920. Charles too had spent time in Australia, arriving in February 1865 and returning—at his father's request—four years later. Eliza'a assistance was now sought in finding a place for him:

My Son, lately returned from Australia, so much wants to get with a good business office, with a view to learning <u>business</u>. He is <u>26</u> yrs. of age but has been working at <u>accounts</u> with a Teacher like a young Boy to get qualified.

I always had a good opinion of a dry salters business. Do you think amongst your City friends you could get him in [?] He is very steady indeed & <u>very pleasing</u>. 6ft

[87] Letter dated 14 March 1870 (ibid., fos. 85–6).   [88] Letter dated 17 [June 1870] (ibid., fo. 98).
[89] Letter dated 29 July 1870 to Linnington Ash (*Lbl* Loan 79).
[90] I am most grateful to Jan Fisher, Fanny's great granddaughter, for information on Samuel's life in Australia.

2 in height. Please try & remember this when your are amongst City people. I am so anxious to get quit of my Sons & I am tired of anxiety & worry. I am unfit for bringing up so many Sons & it kills me. One, my best [Francis], was ordained last Sunday, at Manchester.[91]

In the event Charles entered Gloucester Theological College in 1870 and was ordained by the Bishop of Gloucester and Bristol in 1872; after various curacies he was appointed Rector of Grosmont, Monmouthshire, in 1884, and remained there until he took his own life on 18 March 1914.[92] William Ken, the youngest, had matriculated at Trinity College, Cambridge, in 1866 (but never graduated), and began medical training at St Bartholomew's Hospital, London, in 1869 (qualifying MRCS in 1871); it must have been with considerable relief that Wesley wrote to Walter Parratt in June 1874:

my Sons are now all out in various positions getting their bread. My last left me on friday for Ceylon & if safe is now Steaming down the Coast of Italy. He was delighted with a previous visit to Ceylon when he obtained what seems a fine appointment. You cannot think what a relief it is after more than 35 years Anxiety about Children, to see them on their own [illegible] &, as I think, doing well . . .[93]

Within eighteen months, however, William was back in England and, to judge from Wesley's request that Eliza should 'write Mrs. Wesley a letter about the troubles of the musical profession and ask her to shew it to Willy',[94] apparently having second thoughts about his chosen career. After his father's death he went back to Ceylon but contracted tuberculosis; he died in Chichester in 1879 at the age of thirty-three, and his mother subsequently compiled a manuscript collection of her husband's hymn tunes, 'to the loved Memory of One whose preferences have chiefly guided this selection of his father's hymn Tunes'.[95]

Like many parents, Wesley also found it hard to relinquish responsibility for his children, or to accept that they could stand on their own two feet. '. . . my Son is as docile & attached as a Dog',[96] he had written when trying to secure a minor canon's post for Francis, and he later tried his hardest to get him to move from Hamsteels: 'I fear Durham won't do for my Son. The thing is how to get him away. My Sons have but little tact.'[97] Far more serious, however, were concerns about John, who by the early 1870s was displaying worrying

[91] Letter dated 21 Sept. [1869] (Lbl Add. MS 35019, fo. 52).
[92] Information kindly supplied by Stephen Pickford.
[93] Letter dated 7 June [1874] (Lco Parratt papers).
[94] Undated letter (c.Nov. 1875) (Lbl Add. MS 35019, fo. 121).   [95] Now Lcm MS 4036.
[96] Letter dated 28 Dec. 1873 to Mrs Rance Phipps (Gloucester City Library, Gloucestershire Collection, S23.17(2)).
[97] Letter dated 21 March 1875 (Lbl Loan 79).

symptoms of mental instability, and one suspects that the various references to the illness of one of his sons refer to him. By the end of 1873 he was suicidal and in 1881, at his own request, was placed in Wonford House Asylum, Exeter.[98] Here he outlived all his brothers, dying on 20 July 1924.

But there were bright features in these somewhat dark years, among them the triennial Gloucester Three Choirs Festivals, the belated recognition of his compositions, and new friendships, particularly with Hubert Parry, Walter Parratt, and Dr Linnington Ash. Contact with younger musicians invariably brought out the best in Wesley, and Parry was no exception. As his diaries record, he was a regular visitor to the cathedral, where he had been given the freedom of the organ, while the Wesleys were in turn guests at Highnam. Here, in January 1866, Wesley provided some fascinating insights into his views on music:

Dr Wesley (& Mrs) came to dinner tonight. We got some very interesting conversation out of him. He said that he thought that the reason why Beethoven & more especially Spohr were sometimes (frequently) so unsatisfactory was because that [*sic*] lacked the necessary, and beneficial basis of hard work at Counterpoint; and . . . that the reason why Mendelssohn so excelled was entirely because he had that instruction, and went through that preparation thoroughly. I had a short talk with him over the Full Score of the Lobgesang. He told me that the reason why Spohr so excelled was because he could bring such a marvellous tone out of his orchestra. Mendelssohn could not be sure of it . . . He played some of Bach's Preludes & Fugues & Mendelssohn's 'Lieder ohne Worte'. I played the E major fugue. He says it will be impossible for me to get on well in orchestration without lessons from a London Master.[99]

Regular contact was maintained during Parry's remaining years at Eton and Oxford, but was inevitably broken when he settled in London in 1870. By now, however, Wesley had come to know Parratt, who was already making his mark as an organist and in whom he recognized a kindred spirit. Although born thirty years apart, they shared the same high artistic ideals, and he had wholehearted respect for the younger man: 'your qualities are different from most of them I could easily see',[100] he wrote in 1870. Four years later he shared with him one of his last engagements as a recitalist—at the Victoria Rooms, Clifton (see below). But it was the friendship with Ash, the local physician in Holsworthy, Devon, that had the greatest bearing on his life. Their paths first

---

[98] Admitted at the age of 45, John was described as suffering from 'Chronic Melancholia' and initially had suicidal tendencies (Wonford House Hospital case book 1890, case record 128). He was transferred to Digby Hospital, Exeter, in 1897 and back to Wonford House in 1909.

[99] Parry's diary entry for 6 Jan. 1866 (*ShP*).

[100] Letter dated 11 Jan. 1870 (*Lco* Parratt Papers).

crossed in 1870 when the organ in Holsworthy Parish Church was being rebuilt—at Ash's expense—and Wesley was invited to open it. 'I am so fond of Devon that I should always be willing to take engagements there',[101] he replied to the Rector, the Revd George Thornton. He found in Ash someone who not only enjoyed music but also shared his love of field sports, and thus a friendship was born. As a way of expressing his gratitude to his two Holsworthy friends, he dedicated the new editions of 'O God, whose Nature and Property' and 'I am thine, O save me' (then going through the press) to Rector and physician respectively. When the stage-coach driver refused to carry the parcel with Ash's copies from North Tawton station to Holsworthy it brought back memories of his life at Exeter: Everything was so behindhand, & the people so self-satisfied. How I wish it had been otherwise. Devon is so charming in most respects.'[102]

Renewal of contact with a part of the country of which he was particularly fond also re-awakened the idea—dormant since 1846—of settling there. 'I think if I could hear of a very good place for me, as a musician, in Devon I should be tempted to close with it',[103] he wrote to the Rector, pointedly adding 'But people dont understand the differences, as to quality, amongst professional men'; one suspects, however, that he knew that he would never find a suitable post in the county. But the idea did not die, and with Francis and Charles both looking for parishes the solution seemed obvious: to find a vacant living in Devon. Ash was called upon to help and, in March 1875, succeeded in raising Wesley's hopes. Wesley replied, 'Your account of the living near you was tantalising. I almost wish you had not named it & yet it has given me pleasure to see myself so near the possession of quiet & comfort . . . Could you ask some Clergy & others to tell you of vacancies . . .'[104]

It was, of course, essential that the parish was near a 'clean river',[105] but despite his scouring the clergy list and the list of livings for sale nothing suitable could be found, and Wesley would never enjoy a retirement where he could 'fish a little & roam about in the Winter with a gun'.[106] Yet his memory has been perpetuated in Holsworthy by the two tunes he wrote for the carillon recently installed in the town, again at Ash's expense, and opened on New Year's Day 1874. Wesley's tunes and his arrangement of Mozart's song 'Sehnsucht nach dem Frühlinge' (K. 596) were on the second of the two barrels and could be heard on Mondays, Wednesdays, and Thursdays. As the

[101] Letter dated 8 Feb. 1870 (*Lbl* Loan 79).
[102] Letter dated 20 Oct. [1870] (collection of David Greer).
[103] Letter dated 17 Feb. 1870 to the Revd G. W. Thornton (*Lbl* Loan 79).
[104] Letter dated 23 March 1875 (ibid.).
[105] Letter dated 6 May [1875] to Linnington Ash (ibid.).
[106] Letter dated 8 Feb. 1870 to the Revd G. W. Thornton (ibid.).

Western Morning News reported, this barrel was considered 'far superior to the first, more especially those [tunes] written by Dr. Wesley'.[107] The first tune has since become widely known through the organ piece he based on it, appropriately entitled 'An Air Composed for Holsworthy Church Bells'.

'Holsworthy Church Bells' was one of several organ works written or completed during the final years of Wesley's life when, despite his disaffection with the world, he returned to composition with an enthusiasm not seen since the 1840s. But there was a subtle difference. Whereas thirty years earlier the motivation to compose had invariably come from within and was allied with a fierce detemination to succeed, it was now frequently in response to a commission. Inevitably many of these works suffer from flagging inspiration or the deadening effect of self-imposed restrictions on his naturally expansive style, and while old sketches often provided an initial idea, none of the late anthems, organ pieces, solo songs, or partsongs possesses that sense of inspired vision which raised his best works to such exalted heights. That this should have happened when he was finally acknowledged as one of the leading composers of his generation was particularly ironic, but age and the stresses and strains of a busy professional life had caught up with him: 'I sincerely wish I could give myself up to writing a large serious work for our great Festivals', he had written in December 1867, '[but] Unless I could be quiet & contented this is impossible'.[108] And so it proved to be.

'As soon as my little psalmist is out I am pledged to do organ pieces for the Million',[109] Wesley had told Mrs Bartholomew in August 1871, by which time the first of these—an Andante in C for organ (or harmonium)—had already appeared in *The Musical Standard*.[110] A two-movement Voluntary for Spark's *The Organist's Quarterly Journal* (January 1872) and another Andante for *The Village Organist*[111] followed, leading one to suspect that they had all been intended for the long-awaited collection *Easy Organ Pieces*. That they all incorporate earlier material cannot be in doubt, as diatonic dissonance, chromatic colour and textural interest—in short, all those features so typical of his music in the 1830s and 1840s—are here present. The same is true of the Andante in E minor (issued posthumously in 1877), which, like the 'improvised' fugue noted by Parry, draws on 'To my Request and Earnest Cry'. 'Holsworthy Church Bells' in contrast is a tuneful, harmonically undemanding but perfectly finished piece which bears all the hallmarks of his 'late' style.

---

[107] Quoted in *MS*, new ser., 6 (1874), 36.
[108] Copy of a letter dated 31 Dec. 1867 to Mrs Haigh (formerly in the private library of Novello & Co.).
[109] Letter dated 23 Aug. [1871] to Mrs Bartholomew (*Lcm* MS 3097).
[110] See *MS*, 14 (1871), 40–1.
[111] Not the well-known series edited by John Stainer but a two-vol. collection compiled by the Revd T. R. Matthews.

Like the earlier pieces of church music written at Gloucester, the anthems completed during the 1870s were written to meet the demand from parish church choirs for new but not over-difficult works. Ranging from multi-movement full-with-verse anthems to the brief introits included in *The European Psalmist*, they include at least two which ought to be better known— a short, full setting of the collect 'Lord of all Power and Might' (issued in 1873 as part of Metzler's *The Practical Choirmaster*) and 'Let us now praise famous men' (Edition 'B'). Unpretentious, harmonically restrained, and with sensitive word-setting, the former epitomizes the changes that had taken place in Wesley's conception of and aims for church music during the previous forty years, and provides a perfect illustration of his comment to Parratt shortly before its publication, 'I, more and more, as I get older, dislike pretentious display, and would cling to the serious old Ch. School';[112] even in such a simple work he was able to introduce some welcome irregularity, with opening phrases of four and five bars respectively (see Ex. 6.3). 'Let us now praise famous men', in contrast, is an elaborate four-movement work written for commemoration use at Clifton College, Bristol. For the first time in his career Wesley found himself with a text not of his choosing: 'My reason for not liking to set the words is this—I don't like much solo singing in church', he informed the school organist, W. F. Trimnell, and later commented, 'I did not think I should ever have set words which are all about mankind'.[113] His doubts notwithstanding, he succeeded in producing a work which is full of life and, in many respects, the most successful of his late compositions. Among its more unusal features is an expressive tenor aria, 'There be of them'—his first extended solo for over thirty years—which opens with a beautifully poised melody, supported by simple but imaginative harmony. The anthem closes with an invigorating fugue which builds up to a rousing homophonic climax, but it proved too difficult for the boys, and Wesley subsequently produced an easier—and much weaker—setting, confusingly published as Edition 'A'.

In addition to his work at Clifton, Trimnell was editor of the recently established Collegiate Series, in which four of the new anthems and three secular choral works were published. Of the latter, both *The Mermaid* and 'Arising from the Deep' are typical Victorian partsongs, but *The Praise of Music* is a more substantial two-movement setting for unaccompanied double chorus of verses by Thomas Oliphant. Commissioned by Charles Gounod for his Royal Albert Hall Choral Society, it was the first new work by Wesley to have been heard in a major London venue since the performance of the Benedictus at Drury

[112] Letter dated 22 Feb. 1872, quoted in Worshipful Company of Musicians, *An Illustrated Catalogue of the Music Loan Exhibition . . . at Fishmongers' Hall, June and July, 1904* (London: Novello & Co., 1909), 333.
[113] See 'Clifton College and its Music', *MT*, 46 (1905), 240.

Ex. 6.3. 'Lord of all Power and Might'

Lane on 31 March 1832. By a strange coincidence Gounod wrote to Wesley forty years to the day after that earlier performance: 'I am acquainted with some of your compositions of which I have formed a very high opinion. I should consider it very amiable on your part and most attractive to the public if you would write . . . a chorus (for 4 or 8 voices) of as broad a style and easy in performance as possible.'[114] Offering Wesley the opportunity to conduct his own work, he stressed that he must have the manuscript no later than 25 May; in due course he thanked him for his 'beau morceaux'. The first movement in particular contains some powerful writing, notably where the music moves sequentially through keys a fourth apart—though the impression of eight-part writing is often illusory—and its effect when sung by some 14,000 voices at Gounod's final concert as conductor on 10 July must have been considerable (see Ex. 6.4). It was perhaps on the strength of this that *The Musical Standard* reported that the vacant post of conductor had been offered to Wesley.[115] In the event it went to Joseph Barnby, who subsequently amalgamated the choir with his own.

Such evidence of the continued esteem in which he was held and the renewed interest in his music must have been especially gratifying. How much more so the offer, on the recommendation of the prime minister (W. E. Gladstone), of a knighthood or Civil List pension of £100 per annum. Wesley chose the latter, which was announced on 14 January 1873, 'in recognition of his musical talents', and was continued to Mary Anne after his death.[116] But such recognition had come too late as he was beginning to feel his years and felt unable (as he told Parratt) 'to take up music from where I left it this number of years ago'[117] (i.e. before he had become a father). Even an attempt some two years earlier to interest the conductor Henry Leslie in his large-scale anthems seems to have been somewhat half-heartedly made through the agency of Henry Littleton: it was as though Wesley could no longer bring himself to promote his own music. 'I would write an orchestral Score if they were to be performed', he informed Littleton, 'It is rather hard on me for such things not to be known I think'.[118] But nothing came of this, and it is interesting to find that a suggestion from the Stewards that 'The Wilderness' or another work should be included in the programme of the 1868 Gloucester Three Choirs Festival, too, had borne no fruit.

In turning back to the Three Choirs festivals we return to a series of occasions which both punctuated and framed Wesley's time at Gloucester, besides providing a welcome stimulus to his otherwise uneventful life. The

[114] Letter dated 31 March 1872 (*Lcm* MS 3055).   [115] See *MS*, new ser., 3 (1872), 58.
[116] E[dwards], 'Samuel Sebastian Wesley', 454.   [117] Letter dated 7 June [1874] (*Lco* Parratt papers).
[118] Letter dated 25 March 1872, pasted into a copy of *The Hymnary* (*Lcm* RSCM loan).

Ex. 6.4. *The Praise of Music*

1865 festival had announced his arrival, while that at Worcester ten years later proved to be an unexpected finale, with the intervening years providing their fair share of triumphs and disasters. Yet he constantly confounded those who prophesied that, with such an idiosyncratic technique, he could never hope to succeed as a conductor, and his organization and direction of the Gloucester festivals undoubtedly represented his most important contribution to the musical life of both city and region. That said, the only part he played at Worcester in 1866 was to provoke a lively debate about the reasons for his last-minute absence, for which he pleaded the claims of 'other business'. As the only work of his to be programmed was the morning canticles from the Chant Service in F and he had not been invited to play an organ solo, the general conclusion was that his absence was due to pique, although *The Musical World* suggested that he might have been trying to complete the manifestly unfinished *The European Psalmist*.[119] Calm was restored at Hereford a year later when he conducted the orchestral version of 'Ascribe unto the Lord' and made no objection to acting as piano accompanist for the evening concerts.

But it was at Gloucester that he came into his own, and, with one festival behind him, he must have approached the next rather more confidently. Preparations followed a similar pattern and included visits to London on festival-related business, among them his first trip to the Crystal Palace to hear Schubert's Symphony No. 9 (14 December 1867), recommended to him by George Grove. He was also spotted at one of Boosey's Ballad Concerts in early April, no doubt to meet Charlotte Sainton-Dolby, who was subsequently engaged as principal contralto.[120] The mistake of trying to save money by omitting Sims Reeves was not, however, repeated, and he, Tietjens, and Charles Santley were engaged as principal tenor, soprano and bass respectively. In his choice of oratorios Wesley again adhered to the works of Handel, Mendelssohn, and Spohr, together with Weber's little-known *Praise Jehovah* (an adaptation of the *Jubel-Kantate*) and two contemporary works—Gounod's *Messe solennelle* (1855) and Schachner's *The Return of Israel from Babylon* (1862), first considered in 1865. Although the minutes record the proposal that 'Dr. Wesley's Wilderness or some other of his Works'[121] should be included, he preferred to fulfil a long-held ambition to perform his father's setting of Psalm 111, 'Confitebor tibi, Domine'.[122] Abridged and with 'additional accompaniments' added, it took its place on the first (Tuesday) morning, 8 September, alongside the first part of Haydn's *The Creation*, a short 'Intermezzo religioso'

---

[119] See *MW*, 44 (1866), 599.   [120] See *MW*, 46 (1868), 236.

[121] Minutes of the stewards' meeting of 17 April 1868 (*ThCh*).

[122] An enquiry to Henry Littleton (letter of 21 June 1868) as to whether Novello, Ewer & Co. would publish the work came to nothing, and it remained unpublished until 1978 (Novello & Co. private library).

by the young Hubert Parry, Beethoven's Mass in C, and Mendelssohn's setting of Psalm 42. In so far as keeping programmes to a reasonable length was concerned, Wesley had learnt nothing. As Parry noted, the Thursday morning performance

was the most remarkably lengthy affair I ever had the felicity to sit through; it began at 11.30 and ended about 5.15 [with half an hour for lunch]; and as might have been anticipated for the last half hour or so a complete lassitude took possession of everybody concerned; the principal singers gave up the ghost and sang miserably, the Orchestra simply collapsed, and the Chorus were incapable of the exertion of singing & the audience yet more incapable of listening.[123]

The audience fared no better in the evening, with a programme that lasted from 7.45 until 11.15, and both Parry and the critic of *The Musical Standard* left before the end. In one respect, however, the festival differed considerably from the previous one, as the experiment of placing the chorus and orchestra at the west end was not repeated. With the stewards anxious to avoid the cost of an extra instrument Wesley had agreed to try and use the cathedral organ, but this proved impossible and an organ incorporating the new electro-pneumatic action—enabling the console to be placed in the orchestra—was hired from Bryceson Brothers. Another suggestion made after the last festival—that one of the evening concerts should be replaced by another ball—was not adopted, while a further proposal that sacred works should be included in the evening programmes found no support.

Although the week had its share of mishaps—most notably the (unrehearsed) opening of Beethoven's Mass in C breaking down—there was fairly general agreement that the festival had been a success. Parry particularly enjoyed Spohr's *Die Heilands letzte Stunden*, *Elijah*, and *Messiah* and, at the evening concerts, Mendelssohn's Hebrides Overture, the selection from *Don Giovanni*, and Sullivan's new orchestral song 'I wish to tune my quivering lyre', while *The Musical Standard* praised the performances of Beethoven's Symphony No. 5 and Mendelssohn's *Lobgesang*. Yet, as might have been expected, there was carping from some quarters. Wesley's old adversary Charles Gruneisen, writing in *The Standard*, had nothing positive to say, while the *Pall Mall Gazette* (Davison?) declared that 'the value of the Festivals, from an art point of view, is of the smallest. This ought not to be, but that it needs be, so long as a local organist fills the conductor's seat is obvious . . . There were, however, points of excellence which not even Dr. Wesley could spoil.'[124]

---

[123] Parry's diary entry for 10 Sept. 1868 (*ShP*).   [124] Quoted in *MW*, 46 (1868), 645.

It was not only Wesley who suffered. Parry, whose Intermezzo had been described in *The Musical Standard* as 'a most charming orchestral composition by a highly accomplished young amateur', also found himself a victim of Gruneisen, who described it as a 'kind of voluntary executed by full orchestra'. 'If it had been a playing out of a congregation any intermezzo would suffice', he continued, 'and that of Hubert Parry would have received as much attention as is ordinarily paid to voluntaries after long sermons'.[125] Ten days later Parry called on Wesley, whom he found 'very amusing on the subject of the Festival & the Critics thereon' and who told him that Gruneisen had a grudge against the Gloucester festival and 'wants to do it all the harm he can'.[126]

By the time of his third festival in 1871 Wesley was over sixty, and it was perhaps with this in mind that it was proposed that a select committee be set up to assist him 'in the engagement of the Artistes'.[127] An amendment that help should only be offered 'in case of difficulty'[128] was, however, carried, and he must have breathed a sigh of relief at his escape. As he had already told the meeting, a number of the leading singers were planning a concert tour of America in September, so that when the engagements were made they were for a substantially lower sum than before: £915 12s. 0d., of which over 40 per cent went to Tietjens. Joining her as principal contralto, tenor, and bass were Janet Patey, Vernon Rigby, and A. J. Foli, but the absence of such names as Sims Reeves and Charles Santley was again misconstrued by the press, who accused the stewards of seeking false economies.

The programme followed a similar pattern to that of previous years, with the first morning (Tuesday 9 September) devoted entirely to Handel, with *Jepthah* a late replacement for George Macfarren's unfinished *St John the Baptist*. With *Elijah* and *Messiah* occupying Wednesday and Friday mornings the only remaining space was on Thursday, when a selection from Spohr's *Die Heilands letzte Stunden*, the first performance of William Cusins's *Gideon* (conducted by the composer), and Bach's *St Matthew Passion* were squeezed in. Notwithstanding a specific demand that no morning performance should finish later than 4 p.m., the audience were still in their seats as 5 p.m approached.

The performance of Bach's masterpiece was very much a landmark in the history of the festival, and Wesley was rightly praised for promoting a work which had only been heard a handful of times in this country and never out of London. Its preparation had, however, presented him with a number of

---

[125] Quoted in Jeremy Dibble, *C. Hubert H. Parry: His Life and Music* (Oxford: Clarendon Press, 1992), 60.

[126] Parry's diary entry for 19 Sept. 1868 (*ShP*).

[127] Minutes of the stewards' meeting of 29 April 1871 (*ThCh*).   [128] Ibid.

problems, not least the propriety of Jesus's words on the cross being sung (which were omitted at the request of the stewards),[129] as well as such practical difficulties as how to deal with Bach's use of the oboe d'amore and oboe da caccia. For advice on the latter and on whether it was necessary to divide the orchestra he turned to Joseph Barnby, who had recently given the work in Westminster Abbey: 'Cannot I get the Oboe players to use the Instruments Bach wrote for?'[130] he asked. He also had doubts about the ability of Townshend Smith, organist of Hereford Cathedral, to cope with the organ part and requested the services of 'an accompanyist specially trained for the performance under his direction'[131]—Kendrick Pyne, who had also rehearsed the local festival chorus. 'I fear the Passion Music will give much anxiety',[132] he told Mrs Bartholomew in August, but in spite of the formidable obstacles he faced, not least the difficulty of the unfamiliar music and the shortage of rehearsal time, his worst fears remained unfounded. Even a misunderstanding between conductor and soloists which ruined some numbers was not completely disastrous, and *The Times* was able to declare that 'the execution of this sublime, elaborate, and very difficult music—thanks to the efficient preparatory and general rehearsals . . . was for the most part strikingly good'[133] and, with the young Edward Lloyd making a marked impression as the Evangelist, the performance was one of the highlights of the week.

As in Wesley's two previous festivals, other performances were mixed, owing largely to the *St Matthew Passion*, *Gideon*, *Israel in Egypt*, and *Die Heilands letzte Stunden* having taken all the rehearsal time. *Jepthah* in particular suffered, with 'Band and chorus . . . at times at cross purposes . . . the peculiar and eccentric beat of the conductor being mainly responsible'.[134] With a single rehearsal also sufficing for the Shire Hall concerts it is remarkable that they went as well as they did, with the performances of Mozart's 'Jupiter' Symphony, the selection from Weber's *Preciosa*, and Mendelssohn's *Rondo brillante* in E flat being expecially praiseworthy—though according to *The Musical World* Wesley played little part in the first, as the orchestra 'took the matter in their own hands'.[135] Following the success of Arabella Goddard in 1865 Wesley had engaged Agnes Zimmermann, whose performance of Mendelssohn's *Rondo brillante* (directed by the leader, Prosper Sainton) was another highlight. So too was Kendrick Pyne's playing of Bach's Fugue in B minor (BWV 544) at the close of the opening service.

[129] See Minutes of the stewards' meeting of 14 Aug. 1871 (*ThCh*).

[130] Letter quoted in Spink, 'Samuel Sebastian Wesley', 438.

[131] Minutes of the stewards' meeting of 14 Aug. 1871 (*ThCh*).

[132] Letter dated 23 Aug. [1871] (*Lcm* MS 3097).   [133] Quoted in *MW*, 49 (1871), 587.

[134] Ibid. 576.   [135] Ibid. 595.

While there was criticism, as before, of Wesley's conducting and of the
wisdom of entrusting four days of concerts to a local organist who 'has the misfortune to be somewhat crotchetty in his readings',[136] as much if not more
space was devoted by the press to a serious threat to the festivals—opposition
to the secular concerts and concern about the use of the cathedral. Neither the
Bishop nor the Dean supported the festival, but they had done no more than
absent themselves from Gloucester for its duration. Not so Canon Tinling,
who, having accepted the invitation to preach at the opening service, devoted
a large part of his sermon to arguing that the festival should adopt a more religious tone and (by implication) abandon the Shire Hall concerts and ball,
restrict the musical fare to one daily performance of choral music, and conclude each day with Evensong in the nave, 'free, open, without money and
without price, for all, rich as well as poor, with combined choirs, and with
select preachers, which might give to these Festivals a power of reviving
within us some of the best, the holiest, and the deepest feelings in our fallen
human nature'.[137] Significantly, the 1871 ball was the last.

At the top of the agenda when the stewards met to discuss the 1874 festival
were the points raised by Canon Tinling. Anxious not to dispense with the
evening concerts entirely and having heard from Wesley that the main obsta-
cle to replacing them with additional oratorio performances would be the
'strain on the chorus',[138] they proposed the holding of a general meeting to
discuss this and the question of omitting the final ball and ending the festival
with a cathedral service. In the event, the festival differed from previous ones
only in the replacement of the ball, but change was in the air. Shortly before
it opened there were more serious rumblings:

At the suggestion of the Dean of Worcester, a conference of Cathedral authorities has
been held at Gloucester . . . the outcome of which is that 'important changes' will be
attempted in arranging the Worcester Festival next year. No doubt the changes will
be introduced as 'improvements,' but it is worth remembering that the Music
Meeting, as an institution, has to be protected against a potent and subtle party who
would 'improve it off the face of the earth.' It was after the Gloucester Festival of 1865,
that Earl Dudley offered his seductive bribe to the Dean and Chapter of Worcester,
that he would give a more than princely donation to the languishing Cathedral
Restoration Fund, and guarantee the Clerical Charity an amount equal to its ordinary
income, if the capitular authorities would refuse the use of the Cathedral in which to
hold the accustomed triennial Musical Festival . . . again the opposition originates at
Worcester . . . [and] the new Dean of Worcester is the ostensible leader in the new
movement.[139]

[136] *MW*, 49 (1871), 577.   [137] Ibid. 598.
[138] Minutes of the stewards' meeting of 29 Jan. 1874 (*ThCh*).
[139] Lysons *et al.*, *Origin and Progress of the Meeting of the Three Choirs*, 253–4.

But before looking at the implications of these remarks and the even more pointed ones by Dr Alfred Barry, canon of Worcester and Principal of King's College, London, in his concluding sermon, we must pause and look at the week's events which opened on Tuesday 8 September. In devising what *The Times* described as 'by no means an uninviting selection'[140] Wesley had given a very nineteenth-century flavour to the programme, with the music of Handel represented only by *Messiah*. *Elijah* occupied Wednesday morning, and the other programmes included works by Haydn, Mendelssohn, Rossini, Spohr, and Weber; the real novelty was Rossini's recent *Petite messe solennelle* (heard at Worcester in 1869). Wesley's attempt to give the festival an even stronger contemporary bias, through the inclusion of a new composition by Gounod, had fallen through, despite the latter's offer of a partly completed vocal piece entitled 'L'annonciation' (possibly 'La salutation angélique' for voice, piano, and violin or cello).[141] Neither did an enquiry as to whether he would conduct one of his own works—probably the *Messe solennelle* which was under consideration—come to anything.

The evening concerts included selections from Mozart's *Don Giovanni* and Weber's *Oberon*, numbers from Mendelssohn's incidental music to *A Midsummer Night's Dream*, the slow movement and finale from Beethoven's Piano Concerto No. 5, Mozart's 'Jupiter' Symphony, and two of Wesley's songs—the soprano solo 'Silently, silently' from the *Ode* and 'The Butterfly', a new setting of verses by Lady Flora Hastings. Wesley had also chosen two of his anthems, 'O Lord, thou art my God', which received a rare performance at the opening service, and 'Praise the Lord, O my soul', sung with the Te Deum in E on the final day. Tietjens occupied her customary place at the head of the soloists, together with Zélia Trebelli (contralto), Edward Lloyd (tenor), and Luigi Agnesi (bass), while Agnes Zimmermann was again engaged and created an excellent impression in the Beethoven concerto.

In purely musical terms the 1874 festival was probably Wesley's most successful. Not only were there few of the mishaps which had marred previous years but, as *The Musical Times*, *The Musical World* and *The Times* all agreed, the performances left little to be desired. 'We cannot compliment Dr Wesley too heartily on such a performance',[142] declared *The Times* after *Elijah*, and congratulated him on 'really fine performances'[143] of *Die letzten Dinge* and Rossini's *Petite messe solennelle*. *The Musical World* praised the 'excellent rendering' of Mendelssohn's *Lobgesang*,[144] while Henry Lunn considered that 'the

---

[140] Quoted in *MW*, 52 (1874), 599.
[141] Gounod's reply, dated 11 Nov. 1873, survives as *Lcm* MS 3060.
[142] Quoted in *MW*, 52 (1874), 601.　　　[143] Ibid. 616.　　　[144] *MW*, 52 (1874), 620.

rendering of some works has been the finest within our recollection'.[145] With the evening concerts no less deserving of praise—particularly the selection from *Don Giovanni*, Mozart's 'Jupiter' Symphony, and Beethoven's Piano Concerto No. 5—it was unfortunate that the week should have ended on a decidedly gloomy note. Yet such was the stewards' concern that they called a special meeting at which a resolution expressing

their regret at the general currency of a rumour, to the effect that the discontinuance of the meeting of the Three Choirs on its present footing has been seriously discussed by the authorities of the three Cathedrals, and to place on record their deliberate opinion that such a step would be fatal to the efficiency of the charity, that it would discourage the successful cultivation of sacred music . . . and would deprive the local public of their only opportunity of hearing oratorios, as interpreted by the highest artistic talent of the day'[146]

was carried unanimously. A few hours later their worst fears were fulfilled, as no one who heard Canon Barry arguing that only music intended for church services should be performed in cathedrals could have been left in any doubt as to his meaning. As *The Times* noted, 'the tenor of the discourse was unmistakeable; and if its arguments prevailed there must soon be an end of the Festivals of the Three Choirs'.[147] Wesley played the Dead March in *Saul* 'As a practical comment on the tendency of the sermon'.[148]

For Wesley, who had found much of his career overshadowed by clerical opposition to music, it must have been a profoundly dispiriting time, and when he took his place as organist at Worcester the following year it was merely to play for a succession of cathedral services. Among those present was the young Edward Elgar, for whom his playing was the highlight of an otherwise gloomy week. Many years later (as Ivor Atkins related) he recalled the effect of an especially thrilling outgoing voluntary:

Wesley began with a long extemporisation, designed to lead up to Bach's Choral Prelude '*Wir glauben all an einen Gott*' ['Giant' Fugue, BWV 680], breaking off the extemporisation in an arresting way before entering upon the Prelude. The effect upon Elgar was so great that in after years when he . . . would constantly slip into the old cathedral . . . he almost invariably asked me to play him something, and we always had to end with the *Giant*.[149]

But there were some for whom the 'new' festival was a marked improvement. Among these was W. H. Gladstone (son of the Prime Minister, MP and amateur composer):

---

[145] *MT*, 16 (1874), 637–8.   [146] *MW*, 52 (1874), 618.
[147] Quoted ibid. 616.   [148] Ibid. 618.
[149] E. Wulstan Atkins, *The Elgar–Atkins Friendship* (Newton Abbot: David & Charles, 1984), 475.

Dear Mrs Wesley,

At the expense of leaving you rather abruptly the other day, I gained an admirable place for following your husband's immortal anthem 'Let us lift up', which I did with intense gratitude and sympathy. I am truly glad that the reformed Festival which has proved so successful should owe its principle and excellence to his guiding hand and brain.

It was to me not only an edifying but a touching thing to listen to our Veteran Organist and Prince of Composers revealing himself to us through his own Instrument with that perfect dignity and pathos that always clothes his thoughts but which one so often looks for in vain.

Great as he is now I cannot but think he will be greater still in the eyes of those that come after. May his ripe and vigorous imagination still be long preserved to us.[150]

Little though audience and player were to know it, the so-called 'Mock' festival was to be Wesley's swansong, as three months to the day after Gladstone's eulogy he touched the keys for the last time and within seven months was dead. Yet as both Elgar and Gladstone testified, he had retained to the end his power to move listeners. Although his best days as an organist were past when he arrived in Gloucester, he had contunued to appear as a recitalist throughout his time in the city. He was, as a commentator observed when he opened the new instrument (by Frederick Jardine) in St Thomas's Church, Bury, in March 1868, the 'connecting link between . . . the old and new schools of the organ, possessing as he does the peculiarly close 'touch' of the old school with the elasticity and freedom of the new'.[151] Another old-fashioned feature of his recitals was the very restricted nature of his repertoire—his own works, a handful of fugues by Bach, a small number of instrumental movements by Beethoven, Mozart, and Spohr, and extempore performances. Thus at Bury he played a fugue in C minor by Bach, the overture to Spohr's *Jessonda*, an Andante from a sonata by Mozart, several of his own pieces, and an improvised fugue on a subject handed to him a few minutes earlier. At All Saints', Scarborough, six years later we find a similar programme, with an 'Air' by Mozart, an 'Instrumental Piece' by Spohr, and no fewer than seven of his own works, among them the recently completed 'Holsworthy Church Bells'. A more unusual occasion was the opening in 1869 of the private organ built by Edmund Schulze for T. S. Kennedy of Meanwood Towers, Leeds. Mr Kennedy had been particularly anxious that Wesley should be the first to play it, but the latter, whose nature seemed to become more temperamental by the year, refused to perform before a party of guests and would come only on one condition—that the only people present

---

[150] Copy (by Eliza Wesley) of a letter dated 25 Sept. 1875 (*Lbl* Add. MS 35020, fo. 59).
[151] *The Manchester Courier*, quoted in *MS*, 8 (1868), 136–7.

should be Mr and Mrs Kennedy, Schulze, and their friend Clifford Allbutt. Over fifty years later Allbutt recalled the occasion:

So the master came; appearing and disappearing like a wraith, but a wraith under a radiant halo of illumination. He lifted us up in an organ glory which none of us had known before, or since. For, almost as he sat down, Wesley pulled out every stop he could see, and himself lifted up in the glorious noise for nearly two hours took a long flight of improvisation, mostly in counterpoint and on big combinations. Then he descended to earth, or nearer to it, and strayed delightfully among the several stops. Finally, he turned to Bach, playing the preludes and fugues by the old tradition and giving out the first subject on the great diapasons and rather slowly throughout. It was a wonderful afternoon,—for Wesley himself (as he fully admitted) as well as for us.[152]

Wesley made two of his final appearances in April 1874, first at All Saints' Church, Scarborough (see above), and then at the Victoria Rooms, Clifton. At the latter he had advised on the purchase and re-erection by Bryceson of the organ built by Hill for the Panopticon, Leicester Square, and he shared two programmes with Walter Parratt, accompanying three choral items—Handel's 'Hallelujah' chorus and 'The horse and his rider' (*Israel in Egypt*) and Beethoven's 'Hallelujah' chorus (*Christus am Oelberge*)—and playing two other works at each recital. Parratt did the bulk of the work, contriving to make the audience laugh by inadvertently pulling out a mixture whose 'bleating' produced a 'most comic effect' in one of Mendelssohn's *Lieder ohne Worte*.[153] Although Wesley had complained that he was 'out of all practice, having no organ here [i.e. at Gloucester] to practise on',[154] his performance of two fugues by Bach was the highlight of the day.

Throughout these years he had, of course, continued with his daily duties at the cathedral, seemingly with little complaint on either side. Yet things did not run quite as smoothly as the absence of comment implies, and on one occasion (as Pyne recalled) he was particularly irritable and so 'tantalized the solo singer in the anthem . . . that he . . . stopped and the anthem was finished without him'.[155] He had in addition lost none of his love of fishing and continued to absent himself and leave the supervision of choir and music to his pupils. With the indifferent state of the choir a talking point in the city, one of the minor canons (Isaac Bowman) took it upon himself to try and improve matters, but having dared to criticize the performance of an anthem earned for himself the following rebuke: ' "Sir," said Wesley, drawing himself up; "*I* am

---

[152] Clifford Allbutt, 'Reminiscences of Edmund Schulze and the Armley Organ', *Org*, 5 (1925), 82.
[153] *MS*, new ser., 6 (1874), 296.
[154] Letter dated 26 Dec. 1873 to Walter Parratt (*Leo* Parratt papers).
[155] Pyne, 'Wesleyana', 379.

at the *head* of my profession; *you*, Sir, are a nobody. I am *amazed* at your audacity. *Good afternoon, Sir.*'[156]

Although Wesley was quick to regret his hasty words, Bowman perservered and, at the request of the Dean and Chapter, stated what was needed: 'a little more personal supervision, a little fresh music occasionally by way of sustaining interest, and a weekly practice of the choir'. As he noted, 'the order was given . . . and improvement followed'[157]—though a later comment that the men made no attempt to sing out at the rehearsals suggests that any improvement was limited.[158] The only reference to the music is found in a chapter minute of 21 March 1872, when Wesley's request to take up the offer of an assistant was granted.[159] Matters moved slowly, however, and in October he was still in want (as he wrote to Parratt) of a 'clever assistant' who would welcome a 'good introduction to business';[160] Conrad Clarke was eventually appointed and remained with Wesley until his death. Much of the credit for the avoidance of conflict must lie with the precentor who had learnt never to lose his temper when dealing with Wesley,[161] and who, like Bowman, knew and appreciated both sides of Wesley's nature—'the most cantankerous and the most delightful of all the men he had ever known'.[162] Perhaps, too, Wesley had learnt that it sometimes paid to adopt a low profile (as he confided to Linnington Ash in March 1875): 'I think our Canons must have heard of some of [my] complaints. They have been most civil these last few days. Still, our Crotchety Dean has so alarmed me that I feel most anxious to suit his Society & be quiet that I may attend to writing.'[163]

Yet the good relationship he enjoyed with Precentor Clark had done nothing to alter his views on the desirability of clerical control of the music in cathedrals. 'You see what the Church Musician is subject to', he wrote to Ash, '& I assure you that I have had a sad life amongst the Clergy . . . [who] have such a dreadful power as they can deprive a man of his reputation by a few words or even a look'.[164] It was a subject to which he returned a few weeks later when writing to Joseph Bennett about the publication of the music lists, and it was to Bennett (whom he clearly perceived as an ally) that he outlined his final—and most radical—plan for the reform of cathedral music. During a

---

[156] Ibid. 380.   [157] 'Dr. Wesley and the Minor Canon', *MT*, 40 (1899), 485.

[158] See Alfred Herbert Brewer, *Memories of Choirs and Cloisters (Fifty Years of Music)* (London: Bodley Head, 1931), 4. Writing of the choir when C. H. Lloyd succeeded Wesley, he noted that 'When a full rehearsal . . . took place the men made no attempt to sing out but just whispered their parts . . . and when a new lay clerk was appointed, who showed his zeal and enthusiasm by really singing his part at a rehearsal as it should be sung, his colleagues remonstrated with him at the close of the practice for using his voice unnecessarily!'

[159] Gloucester Cathedral Chapter acts, 1863–92, 170 (*GL*).

[160] Letter dated 4 Oct. 1872 (*Lco* Parratt papers).   [161] See *M* (July 1896), 152.

[162] Ibid.   [163] Letter dated 30 March [1875] (*Lbl* Loan 79).   [164] Ibid.

private dinner at the Norfolk Hotel, Paddington, he put forward his proposal: that the existing arrangement at cathedrals was wasteful and placed musicians in an unfair and unworthy position. When Bennett replied that he was quite prepared to believe that it needed updating Wesley enlarged upon his scheme:

He held that it was useless to attempt amendment of control by Dean and Chapter, and . . . would sweep away all Deans and Chapters with the besom of destruction! I suggested that this was rather a 'large order.' He agreed, but was not every reform, at its inception, a 'large order'? How would the Doctor, having suppressed Deans and Chapters, govern cathedrals? He explained: through a resident clergyman, acting as the rector of a parish church, and having under him a 'sort of curate,' *if necessary*. As for the music, it should be absolutely under the control of the organist; and as for effective preaching, it should be supplied by a Cathedral Board sitting in London, and having at its command a number of the most eloquent orators of the Church; these to go individually the round of the cathedrals, preaching a month at each, and then making way for another.[165]

How he proposed to effect these changes was explained in a later letter:

I should hope the desire to make better use of so large a sum of money (as the endowments of the cathedrals) may serve, especially as this money supports offices which are absolutely obstructive to musical interests . . . I know several persons there (in Parliament) who will encourage all efforts in this direction, and although Nonconformists don't attack the Church, they will be sure to vote for an alteration of the kind in prospect.[166]

He undertook to 'attend to the Parliament' if Bennett would 'work the press', but the latter replied that he had no time for 'exercises of the speculative sort proposed' and no more was heard of it.[167] By now Wesley's health was fast deteriorating. Some six months earlier, in May 1875, he had told Ash that he was 'not quite well' and was thinking of going down to the Lizard with a friend,[168] but whether he actually went is not known. From then onwards he slowly declined, telling Eliza in August that he had been 'ill a long while' and that his liver was 'sluggish'.[169] Could she spare the time to join him if he went to the seaside? By November he was complaining of difficulty in breathing, but was still able to contemplate a visit to London, not least to meet G. J. Stevenson, who wanted information for his *Memorials of the Wesley Family*. He asked Eliza if she could provide accommodation: 'I dont eat solid meat or drink wine, ale of spirits, nor tea or Coffee. I take milk & harty pudding &

---

[165] Bennett, *Forty Years of Music*, 39–40. [166] From a letter dated 7 Nov. 1875 (ibid. 40).
[167] Ibid. 41. [168] Letter dated 6 May 1875 (*Lbl* Loan 79).
[169] Letter dated 30 Aug. 1875 (*Lbl* Add. MS 35019, fo. 109).

broth & perhaps White Fish. Vegetables are good for me, good arrowroot I like but it is hard to get.'[170]

A bad night delayed his departure, but on 22 November he made his last journey to the capital; on setting off to return home he wrote a strangely vale-dictory letter to Eliza to ask whether she would 'come quickly to see me if I send you word that I am very bad':

I had 4 oysters in the City. I dont think they suited me but I much enjoyed them, my mouth is dry & I only drank cold Tea & Mild at dinner. I have got your notes for Mr. Steven[son]'s work, about myself, I mean. I will attend to it at once, (DV) and write to you. Good bye . . . Let me know when you can run down to Gloster.[171]

Putting together material for Stevenson had given Wesley an opportunity to reflect on his life and it is interesting to see what he regarded as his most important achievements. Foremost among his compositions was the volume of *Anthems*, which deserved notice 'for the manner in which the words are expressed and for the new use made of broad massive harmony combined with serious devotional effects', while he also considered that something should be said about his 'style of touching an organ as that has been freely spoken of by the best judges'. Inevitably, there was also a dig at the conditions under which cathedral musicians had to work (which Stevenson declined to include):

this state of things is the natural result of such an anomaly as that of one professional calling being wholly supervised by another—viz, Musicians by Clergymen, with no other laws for order than those of Henry the Eighth's time & the common law which treats organists as the servants of the Clergy so that no recognition of the Musician as an Artist & Gentleman has any place in a Court of Law.[172]

As he told Eliza, he still suffered from 'parched mouth and thirst and short windedness', and two weeks later, on Christmas Day, played for the last time at the cathedral. After Evensong, instead of extemporising or playing a Bach fugue from memory, he asked Conrad Clarke for a full score of *Messiah*, and treated the congregation to the 'Hallelujah' chorus as an outgoing voluntary. Writing to Parry on Boxing Day he expressed the hope that when the 'fair weather' came he would start to feel better, and confided that he found Gloucester 'so depressing' and that moving there had been a mistake.[173] Several weeks in Sandown on the Isle of Wight brought no improvement, and in February he told Eliza that he had been 'always ill since in London'[174] and

---

[170] Lettter dated 17 Nov. [1875] (ibid., fo. 115).
[171] Undated letter [*c*.25 November 1875] (ibid., fo. 121).
[172] Letter dated 10 Dec. 1875 to Eliza Wesley (*Lbl* Add. MS 35019, fo. 124ᵛ).
[173] Letter dated 26 Dec. 1875 (*ShP*).
[174] Letter dated 13 Feb. [1876] (*Lbl* Add. MS 35019, fo. 101).

that the recent cold wind had made matters worse. On his return home he put down all his recent trials and tribulations in a long letter to Ash:

I am worse. I think the cold of Sandown may be the cause but, then, I have been decaying for years. I see it now. I could not walk, latterly & now I stay in the house & hardly walk there. I could no more perform such a journey now as I thought of last week, viz, to you.

My doctor, for the first time, to day, gave me an anema [*sic*] (I believe the term is) & I was surprised at its success. I had been very much bound up. But there must be an [*sic*] disorder going on. I have brought forth very thick small lumps of phlegm strongly tinged with blood. I had hoped the constipation caused my suffering as to difficulty of taking breath, which terrible ailment attacks me at intervals day & night, expecially at night on lying down, but then, the clearance of to day would have relieved me, which it has not done, and my doctor is now about to try to determine where the seat of this lies. To morrow he is to examine me further. Those medical gentlemen I have consulted, here & in London, all say they think my heart is right & my lungs. One or two doubted about my liver, another said the kidneys are in fault . . .

Sir Wm. Gull said my mind had much to do with it. So said my Son & my doctor here. This comes of my getting out of the world when young & remaining out from my love of the Country. Worry worry worry. No delight anywhere. This panting for breath is most dreadful. I eat very spraringly. Only small quantities of light things. Gull told me to live on the cow but I find milk stuffs me up. What I prefer is tea but they won't let me have more than a very little. What can be the real cause of this suffocation?

. . . Glad shall I be if God permits to visit you again.[175]

One fears that the woodcocks for which he thanked Ash remained untasted; on 19 February he made his will, appointing Mary Anne his executrix and leaving everything to her. With each passing week his condition worsened, and in his last surviving letter (written to Sarah Emett on 14 March) he made enquiries about borrowing Eliza's invalid chair; five days later he added a codicil to his will, appointing his brother Matthias Erasmus as joint executor. The end, fortunately, was not far off and he died from Bright's disease—a malfunctioning of the kidneys—on 19 April. Eliza was present and described the scene to Sarah Emett:

To you my dearest Sarah I owe one sad satisfaction of being with my dear brother in his last moments—he died this morng at 11 o'clock.

Last night those around him did not anticipate this change. I did and begged to be called in the night if he was at all worse. The servant came to my door about 7— saying he was not too well—I felt no surprise—Mrs Wesley, Willis & myself—were with him. I went to breakfast—& in a few moments was told he had called for me. My name was the last he mentioned.

[175] Letter dated 17 Feb. [1876] (*Lbl* Loan 79).

His death was so calm and peaceful—it was only ceasing to breathe . . . Poor Mrs. Wesley really feels her loss—it is a trying scene.[176]

At his request Wesley was buried alongside his infant daughter Mary in the Old Cemetery, Exeter, and father and daughter finally shared that peace that they had never known together on earth. The funeral, on 27 April, was a simple, unostentatious affair. Wesley's final departure from Gloucester was to the sound of the tolling of the 'Great Bell' of the cathedral, and the train bearing his coffin then began its long journey to Devon. By a strange coincidence it arrived at St David's Station, Exeter, when a party of singers, among them Sims Reeves and A. J. Foli, was on the platform, and the former sent a floral cross—'an "artist's tribute to genius" '.[177] With the capitular authorities at Exeter having only just learnt that burial was to take place in the city it had been impossible to arrange for the funeral service to be held in the cathedral, so hearse and three mourning coaches made their way slowly up the hill and directly to the cemetery. Wesley's brother-in-law, the Revd Francis Merewether, vicar of Woolhope, officiated while the coffin was carried by his former pupils George Arnold, Francis Gladstone, James Russell, Minto Pyne, and his old friend James Kendrick Pyne. Neither Mary Anne nor Eliza made the journey to Exeter, and the family was represented by his sons John, Francis, Charles, and William (Samuel being in Australia) and his brother Matthias Erasmus. Although Alfred Angel, his successor at the cathedral, and several members of the choir were present, there was no music, and he who had so memorably set the words 'Man that is born of a woman' and 'All go unto one place' was laid to rest in silence, brought back in death to the county he so loved.

In Memory of
Mary Daughter of
Samuel Sebastian Wesley
Of This City
She died February 13th 1840
Aged 9 weeks
Also Of The Above Named
Samuel Sebastian Wesley
Who Died at Gloucester
April 19th 1876
Aged 65 Years
Doctor of Music Oxon

Organist and Succentor
Of Exeter Cathedral
1835–1841

[176] See *Lbl* Add. MS 35020, fos. 25–6.
[177] See *MW*, 54 (1876), 329 (quoting *Exeter and Plymouth Gazette*, 28 April 1876).

Tributes to Wesley's memory were many and varied, but all were in agreement on one point—his pre-eminence both as a composer and as an organist. None, perhaps, captured the essence of the man so well as that in *The Gloucester Journal*:

During the greater part of his life, Dr. Wesley was influenced by a particularly sensitive nervous temperament, which led him to prefer retirement to public life. He probably allowed this feeling to rule when it should have been resisted . . .

He was most decidedly and most emphatically a genius, and was not free from those irritable eccentricities which too frequently accompany the possession of special artistic gifts. With all his attainments he had not the inestimable blessing of a contented mind, and his conversation often gave one the impression that he suffered under the thrall of real or imaginary grievances, and was to some extent at odds with the world in which his lot was cast. Yet those who had no experience of the genial side of his character knew but little of the man. He had a great liking for field sports, was a good shot, and a most accomplished angler—qualities which never yet were found in conjunction with unmitigated moroseness. Dr. Wesley had, besides, a keen sense of humour, and could be a most entertaining and delightful companion.[178]

There was indeed another side to him, familiar to his pupils but unknown to the world at large—the sportsman and lover of the countryside who, freed from the distractions of everyday life, would roam Dartmoor or the Yorkshire dales and, in Spark's words, return 'like a musical giant refreshed with nature's glories and with invigorating air'. 'He not only thus gained health, calmness of mind, and tranquillity of spirit, but his appetite for nature grew with what it fed upon, and, when he returned home, he seemed never to rest until he could again get away to his beloved woods and streams,—and he liked to go *alone*, for more reasons than one.'[179]

Would that we knew what Spark meant by his final cryptic comment! Alongside Wesley's love of the country went a natural understanding of and affection for animals. He would, for example, play with the dean of Gloucester's two huge mastiffs, 'seize them by the forelegs, turn them over and over, and play with them as with children',[180] while his own two dogs, Rob and Gip, were the delight of his life. Rob was the especial favourite, and Kendrick Pyne had vivid memories of their long walks:

He had a habit of stopping occasionally in his walks and meditating in a most unexpected way. As a result of an accident many years before . . . he slightly turned in one foot. 'Rob' Wesley was so much with his master that *he* apparently turned in *his* foot and also stopped to indulge in canine reveries. Rob was an unmusical animal, but Gip,

[178] *GJ* (22 April 1876).   [179] *Musical Memories*, 71–3.
[180] 'Dr. Wesley and the Minor Canon', *MT*, 40 (1899), 485.

I think, really loved the gentle art. One tune Wesley used to perform expecially for Gip's delectation, when his howlings were terrible to listen to; fortunately, any other melody would immediately stop these manifestations.[181]

When Rob died his 'heart was very full, and he went up into the organ loft and relieved it by a mighty wail on the organ, which startled everyone who heard it . . . People asked, "What's the matter with the Doctor?" Those of us who knew understood it—and we loved him all the better.'[182]

Then there was Wesley the practical joker who, having having agreed to play to some companions in the cathedral, would break off and slip out unnoticed, leaving them to ponder what had become of their host. Yet the victims of his humour, particularly his pupils, never seemed to bear him any malice. Pyne related how it was invariably *his* fault if Wesley lost a fish or his line became entangled in a tree, but it was probably Spark who suffered most from his master's whims—as when he accompanied Wesley to Otley for a day's fishing in the river Wharfe. Instructed to secure outside places on the coach and coming off 'second best' after some 'little difficulty about the payment of the fares', on arrival he found himself left to take charge of the rods and net while Wesley slipped away, determined to avoid any demand from the coachman for an extra tip! His troubles were by no means over, however, as Wesley, pleading an inability to wade, persuaded him to carry him across the river and tried to cast a fly in midstream:

I managed just to get through and fall on the bank breathless, and the doctor went clean over my head like a shuttlecock. He got up, and then stood for a moment regarding me with considerable contempt.

'I'm disgusted with you! Surely you could have stood with me for a few minutes while I got that trout. I never behaved so to my master, and often as a boy carried him across the river when he went a fishing.'

'Indeed!' said I; 'what! across the Thames?'[183]

But on another occasion he got his own back. Returning home with Wesley one Friday evening, the latter 'deviated towards Duncan Street, and suddenly went into an oyster shop',[184] instructing his pupil to keep a look out for the vicar. Not having been invited to join his master, Spark conceived a mischievous idea and, shouting out 'Dr Hook, Dr Hook', he saw Wesley drop an unshelled oyster and hastily escape to the privacy of the back room, while he 'bolted, and took care to be out of the great master's way for some days

---

[181] Pyne, 'Wesleyana', *MT*, 40 (1899), 379.

[182] 'Dr. Wesley and the Minor Canon', 485.   [183] W. Spark, *Musical Memories*, 75–6.

[184] Ibid. 80.

afterwards'.[185] Fishing—and doubtless shooting too—was of course responsible for Wesley's many unofficial absences from cathedral duties and, if anecdotes are to be believed, from private lessons as well. And here again, as Nicholas Temperley noted, we encounter a weakness in his moral code—a willingness to condemn dereliction of duty in others, while condoning it in himself.[186] It was the same with financial matters. On the one hand he complained to Mendelssohn that Gauntlett tried to gain influence at St George's Hall because of 'the prospect of deriving some little pecuniary recompense',[187] but on the other he drove a hard bargain himself and attempted to claim expenses to which he was not entitled. His departures from Hereford and Exeter had both been soured by attempts to extract money to which he was not entitled, but it was at the latter that the dark side of his character had been seen at its worst, in the disgraceful attack on the two choristers. Clearly there was a demon within which drove him to such excesses, although it is hard not to read a sense of genuine remorse into his settings of penitential texts—and this is perhaps what makes them so profoundly moving. But as many who knew him testified, he was both quick to anger and quick to repent. His demolition of and subsequent apology to Isaac Bowman has already been mentioned, and a similar example can be seen in a story related by Pyne. Returning triumphantly after being sent to haggle over the price of a pair of old Worcester vases, Pyne was congratulated but was then asked 'did the old man look very poor?'.[188] On replying that he did, he was admonished for beating down such a poor shopkeeper and sent back with the balance. As Pyne knew too well, Wesley had a nose for bargains and his house was full of 'old furniture, curiosities, &c.',[189] so much so that when Mary Anne had to vacate the organist's lodgings in July 1876 no fewer than fifty three razors went under the hammer! Rather less encumbered, she moved to London, where she lived at 57 Finborough Road, West Brompton, until her death on 28 February 1888.

We also learn from Pyne that Wesley was a bon vivant. 'Everything in the way of food and drink had to be of the very best'[190] and, if he was unable to choose them himself, 'woe betide the luckless purveyor if the viands were not up to the mark'.[191] His clothes, too, were invariably ordered from a London tailor although (as Pyne commented) 'his appearance would not always have indicated this'.[192] In this attachment to the good things of life and in his constant worries about money one can surely recognize a reaction to the seeds of

---

[185] W. Spark, *Musical Memories*, 81.

[186] See Nicholas Temperley, 'Wesley, (4) Samuel Sebastian', in Stanley Sadie (ed.), *The New Grove Dictionary of Music and Musicians* (London: Macmillan Publishers Ltd, 1980), 20. 365.

[187] Letter dated 3 Jan. 1846 (*Ob* Mendelssohn Green Books XXIII, 4)

[188] See Pyne, 'Wesleyana', 380.   [189] Ibid.   [190] Ibid.   [191] Ibid.   [192] Ibid. 379.

insecurity planted during his deprived childhood. But there was surely also an element of vanity, seen again in his decision to hide his baldness under a brown wig! Lurking in the background too was the question of his own illegitimate birth, which, although not apparently an active issue, still rankled with some members of the Wesley family. Indeed, twenty-one years after his death Frederick Wesley Newenham, son of his father's half-sister Emma, wrote to *The Methodist Recorder* to denounce those 'masquerading in the name of Wesley, to which they have not an iota of right, further to that derived from my grandfather . . . having formed an unfortunate connection with a domestic servant'.[193]

Fascinating though such reminiscences are, they provide only one side of the picture. Where, throughout this time, was Mary Anne? How did she fit into the household or view her strong-willed and irascible husband who, in his final years, seems to have turned increasingly to his sister Eliza for companionship? And what did his son John mean when he later wrote that his father was 'hard but . . . had a perpetual trouble that he kept to himself', adding 'I know things now I did not then'?[194] What, indeed, did he and his siblings think of the father who worried so much about them (but never taught the eldest 'a note of music')?[195] These questions must perforce remain unanswered, but when one turns to other aspects of his character, not least his jealousy of other musicians, one can speculate with rather more certainty. While his indignation that less worthy candidates held many of the best appointments—principally John Goss at St Paul's Cathedral, James Turle at Westminster Abbey, and George Elvey at St George's Chapel, Windsor—was understandable, his unfair denigration of William Sterndale Bennett (professor of music at Cambridge and principal of the Royal Academy of Music) was not. Bennett's music, he claimed, was barely second-rate and his position due entirely to the efforts of Davison and Mendelssohn! He could rarely find anything positive to say about any of his contemporaries and, as we saw earlier, made a fuss when it was suggested that music by Hopkins and Garrett should be introduced at Gloucester Cathedral. What, one wonders, did he make of George Macfarren, whose seriousness of purpose and compositional rigour matched his own (and who late in life complimented him on 'Ascribe unto the Lord')? At the Gloucester Three Choirs festivals, too, he performed major works by only three living composers: Gounod, Schachner (with influential patronage), and William Cusins—though only Mendelssohn's premature death had removed him from the scene. In such circumstances it is not

---

[193] *MR*, (28 Oct. 1897).
[194] Letter dated 3 Oct. 1894 to George Garrett (private collection).   [195] Ibid.

surprising that his circle of musical friends was small and composed almost entirely of people like William Knyvett and J. G. Emett from his father's generation, and of much younger men, from whom he would have felt no personal threat. Among the latter were Herbert Oakeley (whom he supported in his application for the Reid Chair of Music at Edinburgh in 1865), Walter Parratt (whom he supported when there was a vacancy at Leeds Parish Church in 1869), and Hubert Parry.

But his greatest dislike and suspicion was reserved for the clergy. Was it not they who had not only been responsible for the diversion elsewhere of money intended to support cathedral choirs, but had also been content to preside over the deplorable conditions then prevalent? As an artist in the service of God— for that is how he saw himself—he could not accept such standards without compromising his integrity; he recorded his experiences in *A Few Words*: 'Various attempts to bring capitular bodies to a right understanding with respect to Cathedral music have been made, but always with one result, *i.e.* evasive politeness at first; then, abrupt rudeness; and ultimately, total neglect'.[196] In addition, as he was also only too keenly aware, his attainments as a musician provided him with an entrée to the company of his social superiors, be they Sir Thomas and Lady Acland at Killerton, Gambier Parry and his wife at Highnam, Lord Ashburton at the Grange (where Wesley was a member of the circle which including Henry Taylor and a variety of academics, politicians, and members of the aristocracy),[197] or the guests at a reception given by Mrs Gladstone in Downing Street, but meant nothing in the context of his employment. Not until cathedral musicians were no longer subservient in musical matters to the clergy would he have been content to let his 'sword sleep in my hand' and, as his various schemes for reform show, this was a theme to which he constantly returned. It could indeed be argued that he saw as his life's mission the promotion of the Anglican choral service and the composition of music for use in it.

It is necessity, not choice, that has driven our finest musicians to compose for the theatre, or to occupy their time in tuition, as affording the most lucrative return, instead of giving their attention more immediately to what is known to be a higher department of the Art—that is, Ecclesiastical music. And unless we arrive at some better appreciation of the musician, unless the higher efforts in composition be respected and valued in the same ratio as other works of art, it seems unreasonable to expect that that branch of art will ever again flourish.

Were there a Palestrina at this moment at each of our Cathedrals, he could, in the

---

[196] pp. 10–11.
[197] See Henry Taylor, *Autobiography of Henry Taylor, 1800–1875*, 2 vols. (London: Longmans, Green & Co., 1885), 2. 138.

present crippled condition of the choirs, do nothing, or next to nothing . . . Before our Palestrinas can find a home at Cathedrals, the difficulties of musical composition must be appreciated, *and our artists allowed to rank with men of true eminence in other walks of life*.[198]

Elsewhere he wrote of the universality of music and emphasised its God-given role in Christian worship, to the extent that, he claimed, musicians should consciously strive to imitate God's order of creation:

The principles of Music are of no narrow and limited application: they belong not merely to one country or nation, or even to one world, but are universal and natural: surely then we are warranted in affirming that the good which might here be done should be done for Music's own sake, and in humble imitation of that example of perfect accuracy and order displayed in all His works by the incomprehensible Great Author of all things.[199]

Of Wesley's own faith, underpinning this vision, we know little. A great-nephew of the founder of Methodism and the son of an erstwhile convert to Catholicism, he had been brought up surrounded by the words and music of the Anglican liturgy and was himself a follower of the mid-nineteenth-century 'Broad Church' tradition. Whilst not opposed to the practical reforms of the Tractarians, he cared little for their practices and, as a forward-looking cathedral musician, was resolutely opposed to two of their central theses—the use of Gregorian tones and congregational participation in the offices. To a pupil he wrote:

Your question about Gregorian tones has caused me much pain. I thought I had made a better musician of you. I am sorry for this. I beg to assure you that I am a musician, a protestant, and yours truly, S. S. WESLEY.[200]

In questions of doctrine he probably had little interest, though late in life he expressed concern at hearing of the 'high ch: tendencies' at Helmsley.[201] An early letter to his father, however, reveals an unexpected sense of humility before God, very much at variance with his outward behaviour. One suspects, too, that hidden beneath his later bravado there remained more than a trace of this modesty, which came to the fore in his wonderful responses to sacred texts and surely lay behind his decision to allow a number of grandiose works to end quietly:[202]

---

[198] Wesley, *A Few Words*, 68–9 (editorial use of italic text).
[199] *Reply to the Inquiries of the Cathedral Commissioners*, 8.
[200] [E]dwards, 'Samuel Sebastian Wesley', 455.
[201] Letter dated 13 Nov. 1872 to E. S. Howard (*Mr* MS MAM P12 C, no. 12).

How is Emetts [his father's friend J. G. Emett]? I long to see him. He is the only man I have yet met with, whose every thought, and action, seem guided by the precepts of Jesus Christ—he had had less temptation, perhaps, than most men, but his opportunities for doing good have been proportionally small. I suppose those who have not yielded to temptation to sin, and those who are thoroughly repentant for having sinned, will 'go up highest' by and by. Men are much alike I find, here, and in all other places, those, are thought best, who have most to bestow—and none are contented.[203]

Well might Wesley write that 'none are contented', for few would go through life as discontented as he. Yet for all that (as Pyne wrote), 'his pupils and admirers can always remember his many qualities with veneration, and feel the better for having been in any humble way connected with such a personality'.[204] For posterity that personality lives on his music. No one can hear his most inspired passages without experiencing something of the man who produced them. The sheer thrill of his great climaxes, as in the final movements of 'O Lord, thou art my God', 'To my Request and Earnest Cry', and 'The Wilderness' (where he would call for more and more stops), or the despair of 'Cast me not away, 'Man that is Born of a Woman', and 'Wash me throughly', is the work of someone familiar with extreme emotion and able to translate this into musical terms. That he was able to do this and, in the words of Edward Dannreuther, to produce works which 'contain an expression of the highest point up to that time reached by the combination of Hebrew and Christian sentiment in music'[205] was a truly remarkable achievement.

---

[202] 'Let us lift up our heart', 'O give thanks unto the Lord', 'Praise the Lord, O my soul', 'To my Request and Earnest Cry', 'The Wilderness', the Andante in E flat (*First Set of Three Pieces for a Chamber Organ*), and (by implication) the Andante in F all close quietly.

[203] Letter dated Oct. [1832] (*Lbl* Add. MS 35019, fo. 6).

[204] 'Wesleyana', 381.

[205] *The Romantic Period*, The Oxford History of Music, 6 (Oxford: Clarendon Press, 1905), 297.

7

Wesley the Romantic

LOOKING back at Wesley's life and music we are faced with a remarkable para-dox—a minor composer who, by developing an individual and instantly recognizable musical style, outshone many possessed of greater technical skill. That he did so in the isolated and circumscribed field of Anglican cathedral music makes it difficult, however, to assess his standing in a broader, European context. Difficult, but not impossible, as early in his career he regularly employed the (predominantly German) lingua franca, as familiar in Berlin, Paris, or Vienna as in London. But even in the 1830s this was regularly combined with an old-fashioned and typically English ingredient—a fondness for counterpoint—to fashion a unique blend of ancient and modern. And it was in his grafting of a contemporary harmonic vocabulary on to an old-fashioned contrapuntal technique—what could be described as 'progressive conservatism'—that Wesley's originality lay. Among those who commented on this marriage of the old and the new was Spohr, who noted that the sacred works were 'distinguished by their dignified and, frequently, antique style . . . [with] rich and choice harmonies, and . . . surprizing . . . modulations'.[1]

To understand why Wesley's musical style developed in such marked contrast to that of the majority of his European counterparts, it is necessary to look again at one of the defining characteristics of English music and culture at the time—the unusual degree of interest and respect accorded to anything old. This national characteristic intrigued the Belgian musicologist François-Joseph Fétis, who when visiting London in 1829 marvelled at the 'extraordinary contrast that exists between the degree of civilization to which it [England] has attained over the rest of the world, and the attachment which is shewn to ancient institutions and Gothic usages'. Why, he asked, in the 'finest city of Europe' should the king [George IV] continue 'to inhabit a pile of brick, misnamed the Palace of St. James, merely because the said pile of brick was raised by Henry VI [*recte* VIII]'?[2] This love of the antique embraced 'old' music, kept

---

[1] *Lcm* MS 3071.
[2] 'State of Music in London', *Har*, 7 (1829), 184. St James's Palace continued to be the London home of the sovereign until Queen Victoria moved to Buckingham Palace in 1837.

Acoustic

alive by such bodies as the Madrigal Society and the Concert of Ancient Music, the latter dedicated to the performance of works more than twenty years old, particularly those of Handel. But it was in the (Gothic) cathedrals that music from both the immediate and the more distant past was most frequently performed, with the result that English musicians were better acquainted with—and arguably more receptive to—the styles of previous generations than their European counterparts. England was of course also notable for its contribution to the early nineteenth-century Bach revival (in which Samuel Wesley played such a prominent part). It was from these two old traditions—the English cathedral school and the music of Bach—that Wesley's music acquired its defining characteristic, a tough, gritty polyphonic idiom. Indeed, his own view of the paramount importance of a solid grounding in contrapuntal technique can be judged from his comments to the young Hubert Parry, who recorded that 'he [Wesley] thought that the reason why Beethoven & more especially Spohr were sometimes (frequently) so unsatisfactory was because that [*sic*] lacked the necessary, and beneficial basis of hard work at Counterpoint; and . . . the reason why Mendelssohn so excelled was entirely because he had that instruction, and went through that preparation thoroughly'.[3]

Elsewhere Wesley offered further clues as to why his idiom developed as it did, praising the 'pure and beautiful Spohr',[4] writing of the 'best German writers—Bach, Handel, Mozart', extolling the 'exquisite nature'[5] of the E major Fugue from book 2 of Bach's *Das wohltemperirte Clavier* and the 'exquisite contents'[6] of a volume of his father's manuscripts, and describing some of Gibbons's works (among them 'The Silver Swan') as 'absolutely perfect'.[7] Time and again, as his music demonstrates, he was unafraid to look both backwards and forwards, to draw on the legacy of the cathedral tradition and the music of Bach, as well as the contemporary German school.

In this, of course, his approach mirrored that of his great German contemporary Mendelssohn, and Henry Smart made some interesting observations on the two composers when reviewing Wesley's *Anthems* of 1840. After noting that 'those musicians who know Mendelssohn, and are now but for the first time acquainted with Wesley, will compare notes and thereupon charge the

---

[3] Parry's diary entry for 5 Jan. 1866 (*ShP*).   [4] *A Morning & Evening Cathedral Service*, vii.
[5] Preface to *A Selection of Psalm Tunes*, 2nd edn., 2.
[6] *Lcm* MS 4022. Among the works it contains are the two which Wesley appended to *A Few Words* with the comment that they were 'submitted as proof that talent in the highest order of Ecclesiastical Music can exist in modern times' (p. 77): *Carmen funebre* ('Omnia vanitas') and the six-voice setting of 'Tu es sacerdos'.
[7] *A Morning & Evening Cathedral Service*, vi.

latter with wilfully imitating the German's style, if not with pilfering his ideas; and we anticipate this judgement in the hope of averting it', he continued:

That Wesley and Mendelssohn should fall on similar trains of ideas and similar modes of arranging and working them out, is in nowise astonishing, if the parity of their musical education and likings be considered. Both early imbibed a reverence for the grandest kind of ecclesiastical music and the severest style of organ performance; into both was the wisdom of old Bach instilled at the earliest periods of their musical existence, and both prove by their writings that their love for his sublime composi-tions is, at this day, in no degree diminished. Thus it is evident that the striking simi-larities to which we have referred cannot be rightly viewed otherwise than as kindred inspirations of like minds, journeying towards the same object and lighted by the same guide-star.[8]

But what Smart failed to mention was that Mendelssohn and Wesley differed in one crucial respect—their attitude towards diatonic dissonance. Neither Mendelssohn nor a majority of the composers influenced by Bach sought to emulate the degree of dissonance in the latter's music. Indeed, for those whose training was rooted in the Viennese classical style the concept of an essentially contrapuntal idiom, dependent on the ebb and flow of disso-nance and resolution, would have been alien. Among Wesley's immediate contemporaries only Chopin shared his Bachian reliance on a strong horizon-tal line, and Jim Samson's observation that in the works of both Bach and Chopin 'consistency of figure and contrapuntal integrity . . . provide sufficient justification for severe and often highly unorthodox dissonance . . . [while] the balance between linear and harmonic elements is similar . . . and perceptibly different from the Viennese classical style'[9] is no less applicable to his English counterpart. But Wesley was also influenced by the indigenous polyphonic tradition of the English cathedral school, and it is intriguing to note that when he tired of the more enticing sounds of modern German music, elements of this unruffled, prevailingly diatonic, idiom came to assume greater promi-nence and formed a third element of that 'dignified and, frequently, antique style' described by Spohr.

If one were to ask what it is that stamps Wesley's music indelibly as his own, the answer would surely be his idiosyncratic combination of counterpoint, diatonic dissonance, and, intermittently, chromaticism. Suspensions, passing-notes, appoggiaturas, and pedal-points are all used to create tension between the individual lines, resulting in textures of great vitality. Take, for example, the two passages from the Magnificat in the Service in E quoted in Ex. 7.1. In

---

[8] *MW*, 14 (1840), 233.
[9] Jim Samson, *The Music of Chopin* (London: Routledge & Kegan Paul, 1985), 75.

Ex. 7.1. Service in E, Magnificat

choir, org.

choir, org.

both the musical argument is conceived in terms of the horizontal movement of the parts, with scant regard for the passing dissonance created—chords comprising four adjacent notes (albeit in open position) in the first (G, A, B, C♯ in bar 162 or F♯, G, A, B in bar 164) and a typically baroque blend of accented passing-notes and suspensions in the second. Neither is such writing restricted to choral music or diatonic harmony, as the example of close-position dominant thirteenths, treated as 6–5 appoggiaturas, in the Rondo in C demonstrate (see Ex. 4.8*a*): the sublimation of counterpoint beneath virtuoso writing for the piano is reminiscent in principle, if not in practice, of the example of Chopin.

No less typical are those passages in which the harmonic conflict is with a sustained pedal-point (frequently an inner pedal). In the March in C minor, for example, clashing minor seconds enliven the inner pedal that precedes the return of the main theme (see Ex. 7.2*a*), while a similar pattern can be seen in 'To my Request and Earnest Cry' (Ex. 7.2*b*) and 'I wish to tune my quiv'ring lyre' (Ex. 7.2*c*) where two parts converge chromatically against inverted and inner pedals. It is at such moments that the distance separating Wesley's music from that of his fellow romantics becomes most apparent.

If Wesley's music has a weakness, it lies in his handling of musical structure. Unlike his academy-educated colleagues who benefited from Cipriani Potter's teaching on musical form,[10] he proceeded largely unaided, heavily dependent on the techniques he employed in his extemporizations. We can, surely, recognize the skilled extempore player behind his fondness for episodic forms, bound together either by a recurrent—but not developed—theme, or by one new idea following another, and in his habit of repeating certain stock progressions or phrases. And in the case of the latter, he had, like his father, clearly built up a mental store of ideas upon which to draw for both his impromptu and his finished compositions. The immediate result was that all his works spoke from the same limited phrase book.[11] A good example of this technique can be seen in the Andante in E flat (from the *Second Set of Three Pieces for a Chamber Organ*), where the opening phrase is stated no fewer than five times, almost always with slight variations of harmony or texture. Elsewhere, as in the Symphony, he relied on a ready flow of new ideas, but both approaches have their limitations, and it is significant that he never really mastered the technique of allowing his larger-scale movements to grow organically from their thematic material.

---

[10] See George A. Macfarren, 'Cipriani Potter: His Life and Works', *PMA*, 10 (1883–4), 48–9.

[11] Samuel Wesley's technique was dissected by Edward Hodges, who noted, apropos of his performances at St Mary Redcliffe in 1829, that 'his bold modulations were at first astounding . . . but they anon became familiar . . . [while] many of the passages occurred over and over again' (Hodges, *Edward Hodges*, 52–3).

Ex. 7.2. *a* March in C minor; *b* 'To my Request and Earnest Cry'; *c* 'I wish to tune my quiv'ring lyre'

Choral works, particularly those setting lengthy, continuous passages of prose, make different demands. A regular formal scheme is not necessarily appropriate, and in such circumstances Wesley's practice of continual thematic invention, perhaps in conjunction with a ritornello or partial recapitulation (as in the first movement of 'O Lord, thou art my God'), may be more suitable. Such an approach, in which the changing sentiments of the text are mirrored by the music (as Parry was later to achieve in 'My soul, there is a country'), was both subjective and instinctive—and it was the latter quality which accounted for what Edward Bairstow described as 'those wonderful flashes of inspiration found in the works of all great men—moments when, with the simplest technical means, they could suddenly lift us into the very heavens, or make us hold our breath'.[12] He singled out the 'common cadential 6/4 in F major for organ alone' used to link D major and F major in the quintet from 'O Lord, thou art my God' (see Ex. 7.3), but he could equally well have quoted the remarkable transition from dark B flat minor to radiant B major, with its accompanying change of timbre, at the words 'The unclean shall not pass over it; but the redeemed shall walk there' in 'The Wilderness' (see Ex. 2.1*b*). The new harmony, Alexander Brent-Smith wrote, 'opens new worlds for the redeemed to walk in'; he described the chord as one of two—the other from Bach's *St Matthew Passion*—'which always excite me, even though I know that they are coming'.[13] And it is precisely because of his ability to transcend his limitations and to produce music that is genuinely inspired that Wesley deserves the epithet 'genius'. A flawed and inconsistent genius, perhaps, but a genius none the less. When compared with the polished works of Bennett, Macfarren, or Smart (and later Stanford), his own may appear rough-hewn. Keyboard parts are frequently notated carelessly or contain impossible stretches, while many provide little help for the performer: the Andante in F, for example, contains no dynamic markings or indications for registration or change of manuals. Neither are singers treated more favourably, being asked to move instantaneously from one extreme of a two-octave range to the other, or to maintain the same note for bars on end with no opportunity to breathe. Technically, too, they contain examples of what Frederick Gore Ouseley pedantically described as 'contrapuntal laches and harmonic crudities'.[14] But Wesley's laconic comment 'There is a fifth or two—but never mind—I like 'em' (see Pl. 16) admirably sums up his attitude towards such academic mat-

---

[12] 'The Anthems of Samuel Sebastian Wesley', 309.
[13] 'Significant Chords', *MT*, 63 (1922), 615–6.
[14] 'Modern English Music', in Emil Naumann, *The History of Music*, trans. F. Praeger (London: Cassell & Co., 1886), 2. 1293.

Ex. 7.3. 'O Lord, thou art my God', fourth movement

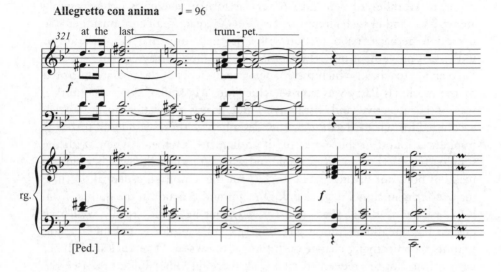

ters. At its best, however, his music speaks from the heart and possesses a
rugged, genuine integrity, as real today as it was a century and a half ago.

It is only when considering what Wesley might have achieved in more propitious circumstances that a note of regret can be allowed to creep in. Would
he have been able to produce further choral or orchestral works that continued the line of development found in his early essays, or maintained the series
of large-scale anthems begun at Exeter?[15] That he did not is a reflection on
both the state of music in England and his own career and character. Successful
large-scale composition demands determination and dedication from the composer. Early in his life he possessed both; by the end he had little of either. Yet
even in the less adventurous works of his later years there are still hints of a
continuing resolve to experiment harmonically, as with the series of parallel
sevenths (bars 163–5) in the second movement of 'Praise the Lord, O my soul'
(see Ex. 7.4) or the idiosyncratic harmonizations of such hymn tunes as
'Orisons' and 'Kerry' (see Ex. 6.2*b*). Indeed, his refusal to subscribe to con-
vention ensured that he had few disciples, and only one of his pupils, George
Garrett, adopted some of his mannerisms and then only in a few early works
(among them his Service in D). Moreover, by the 1860s and 1870s Wesley's
music appeared increasingly old-fashioned as, with the rise of a new genera-

---

[15] It is also tempting to ask whether Wesley would have gained international recognition as an organist
had he remained in London, bearing in mind that Berlioz engaged Henry Smart to play at the first performance of his Te Deum in 1855; Smart withdrew two days before the première.

Ex. 7.4. 'Praise the Lord, O my soul', first movement

choir, org.

tion of composers, a profound change had begun to sweep through English church music. In place of his forthrightly dissonant writing or the vigorous but unsentimental works of Henry Smart or John Goss we find a new style characterized by William Gatens as demonstrating 'tenderness' and 'understatement'[16] and typified by the works of Joseph Barnby (1838–1896) and John Stainer (1840–1901). Only towards the end of the century when the pendulum of fashion had begun to swing back did a few composers attempt to emulate their great predecessor, among them Hubert Parry (1848–1918) and Hugh Blair (1864–1932).

Turning to see how Wesley fits into the rich tapestry of music and musical life, one recognizes a very English figure, whose music shares many characteristics with much written before and since. Foremost among these are a dependence on counterpoint and a willingness to look to the past. In this he followed in the footsteps of his father and other contemporary Bach enthusiasts, and also in those of Robert Pearsall (1795–1856), who had sought inspiration in the works of the Elizabethan madrigalists (though with more than a glance at the *stile antico* composers of the Italian Baroque); taken to extremes, this led to the artistic dead end espoused by Crotch and his like-minded colleagues. More recently Vaughan Williams, Gustav Holst, Herbert Howells, and Edmund Rubbra, to name but four, have all drawn on the example of their Tudor and Stuart predecessors. Howells, in particular, was renowned for the individuality of his harmonic language and the complexity of his contrapuntal textures, and the latter are found also in the works of another individualist who, like Wesley, pursued a doggedly independent path on the fringes of the musical establishment, Havergal Brian. Looking further afield one can find parallels with other composers, among them Anton Bruckner, who also combined contrapuntal rigour with romantic harmony, Hector Berlioz, who made comparable use of unexpected turns of harmony (and whose chromaticism often has a similarly naïve quality), and another

---

[16] *Victorian Cathedral Music*, 170.

renowned improviser, Francis Poulenc, who likewise evolved an instantly recognizable but ultimately limited idiom.

But for all their interest such parallels tell us little about Wesley's very real
achievement. Against a background of indifference (to paraphrase Watkins
Shaw) he successfully restored a sense of value to cathedral music and re-
established it as a living musical form.[17] Yet despite this, his works have often
been relegated to little more than a footnote in the history of English music.
The reasons are varied, but relate to his 'difficult' character, the pattern of his
career, and the tendency among historians to see composers of church and
organ music as a class apart, lying outside the musical mainstream. How else
can one account for his omission—and that of his father and uncle also—from
W. S. Rockstro's *A General History of Music*, published just ten years after his
death?

Although he was marked out from an early age as an outstanding organist,
Wesley's development—and recognition—as a composer was much slower.
Unlike George Macfarren and Sterndale Bennett, who each wrote five symphonies before the age of twenty-two, he was a late developer, and whilst
notices of his earliest published works were encouraging, their message was
usually one of future promise rather than current achievement. Not for him
an editorial devoted to his compositions and musical attainments such as
Schumann gave the twenty-year-old Bennett in the *Neue Zeitschrift für Musik*
in January 1837. And once Wesley had left London he all too easily slipped
from the public eye. By the end of the 1830s his steady trickle of new publications had almost dried up, while the works performed at the Three Choirs
festivals had been heard once and once only. Had his *magnum opus*—the
Anthems—been published in 1840 as it should have been, things might have
been very different. Not only would it have provided a practical demonstration of Gauntlett's belief, expressed in his articles in *The Musical World*, that
Wesley represented a new school of church music composition (see Chapter
2), but it would also have made his anthems readily available to all who wanted
to perform them. As it was they were to remain largely unheard for a further
thirteen years, while Smart's generous review went for nothing. Within a few
years much of his early press support had evaporated, and not until 1859 and
Oakeley's retrospective notice of the 1853 *Anthems* in *The Guardian* did his
stock begin to rise.[18] Thereafter, and for some fifty or sixty years after his
death, his church music enjoyed a period of well-deserved success which
owed much to the improvements in cathedral choirs for which he had long

---

[17] See Watkins Shaw, 'The Achievement of S. S. Wesley', *MT*, 117 (1976), 304.
[18] [Herbert Stanley Oakeley], 'Cathedral Music', *The Guardian* (12 Oct. 1859), 873.

battled. Indeed, in many respects the late nineteenth and early twentieth centuries represented a 'golden age' for cathedral music, with twice-daily choral services, efficient choirs, and sufficient rehearsal time to support a large and varied repertoire, and it was fitting that the centenary of his birth should fall at this time. With Sir Frederick Bridge an indefatigable champion, an elaborate evening service and organ recital were given at Westminster Abbey, at which the Magnificat and Nunc Dimittis in E and no fewer than eight anthems and organ works were performed!

Neither did his music lack advocates in print. F. G. Edwards contributed several valuable articles to *The Musical Times* (including the first well-researched biography), but its most unexpected champion was undoubtedly that staunch Wagnerian Edward Dannreuther, whose remarkable verdict that Wesley's best works 'contain an expression of the highest point up to that time reached by the combination of Hebrew and Christian sentiment in music'[19] has already been quoted. It was a view with which Stanford was wholly in agreement: he praised Dannreuther's 'timely and convincing vindication of the right of the Wesleys to a prominent place in the history of the nineteenth century. Rarely have their great gifts been so wisely and so justly emphasised. Musicians have too long ignored their influence upon the modern renaissance in England, of which they were as undoubtedly as they were unconsciously the forerunners'.[20] H. C. Colles was no less forthright in a centenary essay:

It is not only that these [Wesley's anthems] contain exquisite melodies or that they are examples of the magical effects which can be gained from combined human voices. Their power lies deeper. There is something in the reflective attitude of the musician towards his subject which is specially the outcome of his life in an English Cathedral. They could not have been written by a man who was much concerned with the more strenuous aspects of artistic life. Whether they touch on the sorrows and aspirations of the human soul or on the mysteries of faith, it is with a certain reticence which does not weaken their force, but rather strengthens it. They sum up Wesley's life-long convictions as to the function of Cathedral music. He saw in the cathedral service the means of contemplating in terms of art the deepest emotions and the highest aspirations of humanity. He found the existing organization quite inadequate to its purpose, and he devoted his life to the realization of his ideal.[21]

The fiftieth anniversary of Wesley's death in 1926 was accompanied by discerning tributes from Bairstow and Harvey Grace in *The Musical Times*, to be followed eleven years later by Gerald Spink's series of biographical articles 'Samuel Sebastian Wesley: A Biography'. But the tide had begun to change

---

[19] *The Romantic Period*, 297.
[20] C. V. Stanford, *Studies and Memories* (London: Archibald Constable & Co., 1908), 208.
[21] *Essays and Lectures*, 135.

and, with a growing reaction against all things Victorian, competition from the wealth of rediscovered Tudor music and less time for rehearsal, his works began to slip out of the repertoire. This trend continued in the post-war years; writing in 1953, Denis Stevens could, with a complete lack of irony, describe 'The Wilderness' as a 'tedious' anthem whose closing bars were 'a splendid apotheosis of the mawkish and the maudlin' and offer his 'sincere sympathy' to the 'small solo boy who sounds as if he is genuinely in pain'[22]—words which uncannily echo Crotch's sketch of a chorister 'with his face distorted with agony in the effort to reach the high A in the concluding verse'.[23] By the 1960s only the evening canticles from the Service in E, a handful of anthems, and a few hymn tunes, chants, and organ pieces remained in regular use, but the centenary of Wesley's death in 1976 gave his cause a fillip, with the revival by the BBC of the orchestral versions of 'The Wilderness' and 'Ascribe unto the Lord', the Symphony, and 'I have been young but now am old' and the publication a year later of the first full-length biography, Paul Chappell's *Dr. S. S. Wesley*. Since then not only has Donald Hunt produced a second study, *Samuel Sebastian Wesley*, but there has also been a steady growth of interest in all aspects of nineteenth-century British music, marked by the publication of books devoted to both the period (Nicholas Temperley's *The Romantic Age*) and specifically to cathedral music (William Gatens's *Victorian Cathedral Music in Theory and Practice*). Both Temperley and Gatens offer valuable insights into Wesley's music, and the latter places it in the context of a more general theory of Victorian church music.

With the benefit of hindsight we can recognize in Wesley's life and works a quintessentially romantic figure, striving for the unattainable, conceiving art as a means of escape from everyday matters, and speaking the musical language of romanticism as though born to it. But it was in his two intertwined beliefs—of the musician as an artist, and of the choral service, with its combination of words, music, ceremonial, and (in the broadest sense) architecture, as representing the pinnacle of religious art—that his romantic vision found its clearest expression. Like his contemporaries Berlioz, Wagner, and Schumann, he felt the need to expound his ideas in a series of manifestos, and his various publications provide our clearest picture of 'Wesley the artist'. Such an outlook, however, ran completely counter to the ethos of the contemporary Anglican church, in which, as he repeatedly complained, musicians were all too frequently viewed as subservient menials. And it was his stubborn nature and refusal to conform that ultimately thwarted his career. Despite this, his

---

[22] 'Gramophone Notes: English Church Music', *MT*, 94 (1953), 119.
[23] Bumpus, *A History of English Cathedral Music*, 370.

contribution to English music, seemingly small and insignificant though it is, shows the hand of a master who, inspired by a passionate belief in the value and importance of his art, strove against all the odds to bring to his chosen field—English cathedral music—the dignity and strength of purpose it had for so long lacked.

APPENDIX 1

Syllabus and Music Illustrations for Wesley's Lectures on Church Music at the Liverpool Collegiate Institution, 12 March–12 April 1844

Lecture 1

Introduction—Church music, its early state—Chants of the early church—St Ambrose—St Gregory—Antiphony

Illustrations

'As from the Power of sacred lays' [*Ode for St Cecilia's Day*]	Handel
Chants of St Ambrose and St Gregory	
Te Deum	Ascribed to St Ambrose
Modern chant	[James] Turle
Chorus 'In exitu Israel'	S. Wesley
Motett 'Be not afraid' ['Fürchte dich nicht']	Bach
Psalm 'Out of the deep' [Psalm 130, Op. 85 No. 3]	Spohr

Lecture 2

Progress of the art from the time of St Gregory to the reign of Henry 8th—Extemporaneous descant—Introduction of counterpoint—The 'Church School of Music'—its claims to notice at the present day—Josquin du Prey—The monasteries and their spoliation

Illustrations

Anthem 'Call to remembrance'	R. Farrant
Anthem 'Hide not thou thy face'	R. Farrant
Miserere	Beethoven
Requiem	Josquin du Prey
First movement of the Requiem	Mozart
Anthem 'O Lord the maker'	King Henry 8th
Anthem 'O Lord thy word' [from *The Actes of the Apostles*]	Tye
Psalm 'How excellent' [Psalm 84]	Spohr

Lecture 3

State of music at the Reformation—King Henry the Eighth—His reign continued to
that of Edward the Sixth—The choral services—Marbeck's 'Book of Common
Prayer, noted'—Robert White—Prescription of Commissioners—Dr Tye's 'Acts
of the Apostles'—The rubric 'To be said or sung'

Illustrations

Anthem 'Lord, who shall dwell'	Robert White
Anthem 'Laudate Nomen' [from	
The Actes of the Apostles]	Tye
Anthem	Tye
Chorus 'Then round about the Starry Throne'	
[from *Samson*]	Handel
Chorus	Mozart
Kyrie Eleison [Mass in C?]	Beethoven
Tallis' Responses	Tallis
Anthem 'Lord, for thy tender mercies' sake'	Farrant
Chorus 'Beloved Lord'	
[from *Des Heilands letzte Stunden*]	Spohr

Lecture 4

Reign of Queen Mary—Byrd—Palestrina—Re-establishment of Protestantism—The
injunctions of Queen Elizabeth—Metrical Psalmody—Gibbons

Illustrations

Motett 'Laetentur coeli'	Byrd
Anthem 'We have heard'	Palestrina [adapted H. Aldrich]
Motett 'Exaltabo te Domine'	Palestrina
Chorals	Tallis, Bach, Mendelssohn, Spohr
Motett 'As the fathers with compassion'	Bach
Anthem 'Almighty and everlasting God'	Gibbons
Anthem 'Hosanna'	Gibbons

Lecture 5

The school of Venice—The Gabrieli family—The state of music at Venice, in the 16th
century—The Church of St. Mark—Reign of King James 1st—Decline of cathedral
music in England—MS on the subject preserved in the Library of George IV

Illustrations

Anthem 'Plead thou my cause'	A. Willaert
Hymn 'Sancta Maria'	G. Gabrieli
Motett 'Ego dixi Domine'	G. Gabrieli
Motett 'Et exultavit Spiritus meus'	Orlando di Lasso
Part of a Miserere	Allegri
Anthem	Gibbons
Chorus 'Et vitam venturi'	Perti

Lecture 6

Ecclesiastical music in the 18th and 19th centuries—Decline of the Vocal school in
    cathedrals—Purcell—Dr. Creyghton—Croft—Bach—Handel—Marcello

Illustrations

Anthem 'O give thanks'	Purcell
Anthem 'Thou knowest Lord'	Purcell
Anthem 'I will arise'	Creighton [*sic*]
Duett 'Qual anelante' [from Psalm 41]	Marcello
Anthem 'Sing unto the Lord'	Croft
Motett 'Jesus, thou that only'	
['Jesu, meine Freude'?]	Bach

Lecture 7

Subject continued

Illustrations

Anthem 'O where shall wisdom be found'	Boyce
Motett 'Lord God of Heaven'	
[from *Die letzten Dinge*]	Spohr
Anthem 'Turn thy face'	Attwood
Trio 'Jesus, heavenly Master'	
[from *Des Heilands lezte Stunden*]	Spohr
Quartett 'Recordare' [Requiem]	Mozart
Chorus 'All Kings'	
['Give the King thy judgements']	Dr. Boyce

Lecture 8

The choral service—Its resuscitation—St Mark's College, Chelsea—The Parish
    Church, Leeds

Illustrations

Psalm 'As the Heart [*sic*] pants' [Psalm 42]	Mendelssohn
Chorus 'Tu es Sacerdos'	S. Wesley
Anthem 'Omnia vanitas'	S. Wesley
Part of a psalm 'Not unto us' [Psalm 115]	Mendelssohn
Motett 'God is my shepherd' [Psalm 23]	Spohr

APPENDIX 2

Organs Opened by Samuel Sebastian Wesley

Date	Place	Builder
6 November 1832	Hereford Cathedral	J. C. Bishop
12 February 1835	Penzance Parish Church	Henry Crabbe
3 November 1838	Exeter Cathedral	John Gray
5 November 1838	Bath Abbey	John Smith
14 October 1841	Leeds Parish Church	Greenwood Brothers
9 September 1842	Pontefract Parish Church	Booth
21 June 1844	St Jude's Church, Bradford	J. Ward
11 September 1844	St James' Church, Bradford	Gray & Davison
18 September 1844	St John's Church, Dewsbury Moor	Joseph Hampshire
2 October 1844	Liverpool Collegiate Institution	Bewsher
21 November 1844	St Giles' Church, Camberwell	J. C. Bishop
26 April 1846	Wortley Parish Church	Messrs Holt
25 June 1846	Tavistock Parish Church	J. W. Walker
25 February 1847	St Matthew's Church, Manchester	Unknown
8 February 1850	St George's Church, Leeds	Messrs Holt
15 August 1850	St Margaret's Church, Lee	J. C. Bishop
January 1851	Upton Church, Torquay [but opened in Royal Public Rooms, Exeter]	H. P. Dicker
25 October 1851	St Jude's Church, Southsea	George Smith
3 June 1854	Winchester Cathedral	Henry Willis
28 November 1854	Winchester Cathedral [complete]	Henry Willis
29 May 1855	St George's Hall, Liverpool	Henry Willis
10 September 1861	Holy Trinity Church, Winchester	Henry Willis
3 November 1863	Agricultural Hall, Islington	Henry Willis
13 May 1866	Christ Church Spa, Gloucester	John Nicholson
4 April 1867	High Street Methodist Chapel, Huddersfield	Conacher
19 March 1868	St Thomas' Parish Church, Bury	F. Jardine
1869	T. S. Kennedy, Meanwood, Leeds	Schulze
1873	Parish Church, Holsworthy	Unknown
12 April 1874	All Saints' Church, Scarborough	J. M. & C. Corps
29 April 1874	Victoria Rooms, Clifton	Bryceson

WORK-LIST

This work-list includes the following information on Wesley's works (apart from the hymn tunes and Anglican chants: see below): title, scoring, date of composition, location of manuscript (if known), and details of first and later editions, plate numbers, and reviews; where a work is from a collection, reviews are noted under the collection title. Unless otherwise stated all manuscripts are autograph and all editions were published in London. Details of where hymn tunes and Anglican chants were published are given, together with the texts with which they were first associated; except where a cross-reference to another section of the list is given, further details of hymn and chant collections may be found in the Bibliography. To aid identification chants are also provided with a coded melodic incipit, using numerals to represent the degrees of the scale (1 = tonic, 2 = supertonic, etc.); slurred pairs of notes are indicated by underlining and accidentals by the appropriate symbols. Wesley's anthems are being published in three volumes in the series Musica Britannica: A. 1–3, 5–12 (vol. 58); A. 4, A. 20 (vol. 63), and A. 13–19, 21–37 (in preparation).

Contents

A.   Church anthems and introits
B.   Service settings
C.   Hymn tunes
D.   Anglican chants
E.   Solo songs
F.   Vocal works with orchestral accompaniment
G.   Glees and partsongs
H.   Choral works with orchestral accompaniment
I.   Orchestral and stage works
J.   Organ music
K.   Piano music
L.   Arrangements and editions
M.   Writings and compilations

Abbreviations

General

arr.	arranged
CM	common metre
DLM	double long metre
LM	long metre

orch   orchestra
org   organ doubling the voices
org acc   independent organ accompaniment (church music only)
rev.   revised edition
SM   short metre
wm   watermark
★   no extant copy

Bibliographical

Wesley's Own Collections

2nd Set (1842)	*A Second Set of Three Pieces for a Chamber Organ* (London: Cramer, Addison & Beale, [1842]); review: *ME*, no. 11 (1843), 74–5.
2nd Set (1868)	*Second Set of Three Pieces for a Chamber Organ* (London: Novello, Ewer & Co., [1868]).
3 Pieces (1842)	*Three Pieces for a Chamber Organ* (London: Cramer, Addison & Beale, [1842]); review: *ME*, no. 11 (1843), 74–75.
3 Pieces (1868)	*First Set of Three Pieces for a Chamber Organ* (London: Novello, Ewer & Co., [1868]).
Anthems (1840)	*Anthems* (n.p., [1840]); review: *MW*, 14 (1840), 231–3, 243–4, 277–8.
Anthems (1853)	*Anthems*, vol. 1 (London: Addison & Hollier, [1853]); review: *Ath*, 15 (July 1854), 884.
Collects	*Sacred Songs: The Collects for the First Three Sundays in Advent* (London: Coventry, [1848]).
EP	*The European Psalmist* (see M. 8)
HM	*Special Hymns to be Used at the Consecration of the Church of St. John the Baptist, Hamsteels, Durham, July 6th, 1875* (London: Novello, Ewer & Co., [1875]).
K	*A Selection of Psalms and Hymns, Arranged . . . by the Rev. Charles Kemble* (see M. 7)
PS	*The Psalter, with Chants* (see M. 2)
W	*The Welburn Appendix* (see M. 9)

Other Collections

A&M[68]	*Hymns Ancient and Modern*, new edn. (1868)
A&M[75]	*Hymns Ancient and Modern*, rev. and enlarged edn. (1875)
BM	Bennett and Marshall (eds.), *Cathedral Chants*
CaC	Blakeley (ed.), *The Canticle Chant Book*
CH	Sullivan (ed.), *Church Hymns with Tunes*
CoC	Trimnell (ed.), *The Collegiate Chant-Book*

H	Hawes (ed.), *A Collection of Chants, Sanctuses, & Responses*
Hy	*The Hymnary*
NP	Hackett (ed.), *The National Psalmist*
NV	Tate and Brady, *A New Version of the Psalms of David*
P	Novello (ed.), *The Psalmist*
SoP	Evans-Freke (ed.), *The Song of Praise*

A. Church Anthems and Introits

1   'Tho' Round thy Radiant Throne on High' (ss, SS, org acc), *c*.1827? Manuscript: *Lbl* Add. MS 35039.

2   'Glory to God on high' (SSAATTBB, org), *c*.1831? Manuscript: *Lcm* MS 4030.

3   'O God, whose Nature and Property' (SATB, org), 1831. Manuscript: *H* MS C.9.xii (1834?). Editions: W. Hawes, [1831], pl. no. 598; Novello, Ewer & Co., [1870], pl. no. 4486 (rev.). Reviews: *Har*, 9 (1831), 221; *MT*, 15 (1871), 54.

4   'The Wilderness and the Solitary Place' (b, sattb, SSATB, org acc), 1832. Manuscript: *H* MS C.9.xii (1834). Editions: *Anthems* (1840); *Anthems* (1853) (rev.); Hall, Virtue & Co., [1862] (rev.); Novello, Ewer & Co., [1868] (rev.). Orchestral version, 1852. Manuscript: *Lcm* MS 4030 (score), MS 6855 (parts); alternative orchestral version (part autograph), *c*.1859. Manuscript: *Cfm* Mus Ms 216.

5   'Blessed be the God and Father' (s, SATB, org acc), 1834. Manuscript: *H* MS C.9.xii (1834?). Editions: *Anthems* (1853); Hall, Virtue & Co., [1862] (rev.); Novello, Ewer & Co., [1868] (rev.).

6   'Trust ye in the Lord' (s, SATB, org acc), *c*.1835. Manuscript: *Lcm* MS 4030 (incomplete).

7   'O give thanks unto the Lord' (s, satb, SATTB, org acc), *c*.1835. Editions: *Anthems* (1853); Novello, Ewer & Co., [1870], pl. no. 4331 (rev.).

8   'All we like sheep' (SSATB), *c*.1836. 5 bar fragment. Manuscript: in private possession.

8   'Let us lift up our heart' (b, satb, SSAATTBB, org acc), *c*.1836. Editions: *Anthems* (1853); Novello, Ewer & Co., [1870], pl. no. 4331 (rev.).

9   'O Lord, thou art my God' (b, ssattb, SSAATTBB, org acc), *c*.1836. Editions: *Anthems* (1840); *Anthems* (1853) (rev.); Novello, Ewer & Co., [1870], pl. no. 4331 (rev.).

10 'To my Request and Earnest Cry' (b, SSAATTBB, org acc), *c*.1836. Edition: *Anthems* (1840) (movements 1 and 2 only). Manuscript: *Lbl* Add. MS 40636 (last movement only).

11 'Wash me throughly from my wickedness' (s, SATB, org acc), *c*.1840. Editions: *Anthems* (1853); Novello & Co., [1863] (rev.).

12 'Man that is Born of a Woman' (SATB, org acc), *c*.1845. Editions: *Anthems* (1853); Novello, Ewer & Co., [1870], pl. no. 4331 (rev.).

13 'Cast me not away from thy presence' (SSATTB, org), 1848. Manuscript: sketch in collection of Robert Pascall. Editions: *Anthems* (1853); Novello, Ewer & Co., [1870], pl. no. 4331 (rev.).

14 'The Face of the Lord' (ssaattbb, SATTB, org), 1848. Editions: *Anthems* (1853); Novello, Ewer & Co., [1870], pl. no. 4331 (rev.).

15 'Blessed is the man that feareth the Lord' (SATTB, org), 1849? Manuscript: *LPC* (S part, not autograph). Edition: Novello & Co., 1908. The portrait of Wesley by Briggs (1849) shows him resting his hand on the unfinished manuscript.

16 'Hear thou in heaven' (SATTB, org), 1849? Manuscript: *LPC* (S part, not autograph). Edition: Novello & Co., 1908.

17 'I will wash my hands in innocency' (SATB, org), *c.*1849. Manuscript: *LPC* (S part, not autograph). Edition: Novello & Co., 1908.

18 'O Lord, my God' (Solomon's Prayer) (SATB, org), *c.*1850. Editions: *Anthems* (1853); Hall, Virtue & Co., [1862] (rev.).

19 'Thou wilt keep him in perfect peace' (SATTB, org acc), *c.*1850. Manuscript: *WC* (T and B parts). Editions: *Anthems* (1853); Hall, Virtue & Co., [1862] (rev.).

20 'Ascribe unto the Lord' (sssattb, SSATB, org acc), 1851. Editions: *Anthems* (1853); Novello & Co., [1865], pl. no. 3463 (rev). Orchestral version, 1865. Manuscript: *Lcm* MS 4034 (score and parts).

21 'By the Word of the Lord' (satb, SATTB, org acc), 1854. Manuscripts: *Lcm* MSS 4030, 4031 (both incomplete). Written for the opening of the new organ in Winchester Cathedral, 3 June 1854.

22 'I am thine, O save me' (SATTB, org acc), 1857. Editions: supplement to *The Musical Remembrancer* (1857); Novello, Ewer & Co., [1870], pl. no. 4485 (rev.).

23 'All go unto one place' (SATB, org acc), 1862. Manuscript: fragment in private possession. Edition: Hall, Virtue & Co., [1862]. Review: *MW*, 40 (1862), 83. Written in memory of the Prince Consort.

24 'Praise the Lord, O my soul' (s, ssatb, SATB, org acc), 1861. Editions: Hall, Virtue & Co., [1862]; Novello, Ewer & Co., [1868] (rev.). Review: *MS*, 1 (1862), 11–12. Written for the opening of the organ in Holy Trinity Church, Winchester, 10 Sept. 1861.

25 'Give the King thy judgements' (ssattbb, SSAATTB, org acc), 1863. Manuscript: *Lcm* MS 4032, 1863. Edition: Novello, Ewer & Co., [1870]. Written to celebrate the marriage of the Prince of Wales, 10 March 1863.

26 'God be merciful unto us' (b, satb, SATB, org acc), 1866. Manuscript: *Lbl* Add. MS 40636 (S & T parts). Edition: Novello, Ewer & Co., [1867], pl. no. 3734. Review: *MT*, 16 (1874), 482. Written for the marriage of George Watson, 1 Jan. 1867.

27 'Blessed be the Lord God of Israel' (SATB, org acc), 1868. Edition: Novello, Ewer & Co., [1868], pl. no. 4152. Review: *MW*, 47 (1869), 851, 864. Published simultaneously as a supplement to *MT*.

28 'I will arise' (D major) (SATB, org), 11 Nov. 1869. Manuscript: *Lbl* Add. MS 40636. Edition: *EP*, no. 724.

29 'I will arise' (F major) (SATB, org), *c.*1869. Manuscript: *Lbl* Add. MS 40636.

30 'At thy right hand' (SATB, org), 1869. Manuscript: *Lbl* Add. MS 40636. Edition: *EP*, no. 725. Written to follow Samuel Wesley's 'O remember not our old sins'.

31 'Blessed is the man' (ATTB, org), *c.*1870. Manuscript: *Lbl* Add. MS 40636. Edition: *EP*, no. 729.

32 'Turn thee again' (SATB, org), *c.*1870? Edition: *EP*, no. 723.

33 'Lord of all Power and Might' (SATB, org), Jan. 1873. Manuscript: *Lbl* Add. MS 40636. Edition: *The Practical Choirmaster* (March 1873), no. 1 (Metzler & Co.), pl. no. M.3608.

34 'Let us now praise famous men' (Edition 'B') (t, satb, SATB, org acc), 1873. Manuscript: Perkins Library, Southern Methodist University, Dallas. Edition: Novello, Ewer & Co. and Weekes & Co., [1875] (Collegiate Series, no. 46). Written for Founder's Day at Clifton College, Bristol.

35 'Let us now praise famous men' (Edition 'A') s, SATB, org acc, 1874. Manuscript: Southern Methodist University, Dallas. Edition: Novello, Ewer & Co. and Weekes & Co., [1875] (Collegiate Series, no. 14). Written for Founder's Day at Clifton College, Bristol.

36 'O how amiable are thy dwellings' (SATB, org acc), 1874? Manuscript: *Lbl* Add. MS 40636 (last movement only). Edition: Novello, Ewer & Co. and Weekes & Co., [1874] (Collegiate Series, no. 18).

37 'Wherewithal shall a young man cleanse his way' (s/t, SATB, org acc), 1875? Manuscript: *Lbl* Add. MS 40636 (incomplete). Edition: Novello, Ewer & Co. and Weekes & Co., [1875] (Collegiate Series, no. 19).

38 'The Lord is my shepherd' (sb, SATB, org acc), 1875? Edition: Novello, Ewer & Co. and Weekes & Co., [1875] (Collegiate Series, no. 40).

39 *Twelve Anthems.* Advertised 1863 (see *MT*, 11 (1863), 55), but never published.

B. Service Settings

1 *A Morning & Evening Cathedral Service* [Service in E] (ssaattbb, SSAATTBB, org acc), *c.*1834–43? Manuscript: *Exc* MS D & C Exeter Mus/2/24 & Mus/2/26 (B part Kyrie no. 2, Creed and Sanctus, not autograph); *Lbl* Add. MS 40636 (Sanctus); Te Deum, Creed, Kyrie (unpublished), and Nunc Dimittis in collection of Robert Pascall. Editions: Chappell, 1845, pl. no. 6697; Novello, Ewer & Co., [1865], pl. no. 6697. Reviews: *LI* (10 Feb. 1844), 7; *MP* (26 Feb. 1844), 3; *Sp*, 17 (1844), 234–5; *ILN*, 6 (1845), 229.

2 Versicles and Responses, *c.*1846. Lost.

3 Gloria in Excelsis in C (SATB, org), *c.*1846. Edition: Novello, Ewer & Co., [1869], pl. no. 4189. Reviews: *MS*, 10 (1869), 287; *MT*, 13 (1869), 688.

4a *Magnificat and Nunc Dimittis, A Chant* [Chant Service in F (Evening)] (SATB, org), 1846? Manuscript: *LPC* (S part, not autograph). Edition: Chappell, [1851]; Arthur Hall, Virtue & Co., [1855]; Arthur Hall, Virtue & Co., [1859]; Novello, Ewer & Co., [1865]. Review: *MS*, 1 (1862), 11.

4b *A Chant Service* [Chant Service in F (Morning)] (SATB, org), 1855? Editions: A. Hall, Virtue & Co., [1855]; Arthur Hall, Virtue & Co., [1859]; Novello, Ewer & Co., [1865]. Review: *MS*, 1 (1862), 11.

5   Deus Misereatur in F (satb, SATB, org), 1858. Manuscript: *Lbl* Add. MS 40636.
6   *A Short, Full, Cathedral Service in F* [Service in F] (SATB, org), 1868–9.
     Manuscript: *H* MS R.10.xviii (lacking Creed and part of Responses to the
     Commandments). Edition: Novello, Ewer & Co., [1869], pl. no. 4277.
     Reviews: *MS*, 11 (1869), 83; *MT*, 15 (1872), 595.
7   Chant Service, 'Letter B' (SATB, org), 1869. Edition: Novello, Ewer & Co.,
     [1869].
8   Responses to the Commandments in F sharp minor, *c.*1870. Manuscript: *Lbl*
     Add. MS 40636. Edition: *EP*, no. 617.
9   Responses to the Commandments in F, *c.*1870. Edition: *EP*, no. 623.
10   Sanctus in D, *c.*1870. Manuscript: *Lbl* Add. MS 40636. Edition: *EP*, no. 616.
11   Sanctus in F, *c.*1870. Edition: *EP*, no. 622.
12   Chant Service in G, 1872? Edition: *EP*, no. 730.

C. Hymn Tunes

Name/key	Metre	Text incipit	Collection, MS
Abbey Dore	6.6.4.6.6.6.4	'Glory to God on high!'	*EP* 552, *K* 98
Achill	CM	'O all ye people, clap your hands' (Ps. 47 *NV*)	*EP* 111
Alleluia	8.7.8.7.8.7.8.7	'Alleluia, sing to Jesus'	*A&M*[68] 350, *EP* 392
Almsgiving	LM	'Almighty Father, heaven and earth'	*Hy* 522
Arimathea	10.10	'Draw nigh, and take the body of the Lord'	*EP* 587
Arran	6.6.6.6	'Thy way, not mine, O Lord'	*EP* 532, *K* 120, *W* 31
Ashburton	8.7.8.7.4.7	'Pilgrims here on earth'	*EP* 458, *K* 23, *SoP* 35
Askelon	10.10.7	'Sing Alleluia forth in duteous praise'	*EP* 562
Atonement	10.10.10.4	'O man of sorrows'	*EP* 571
Aurelia	7.6.7.6.7.6.7.6	'The Church's one foundation', 'Jerusalem the golden'	*A&M*[68] 320, CH218, *EP* 451, *K* 122, *SoP* 489
Avebury	6.5.6.5.6.5	'We close the weary eye'	*EP* 600
Baptism	10.6.10.6.8.8.4	'O Father, thou who hast created all'	*EP* 329
Bath New (Bath)	DSM	'O where shall rest be found'	*EP* 460, *K* 121

p. 376

Name/key	Metre	Text incipit	Collection, MS
Be not afraid	7.7.7.7	'When the dark waves around us roll'	*CH* 549
Bedminster	6.6.6.6	'We love the place, O God'	*EP* 432
Berea	7.7.7.7.7.7	'Christ the wisdom and the power'	*SoP* 580
Beverly	6.6.6.4	'Jesus, Immanuel'	*EP* 613
Bickleigh	8.7.8.7.4.7.	'Lo! He comes with clouds descending!'	*EP* 452, *K* 31
Bolton	8.8.8.8.8.8	'O God, of good th'unfathom'd sea'	*EP* 328
Bovey	8.8.6.8.8.6	'O God, mine inmost soul convert'	*EP* 538, *K* 55
Bozrah	7.6.7.6.7.7	'Who is this with garments dyed?'	*EP* 567
Brecknock	8.8.8.8.8.8	'Thou hidden love of God'	*EP* 517
Brierly	6.6.6.6	'O God, descend and bless'	W 28, *Lbl* Add. MS 40636
Brisbane	8.8.6.8.8.6	'Thou God of power and God of love'	*EP* 545, *K* 9
Brixton	7.7.7.6	'In the dark and cloudy day'	*EP* 493, *W* 97
Bude	CM	'Alas! what dangers hourly rise'	*EP* 208
Bulmer	6.6.4.6.6.4	'The Lord almighty reigns'	*W* 105
Bury	8.4.8.4.8.8.8.4	'God who madest earth and heaven'	*EP* 424
Byford	6.6.6.4	'So guide our steps, O Lord'	*EP* 305b
Calne	6.6.6.6.7.7	'Angels, assist to sing'	*EP* 606
Calvary	8.7.8.7.7.7	'He who once in righteous vengeance'	*EP* 425
Camberwell	CM		*Lcm* MS 4038
Celestia	11.10.11.10.9.11	'Hark, hark, my soul'	*EP* 602, *SoP* 558
Chesham	6.6.4.6.6.4	'The Lord almighty reigns'	*W* 34
Clifton	CM	'My God, to thee I now commend'	*EP* 211
Colchester	8.8.8.8.8.8	'Would Jesus have the sinner die?'	*EP* 490
Collingham	8.8.8	'O sons and daughters, let us sing'	*EP* 438, *W* 57
Communion	6.4.6.4.6.6.4	'Nearer, my God, to thee'	*EP* 524, *K* 123

Name/key	Metre	Text incipit	Collection, MS
Corinth	8.7.7.7.8.5	'Some sweet savour of thy favour'	*EP* 526, *K* 131
Cornwall	8.8.6.8.8.6	'Thou God of glorious majesty'	*EP* 441
Devon	11.9.11.9	'Come away to the skies'	*EP* 309
Dies Irae	8.8.8.8.8.8	'Day of wrath, O day of mourning'	*EP* 547
Dinmore	CM	'O God, unseen, yet ever near'	*EP* 122
Donnington	6.6.4.6.6.4	'Lowly and solemn be'	*EP* 588
Dorcas	8.8.8.4	'O Lord of heaven and earth and sea'	*SoP* 484
Dover	8.6.8.4	'Our blest redeemer, ere he breathed'	*EP* 423
Downton	CM	'O that the Lord would guide my ways'	*EP* 89
Dulverton	8.6.8.6.8.8.8.8	'Salvation, O the joyful sound'	*EP* 445, *K* 86
Eden	6.4.6.4.6.7.6.4	'There is a happy land on high'	*EP* 527, *K* 125
Ellingham	10.10.10.10	'Father of heaven, in whom our hopes confide', 'Abide with me, fast falls the eventide', 'Go forth and reap'	*EP* 457, *K* 111, *W* 53, *SoP* 8
Elwell	CM	'God's time with patient faith expect'	*EP* 143
Engedi	8.6.8.8.6	'Eternal light! Eternal light'	*EP* 595
Epiphany	11.10.11.10	'Brightest and best of the sons of the morning'	*EP* 528, *K* 124
Epworth	8.7.8.7.8.7.8.7	'Peace be to this congregation'	*EP* 558, *K* 87
Eternity	7.7.7.5	'When the day of toil is done'	*SoP* 511
Euphrates	8.8.8.8.7	'When our latest breath is falling'	*EP* 570
Ewyas Harold	6.6.8.6.4.4.4.7	'From Egypt lately come'	*EP* 459, *K* 96
Excelsior	6.5.6.5.6.5.6.5	'Onward, Christian soldiers'	*EP* 585
Eyton	8.6.8.6.8.6	'Saviour of sinners, now we pray'	*EP* 114
Faith	7.6.7.6.7.6.7.6	'God of my salvation, hear'	*EP* 553, *K* 103

Name/key	Metre	Text incipit	Collection, MS
Fowler	6.10.6.10	'O why should I have peace?'	EP 596
Gilboa	6.5.6.5.6.5.6.5	'Saviour, blessed saviour'	EP 574
Gilead	8.8.8.6	'Lo, the storms of life are breaking'	EP 581
Glasbury	11.11.11.11	'The Lord is our refuge'	EP 534, K 54
Glastonbury	9.8.9.8.9.8.9.8	'Bread of the world, in mercy broken'	EP 584
Gonville	SM	'Ye souls devout, give ear'	W 42
Grace Dieu	9.8.9.8	'There is a rest from sin and sorrow'	EP 607
Gratitude	8.8.8.8.8.8.8.8	'The Lord, our salvation and light'	EP 551, K 105
Grosvenor	7.8.7.8	'Jesus lives! no longer now'	EP 431
Gweedore	6.6.6.6.8.8	'My trust is in the Lord'	EP 530, K 16
Hampstead	6.6.8.6.6.8	'How pleased and blest was I'	EP 614
Hampton	LM	'Return, my wand'ring [*recte* roving] heart, return', 'How shall the young preserve their ways' (Ps. 119: 9–16, *NV*)	NP 62, EP 8, K 10, W 8, Mr MS MAM P 12 C
Hamsteels No. 1	LM	'God, in thy name these walls we raise'	HM
Hamsteels No. 2	LM	'Eternal power, whose high abode'	HM
Harbridge	8.8.8.6	'Just as I am, without one plea'	EP 536, K 115
Harewood	6.6.6.6.8.8	'Rejoice the Lord is king', 'Christ is our corner stone'	NP 122, EP 410, A&M⁷⁵ 239, W 58, Mr MS MAM P 12 C
Haven	8.5.8.3.8.5.8.3	'Art thou weary, art thou languid'	EP 564
Haverhill	6.4.6.6	'The sun is sinking fast'	EP 605
Havilah	8.8.8.8	'A mighty, a fathomless deep'	EP 576
Hawarden	8.8.8.8.8.8.8.8	'There is a blessed home'	EP 601
Hawkridge	8.6.8.6.8.8.8.6	'O Thou in whom we all are one'	EP 300

Name/key	Metre	Text incipit	Collection, MS
Hereford	LM	'My soul, inspired with sacred love' (Ps. 103, *NV*)	*EP* 54, *Lcm* MS 4037
Holsworthy	DLM	'Lord cause thy face on us to shine'	*EP* 74
Hornsey	8.7.8.3	'On the resurrection morning'	*EP* 611, *SoP* 493
Houghton (Houghton-le-Spring)	7.7.7.7.7.7	'Rock of ages, cleft for me'	*EP* 448, *K* 97, *Hy* 499, *SoP* 355, 537
Hymn for All Nations	7.7.7.7.7.7.7.7	'Glorious God, on thee we call'	Pub. Thomas Hatchard, 1851; *Lcm* MS 4038
Hymn for Christmas	8.8.8.8.8.8	'O come, loud anthems let us sing'	*Lbl* Add. MS 40636
Iona	7.7.7.5	'Three in one, and one in three'	*EP* 422, *W* 76
Jersey	7.6.7.6.7.7.7.6	'Rise, my soul, and stretch thy wings'	*EP* 515, *K* 94
Jerusalem	6.8.6.4	'Lo! on the inglorious tree'	*EP* 557
Keila	6.6.6.6.6.6	'When morning gilds the skies'	*EP* 582
Kensington	DLM	'The spacious firmament on high'	*EP* 446, *K* 91
Kerry	LM	'Sun of my soul, thou saviour dear'	*EP* 500
Kilkhampton	CM	'O Thou from whom all goodness flows'	*EP* 230
Killerton	8.8.7.8.8.7	'Come pure hearts, in sweetest measure'	*EP* 434
Lebanon	8.8.8.6	'Lo, the storms of life are breaking'	*EP* 577
Leintwardine	8.8.8.8.8.8	'Grant us dear Lord, from evil ways'	*EP* 270
Leominster	LM	'The Lord in righteousness arrayed'	*EP* 84
Lincoln	DSM	'A few more years shall roll'	*SoP* 232
Llanthony	LM	'Pass a few swiftly-fleeting years'	*EP* 429a
Londesborough	7.8.7.8	'Fear no more the clanking chain'	*EP* 609

✓

Name/key	Metre	Text incipit	Collection, MS
Lowthorpe	6.8.8.6	'Now are we truly blest'	*W* 15
Lucerna	6.4.6.4	'Today the saviour calls'	*EP* 555
Lusatia	8.3.3.6.8.3.3.6	'Ere I sleep, for every favour'	*EP* 593
Mara	6.6.8.6.8.8	'Friend after friend departs'	*EP* 554
Martyrs	7.6.7.6.7.6.7.6	'Let our choir new anthems raise'	*EP* 415
Masham	SM		*K* 42
Mason	10.4.10.4.10.4.10.4	'Maternal earth! receive this kindred dust'	*W* 63
Mispah	8.3.3.6.8.3.3.6	'Ere I sleep, for every favour'	*EP* 599
Morning	LM	'Wake, and lift up thyself, my heart'	*EP* 3, *W* 11
Morning Hymn	LM	'New every morning is the love'	*EP* 42, *K* 108
Nazareth	7.7.7.11.11.8	'Christ is born! exalt his name!'	*EP* 568
Nebo	7.5.7.5.7.7	'Every morning the red sun'	*EP* 575
Netley	6.6.10.6.6.10	'Thou who didst stoop below'	*EP* 612
Northchurch	5.5.5.5.6.5.6.5	'Breast the wave, Christian'	*EP* 608
Nunnington	10.10.11.11	'Our Father and Lord, almighty art thou'	*EP* 447
Orisons (A)	10.10.10.10	'Abide with me, fast falls the eventide'	*EP* 539, *K* 126A
Orisons (B)	10.10.10.10	'Abide with me, fast falls the eventide'	*EP* 540, *K* 126B
Patmos	10.4.10.4.10.10	'Lead, kindly light'	*EP* 569
Paradise	8.6.8.6.6.6.6.6	'O paradise, O paradise'	*EP* 583
Pilgrimage	7.6.7.6	'O happy band of pilgrims'	*SoP* 487
Plymouth	8.8.4.8.8.4	'What care the saints of God'	*EP* 40
Providence	6.5.6.5	'O! Let him whose sorrow'	*EP* 439
Prussia	8.4.7.8.4.7	'Come, my soul, thou must be waking'	*EP* 565
Radford	9.8.9.8	'The day thou gavest, Lord, is ended'	*CH* 32
Redemption	11.11.12.11.10.10	'Sion, the marvellous story be telling'	*EP* 543, *K* 128
Refuge	10.10.10.10	'Abide with me, fast falls the eventide'	*EP* 580

Name/key	Metre	Text incipit	Collection, MS
Resignation	13.11.13.11	'Thou art gone to the grave'	*EP* 525, *K* 127, *SoP* 458
Rock of ages	7.7.7.7.7.7	'Rock of ages, cleft for me'	*Lbl* Add. MS 40636
Ross	7.7.7.7	'As the sun doth daily raise'	*CH* 3
St Athanasius	7.7.7.7.7.7	'Holy, holy, holy, Lord'	*SoP* 116
St Michael New	10.10.6.6.10	'O Captain of God's host'	*EP* 492
St Michael New (alternative version)	10.10.6.6.10	'O Captain of God's host'	*EP* 493a, *Hy* 376
St Paul's	CM		*Lcm* MS 4038
St Sebastian			also published as Houghton (see above)
Sennen	DCM	'Lord I believe a rest remains'	*EP* 488
Sepulchre	4.4.7.7.6	'O darkest woe!'	*EP* 556
Seraphim	8.5.8.5.8.7	'Angel-voices ever singing'	*SoP* 206
Sheffield	6.6.7.7.7.7	'Worthy, O Lord, art thou'	*EP* 428
Shillingstone	4.6.4.6.4.6.4.6	'Sleep thy last sleep'	*EP* 563
Skipton	6.6.8.6.6.8	'Jerusalem divine'	*EP* 426
Southam	LM	'Inspirer and hearer of prayer'	*EP* 43
Sparsholt	CM	'We magnify thee day by day' (Te Deum, *NV*)	*EP* 161
Spilsby	CM	'O bounteous Lord, thy grace and strength'	*EP* 100
Spofforth	5.5.5.11	'Come let us anew'	*EP* 427
Sugwas	6.6.6.4	'So guide our steps, O Lord'	*EP* 305a
Supplication	11.11.11.5	'Lord of our life, and God of our supplication'	*EP* 586
Syracuse	CM		*P* 226
Time	8.8.8.4	'The radiant morn hath passed away'	*EP* 566
Tintern	6.5.6.5.6.5	'When day's shadows lengthen'	*EP* 594
Trinity	11.12.12.10	'Holy, holy, holy, Lord God almighty'	*EP* 454, *K* 130, *SoP* 115
Triumph	8.6.8.6.4.10	'Who shall ascend the holy place?'	*EP* 573

Name/key	Metre	Text incipit	Collection, MS
Vespertine	6.6.8.6.6.8	'The moon hath risen on high'	*EP* 511b
Vigilance	7.7.7.3.7.7.7.3	'Christian, seek not yet repose'	*EP* 578
Welburn	6.6.4.6.6.4	'O God, thou God of love'	*W* 86
Wensley	LM	'All praise, to thee, my God this night'	*EP* 22
Weston	7.7.7	'Lord, in this, thy mercy's day'	*EP* 419
Westbury	DSM	'Thou art gone up on high'	*EP* 523
Wetherby	CM	'Awake, ye saints, and raise your eyes'	*EP* 88
Whitby	8.8.8.3	'Fierce rag'd the tempest o'er the deep'	*EP* 610
Whitstone	6.6.6.6	'Jesu, meek and lowly'	*EP* 440
Wigan	6.6.4.8.8.4	'Behold the Lamb of God'	*EP* 430
Wimbledon	8.8.8.4	'My God, my Father, while I stray'	*EP* 514, *K* 106
Winscott (A)	LM	'Sun of my soul, thou Saviour dear'	*EP* 370
Winscott (B)	LM	'Sun of my soul, thou Saviour dear'	*EP* 589
Winsford	8.8.8	'The strife is o'er, the battle done'	*EP* 433, *W* 85
Winton	6.6.8.8.4	'Arise, my soul, arise'	*W* 93
Wrestling Jacob	8.8.8.8.8.8	'Come, O thou traveller unknown'	*EP* 401
In C	CM	'Dread Trinity in unity'	*Hy* 29
In C	7.7.7.7.7.7	'Christ, whose glory fill the skies'	*Hy* 58
In C	7.6.7.6	'Brief life is here our portion'	*Hy* 199
In D	8.8.8.8.8.8	'O come, loud anthems let us sing'	*Hy* 135
In D	6.10.6.10	'Ye angel hosts above'	*Hy* 630
In E	8.3.3.6	'Jesu, let thy sufferings ease us [*recte* me]'	*Hy* 44
In E♭	LM	'Behold, the radiant sun on high'	*Hy* 66
In E♭	8.8.8.4	'O Lord of heaven, and earth, and sea'	*Hy* 524

Name/key	Metre	Text incipit	Collection, MS
In E♭	8.7.8.7.8.7.8.7	'He is coming'	*Lbl* Add. MS 40636
In F	CM	'Through all the changing scenes of life'	*Hy* 624
In G	7.6.7.6.7.6.7.6.7.6	'The world is very evil'	*Hy* 109
In G	SM	'Far from our heavenly home'	*Hy* 203
In G	CM	'All ye who seek for sure relief'	*Hy* 596

D. Anglican Chants

No.	Key	Melodic incipit	Text	Collection, MS, comments
Single chants				
1	B♭	567171	Pss. 136 and 138	*PS* 144, *EP* 637, *Lcm* MS 4035
2	C	15162	Ps. 105	*Lbl* Add. MS 40636
3	C	51366	Ps. 105	*Lbl* Add. MS 40636
4	D	56717	Te Deum ('We praise thee')	*CaC*, p.10/6a, = no. 5, differently harmonized
5	D	56717	Ps. 106	*Lbl* Add. MS 40636 = no. 4, differently harmonized
6	D	34362	Ps. 107	*Lbl* Add. MS 40636
7	D	33233	Te Deum ('Thou art the King')	*CaC*, p.10/6b
8	D	17654	Te Deum ('We believe')	*CaC*, p.10/6c
9	E	3555♯4♮4	Pss. 108–9	*Lbl* Add. MS 40636, unattributed
10	E/e	33215	Pss. 108–9	*Lbl* Add. MS 40636 unattributed
11	e/E	53213		*EP* 627
12	e	3342♮2		*EP* 641; = no. 26, transposed
13	e	5♯7122		*EP* 642
14	e	55564		*EP* 670
15	E♭	32123	Pss. 91–2	*Lbl* Add. MS 40636; = no. 23, transposed
16	E♭	34321	Ps. 103	*Lbl* Add. MS 40636
17	E♭	51653		*EP* 636

No.	Key	Melodic incipit	Text	Collection, MS, comments
18	E♭	35517		*EP* 652, *Lcm* MS 4035
19	F	353214		*EP* 625
20	F	33211		*EP* 643
21	F	33422		*EP* 647
22	F	54326		*EP* 651, *K* 186
23	F	34321		*EP* 659; = no. 15, transposed
24	F	176217	Ps. 107	*Lbl* Add. MS 40636
25	F	333322	Pss. 110–13	*Lbl* Add. MS 40636
26	f♯	33424 2	Pss. 142–3	*PS* 150; = no. 12, transposed
27	f♯	33425		*EP* 668
28	G	13251	Ps. 103	*Lbl* Add. MS 40636
29	G	23♯453	Ps. 104	*Lbl* Add. MS 40636
30	G	13243	Ps. 104	*Lbl* Add. MS 40636

Double chants

1	B♭	56715		*EP* 706
2	c	513211		*EP* 710
3	D	343321		*EP* 702
4	d	53421		*EP* 676
5	d	54365		*EP* 714
6	d	53121		*EP* 720
7	e	35517		H
8	E♭	31353		*EP* 699
9	E♭	54324	Pss. 110–13, Ps. 103	*EP* 715, *Lcm* MS 4035; = no. 10, transposed
10	F	54324		*PS* 104, *EP* 679; = no. 9, transposed
11	F	33353		*EP* 687
12	F	32343	Pss. 132–5	*PS* 141, *EP* 713, *BM* 179
13	F	35314		*EP* 719
14	F	31277	Ps 105	*EP* 722, *Lbl* Add. MS 40636
15	F	346716	Pss. 15–16	*CoC* 12

Benedicite in D   *EP* 728

E. Solo Songs

1 'You told me once', 1831? Edition: W. Hawes, [1831], pl. no. 451. Review: *Har*, 10 (1831), 246.

2 'When we Two Parted' (words Byron), 1832? Manuscript: *Lbl* Add. MS 40636 (late 19th-century copy). Edition: W. Hawes, [1832].★ Review: *Har*, 11 (1832), 258.

3 'The Smiling Spring' ('I beheld her from my casement': words trans. from De Beranger), 1832? Edition: J. Dean, [1832], pl. no. 227. Review: *Ath* (10 November 1832), 733. Dedicated to Henry Mullinex.

4 'Wert thou Like me' (words Walter Scott), 1832. Manuscript: *Lcm* 4031, dated 29 December 1832. Editions: Mori & Lavenu, [1835], pl. no. 3597★; Novello, Ewer & Co., [1876].

5 'Did I Possess the Magic Art' (words Samuel Rogers), *c*.1833? Edition: Mori & Lavenu, [1835], pl. no. 3596.

6 'There breathes a living fragrance' (words anon.), 1833. Manuscript: *Lbl* Add. MS 40636 (incomplete copy).

7 'The Bruised Reed' (words W. H. Bellamy), 1834. Manuscripts: *Lcm* 4038, 1834; *Mr* MS MAM P 12 C. Edition: *NP* (1839).

8 'Blessed are the dead who die in the Lord' (words Byron), 1835? Edition: Mori & Lavenu, [1835], pl. no. 3621.

9 'There be none of beauty's daughters' (words Byron), 1835? Editions: Mori & Lavenu, [1835], pl. no. 3644 (lost; copy by Addison, Hollier, and Lucas printed from the original plates, *Lcm*); Novello, Ewer & Co., [1876]. Orchestral version. Manuscripts: *Lcm* 4031 (2 incomplete scores); *Lcm* 4032 (late 19th-century copyist's score).

10 'Orphan Hours' (words Shelley), *c*.1836. Manuscript: *Lbl* Add. MS 40636 (wm 1836). Edition: Cramer & Co. and Novello, Ewer & Co., [1867]. Review: *MS*, 7 (1867), 193.

11 'By the Rivers of Babylon' ('We sat down and wept': words Byron), 1845–50? Manuscript: *Lbl* Add. MS 40636. Edition: Novello and Co., [1867]. Review: *MS*, 7 (1867), 193. Sketches for a different setting of the same words are also found in Add. MS 40636.

12 'Almighty God, O give us grace' (words W. H. Bellamy), 1848. Edition: *Collects*.

13 'Most Blessed Lord' (words W. H. Bellamy), 1848. Edition: *Collects*.

14 'Lord Jesu Christ' (words W. H. Bellamy), 1848. Edition: *Collects*.

15 'For Charity's Sake' (words M. F. Tupper), 1849. Edition: Liverpool: James Smith; London: Chappell, [1849], pl. no. 8237. Written for the Liverpool Charitable Fetes, 8–10 August 1849.

16 'Shall I tell you whom I love?' (words William Browne), *c*.1860. Edition: Chappell & Co.; Novello; Hall, Virtue & Co., [1861]. With cello obbligato and alternative German text, 'Hoher Muth, und süsse Minne'. Also issued as a part-song (see G. 5).

17 'The Butterfly' ('Butterfly, butterfly'; words Lady Flora Hastings), 1874? Edition: J. B. Cramer; Lamborn Cock, [1874–6]. First known performance at the 1874 Gloucester Three Choirs Festival.

F. Vocal Works with Orchestral Accompaniment

1   'Agnus Dei' (Latin) (s or t, org/piano/orch), *c.*1830. Manuscript: <u>Lbl</u> Add. MS
    40636 (late 19th-century copies).

2   *Abraham's Offering* ('Take thou my son, my only son': words W. H. Bellamy)
    (bar, orch), 1834. Manuscript: *Lcm* MS 4030 (wm 1828).
    ——— 'There be none of beauty's daughters' (words Byron): see E. 8.

3   'I have been young and now am old' (words Bible), (bar, orch), 1848?
    Manuscript: *Lcm* 4030 (wm 1846).

4   'The Song of the Seamstress' ('They tempt me from my native land': words
    W. H. Bellamy), s, orch, 1864. Announced on the programme for the closing
    ceremony of the 1864 North London Working Men's Industrial Exhibition (see
    Lbl Add. MS 35020, fo. 77), but no copy known.

G. Glees and Partsongs

1   'I wish to tune my quiv'ring lyre' (words Byron from Anacreon) (ATTBB), 1833.
    Manuscript: *Mp*, dated 31 May 1833. Edition: D'Almaine & Co., [1837–8].
    Dedicated to William Shore. Review: *MW*, 11 (1839), 211–12.

2   'At that Dread Hour' (words William Linley) (ATTB), 1834. Manuscript: *Mp*.
    Edition: D'Almaine & Co., [1837–8]. Review: *MW*, 11 (1839), 211–12.

3   'Fill me Boy as Deep a Glass' (words T. Moore from Anacreon) (ATTBB), 1834.
    Manuscript: *Mp*.

4   'When Fierce Conflicting Passions Rend the Breast' (words Byron from
    Euripides) (ATTBB), 1837. Editions: D'Almaine & Co., [1837–8];* Novello,
    Ewer & Co., [1876], pl. no. 9317. Review: *MW*, 11 (1839), 211–12.

5   'Shall I tell you whom I love?' (words William Browne) (SATB, cello obbligato,
    piano acc), 1862? Editions: Hall, Virtue & Co., [1862];* Cramer & Co., [1868].

6   'The Praise of Music' ('Sing we in chorus': words Thomas Oliphant) (SSAAT-
    TBB), 1872. Manuscript: Sotheby's sale 13 March 1978. Edition: Novello, Ewer
    & Co. and Weekes & Co., [1874] (Collegiate Series, no, 2).

7   'The Mermaid' ('When the pale moon': words Charles A. Burroughs) (SATB),
    1873? Manuscript: Sotheby's sale 13 March 1978. Edition: Novello, Ewer & Co.
    and Weekes & Co., [1874] (Collegiate Series, no. 3).

8   'Arising from the Deep' (words anon.) (SATB), 1873? Manuscript: Sotheby's
    sale, 13 March 1978. Edition: Novello, Ewer & Co. and Weekes & Co., [1874]
    (Collegiate Series no 6).

H. Choral works with orchestral accompaniment

1   'Young Bacchus in his Lusty Prime' (words anon.) (t, TTB, orch), *c.*1830. Manu-
    script: *Lcm* MS 4031 (copied by 'Coad Copyist 6 Royal St. Lambeth', wm 1829).

2   'Gloria in Excelsis' (Latin) (b, SATB, orch), c.1830. Manuscript: *Lcm* MS 4030
    (opening fragment of copyist's score).

3 'Benedictus qui venit' (Latin) (satb, org/orch), 1832 (org), 1833 (orch). Manuscripts: *Lcm* MS 4034 (vocal score, wm 1830); *Lcm* MS 4030 (full score, 1833; final leaf copied from orchestral parts by F. G. Wesley).

4 'Sanctus' and 'Osanna' (Latin) (SATB, orch), 1834? First performed at the Hereford Three Choirs Festival, 10 September 1834. Lost.

5 'Millions of Spiritual Creatures' (words J. Milton: *Paradise Lost*) (satb, orch), 1835. Manuscript: *Lcm* MS 4030 (wm 1833).

6 *Ode to Labour* ('When from the great creator's hand': words W. H. Bellamy) (ssatb, SATTBB, org/orch), 1864 (org), 1865 (orch). Manuscripts: *Lcm* 4039 (full score), 1865; *Lbl* Add. MS 40636 (no. 5 only, full score). Edition (vocal score): Cramer & Co., Novello & Co. and Virtue & Co., [1864].

I. Orchestral and stage works

1 Ballet music *c.*1825. Manuscript: *Cfm* MS MU 698 (wm 1809).

2 *The Dilosk Gatherer or the Eagle's Nest*, 1832. Manuscript: *Lbl* Add. MS 33819 (set of parts), Add. MS 33816 (vocal score of glee and song), not autograph.

3 Overture in E, 1832? Manuscript: *Lbl* Add. MS 35010 (set of parts, lacking clarinet, copied by J. Hedgeley, 1834, wm 1834).

4 Symphony, 1834–5? Manuscript: *Lcm* MS 4033 (wm 1833–4).

5 Concertante (2 flutes, 2 oboes, 2 clarinets, 2 bassoons, 4 horns), 1835. Written for the Gloucester Three Choirs Festival 1835. Lost.

J. Organ Music

1 *God save the King, with Variations*, 1829. Editions: W. Hawes, [1831], pl. no. 484; Novello, Ewer & Co., [1869] (rev. as *The National Anthem, with Variations*), pl. no. 4368. Reviews: *At*, 6 (1831), 396; *Har*, 10 (1831), 196.

2 Andante in A, *c.*1830? Manuscript: *Lbl* Add. MS 40636, 1870–6? Edition: Novello, Ewer & Co., [1877], pl. no. 5560. Reviews: *MMR*, 7 (1877), 192; *MT*, 19 1878, 36.

3 *A Selection of Psalm Tunes Adapted Expressly to the English Organ with Pedals, c.*1832? Manuscript: *Lcm* MS 4031 (fragment). Editions: J. Dean, [1834], pl. no. 338; R. Cocks & Co., [1842] (rev.), pl. no. 3126. Reviews: *MW*, 17 (1842), 344; *LI* (1 April 1843), 7.

4 Choral Song, *c.*1832? Editions: *3 Pieces* (1842); *3 Pieces* (1868).

5 Introduction and Fugue in C sharp minor, 1835? Editions: J. Dean, [1836]★; Novello, Ewer & Co., [1876?]; Novello, Ewer & Co., [1869] (rev.), pl. no. 4191. Reviews: *MW*, 2 (1836), 143; *MW*, 8 (1838), 100; *MS*, 10 (1869), 181.

6 Larghetto in F minor, 1835–6? Manuscript: *Lbl* Add. MS 40636 (Wesley's title 'For the organ 5 parts'). Edition: Novello, Ewer & Co., 1893.

7 Andante in E flat (4/4), *c.*1840. Editions: *3 Pieces* (1842); *3 Pieces* (1868).

8 Andante in F, *c.*1840. Editions: *3 Pieces* (1842); *3 Pieces* (1868).

9   Andante in E flat (3/4), c.1841. Editions: *2nd Set* (1842); *2nd Set* (1868).

10 Andante in G, c.1841. Editions: *2nd Set* (1842); *2nd Set* (1868).

11 Larghetto in F sharp minor, c.1841 (left untitled by Wesley; title added by George Garrett). Editions: *2nd Set* (1842); *2nd Set* (1868).

12 Andante in D, 1846. Manuscript: Author's collection, 'Leeds. Decr 27th. 1846. Played at the Parish Church extemporaneou[sly] and written at the request of Mr Martin Cawo[od]'.

13 Andante Cantabile in G, 1863. Editions: Messrs Virtue, [1864]; Novello, Ewer & Co., [1868]. Review: *MS*, 2 (1864), 201.

14 Andante in C (*The Musical Standard*), 1870. Edition: under the title *For Organ or Harmonium* in January 1871, *MS*, 14 (1871), 40–1.

15 Voluntary: Grave and Andante, c.1871. Edition: in The Organist's Quarterly Journal, vol. 3 (Metzler, 1872).

16 Andante in C (*The Village Organist*), 1872. Manuscript: *Lbl* Add. MS 40636 (copyist's score corrected by Wesley). Edition: in *The Village Organist*, vol. 2, ed. T. R. Matthews (Novello, Ewer & Co., [1872]). Review: *MT*, 15 (1872), 572.

17 'An Air Composed for Holsworthy Church Bells', 1873–4. Manuscript: *Lbl* Add. MS 40636. Edition: Novello, Ewer & Co., [1877], pl. no. 5495. Reviews: *MMR*, 7 (1877), 94; *MT*, 18 (1877), 345.

18 Andante in E minor. Manuscript: *Lbl* Add. MS 40636. Edition: Novello, Ewer & Co., [1877], pl. no. 5591.

19 *Easy Organ Pieces*. Advertised in 1863 (see *MT*, 11 (1863), 55), but never published.

K. Piano Music

1   Waltz in E, 1830. Edition: supplement to *The Harmonicon*, September 1830: *Har*, 8 (1830), 366–7.

2   *An Introduction and Rondo on an Air from Spohr's Azor and Zemira*, c.1831. Edition: W. Hawes, [1831].★

3   *Original Air, with Variations*, dedicated to J. B. Cramer, 1831? Edition: J. Dean, [1832].★ Reviews: *At*, 7 (1832), 92; *Har*, 10 (1832), 15.

4   Rondo 'La Violette', c.1832? (advertised in *LI* (2 July 1842), 4).★

5   Dance in D, 1833–34? Manuscript: *Lcm* MS 4031 (wm 1833).

6   Rondo in G, 1834? Manuscript: *Lcm* MS 4038. Edition: Mori & Lavenu, [1835–6].★

7   Piece in E minor, 1834. Manuscript: *Lcm* MS 4038.

8   Presto in C minor, 1834. Manuscript: *Lcm* MS 4038, 23 April 1834. Unfinished.

9   March (C minor) and Rondo (C major),1842. Editions: Cramer, Addison & Beale, [1843];★ Novello, Ewer & Co., [1868], pl. no. 3988. Review: *ME*, no. 13 (1843), 90.

10 *Jeux d'esprit: quadrilles à la Herz*, 1846. Edition: Chappell & Co., [1847], pl. no. 7506. Also published in an arrangement for piano duet.★

L. Arrangements and Editions

1   James Connolly, 'O when do I Wish for thee' (melody and words James Connolly), arr. for voice and piano, 1832. Edition: J. Dean, [1832], pl. no. 149.

2   Edward Harwood, 'Vital Spark of Heavenly Flame' (melody Edward Harwood; words Alexander Pope), arr. for voice and piano, 1832. Edition: J. Dean, [1832], pl. no. 167.

3   John Hullah, *The Psalter or Psalms of David in Metre*, 6 tunes harmonized, 1843. Edition: J. W. Parker, 1843.

4   Kozeluch, *An Air with Variations*, arr. for organ, *c*.1830. Manuscript: *Lcm* MS 4031.

5   W. A. Mozart, *New and Complete Edition of Mozart's Favorite Songs, Duets & Trios*, rev. Wesley. Edition: Chappell, [1849–51]): 36 numbers. Reviews: *Ath* (15 Dec. 1849), 1279; *MW*, 29 (1851), 619.

6   W. A. Mozart, *Ten Songs by Mozart*, arr. Wesley. Edition: Chappell and Co., [1861]. Issued as *Chappell's Musical Magazine*, no. 4.

7   William Owen, 'By the Streams of Babylon' 'Wrth Afonydd Babilon' (SATB, org/piano), accompaniment by Wesley. Edition: J. A. Novello, [1854].

8   John Reading, 'Dulce domum', arr. for 2 voices & bass, *c*.1850. Manuscript: *Lcm* MS 4038.

9   Louis Spohr, Witches' Rondo (from *Faust*), arr. for piano solo, 1832? Manuscript: *Cfm* MS MU 691 (marked up for engraving and bearing the pl. no. 738, implying publication by W. Hawes in 1832).

10   Louis Spohr, Psalm 24, 'The earth is the Lord's', adapted to English words by W. T. Freemantle, rev. Wesley. Edition: Novello, Ewer & Co., [1874].

11   Edward Stephen, *The Storm of Tiberias* (Ystorm Tiberias), accompaniment rev. Wesley. Edition: Bethesda: R. Jones, 1857.

12   Samuel Wesley, March in B flat, arr. for full orchestra, *c*.1830. Manuscript: *Lcm* MS 4031 (wm. 1828).

13   Samuel Wesley, 'Thou, O God, art praised in Sion' (SATB, org), ed. S. S. Wesley, 1865. Edition: Novello & Co., [1865], pl. no. 3458.

14   Samuel Wesley, 'Confitebor tibi, Domine' (satb, SSATB, orch), additional accompaniments added to nos. 2, 3, 6–9, 13–15, 1868. Manuscript: *Lcm* MS 4121 (copyist's score with autograph additions).

15   Samuel Wesley, 'Peace troubled soul' (from 'Who is the trembling sinner'), arr. for SATB by S. S. Wesley, *c*.1870. Edition: *EP*, no. 727.

16   *The Hundredth Psalm*, arr. with varied harmonies, 1864. Edition: Novello & Co., [1864], pl. no. 3348. Review: *MS*, 6 (1867), 37. Orchestral version: lost (but organ arrangement by C. S. Jekyll published by Goodwin & Tabb).

17   'Light o' Love' (old ballad), harmonized, *c*.1838? Manuscript: collection of Robert Pascall.

M. Writings and Compilations

1 Preface to *A Selection of Psalm Tunes*, 2nd edn., 1843. See J. 3

2 *The Psalter, with Chants*, 1843. Editions: Leeds: T. W. Green; London: J., G., F., and J. Rivington, 1843; Leeds: T. W. Green; London: J., G., F., and J. Rivington, 1846. Reviews: *MW*, 18 (1843), 205; *LI* (17 June 1843), 7; *Ath* (31 Aug. 1844), 797; *LI* (10 Oct. 1846), 5.

3 Preface to *A Morning & Evening Cathedral Service*, 1845. See B. 1

4 [Address on cathedral music, 1849]. Edition: [without imprint, 1849]. Written in collaboration with Edward Taylor.

5 *A Few Words on Cathedral Music and the Musical System of the Church, with a Plan of Reform*, 1849. Edition: F. & J. Rivington, 1849. Reviews: *ChR*, 18 (1849), 373–403, *passim*.

6 *Reply to the Inquiries of the Cathedral Commissioners, Relative to Improvement in the Music of Divine Worship in Cathedrals*, 1854. Edition: Piper, Stephenson, and Spence, [1854]. Review: *Ath* (1 April 1854), 404–5.

7 *Words of Anthems used in Cathedral and other Churches*, 1869. Edition: Gloucester: E. Nest, [1869].

8 *A Selection of Psalms and Hymns, Arranged . . . by the Rev. Charles Kemble*, 1864. Editions: John F. Shaw, 1864; [as *Wesley's Tune Book*] John F. Shaw & Co., 1866. Review: *MS*, 3 (1864), 177.

9 *The European Psalmist*, 1872. Edition: Novello & Co., Boosey & Co., Hamilton, Adams, & Co., 1872.

10 *The Welburn Appendix of Original Tunes*, 1875. Edition: Novello, Ewer & Co., [1875].

BIBLIOGRAPHY

Books and Articles

ABRAHAM, GERALD, *Chopin's Musical Style* (London: Oxford University Press, 1939).

ALLBUTT, CLIFFORD, 'Reminiscences of Edmund Schulze and the Armley Organ', *Org*, 5 (1925), 78–86.

ATKINS, E. WULSTAN, *The Elgar–Atkins Friendship* (Newton Abbot: David & Charles, 1984)

'Aurelia', *MT*, 47 (1906), 676–8.

AYLMER, GERALD, and TILLER, JOHN (eds.), *Hereford Cathedral: A History* (London: The Hambledon Press, 2000).

BAIRSTOW, EDWARD C., 'The Anthems of Samuel Sebastian Wesley', *MT*, 67 (1926), 308–9.

BARRETT, PHILIP, *Barchester: English Cathedral Life in the Nineteenth Century* (London: SPCK, 1993).

—— 'English Cathedral Choirs in the Nineteenth Century', *Journal of Ecclesiastical History*, 25 (1974), 15–37.

—— 'John Merewether, Dean of Hereford 1832–50', *The Friends of Hereford Cathedral Annual Report* (1977), 23–39.

BELL, JAMES, *A New and Comprehensive Gazetteer*, 4 vols. (Glasgow and Edinburgh: A. Fullarton & Co., 1836).

[BELLAMY, W. H.], *The Collects for the Sundays and Holydays throughout the Year, in the Order in which they Occur in the Book of Common Prayer, Rendered into Verse* (London: Hatchard and Son, 1848).

BENHAM, GILBERT, 'Interesting London Organs, XXXV: St. Giles's Church, Camberwell', *Org*, 13 (1933–4), 46–51.

—— 'The Organ at St. George's Hall, Liverpool', *Org*, 6 (1926), 145–9.

BENNETT, JOSEPH, *Forty Years of Music, 1865–1905* (London: Methuen, 1908).

BLANCH, WILLIAM HARNETT, *Ye Parish of Camerwell: A Brief Account of the Parish of Camberwell, its History and Antiquities* (London: E. W. Allen, 1875).

BODEN, ANTHONY, *Three Choirs: A History of the Festival* (Stroud: Alan Sutton, 1992).

BRADLEY, IAN, *Abide with me: The World of Victorian Hymns* (London: SCM Press, 1997).

BRENT-SMITH, ALEXANDER, 'Significant Chords', *MT*, 63 (1922), 615–16.

BREWER, ALFRED HERBERT, *Memories of Choirs and Cloisters (Fifty Years of Music)* (London: Bodley Head, 1931).

BRIDGE, FREDERICK, *A Westminster Pilgrim: Being a Record of Service in Church, Cathedral, and Abbey, College, University, and Concert-Room* (London: Novello & Co., [1919]).

BROWN, JAMES WALTER, *Round Carlisle Cross* (Carlisle: Charles Thurnam & Sons, 1951).

BROWNE, NIGEL, 'Henry Philip Dicker, Organ Builder', *BIOSJ*, 22 (1998), 140–60.

BUMPUS, JOHN S., 'The Church Compositions of Samuel Sebastian Wesley', *MN*, 29 (1910), 139–41, 179–81, 199–200, 224–6, 240–1.

——*A History of English Cathedral Music*, 2 vols. (London: T. Werner Laurie [1908]).

——'A Letter of S. S. Wesley', *MN*, 26 (1904), 251.

——'A Letter of S. S. Wesley', *MN*, 27 (1904), 384, 402–3, 426–7.

——*The Organists and Composers of S. Paul's Cathedral* (London: for the author, 1891).

——'Wesley and the Cathedral Service', *MN*, 29 (1910), 40–1.

BURCHELL, DAVID, 'The Role of Pedals in the Accompaniment of English Hymnody, 1810–1860', *BIOSJ*, 25 (2001), 56–77.

BURNEY, CHARLES, *A General History of Music*, 4 vols. (London, 1776–89); ed. F. Mercer, 2 vols. (New York, 1935, repr. 1957).

CALDWELL, JOHN, *The Oxford History of English Music*, 2 vols. (Oxford: Clarendon Press, 1991–9).

CARRINGTON, DOUGLAS, *St. George's Hall: The Hall, Organ and Organists* (Liverpool: Liverpool City Council, 1981).

'Cathedral Service', *QMMR*, 6 (1824), 17–27, 310–17.

CHAPPELL, PAUL, *Dr. S. S. Wesley, Portrait of a Victorian Musician* (Great Wakering: Mayhew-McCrimmon, 1977).

'Church Music in Leeds', *PC*, 3 (1850), 148–50.

CLARKE, W. K. LOWTHER, *A Hundred Years of Hymns Ancient & Modern* (London: William Clowes & Sons, 1960).

'Clifton College and its Music', *MT*, 46 (1905), 237–41.

CLUTTON, CECIL, and NILAND, AUSTIN, *The British Organ*, 2nd edn. (London: Eyre Methuen, 1982).

COLEMAN, HENRY, 'James Kendrick Pyne: A Link with a Forgotten Past', *Org*, 40 (1960–1), 8–15, 92–8.

COLLES, H. C., *Essays and Lectures* (London: Oxford University Press, 1945).

CROTCH, WILLIAM, *Substance of Several Courses of Lectures on Music* (London: Longman, Rees, Orme, Brown, and Green, 1831).

DANNREUTHER, EDWARD, *The Romantic Period*, The Oxford History of Music, 6 (Oxford: Clarendon Press, 1905).

DAVID, HANS, and MENDEL, ARTHUR, *The Bach Reader*, rev. edn. (London: J. M. Dent & Sons, 1966).

DAVISON, HENRY (ed.), *From Mendelssohn to Wagner: Being the Memoirs of J. W. Davison* (London: Wm. Reeves, 1912).

DAWE, DONOVAN, *Organists of the City of London, 1666–1850: A Record of One Thousand Organists with an Annotated Index* (for the author, 1983).

DIBBLE, JEREMY, 'Hubert Parry and English Diatonic Dissonance', *BMSJ*, 5 (1983), 58–71.

——*C. Hubert H. Parry: His Life and Music* (Oxford: Clarendon Press, 1992).

DICKSON, W. E., *Fifty Years of Church Music* (Ely: T. A. Hills & Son, 1894).

—— *A Letter to the Lord Bishop of Salisbury, on Congregational Singing in Parish Churches* (Oxford: J. H. & J. Parker, 1857).

'Dr. J. Kendrick Pyne', *MT*, 49 (1908), 636–41.

'Dr. Wesley and the Minor Canon', *MT*, 40 (1899), 484–5.

DYER, SAMUEL, *The Dialect of the West Riding of Yorkshire: A Short History of Leeds and other Towns* (Brighouse: J. Hartley, 1891).

EDWARDS, F. G., 'Wesley, Samuel Sebastian (1810–1876)', in Leslie Stephen and Sidney Lee (eds.), *Dictionary of National Biography* (London: Smith, Elder, 1908–9), 6. 1231–3.

E[DWARDS], F. G., 'Bach's Music in England', *MT*, 37 (1896), 585–7, 652–7, 722–6, 797–800.

[EDWARDS, F. G.], 'Samuel Sebastian Wesley', *MT*, 41 (1900), 297–302, 369–74, 452–6.

—— 'Wesley's "Wilderness"', *MT*, 45 (1904), 170–2, 238–9, 306–7.

—— 'The Metamorphosis of a Well-Known Anthem', *MT*, 41 (1900), 522–4.

—— 'Wesley in E', *MT*, 48 (1907), 662–4, 797–9.

EHRLICH, CYRIL, *First Philharmonic: A History of the Royal Philharmonic Society* (Oxford: Clarendon Press, 1995).

ELVEY, MARY, *Life and Reminiscences of George J. Elvey, Knt* (London: Sampson Low, Marston & Co., 1894).

ELVIN, LAURENCE, *Bishop and Son, Organ Builders* (Lincoln: for the author, 1984).

—— *Family Enterprise: The Story of Some North Country Organ Builders* (Lincoln: for the author, 1986).

EVERITT, WILLIAM, *Memorials of Exmouth* (Exmouth: T. Freeman, 1883).

[FEARON, W. A.], *The Passing of Old Winchester* (Winchester: Warren & Sons, 1924).

FÉTIS, F.-J., 'State of Music in London', *Har*, 7 (1829), 181–6, 214–20, 241–6, 275–81.

FISHER, JAN, *The Rockie Road from Epworth: the Wesleys in Australia* (privately printed, 2001).

FORD, ERNEST, 'The Wesleys', *MMR*, 47 (1917), 152–3.

FOSTER, MYLES BIRKET, *Anthems and Anthem Composers: An Essay upon the Development of the Anthem from the Time of the Reformation to the End of the Nineteenth Century* (London: Novello & Co., 1901).

—— *History of the Philharmonic Society of London, 1812–1912: A Record of a Hundred Years' Work in the Cause of Music* (London: John Lane, 1912).

FROST, MAURICE (ed.), *Historical Companion to Hymns Ancient & Modern* (London: William Clowes & Sons, 1962).

GARRETT, GEORGE M., 'S. S. Wesley's Organ Compositions', *MT*, 36 (1894), 446–9.

GATENS, WILLIAM J., *Victorian Cathedral Music in Theory and Practice* (Cambridge: Cambridge University Press, 1986).

GAUNTLETT, H. J., 'English Ecclesiastical Composers of the Present Age', *MW*, 2 (1836), 113–20.

—— 'The Gresham Prize', *MW*, 2 (1836), 81–6, 97–101.

GAUNTLETT, H. J., 'The Musical Profession; and the Means of its Advancement Considered. No. 1.—Cathedrals and Collegiate Churches', *MW*, 3 (1836), 129–35.

GEDGE, DAVID, 'The Reforms of S. S. Wesley', *Org*, 67 (1988), 126–36; 68 (1989), 41–51.

GODMAN, STANLEY, 'Bach's Music in England, 1835–1840', *MMR*, 83 (1953), 32–9, 69–71.

—— 'The Early Reception of Bach's Music in England', *MMR*, 82 (1952), 255–60.

GRACE, HARVEY, 'The Organ Music of Samuel Sebastian Wesley', *MT*, 67 (1926), 309–12.

GRAVES, C. L., *Hubert Parry: His Life and Works*, 2 vols. (London: Macmillan & Co., 1926).

—— *The Life & Letters of Sir George Grove, C.B.* (London: Macmillan & Co., 1903).

GROVE, GEORGE (ed.), *A Dictionary of Music and Musicians (A.D. 1450–1889)* (London: Macmillan & Co., 1879–90).

HADDOCK, GEORGE, *Some Early Musical Recollections of G. Haddock* (London: Schott & Co., 1906).

HADOW, W. H., *English Music* (London: Longmans, Green & Co., 1931).

HAWKINS, JOHN, *A General History of the Science and Practice of Music*, 5 vols. (London, 1776).

'Henry Willis', *MT*, 39 (1898), 297–303.

HIEBERT, ARLIS JOHN, 'The Anthems and Services of Samuel Sebastian Wesley (1810–76)', Ph.D. dissertation, George Peabody College, Nashville, Tenn., 1965.

HODGES, FAUSTINA H., *Edward Hodges* (New York: E. P. Putnam's Sons, 1896).

HOGARTH, GEORGE, *Musical History, Biography and Criticism* (London: John W. Parker, 1835).

HOPKINS, EDWARD J., and RIMBAULT, EDWARD F., *The Organ, its History and Construction*, 3rd edn. (London Robert Cocks & Co., 1877).

HORTON, PETER, "A Clever Thing, but not Cathedral Music": *CMS*, 94th Annual Report (2000), 9–19.

—— ' ". . . the highest point up to that time reached by the combination of Hebrew and Christian sentiment in music"', in Peter Horton and Bennett Zon (eds.), *Nineteenth-Century British Music Studies*, 3 (Aldershot: Ashgate, 2003).

—— 'Modulation Run Mad', in Jeremy Dibble and Bennett Zon (eds.), *Nineteenth-Century British Music Studies*, 2 (Aldershot: Ashgate, 2002), 223–34.

—— 'The Music of Samuel Sebastian Wesley (1810–1876)', D.Phil. dissertation University of Oxford, 1983.

—— 'The Natural Romantic', *Choir & Organ*, 9/2 (2001), 71–5.

—— ' "A Organ should be *an Organ*": S. S. Wesley and the Organ in St George's Hall, Liverpool', *BIOSJ*, 22 (1998), 84–125.

—— 'Samuel Sebastian Wesley at Leeds: A Victorian Church Musician Reflects on his Craft', in Nicholas Temperley (ed.), *The Lost Chord: Essays on Victorian Music* (Bloomington and Indianapolis: Indiana University Press, 1989).

—— 'Samuel Sebastian Wesley: "One of the finest and most dignified extempore players of his day"', *The Organist*, 1/1 (1990), [2]–[4].

—— 'St George's Hall, Liverpool: S. S. Wesley, W. T. Best and the Town Hall Tradition', *The Organ Yearbook*, 28 (1998–9), 103–16.

—— 'The Unknown Wesley: The Early Instrumental and Secular Vocal Music of Samuel Sebastian Wesley', in Bennett Zon (ed.), *Nineteenth-Century British Music Studies*, 1 (Aldershot: Ashgate, 1999), 137–78.

HUNT, DONALD, *Samuel Sebastian Wesley* (Bridgend: Seren Books, 1990).

HUTCHINGS, ARTHUR, *Church Music in the Nineteenth Century* (London: Herbert Jenkins, 1967).

—— 'Could "Jubilee" have been "Centenary"?', *ECM*, 1977, 31–8.

ILLING, ROBERT, 'The Chamber Organ in Killerton House', *MO*, 80 (1957), 299–300.

JEBB, JOHN, *The Choral Service of the United Church of England and Ireland: Being an Enquiry into the Liturgical System of the Cathedral and Collegiate Foundations of the Anglican Communion* (London: John W. Parker, 1843).

[——] T, W. Green, *Dialogue on the Choral Service* (Leeds, 1842).

—— 'Three Lectures on the Cathedral Service of the Church of England', *The Christian's Miscellany*, no. 3 (May 1831), 1–30.

JOHNSTONE, H. DIACK, and FISKE, ROGER (eds.), *The Eighteenth Century*, The Blackwell History of Music in Britain, 4 (Oxford: Blackwell Reference, 1990).

JOHNSTONE, KENNETH I., *The Armley Schulze Organ: A History, Descriptions and Appreciation of the Edmund Schulze Organ in St. Bartholomew's Church, Armley, Leeds* (Leeds: [St Bartholomew's Church], 1978).

JULIAN, JOHN, *A Dictionary of Hymnology: Setting Forth the Origin and History of Christian Hymns of all Ages and Nations*, 2nd revised edn. (London: John Murray, 1907; facs. repr. 1957).

KASSLER, MICHAEL, and OLLESON, PHILIP, *Samuel Wesley (1766–1837): A Source Book* (Aldershot: Ashgate, 2001).

LANGLEY, LEANNE, 'The English Musical Journal in the Early Nineteenth Century', Ph.D. dissertation, University of North Carolina at Chapel Hill, 1983.

LEVIEN, JOHN MEWBURN, *Impressions of W. T. Best (1826–1897), Organist at St. George's Hall, Liverpool, the Handel Festival, &c.* (London: Novello & Co., 1942).

—— *Sir Charles Santley: A Lecture* (London: Novello & Co., [1930]).

LIGHTWOOD, J. T., *Samuel Wesley, Musician: The Story of his Life* (London: Epworth Press, 1937)

—— 'S. S. Wesley—a Sad Story', *CMJ*, 32 (1941), 101–2, 117–18.

LINDLEY, SIMON, *The Organs, Organists & Choir of Leeds Parish Church: a Brief History*, 2nd edn. (Leeds, 1978).

LONG, KENNETH R., *The Music of the English Church* (London: Hodder and Stoughton, 1971).

LUCAS, STANLEY, 'Samuel Sebastian Wesley', *MO*, 47 (1933), 144–5, 340–2.

LYSONS, DANIEL, et al., *Origin and Progress of the Meeting of the Three Choirs of Gloucester,*

Worcester & Hereford, and of the Charity Connected with it (Gloucester: Chance and Bland, 1895).

'M', 'Samuel Sebastian Wesley', *M*, June 1896, 131–2.

MACFARREN, GEORGE A., 'Cipriani Potter: His Life and Works', *PMA*, 10 (1883–4), [41]–56.

MADAN, MARTIN, *Thelyphthora, or A Treatise on Female Ruin* (London, 1780–1).

MANSFIELD, ORLANDO A., 'W. T. Best: His Life, Character and Works', *MQ*, 4 (1918), 209–49.

MARRYAT, FLORENCE, *Nelly Brooke: A Homely Story*, 3 vols. (London: Richard Bentley, 1868).

MATTHEWS, BETTY, *The Organs and Organists of Exeter Cathedral* (Exeter: Dean and Chapter of the Cathedral Church of St Peter in Exeter, [1965]).

—— *The Organs and Organists of Winchester Cathedral*. 2nd revised edn. (Winchester: Friends of Winchester Cathedral, 1975).

—— *Samuel Sebastian Wesley, 1810–1876: A Centenary Memoir* (Bournemouth: Kenneth Mummery, 1976).

—— 'Samuel Sebastian Wesley at Winchester', *MO*, 87 (1963–4), 33, 35.

——, ed., *The Royal Society of Musicians of Great Britain: List of Members, 1738–1984* (London: Royal Society of Musicians, 1985).

MILLER, C. E., 'Some Organists I have Known', *MO*, 57 (1934), 342.

MOBERLY, C. A. E., *Dulce domum: George Moberly, his Family and Friends* (London: John Murray, 1911).

NEIGHBOUR, O. W. and TYSON, Alan, *English Music Publishers' Plate Numbers in the First Half of the Nineteenth Century* (London: Faber and Faber, 1965).

NETTEL, REGINALD, *The Orchestra in England: A Social History* (London: Jonathan Cape, 1946).

OAKELEY, EDWARD M., *The Life of Sir Herbert Stanley Oakeley* (London: George Allen, 1904).

[OAKELEY, HERBERT STANLEY], 'Cathedral Music', *The Guardian* (12 Oct. 1859), 872–3.

OAKELEY, HERBERT STANLEY, 'Wesley, Samuel Sebastian', in George Grove (ed.), *A Dictionary of Music and Musicians (A.D. 1450–1889)* (London: Macmillan & Co., 1890), 4. 447–8.

OLLESON, PHILIP, *The Letters of Samuel Wesley: Professional and Social Correspondence, 1797–1837* (Oxford: Clarendon Press, 2001).

—— *Samuel Wesley: The Man and his Music* (Woodbridge: Boydell and Brewer, 2003.

'On the Formation of an English School of Music', *Har*, 9 (1831), 108–10.

'On the State of Music in England', *Har*, 8 (1830), 17–18.

OUSELEY, F. A. GORE, 'Modern English Music', in Emil Naumann, *History of Music*, trans. F. Praeger (London: Cassell & Co., 1886), 2. 1274–314.

PARKER, ANDREW, *Winchester Cathedral Organs: One Thousand Years* (Winchester: Friends of Winchester Cathedral, 1994).

The Parish Choir or Church Music Book, 3 vols. (London: John Olliver, 1846–51).

Pazdírek, Franz (ed.), *Universal-Handbuch der Musikliteratur aller Zeiten und Volken* (Vienna: Pazdírek & Co., [n.d.]).

Pearce, C. W., *The Evolution of the Pedal Organ* (London: Musical Opinion, 1927).

—— *The Life and Works of Edward John Hopkins* (London: Vincent Music Co., [1910]).

Phillips, C. Henry, *The Singing Church: An Outline History of the Music Sung by Choir and People* (London: Faber and Faber, 1945).

Pigot and Co.'s London Alphabetical and Classified Commercial Directory (London: J. Pigot & Co., 1838).

Pigot and Co.'s London & Provincial New Commercial Directory, for 1823–4 (London: J. Pigot & Co., [1823]).

Practical Remarks on Cathedral Music: see Stevens, C. A.

Prendergast, William, 'Notes on Samuel Sebastian Wesley', *Sammelbände der Internationalen Musik-Gesellschaft*, 13 (1912), 350–5.

Pyne, J. Kendrick, 'Dr. Samuel Sebastian Wesley', *ECM*, 5 (1935), 4–8.

—— 'Wesleyana', *MT*, 40 (1899), 376–81.

Rainbow, Bernarr, *The Choral Revival in the Anglican Church (1839–1872)* (London: Barrie & Jenkins, 1970).

Rannie, Alan, *The Story of Music at Winchester College, 1394–1969* (Winchester: P. & G. Wells, 1970).

Redlich, Hans F., 'The Bach Revival in England (1750–1850): A Neglected Aspect of J. S. Bach', *Hinrichsen's Seventh Music Book*, ed. Max Hinrichsen (London: Hinrichsen, 1952).

Reid, Charles, *The Music Monster: A Biography of James William Davison* (London: Quartet Books, 1984).

Rennert, Jonathan, *William Crotch: Composer, Artist, Teacher* (Lavenham: Terence Dalton, 1975).

Ringer, Alexander L., 'Beethoven and the London Pianoforte School', *MQ*, 56 (1970), 742–58.

Rohr, Deborah, *The Careers of British Musicians, 1750–1850: A Profession of Artisans* (Cambridge: Cambridge University Press, 2001).

Routh, Francis, *Early English Organ Music, from the Middle Ages to 1837* (London: Barrie & Jenkins, 1973).

Routley, Erik, *The Musical Wesleys* (London: Herbert Jenkins, 1968).

—— *The Music of Christian Hymnody: A Study of the Development of the Hymn Tune since the Reformation, with Special Reference to English Protestantism* (London: Independent Press, 1957).

—— 'Samuel Sebastian Wesley and "The European Psalmist"', *HSB*, 7 (1973), 221–35.

—— 'Victorian Hymn-Composers—I: Samuel Sebastian Wesley', *HSB*, 2/1 (1948), 2–5; 2/2 (1948), 4–11.

'St. Mary Redcliffe Church, Bristol', *MT*, 47 (1906), 725–35.

Samson, Jim, *The Music of Chopin* (London: Routledge & Kegan Paul, 1985).

'Samuel Sebastian Wesley Commemoration', *MN*, 29 (1910), 148–50.

'Samuel Sebastian Wesley: d. April 19, 1876', *MT*, 67 (1926), 305–7.

SCHWARZ, JOHN I., 'The Orchestral Music of Samuel Wesley', Ph.D. dissertation, University of Maryland, 1971.

——'Samuel and Samuel Sebastian Wesley, the English Doppelmeister', *MQ*, 49 (1959), 190–206.

The Seven Sermons Preached at the Consecration and Re-Opening of the Parish Church of Leeds, with an Introduction (Leeds: T. W. Green, 1841).

SHAW, WATKINS, 'The Achievement of S. S. Wesley', *MT*, 117 (1976), 303–5.

——'Church Music in England from the Reformation to the Present Day', in Friedrich Blume et al., *Protestant Church Music* (London: Victor Gollancz, 1975), 691–732.

—— *The Organists and Organs of Hereford Cathedral* ([Hereford]: Friends of Hereford Cathedral, 1976).

—— 'Samuel Sebastian Wesley (d. 19 April 1876): Prolegomenon to an Imagined Book', *ECM*, 20 (1976), 22–30.

—— *The Succession of Organists* (Oxford: Clarendon Press, 1991).

—— *The Three Choirs Festival: The Official History of the Meetings of the Three Choirs of Gloucester, Hereford and Worcester, c.1713–1953* (Worcester: Ebenezer Baylis & Son, 1954).

SHINN, GEORGE, 'Dr. Wesley's Organ Performance at the Agricultural Hall', *MN*, 29 (1910), 42.

'Short Notes on Chanting the Psalms.—No. 2', *PC*, 1 (1846), 6–7, 14–15.

SMITH, G. H., *A History of Hull Organs and Organists, together with an Account of the Hull Musical Festivals, and the Formation of the Various Musical Societies in the Town* (London: A. Brown & Sons, [n.d.]).

SPARK, FREDERICK R., *Memories of my Life* (Leeds: Fred. R. Spark & Son, [1913]).

SPARK, WILLIAM, *Musical Memories*, 3rd edn. (London: W. Reeves, [1909])

—— *Musical Reminiscences: Past and Present* (London: Simpkin, Marshall, Hamilton, Kent & Co., 1892).

—— 'Samuel Sebastian Wesley', *MT*, 17 (1876), 490–1.

SPINK, GERALD W., 'Samuel Sebastian Wesley: A Biography', *MT*, 78 (1937), 44–6, 149–50, 239–40, 345–7, 432, 438–9, 536–8.

—— 'Walter Scott's Musical Acquaintances', *ML*, 51 (1970), 61–5.

STAINER, JOHN, and BARRETT, WILLIAM, *Dictionary of Musical Terms*, rev. edn. (London: Novello & Co., 1898).

STANFORD, C. V., *Pages from an Unwritten Diary* (London: Edward Arnold, 1914).

—— *Studies and Memories* (London: Archibald Constable & Co., 1908).

—— and FORSYTH, CECIL, *A History of Music* (London: Macmillan & Co., 1916).

STATHAM, HENRY HEATHCOTE, *The Organ and its Position in Musical Art: A Book for Musicians and Amateurs* (London: Chapman and Hall, 1909).

STEPHENS, W. R. W., 'Hook, Walter Farquhar (1798–1875)', in Leslie Stephen and Sidney Lee (eds.), *Dictionary of National Biography* (London: Smith, Elder, 1907), 9, 1170–3.

STEPHENS, W. R. W., *The Life and Letters of Walter Farquhar Hook*, 2 vols. (London: Richard Bentley & Son, 1878).

[STEVENS, C. A.], *Practical Remarks on the Reformation of Cathedral Music* (London: Francis & John Rivington, 1849).

STEVENS, DENIS, 'Gramophone Notes: English Church Music', *MT*, 94 (1953), 119.

STEVENSON, GEORGE J., *Memorials of the Wesley Family* (London: S. W. Partridge & Co., [1876]).

SUMNER, W. L., *Father Henry Willis, Organ Builder, and his Successors* (London: Musical Opinion, [1955])

[TAYLOR, EDWARD], *The English Cathedral Service—its Glory, its Decline, and its Designed Extinction* (London: Simpkin, Marshall & Co., 1845).

TAYLOR, HENRY, *Autobiography of Henry Taylor, 1800–1875*, 2 vols. (London: Longmans, Green & Co., 1885).

TEMPERLEY, NICHOLAS, 'Instrumental Music in England, 1800–1850', Ph.D. dissertation, University of Cambridge, 1959.

—— 'London and the Piano, 1760–1860', *MT*, 129 (1988), 289–93.

—— 'Mendelssohn's Influence on English Music', *ML*, 43 (1962), 224–33.

—— 'Mozart's Influence on English Music', *ML*, 42 (1961), 307–18.

—— *The Music of the English Parish Church*, 2 vols. (Cambridge: Cambridge University Press, 1979).

—— 'Samuel Wesley', *MT*, 107 (1966), 108–110.

—— (ed.) *The Romantic Age, 1800–1914*, The Athlone History of Music in Britain, 5 (London: Athlone Press, 1981).

—— 'Wesley, (4) Samuel Sebastian', in Stanley Sadie (ed.), *The New Grove Dictionary of Music and Musicians* (London: Macmillan Publishers Ltd, 1980), 20. 363–8.

TEMPERLEY, NICHOLAS, AND HORTON, PETER, 'Wesley: (5) Samuel Sebastian Wesley', in Stanley Sadie (ed.), *The New Grove Dictionary of Music and Musicians*, 2nd edn. (London: Macmillan Publishers Ltd, 2001), 27. 312–8.

TERRY, R. R., *A Forgotten Psalter and Other Essays* (London: Oxford University Press, 1929).

THISTLETHWAITE, NICHOLAS, 'Bach, Mendelssohn, and the English Organist: 1810–1845', *BIOSJ*, 7 (1983), 34–49.

—— *A History of the Birmingham Town Hall Organ* (Birmingham: Birmingham City Council, 1984).

—— *The Making of the Victorian Organ* (Cambridge: Cambridge University Press, 1990).

TOVEY, DONALD, and PARRATT, GEOFFREY, *Walter Parratt: Master of the Music* (London: Oxford University Press, 1941).

WALKER, ERNEST, *A History of Music in England*, 3rd edn., rev. and enlarged by J. A. Westrup (Oxford: Clarendon Press, 1952).

WATSON, HENRY, *A Chronicle of the Manchester Gentlemen's Glee Club* (Manchester: Charles H. Barber, 1906).

WEBSTER, DONALD, *'Parish' Past and Present: 275 Years of Leeds Parish Church Music* (Leeds: Leeds Parish Church Old Choirboys' Association, 1988).

'Wesley Appreciation', *MN*, 29 (1910), 137.

'The Wesley Centenary', *MN*, 28 (1910), 667–9.

'The Wesley Commemoration Service', *MN*, 29 (1910), 11.

'The Wesley Pedigree', *MR* (11 Nov. 1897).

WESLEY, SAMUEL SEBASTIAN, *A Few Words on Cathedral Music and the Musical System of the Church, with a Plan of Reform* (London: F. & J. Rivington, 1849).

—— *Reply to the Inquiries of the Cathedral Commissioners, Relative to Improvement in the Music of Divine Worship in Cathedrals* (London: Piper, Stephenson, and Spence, [1854]).

—— preface to *A Morning Evening Cathedral Service* (London: Chappell, [1845]).

—— preface to *A Selection of Psalm Tunes Adapted Expressly to the English Organ with Pedals*, 2nd edn. (London: R. Cocks & Co., [1842]).

WESTON, AGNES, *My Life among the Bluejackets* (London: James Nisbet & Co., 1909).

WILLIAMS, PETER, *The Chromatic Fourth during Four Centuries of Music* (Oxford: Clarendon Press, 1997).

—— 'J. S. Bach and English Organ Music', *ML*, 44 (1963), 140–51.

WINTERS, WILLIAM, *An Account of the Remarkable Musical Talents of Several Members of the Wesley Family, Collected from Original Manuscripts*, &c (London: F. Davis, 1874).

WORSHIPFUL COMPANY OF MUSICIANS, *An Illustrated Catalogue of the Music Loan Exhibition . . . at Fishmongers' Hall, June and July, 1904* (London: Novello & Co., 1909).

YEATS-EDWARDS, PAUL, *English Church Music: A Bibliography* (London: White Lion Publishers, 1975).

Collections of Psalms, Hymns, and Anthem Texts

Anthems Used in the Cathedral Church of Durham (Durham: Andrews & Co., 1871).

AYLWARD, THEODORE EDWARD (ed.), *The Sarum Hymnal, with Proper Tunes* (Salisbury: W. P. Aylward and Brown & Co., [1869]).

CALVERT, JOHN (ed.), *A Collection of Anthems Used in Her Majesty's Chapel Royal, the Temple Church and the Collegiate Churches and Chapels in England and Ireland* (London: George Bell, 1844).

The Cathedral Psalter, Containing the Psalms of David, Together with the Canticles and Proper Psalms for Certain Days Pointed for Chanting (London: Novello, Ewer & Co., [1875]).

A Collection of Anthems used in the Parish Church of Leeds, 4th edn. (Leeds: Joseph Johnson, 1859).

A Collection of Anthems, Introits, etc., Used in the Parish Church of St. John, Bradford (Bradford: R. Thornton Dale, 1873).

COTTERILL, THOMAS (ed.), *Selection of Psalms and Hymns*, 9th edn. (London: T. Cadell, 1820).

DEACLE, E. L. Y. (ed.), *Anthems Used in Chester Cathedral and Adapted for Parochial Choirs* (Chester: Phillipson and Golder, 1869).

DIBB, J. E., *Key to Chanting. The Psalter . . . and Portions of the Morning and Evening Services of the Church, Appointed to be Sung or Chanted, with a Peculiar Arrangement to Facilitate the Practice* (London, 1831).

ELVEY, STEPHEN, *The Psalter or Canticles and Psalms of David, Pointed for Chanting, upon a New Principle; with Explanations and Directions* (Oxford: John Henry and James Parker, 1856).

HARRIS, JOSEPH JOHN (ed.), *A Collection of those Portions of the Psalms of David, Bible and Liturgy which have been Set to Music, and are Sung as Anthems in the Cathedral and Parish Church of Manchester*, 3rd edn. (Manchester: sold at the Depository of the Society for Promoting Christian Knowledge, 1856).

HEBER, REGINALD (ed.), *Hymns Written and Adapted to the Weekly Church Service of the Year* (London, 1827).

JANES, ROBERT, *The Psalter; or Psalms of David, Carefully Marked and Pointed . . .* (Ely: T. A. Hills, 1837).

MARSHALL, WILLIAM (ed.), *A Collection of Anthems Used in the Cathedral and Collegiate Churches of England and Wales* (Oxford: John Henry Parker, 1840).

MILMAN, H. H. (ed.), *Selection of Psalms and Hymns Adapted to the Use of the Church of St. Margaret, Westminster* (London: J. B. Nichols and Son, 1837).

NELSON, HORATIO, third EARL NELSON (ed.), *The Sarum Hymnal* [words only] (Salisbury: Brown & Co. and W. P. Aylward, 1868).

OUSELEY, FREDERICK ARTHUR GORE, and MONK, EDWIN GEORGE, *The Psalter, with the Canticles and Hymns of the Church Pointed for Chanting* (London: J. Alfred Novello, 1861).

PEARCE, THOMAS (ed.), *A Collection of Anthems Used in His Majesty's Chapels Royal, and Most Cathedral Churches in England and Ireland*, new edn., with additions (London: C. & J. Rivington, 1826).

The Psalter Newly Pointed (London: Society for Promoting Christian Knowledge, 1926).

TATE, NAHUM, and BRADY, NICHOLAS, *A New Version of the Psalms of David, Fitted to the Tunes Used in Churches* (Oxford: Printed at the University Press, 1847).

TERROTT, WILLIAM MULREADY (ed.), *Anthem Book: Containing the Words of all the Anthems Commonly Sung in the Cathedrals and Collegiate Churches of England and Ireland* (London: Joseph Masters, 1856).

Editions of Music

ADAMS, THOMAS, *Six Organ Pieces, Composed and Inscribed to T. Attwood Esqr.* (London: J. Alfred Novello, [c.1825]).

BARNBY, JOSEPH, *Original Tunes to Popular Hymns for Use in Church and Home* (London: Novello, Ewer & Co., 1869).

BARNETT, JOHN, *Lyric Illustrations of the Modern Poets*, 2nd edn. (London, 1877).

BENNETT, ALFRED, and MARSHALL, WILLIAM (eds.), *Cathedral Chants* (London: Mori and Lavenu, [1829]).

BLAKELEY, WILLIAM ARTHUR, *The Canticle Chant Book: Containing the Canticles and Hymns of the Church, Pointed for Chanting, together with Upwards of Six Hundred Appropriate Chants* (London: Weekes & Co., [1875]).

CAMIDGE, JOHN, *Cathedral Music* (London: Preston, 1828).

CLARKE-WHITFELD, JOHN, *Cathedral Music* (London: Broderip and Wilkinson, 1800–05).

—— *Twelve Vocal Pieces, Most of them with Original Poetry, Written Expressly for this Work* (London: for the author, [1816]).

EVANS-FREKE, VICTORIA (ed.), *The Song of Praise; or Psalm and Hymn Tunes . . . for a Church Psalter and Hymnal* (London: George Routledge and Sons, [1875]).

GARRETT, GEORGE, *Cathedral Services in Score . . . Composed & Dedicated to Mrs. C. J. Ellicott* (London: Novello & Co., [1864]).

GAUNTLETT, H. J., and KEARNS, W. H. (eds.), *The Comprehensive Tune Book* (London: Houlston and Stoneman, 1846).

HACKETT, CHARLES DANVERS (ed.), *The National Psalmist* (London: Coventry and Hollier, [1839]).

HAVERGAL, WILLIAM HENRY (ed.), *Old Church Psalmody* (London: J. Hart, [1847]).

HAWES, WILLIAM (ed.), *A Collection of Chants, Sanctuses & Responses to the Commandments . . . Selected from Antient & Modern Composers* (London: W. Hawes, [1830]).

HAYCRAFT, HENRY, *Sacred Harmony* (London: R. Addison, [1851]).

—— *A Selection of Sacred Music* (London: Mori and Lavenu, [1837]).

HULLAH, JOHN (ed.), *The Psalter or Psalms of David in Metre* (London: J. W. Parker, 1843).

HUNT, JOHN, *Songs, by the Late John Hunt, Organist of Hereford* (London: Cramer, Addison, and Beale, [n.d.]).

The Hymnary: A Book of Church Song (London: Novello, Ewer & Co., 1872).

Hymns Ancient and Modern: see Monk, William Henry.

Hymns Ancient & Modern Revised (London: William Clowes and Sons, [1951]).

LINLEY, WILLIAM, *Eight Glees* (London: W. Hawes, [1832]).

MATHER, SAMUEL (ed.), *Christian Psalmody* (London: T. Cadell, 1831).

MONK, WILLIAM HENRY (ed.), *Hymns Ancient and Modern for Use in the Services of the Church, with Accompanying Tunes* (London: Novello & Co., [1861]).

—— *Hymns Ancient and Modern for Use in the Services of the Church, with Accompanying Tunes . . . with Appendix* (London: William Clowes and Sons, [1868]).

—— *Hymns Ancient and Modern for Use in the Services of the Church, with Accompanying Tunes . . . Revised and Enlarged Edition* (London: William Clowes and Sons, [1875]).

NOVELLO, VINCENT (ed.), *The Psalmist* (London: J. Haddon, 1839–44).

Novello's Collection of Anthems by Modern Composers, 1 (London: Novello, Ewer & Co. [1871]).

SALE, J. B. (ed.), *Psalms and Hymns for the Service of the Church* (London: the Editor, 1837).

SMART, HENRY, *A Choral Book Containing a Selection of Tunes Employed in the English Church* (London: Boosey & Co., [1857]).

——— *Henry Smart's 50 Preludes and Interludes* (London: Boosey & Co., [1862]).

SMITH, JOHN STAFFORD, *Anthems Composed for the Choir-Service of the Church of England* (London: for the Author, [1793]).

STEGGALL, CHARLES, *Church Psalmody* (London: Addison & Hollier, [1849]).

STEVENSON, JOHN, *Morning and Evening Services and Anthems* (London: J. Power, 1825).

SULLIVAN, ARTHUR (ed.), *Church Hymns with Tunes* (London: Society for Promoting Christian Knowledge, 1874).

TRIMNELL, W. F. (ed.), *The Collegiate Chant-Book* (London: Weekes & Co., [1880]).

WAITE, J. J., and G., H. (eds.), *The Hallelujah; or, Devotional Psalmody: Being a Collection of Choice and Standard Tunes, Ancient and Modern* . . . (London: John Haddon & Co., [1851]).

WALMISLEY, THOMAS ATTWOOD, *Cathedral Music* (London: Ewer & Co., 1857).

INDEX OF WORKS

Numbers in bold refer to musical examples or facsimiles

INDEX

Buildings are indexed by name rather than location

Index

SSW contextualized in Austrian church
archives + Architecture -ne-